The End of Obscenity

THE TRIALS OF
LADY CHATTERLEY,
TROPIC OF CANCER,
AND FANNY HILL

Charles Rembar

INTRODUCTION BY
NORMAN MAILER

SIMON AND SCHUSTER
NEW YORK

To Billie Ann

———————◆———————

Acknowledgments

I thank:

James H. Silberman, a wise editor.

Barney Rosset, an extraordinary publisher. He must be counted a creator of the book, since he started the chain of events that form its story.

Walter Minton, who brought out the work that completes the story—like Rosset, he is one of those clients who make the practice of law a pleasure, with their quick understanding of the issues and a willingness to go for the main goal.

Friends who read and commented on the manuscript: Victor Brudney, Ivan Von Auw, Nancy Wechsler, Louis Lusky, Elizabeth Hull Froman and George Gallantz. I am grateful, with good reason, to all of them, but I must make particular mention of the last two. Gallantz brought to bear an invaluable combination of no-nonsense tough-litigator realism and sensitive literary judgment, and both he and Mrs. Froman excel in an art form that has limited but appreciative audiences—the marginal note—thus providing delight along with assistance.

Ellis B. Levine, who did much of the research for the chapter called "Tropical Storm."

Margaret Ann Harrell, a gifted book-tuner—a lass with a delicate ear.

Author's Note

The excerpts of trials and arguments that appear in this book have had no editing apart from punctuation—court stenographers are excellent at catching sounds, but they are not so good on rests, and no witness says "comma" —the correction of an occasional word where there was an obvious mistake in stenography or transcription, and, at a few points only, the use of italics where vocal stress was especially important to the meaning. Books dealing with the law sometimes indulge in revision of what was said in court, not to change the substance, but because extemporaneous speech, put on paper, tends to read poorly and is often downright embarrassing. The indulgence damages accuracy and deadens flavor. Accordingly, apart from the small efforts to make reproduction more exact, I have used the official court reporters' transcript of their notes, without any attempt to spare the literary sensitivities of the reader or the ego of the speaker.

The description of the affairs of clients, and conversations with them, is in each instance with the client's permission.

Contents

Introduction

THE BOOK in your hand is a quiet and essentially modest account of a legal revolution led by a few determined and extraordinary publishers. When I think of Barney Rosset and Walter Minton, I am reminded on the instant of Civil War generals: Sherman and Grant race to the fore. They are men who are determined to take a hill even if it takes all summer and chews up half their resources. It was thus Minton's and Rosset's great good fortune to have on their side one of Lee's lieutenants, a Light-Horse Harry named Charles Rembar, and the purpose of this foreword is not to take up the arguments of the book, but rather to relieve its modesty with an account of the author. Light-Horse Harry was a great cavalryman, and his strategy and tactics were bold, luminous, witty, and exceptionally well-balanced, but men endowed with the combative graces do not often write about themselves. So I will repair the lack of personal memoir and give you an introduction to the author.

He is my cousin, Mr. Charles Rembar, the son of my mother's oldest sister, and he is the closest to an older brother I will ever come. Since he is eight years older than me (although I fear he does not look it) he was very much an older brother all through my childhood, and I worshiped him (with enormous funds of love and envy) because he was a hero. He was one of the few people I've ever known who had a happy look on his face when he came to bat in the late innings with men on base, his side behind, and the need for a homer prominent in everyone's head. Indeed he had his smile because it was slightly better than even money he was going to hit that homer. In fact, he would. This is not hyperbole. If I saw him in a hundred baseball games, there must have been fifty late-inning spots of exactly the sort I describe: he probably hit thirty-six homers out of fifty. In fact, we usually didn't believe it if he didn't give us our expected spark of apocalypse when the ball rocketed over the center fielder's head. Often as not, Cy Rembar's homers would land in the tennis court at the end of our playing field, for that after all was the place where he would pull out all the winning sets from all the tennis players who were more trained than he, more devoted, more fanatical and less humorous. Ditto for football. Ditto for getting the best-looking girls. Because of Cy Rembar, I used to believe in Jack Armstrong.

Those were Depression years. Much gloom abounded in everyone, but he was the bright spot, man. He was the only figure I encountered in my childhood who seemed to believe it was more natural to win than to lose and that life was therefore to be enjoyed rather than decried.

Since then, he's gotten a little older, not a great deal so far as I can see, and it's a shock to realize I'm as tall as he is today and weigh—I do not brag of this—thirty pounds more. But he's still the one man in all the world whose good opinion is gold to me, because Rembar is not only a winner, but a man with a subtle moral force. While he was never religious, probably never will be, and so far as I know evolved no elaborate set of ethics other than a profound respect for the law, which served to house the architecture of his ability to reason, that particular ability in him precisely to reason has become a force which approaches the power of a mighty muscle, for in close tactical argument and debate on any subject improvised at the drop of a coin, he is doubtless one of the world's best and most brilliant quick reasoners. Which is to say he can be as bad as a boil on the royal behind if he beats you in a tactical brush on your favorite theme. But I have been led astray by Rembar's annoying power to reason. I was speaking of his moral force. It comes, I suppose, from a reliance on taste, a sort of implicit sense that manners, if they are excellent enough, can serve as a substitute for metaphysics. (Doubtless they so serve because exquisite manners call upon that reservoir of natural grace and animal philosophy which existentialists like myself are always trying to chart.) No matter how, he's a modest moral force in any room in which he finds himself because he's a clean man, and looks for clean issues to complex problems, and does it with good will. Consider what a recommendation is this when the man has been my lawyer for twenty years and charges solid fees. But it is true. He looks for moral issues in his activities. And still plays baseball. And still might take a girl away from me if he chose to. Although I hope the odds have closed.

And I take pleasure in this book by him because I had a little to do with the commencement of his interest in these problems. Yes, back years ago with *The Deer Park,* and years before, we used to argue (since it was a matter of direct moment to me) about the defense of serious works of literature which were on the face of their language or situation obscene, and I used to fulminate against those thumbscrews of the law which required the defense to engage respectable witnesses who had then all but to perjure themselves in order to swear that the particular erotic work was moral and aroused them not at all. I would cry out, "Why can't a novel just once be defended as erotic and valuable as well?" and Rembar would give me a short lecture, most clearly presented, about the subtle if sometimes retarded relation of the law to reality, and how perhaps the time was coming.

Well, it has come. A war has been won. Writers like myself can now write about any subject; if it is sexual, and we are explicit, no matter, the American writer has his freedom. Rembar has done as much as anyone to forge that freedom. We can all congratulate ourselves.

He is, however, as I would remind you, a moral man, and so I was pleased to see as I read through these pages that he is troubled just a hint by the liberties won, just indeed as I am troubled. For back of the ogres of censorship and the comedies of community hypocrisy, there still rests the last defense of the censor, that sophisticated argument which might urge that sex is a mystery and men explore it and detail it and define it and examine it and eventually disembowel it of privacy at their peril. It is the argument of tradition against the power of reason. Rembar—we will repeat—personifies the positive attractions of the life of reason, but he is sufficiently instinctive as a gent to waste no time congratulating himself on heroic victories. Like the noblest (one revenges oneself on an older brother by drowning him in superlatives), yes, like the noblest of Lee's lieutenants, he wonders privately and with concern if his cause is altogether just. So, too, do I. It is my cause as well. And like many another American writer, about to embark on a literary trip through some of the aesthetic territory Rembar's cases have helped one to enter, I brood, too, about undue exposure of the mystery, and console myself with the second argument—that the inroads of science and industry, advertising, bad art, industry and commerce also invade the mysteries of existence. And thus the poet must be there as well to trim the lamp and anoint that numbing of the flesh which serves the technician's electrodes and probes. The novelist may help to sink the ship of sex before all is done, but it might be even worse without a literary exploration or two. For next to the mystery is the disease. It is the disease of the twentieth century, that ill so ubiquitously spawned by the anomalies of reason and the maceration of instinct, all the promiscuous pills of all that labyrinthine and technological vat. So when I question the value of the inquiry I would make—and, repeat, now have via Rembar, Minton, Rosset, and some others, yes, now have real freedom to make—I lave the edge of my doubt with the certainty that some one of us artists must manage to be there to arrest the doctor when he also marches into the door of the mystery. Because the doctor takes flashbulbs into the womb, whereas we—if we are good enough—will take the herbs of some of the good words and balm the helpless exposure of the girl with aromatics and spice. Perhaps life continues on a certain irreducible minimum of art. Without that, no life. That is the modus operandi of the advocate whose opinions and deeds you are now ready to encounter. Welcome to my racket, Cousin Cy, Gentleman Sword.

NORMAN MAILER

❀

Then the first thing will be to establish a censorship of the writers of fiction, and let the censors receive any tale of fiction which is good, and reject the bad; and we will desire mothers and nurses to tell their children the authorized ones only. . . . The doings of Kronos, and the sufferings which in turn his son inflicted upon him, even if they were true, ought certainly not to be lightly told to young and thoughtless persons; if possible, they had better be buried in silence. But if there is an absolute necessity for their mention, a chosen few might hear them in a mystery. . . .

PLATO, *The Republic*

Chapter XX. That in a Free State every man may Think what he Likes, and Say what he Thinks.

How much better would it be to restrain popular anger and fury, instead of passing useless laws, which can only be broken by those who love virtue and the liberal arts, thus paring down the state till it is too small to harbor men of talent.

SPINOZA, *Theologico-Political Treatise*

Congress shall make no law . . . abridging the freedom of speech, or of the press. . . .

United States Constitution, Amendment I

The End of Obscenity

As Long As It
Doesn't Offend
Our Own Ideas

IN 1930 THEODORE DREISER'S AN AMERICAN TRAGedy was held to be "lewd and obscene." A bookseller had been convicted of crime for selling the book, and one of America's most distinguished courts—the Supreme Judicial Court of Massachusetts—affirmed the conviction. The judges, "even assuming great literary excellence, artistic worth and an impelling moral lesson in the story," were unanimous that the book must be banned. Four years later the libertarians won one: New York federal courts held James Joyce's *Ulysses* not obscene. The *Ulysses* decision impressed the literary world, but not the other courts.

In the 1940's Lillian Smith's *Strange Fruit* was suppressed in Massachusetts (a commonwealth celebrated for its institutions of higher learning), and Edmund Wilson's *Memoirs of Hecate County* in New York (the national center of publishing and other cultural pursuits). From the present point in time it is hard to think of Miss Smith's sermon on racial hatred as the occasion of an anti-obscenity prosecution (in Mass., remember, not Miss.). As for *Hecate County*, there was only one chapter in the book that had much to do with sex, and its tone was scarcely lascivious. Yet these are not ancient cases.

With innocents so much in trouble, it was not remarkable that in 1953 a Customs ban on Henry Miller's *Tropics* was sustained by a high federal court in California. What may be remarked is that the court repeated almost verbatim a test of obscenity formulated by British courts about a century earlier. It was, in fact, the prevailing test.

This book is several things. It is a narrative of some cases in court that drew considerable public attention though they involved no violence and touched hardly anybody's pocketbook—cases that continue to be argued, publicly and privately, long after the courts have decided them. It is an attempt to offer an insight, to those who are not part of it, into how our legal system works. It is a comment on our Constitution, and particularly on its assurance of free speech and a free press.

It is also the story of an idea, a legal concept. In 1956 the concept did not exist at all. In 1966 it was full grown and dominant, and turned a hard hand against censorship, and laid an exceedingly gentle one on the freedom to write and publish.

The idea was this: no matter what the courts and the legislatures had traditionally deemed "obscene"—no matter what the term meant to laymen or to lawyers—the government could not suppress a book if it had merit as literature. It would not need much; if there was any discernible value, the First Amendment must intervene.

In the cases this book tells about, the government tried to stop the publication of *Lady Chatterley's Lover*, *Tropic of Cancer* and *Fanny Hill*. Before these cases, literary merit had occasionally been a factor in obscenity prosecutions, but a subordinate one. The ultimate question was whether the writing was lustful—that is, whether it excited a sexual response. If it did, it was obscene, and if it was obscene it could be banned and its author and publisher sent to jail. Now, only a few years later, the law is that the sexual content of a book, and the sexual stirrings it may provoke in its readers, cannot condemn a work that has any literary value.

The concept did not, of course, by itself bring about the change; the development of the law is affected by developments in the culture as a whole. But it works both ways: courts are influenced by what is going on in the world around them, and at the same time their decisions help to shape that world. The pace and nature of events in race relations, for example, would not have been the same were it not for the judicial decisions on integration.

The Supreme Court, said Mr. Dooley, follows the results of the last election. He was only partly right. The Court is not a legislature fulfilling the wishes of a current majority. It is a group of lawyers reading a constitution that was meant to give a permanent pledge of certain liberties, regardless of what the current majority would like. While in a measure the Court is responsive to popular attitudes, it is at the core proof against them. And Mr. Dooley neglected the important converse: the electorate, in about the same measure, has its reflexes conditioned by decisions of the Court.*

Nor is there any inevitability about progress in the law. The case with which this story ends was decided in favor of the book by a vote of six to three. On the same day, in two other cases, publishers were given prison sentences. The degree of freedom now enjoyed by writers would probably have been gained sooner or later, but it could easily have been later, and the word "probably" leaves room for the chance that when the law is slow to move, history may change its mind and turn the other way. In any event, whatever would have happened someday, the law this day might be quite different if there had been a different Presidential choice, on an occasion or two, when there was a vacancy on the bench. It might also be quite different if different arguments—on either side—had been presented to the courts.

For some time now it has been noticed that judges are impelled to decide the way they do (quite apart from corruption) by factors other than, or at least in addition to, the legal principles stated in their opinions. But what modern jurisprudence calls "the inarticulate hypothesis" has come to play a smaller role by reason of the very fact that our philosophers have made

---

* As used in this book, "the Court" is always the Supreme Court, and "Justice" is one of its members—the capitals being used for identification, and meaning no disrespect to other courts and judges.

our judges aware of it. Particularly with a court as self-conscious, as literate and as exposed as the United States Supreme Court, the legal theory offered as the basis for its judgment is crucial.

The legal theory offered in defense of the three books I named has to do with the meaning of the First Amendment. The Amendment contains our guaranty of free expression. The guaranty is not unlimited. One of its limits, people had long assumed, and the Supreme Court in 1957 confirmed, is the obscene.

The First Amendment also contains guaranties against laws "respecting an establishment of religion or prohibiting the free exercise thereof" and laws abridging the rights of assembly and petition. In this book we are concerned only with free expression; references to the Amendment are to be read with that aspect of it in mind. For convenience, the terms "speech" and "freedom of speech" will sometimes be used (along with the broader term "expression") to refer both to speech and to the press, to writing as well as talk.

And the restriction on free expression we are concerned with is that imposed by anti-obscenity laws. There are other restrictions that the law imposes. Slander and libel—false statements harmful to reputation—may lead to the payment of damages, a possibility that inhibits the speaker or writer. A conscious misrepresentation on which another person relies, and as a result of his reliance suffers, is fraud; the law holds the liar responsible and, as with defamation, the prospect of paying damages is a restraint. Fraud also brings criminal penalties—under the false-advertising statutes, for instance, or under the Securities Act. To take an example close to our subject, advertising a book as obscene which is in fact quite innocent will involve the advertiser not with the anti-obscenity laws but with the mail-fraud statute.

But false statements are not the only ones subject to restraint. The law demands a buttoned lip where information is given in confidence; disclosure of trade secrets may make one liable in damages. More than money is involved when the secrets are the government's; certain things are kept quiet for purposes of national security, and breaches are crimes. Then there are utterances that create a "clear and present danger." The classic example is the cry of "Fire!" in a crowded theater, but the utterance need not be factual at all; it may be exhortation. And there are restraints on expression that we hardly think of in terms of freedom: a writer who without permission repeats too large a portion of this book—or of any book in copyright—may pay heavily in court. The law interferes with the plagiarist's freedom of speech.*

Freedom of speech is an abstraction. Since it is an abstraction, and not ordinarily a felt need, it is sometimes hard to understand. Five-star national hero, President of Columbia University, President of the United States Dwight D. Eisenhower, made a civil-libertarian address at Dartmouth College on June 14, 1953. "Don't join the bookburners," he urged. "Don't think you are going to conceal faults by concealing evidence that they ever existed. Don't be afraid to go into your library and read every book, *as long as that document does not offend our own ideas of decency*." (The italics are ruefully supplied.)

The need is not felt because people are not ordinarily inhibited, by the power of government, from saying what they want to. Forces outside the law may limit speech—economic pressure, social disapproval, parental discipline. But falsehood and the subject of this book apart, the government permits us to say and to write pretty much what we choose. Where expression rather than action is concerned, the feeling of constraint by force of law is, in our society, a rare one.

More often encountered is the complaint that there is not enough restriction, that there are those the government ought to silence. Radicals should not be allowed to preach godless social-

---

* That it should, to the extent it does, is not as clear as it may seem. Copyright is a monopoly that puts a toll on access to art and information. The monopoly is justified, I feel, for a number of reasons, but it impairs free speech: a speaker need not be an originator. It may be observed that censorship and copyright have closely connected origins; the Crown-chartered Stationers' Company served both to limit printing according to the Crown's desires and to establish exclusive rights of private ownership in the works printed.

ism; John Birchers should not be allowed to circulate their obloquies. The specific expression we fear or hate is very real, while the theory that everybody ought to be able to say or write what he chooses is usually experienced as no more than that—a theory.

The First Amendment finds especially few subscribers among those who, were it not for the Amendment, would most likely be silenced. The domestic Communists of the thirties and the New York streetcorner Nazis of the early sixties provide familiar examples of the view that freedom of speech means freedom-for-me. They wanted to be free to speak as they pleased, but freedom of speech as a general matter did not interest them (and if they had gained power, it would immediately have been extinguished). Even John Milton, whose *Areopagitica* is a fundamental document in the history of liberty, denied its application to Catholics and atheists, and Martin Luther's loud demands for freedom turned out to be no more than demands that he be free.

In our time and in our country, freedom of expression is experienced as a need mainly by two classes of people—writers and lawyers.* Writers, of course, feel it directly. Lawyers are people who by nature have emotions about abstractions, and by practice are invested with their clients' needs. To appreciate a law or a constitution, it is necessary to undertake an essay in imagination; you must appreciate how it works in situations that do not directly affect you. Like other beneficial exercises, this is not easy; it imposes an awkward strain, and there are creaks and groans until it is learned.

Most of you who read this book belong to a minority. In each of the three cases I tell about, the decision would have gone the other way if it had been put to a popular vote. A majority of the people were opposed to the publication (a legitimate point

---

* The term "lawyers" includes judges. The term "writers" includes dramatists as well as essayists, novelists, poets, and, for this purpose, directors and producers who contribute to the content of a play or a film. It does not include all producers for the stage or screen, whose interest in avoiding restraint is often commercial rather than artistic; their concern is not the right to speak freely, but the right to make money, and the Constitution, while it recognizes both rights, does not equate them.

of view) and would therefore have had the law suppress it (an illegitimate deduction). The First Amendment stands between the personal preference and the desired governmental action. But the majority does not really accept the Amendment.

Any doubt about the nature of majority sentiment ought to be dispelled by the fact that in 1965 Mayor Robert Wagner of New York City led a drive to enact additional anti-obscenity legislation. Whatever other appraisals of Mayor Wagner might be made, it is indisputable that he had a fine instinct for avoiding minority positions. Part of the fuel for the anti-obscenity movement was supplied by the *New York Daily News*. The paper began with an editorial, and two months later a lead story hailed the result—another anti-obscenity bill. The headline read: BLAME COURTS FOR FLOOD OF PRINTED FILTH. The legislation, said the story, "comes hard on the heels of overwhelming public response to an editorial printed in the *News* on February 15." The *News* had the second largest circulation of all the papers in the United States, and the largest in New York City. It had generally been assumed that one reason for its success was the use of sex in its stories and photographs. The crusade did not invalidate the assumption. A *Wall Street Journal* article, published about two years later, summarized the situation; *its* headline read: NEW YORK DAILY NEWS STAYS NO. 1 WITH CRIME, SEX, PHOTOS—& CHANGE. The article, among other things, quoted an editor of the *News*:

> "If Rusk wants to launch a trial balloon, he calls Scotty Reston" of the *New York Times*, he says. "If the cops knock off a cat house on Seventy-second Street, they call us."

We all know where the blame lies. The *News* has told us. With the courts.

In the mid-1950's "a national cross-section" was asked this question: "if a person wanted to make a speech in your community against churches and religion, should he be allowed to speak or not?" Thirty-seven percent said "Yes"; 60 percent said "No"; 3 percent had no opinion. Two years earlier the Gallup Poll inquired whether an individual "known to favor communism" should be allowed to make a speech; 29 percent thought he should; 67 percent thought not; 4 percent had no opinion.

The phenomenon is not confined to the Philistines.* In 1965 Pablo Picasso went to court for an injunction against the distribution of Françoise Gilot's *Life with Picasso*. He said the book was "an infringement of my personal privacy and an attack on my honor." In Picasso's support, forty-four artists (including Labisse, Manessier, Miró and Soulages) issued a manifesto. It included the following:

> Françoise Gilot has committed an intolerable attack on individual liberty and private property. Any man—above all, a great man—can refuse to have the secrets of his personal life spread before the public gaze and strewn in the market place, especially when such facts are distorted by spite.

If the book lied, Picasso could talk back, or establish the truth in a suit for libel; the complete suppression that an injunction imposes is, if we are interested in freedom, too brutal a remedy. If privacy rather than libel was the concern, the manifesto had it backwards. It singled out for particular solicitude the "feelings of a great man," thus urging the same principle that would give a large car with a low license number immunity from parking tickets. But here the needs of society go beyond democratic equality: the ordinary person should be favored. The undistinguished have, as compensation for the want of celebrity, a claim on comfort—the privilege of being left alone. Our law recognizes that society has a valid interest in the exceptional individual who creates the things society values, and a quantum of privacy must be paid out when a quantum of fame is accorded.

There is a nice irony, but no paradox, in the fact that this strident protest against freedom of speech should come from the artists of Paris. A voyage in logic (upon which Parisian intellectuals easily embark) will lead to the idea that expression should

---

* The historical Philistines are owed an apology by Carlyle and the rest of us who use their name in this sense. There is evidence that in the period the Bible speaks of, they were people of a higher culture than their enemies the Hebrews. This knowledge not only deprives the arts of a convenient epithet; it puts a new light on the story of David and Goliath. We can now picture a tall, portly gentleman, his hand extended, saying amiably, "Hello, little boy"—when, right between the eyes . . .

be free, but it takes a great effort of will to hold to the idea when the specific expression is hurtful, even abhorrent.

Nevertheless, and remarkably, expression in this country is largely free of legal restraint. Government, long regarded as the oppressor, is in this respect ahead of those it governs. There are instances, relatively few (though far too many), in which officials interfere with freedom of speech. But in doing this, they are not enforcing the law; they are violating it. Their conduct draws criticism and protest, and if it reaches the courts, condemnation and undoing. The judiciary, particularly the upper courts, have led the way, and we now have a degree of freedom equaled only in a few other countries—so far as literature is concerned, almost nowhere. (Even the constitution of that traditional model of democracy, the Swiss Confederation, and such new constitutions as those of India, Burma, Libya, Nigeria and Zambia, make expression subject to "reasonable" regulations, thus assuring their citizens nothing more than freedom-by-sufferance.)

Censorship is old, as old as history. The idea that the government should not interfere with freedom of speech—should even protect it—has been with us only a few centuries. A few centuries is a brief period in all of history, and not till the last of them has the kind of freedom that is the subject of this book been at issue. Until recently there was no contest: almost nothing that seriously offended certain prevailing concepts of morality and decency was allowed to be published. Now the fighting, which seems just begun, in a short time draws to its close. The radical nature of the change and the rapidity with which it has occurred earn it the name revolution. By the measurements of the law, it has happened in an instant, and it has happened against the wishes of a majority.

Where First Amendment freedoms are involved, however, the majority does not rule. Our fundamental law is designed to protect the dissident and the unpopular. The legal question in an obscenity case is not whether it is a good thing or a bad thing that the particular book be published, but whether its publication is protected by that puzzling abstraction, the First Amendment.

The puzzle is what it covers, how far it goes. But there is an anterior question: why do we have it at all? *

The reasons usually advanced in support of free speech are concerned with its value to society. Unhampered expression, according to the classic argument, will produce a great deal that is wrong or worthless, but restrictions on expression will cover and kill a great deal that is good. In the free interchange of ideas, the truth will emerge. "The best test of truth," said Justice Holmes, "is the power of the thought to get itself accepted in the competition of the market." (The figure of speech, an interesting conjunction of capitalism and intellectual freedom, was also used by Jefferson.)

There are other reasons why a good society must have free speech. One is that if there is to be a democratic government— if, as our Declaration of Independence tells us, governments "derive their just powers from the consent of the governed"— then the governed must be free to say what they think. Another is that suppression tends to make a society brittle; the conflicts are congealed. Freedom of expression is necessary not only because the ideas themselves may be valuable to the society, but also to avoid a fatal arteriosclerosis in the body politic.

I concur in these arguments, but I feel they take up too much room in the reasoning of those who support the First Amendment freedoms. Among the things that make life valuable is the kind of internal activity that can roughly be called thought. This includes both thought in the strict sense, whose higher products are philosophy and science, and thought in its emotive aspects, whose higher product is art. But thought is

---

* No extended treatment of the philosophy and history of freedom of expression is undertaken here. There is, of course, a great literature on the subject. For those who wish to go further, I particularly recommend *Toward a General Theory of the First Amendment*, by Thomas I. Emerson (New York: Vintage Books, 1967), *Catholic Viewpoint on Censorship*, by Harold C. Gardiner, S.J. (New York: Doubleday, 1958) and *Versions of Censorship*, by John McCormick and Mairi MacInnes (New York: Anchor Books, 1962).

frustrated and tends to rot if it must be contained within the individual. In *Areopagitica*, Milton's general arguments became intensely personal at one point: "Give me liberty to know, to utter, and to argue freely according to conscience, above all liberties."

Aside from the collective benefit that comes from the free interchange of ideas, there is direct personal benefit for the individual concerned. Each of us should have the right to speak his thoughts and to hear the thoughts of others. It makes us feel good.

On the other hand, there are serious points to be made against freedom of expression. I have mentioned some arguments pro, and I do not propose to weigh them against the arguments con. Our Constitution is based on the premise, among others, that freedom of expression is both necessary and desirable, and in my view the young United States made a wise choice. But do not assume the choice was simple.

Consider, for example, the case of Father Charles E. Coughlin, the "radio priest." A 1934 survey showed that Americans considered him the nation's most important public figure apart from the President (whom Coughlin called "a great liar and betrayer"). Fairly typical of what he gave his vast audience was the statement that a New York banking firm under the control of Jews (which it wasn't) had helped finance the Russian Revolution (which it didn't). There was a good possibility that Coughlin, together with the frenzied anti-Semite Gerald L. K. Smith and the economic quack Dr. Francis E. Townsend, might have combined to make Huey Long President, a possibility ended by the murder of Long (which perhaps opens a question about another widely accepted postulate—that political assassination is in all circumstances unthinkable). Coughlin was eventually silenced by the Roman Catholic Church. His archbishop forced him to submit his talks to a board of censors, who "cut the heart out of the sermons. . . . That was the beginning of the end."

In the 1930's, there was a substantial possibility that Nazi doctrine would go beyond the Rhine, even beyond the Mississippi. Hitler was a great orator. One of the few things a great orator cannot deal with is a muzzle. That is to say, censorship. I mention this; I do not think it negates the premise.

The Law
---
to the Time
---
of Chatterley

IN THE MIDFIFTIES, ANTI-OBSCENITY LAWS WERE attacked as unconstitutional. The attacks were repelled. Freedom of expression, said the Supreme Court, does not extend to expression that is obscene.

Publishers fretted, with reason, about words and scenes in serious novels. Rinehart & Company, who had put out Norman Mailer's first two books, stuck at his third. It was *The Deer Park*, and they had contracted to publish it. After the manuscript had been set in type, however, the company came to the conclusion that it was unpublishable because it was obscene. A contract to perform an illegal act is not enforceable, and Rinehart, strongly convinced of the illegality because of one passage in particular, felt relieved of its obligation to publish. On the author's behalf, I disagreed, and offered to test the issue in a suit for the advance royalties. Rinehart held to its position, but faced with the suit, paid Mailer for the privilege of not publishing his book. Despite the obvious desirability of adding an extravagantly gifted writer to their list, six other houses turned the book down before Walter Minton celebrated his ascension to the presidency of Putnam by taking a chance on it.*

---

* The lawyer for one of them presented me with a memorandum of

In England, about the same time, respected publishers came near going to prison. Frederick Warburg boldly entered the dock in the Old Bailey and felt the terror of the criminal law. The charge was on *The Tightrope*, by Stanley Kauffman (retitled *The Philanderer* for British readers)—a novel quite innocuous by today's standards. It took an exceptional charge to the jury by an exceptional British judge, Mr. Justice Stable, to save Warburg, and in subsequent cases other British judges refused to accept Stable's view of the law. The climate is indicated by a remark the defendant himself made in recounting his experience. Warburg noted Edmund Gosse's statement that he "would rather see English literature free than decent" and wondered "whether [Gosse] was not going a bit too far."

When books like these created so much danger, it took a brave publisher to raise up a book that had long been consigned to the underworld of the obscene. In 1959 Barney Rosset of Grove Press announced the open publication of *Lady Chatterley's Lover*. Reactions ranged from approving through disapproving to horrified. Some felt that Grove was doing a disservice to the cause of freedom—that to bring out *Lady Chatterley* was an act of wild extremism and its consequence would be increased repression. Among those who were sympathetic, many were sorrowful. They considered the publication more than brave; they considered it suicidal.

Not only did the Lawrence novel devote more of its pages to the act of sex and deal with it in greater detail than anything ever before sold over the counter; it had language that had never been seen in a book openly circulated, except when used for tangential and occasional purposes, and not often then. It was one thing to put into the dialogue of soldiers the four-letter words to which people felt them entitled—the punctuation and italics of fighting men. It was quite another to have a principal character use the words in their primary, literal sense, and not for some distant reference, but as part of what was going on before the reader's very eyes. This was too much. *Lady Chatter-*

---

over a hundred excerpts arranged under headings such as "Must be deleted," "Must be changed," "Should be changed." Nowhere in his catalogue was the passage that Rinehart thought fatal.

ley's Lover presented the forbidden acts in forbidden detail, and described them in forbidden language.*

The United States government had declared the book obscene. There was a Post Office ruling barring it from the mails. If Customs found a copy in the luggage of a returning traveler, it was confiscated. These officials were by no means reactionary. Despite a few discordant judicial utterances, and despite the fact that liberal commentators of the 1950's, apparently in an effort to urge the law along, described it as having made some progress, the law essentially was not very different from what it had been in 1868.

In 1868 the first important judicial opinion on obscenity was handed down. The date suits the notion that there had been a classic age of freedom which ended when a Victorian blight descended upon literature. It is not so. Books thought to be obscene had for a long time been liable to suppression. It was just that before this date there were few reported opinions on the subject, and no judicial attempt to define the term.

In the beginning, censorship-in-advance took care of the matter, and censors, unlike judges, feel no need to explain their actions, or to develop principles that will govern their use of power. Almost from the date of its invention, printing was subject to ecclesiastical and royal control. In seventeenth-century England, the Crown, the Star Chamber and Parliament took turns deciding what might be published. Printing was a licensed privilege. You could then no more publish a book without official approval than you can now open a saloon.

Licensing of printing disappeared from England at the end of the seventeenth century, and has never existed in the United

---

* Not that soldier talk presented no problems. Mailer again furnishes an example. *The Naked and the Dead*, in 1948, had created worries for its publishers. The author had discussed obscenity problems with me while the work was being written, and I had suggested what was then a new spelling —"fug"—for the most worrisome word. I advocated this partly because it might reduce the risk of suppression, and partly on the ground that it was phonetically closer than was the classic spelling to the prevailing GI gutturals.

States. But at just about the time licensing ended, the English courts decided that publishing an obscene book was a common law crime—that is, an act pronounced criminal by the courts although not prohibited by any statute. (The theory is that the illegality is established by custom and tradition. Some traditions seem to lie around unnoticed for a long time.)

The threat of prosecution was enough to drive a book underground. Neither the author nor the original publisher of *Fanny Hill* was brought to court, but the book disappeared from public view. (It was a near thing for John Cleland and his publisher though; twelve years after the publication of *Memoirs of a Woman of Pleasure*—the name Cleland gave his work—a dealer named Drybutter was put in the pillory for selling it.) The cases that did go to court contributed little to doctrine. A criminal case does not ordinarily involve a judicial opinion unless there is an appeal, and in obscenity prosecutions there were very few appeals until well into the nineteenth century.

The English common law was adopted by the courts of the United States, and with it the rule that it was a crime to publish an obscene book. Our first reported case, appropriately, involved that prima ballerina of the law of obscenity, *Fanny Hill*. It was decided in 1821, in Boston. (Six years earlier in Pennsylvania, there had been a conviction of a group of entrepreneurs who exhibited a painting "representing a man in an obscene, impudent and indecent posture with a woman.") In the Boston case two booksellers were convicted. On their appeal, the upper court discussed a number of points raised by the defense but said absolutely nothing about whether the book was obscene. Apparently the answer was obvious.

Twenty years later, in a typically xenophobic approach, Congress moved to guard against infection from abroad; in passing a tariff act, it authorized Customs officials to confiscate pictures. But this was a rather limited statute, and we still had no definition of obscenity.

England sent us one. It came in the form of judicial interpretation of a statute. Parliament, in 1857, enacted the first major piece of anti-obscenity legislation, Lord Campbell's Act. When people get morally indignant they are apt to pass laws against things that are already illegal. Lord Campbell's Act was an example.*

The Victorians in general were probably more exercised than their predecessors about the evils of obscenity. But there were also Victorians who were exercised about the evils of suppression; they were outnumbered, but they fought. Campbell was a former Lord Chief Justice, and brought up his bill in the House of Lords. It encountered strong and spectacular opposition from Lord Lyndhurst, himself a former Chief Justice. (He was born John Singleton Copley, a son of the painter who had migrated from America to England.) Lyndhurst evidently won the debate and lost the argument. The bill became the Obscene Publications Act. As usual, wit was on the side of freedom, and the votes were on the side of suppression.†

The Act had to do with procedures for stamping out the crime, not with saying what it was. Definition came eleven years afterward, from the courts—particularly from another Lord Chief Justice, Lord Cockburn—in the case of *Queen* v. *Hicklin*. The case involved an anti-Catholic pamphlet, more libelous than

---

* Another, more recent, was the congressional tautology declaring it a crime to burn a draft card, when it was already a crime to be without one's draft card. Lord Campbell's Act at least affected the procedures for punishing obscene publication; the card-burning statute made no change in the penalties that already existed, which would apply whether one burned his card, threw it out the window or chewed it up and swallowed it.

† Campbell had recently published a voluminous work called *The Lives of the Chief Justices.* Lyndhurst was one of the subjects, and it is a fair guess he was not pleased; then eighty-five years old, he made a vigorous attack on the bill and its author. The attack was described both as "one of the most amusing speeches" ever made in Parliament and as "either a scandalous exhibition of senile depravity or the vicious outburst of a temperament which years could not impair." Even the victim of the forensic violence gave it an offended, and puzzled, tribute. Campbell put out a supplement to his earlier biographical work, and in it he wrote: "For some unaccountable reason, Lyndhurst violently opposed this measure, and on the second reading he delivered a most elaborate, witty, unfair, and, I must add, profligate speech against the bill, and moved that it be read a second time that day three months." Whatever else one may think of Lord Campbell and his Act, he must be respected as a man who, having the last word, used it to affirm the quality of a polemic of which he was the target.

obscene, published by the Protestant Electoral Union. Cockburn formulated a test of obscenity that had an enduring and baleful influence in both Great Britain and the United States. "I think," he said, "the test of obscenity is this, whether the tendency of the matter charged as obscenity is to deprave and corrupt those whose minds are open to such immoral influences, and into whose hands a publication of this sort may fall."

Note how thoroughly repressive this is. The Crown need not demonstrate that harm will occur, or even that it is likely—all that is needed is a "tendency." *

And what kind of tendency did the Lord Chief Justice have in mind? A tendency, he said, "to deprave and corrupt." This meant something more than, or less than, or in any case other than, the advocacy of immorality. Most of the books condemned by the Act deplored what they depicted. The depiction would be enough.†

And whose liability to corruption? Those "whose minds are open to such immoral influences." Now since the minds of most of us are open to influence, whether moral or immoral, this means a publication that might turn anybody in the direction of immorality must be banned. "Anybody," of course, includes children, a point the *Hicklin* test makes doubly clear in its next and final phrase:—"into whose hands publication of this sort may fall." The phrase perhaps saves the case where a book is kept under lock and key and shown only to selected readers. But so far as general circulation is concerned, we are reminded that it may reach those who are particularly susceptible. The court's

---

* This is similar to the pattern of our antitrust law. The existence of an economic combination that may operate as a monopoly, although it has not yet done so, is enough to violate the law. The theory is that such combinations have a tendency to act in ways unfair to competitors and bad for the general economy. But there is a significant difference between the two situations: the realization of the tendency—the history of savage business practices on the part of such combinations—was well documented when the antitrust acts were passed. Congress was dealing not with merely conceivable consequences, but with historical fact.

† The most common agent of corruption is money. The consensus on this point is reflected in the familiar cynical question "What's his price?" Under the *Hicklin* test, could money be described in frank detail? Would we then suppress the *Wall Street Journal?*

language induces the image of tender plump pink hands that should not be holding open such books, but should be playing with dolls, or pulling wings off insects.

The outrageous immoral fact is that the only kind of immorality toward which all this is directed is sexual immorality. Nothing has ever been censored on the ground that it had a tendency to promote dishonesty or cruelty or cowardice. No significant legislative attempt has ever been made to suppress books except to preserve the political order, the established piety or theoretical standards of sexual behavior.*

Meanwhile, things had been stirred up in the United States. Most of the stirring was done by Anthony Comstock. Remembered as an old bluenose, Comstock was in fact a young bluenose. In his early twenties he had made his reputation as a crusader against vice. In 1873, at the age of twenty-eight, he set a standard for all future congressional lobbyists to shoot at: singlehanded, he got Congress to pass the archetype of American anti-obscenity legislation. There are very few Acts of Congress that bear the name of anyone other than a senator or representative; the mark of the man is that this statute became known as the Comstock Act. On the day of its passage, its author made a diary entry: "Oh how can I express the joy of my Soul or speak the mercy of God!"

Comstock's famous organization, the New York Society for the Suppression of Vice, has not been heard from for a number of years. It appears as a complainant in the law reports until the 1930's (when it was under the direction of John Sumner) and then vanishes. Upon inquiry at the New York bureau that keeps records of the formation and dissolution of corporations, I found that the Society for the Suppression of Vice never died. It first changed its name, then merged, and now lives on, corporately, as the Police Athletic League.

This rich vein of repressive legislation—sometimes referred

---

* In recent years, there have been some small attempts to restrict the portrayal of violence; the chief effect has been to tone down comic books, and to remit impressionable young minds to television and the newspapers for their daily ration of sadism.

to as the Comstock Load—provided the model for most American anti-obscenity statutes, which endured unchanged until a
short time ago. In the last few years, congressmen and state
legislators, apprised of the existence of the First Amendment
and deeply alarmed by it, have begun to fashion new statutes in
an effort to overcome the recent decisions of the courts.

They had no problem with earlier decisions. American courts
had eagerly adopted the *Hicklin* test and used it to define obscenity in applying both the Comstock Act and the similar statutes that every state but one eventually enacted.*

In two respects the *Hicklin* rule was modified after a time.
Lord Cockburn had focused on "matter" rather than books.
This permitted prosecutors to proceed against selected pages or
paragraphs, and courts to condemn a work though neither judge
nor jury had read it through. By the end of the 1940's, however,
the prevailing view was that a book should be judged as a whole,
not on the basis of isolated passages. The other change had to do
with *Hicklin*'s solicitude for the susceptible. It was gradually
realized that what was published for the world at large could not
be governed by rules designed for minors; adult reading could
not be reduced to the level of a child's bookshelf.

These modifications were sensible but peripheral. In its essence—"the tendency of the matter to deprave or corrupt"—
Hicklin survived and flourished. The courts decided whether
publication was permissible by deciding whether the book under
attack was "lustful." If it was, it was obscene, and its author and
publisher criminals. As to how provocative a book must be to
rate as lustful, the answer, of course, was subjective, and some-

---

* Both the federal act and the typical state statute referred to material
"obscene, lewd, lascivious, filthy" and, depending on the legislators' fancy,
one or more additional near-synonyms. The courts, however, found it unnecessary to go beyond "obscene," treating the rest as redundant.

The exception is New Mexico, which has no state law on the subject,
but some of whose municipalities have anti-obscenity ordinances, thus taking local option and brown-bagging into an unaccustomed field. New
Mexico officials, however, maintain that there is no greater incidence of
sexual immorality in New Mexico than anywhere else.

what more charitable answers were given as time went on. But while the law of obscenity dropped a few gables and dormers as the memory of Campbell's queen and Comstock's Congress began to fade, the underlying idea of *Hicklin* was not relinquished until a moment ago.

It seemed to suffer no damage from—it even prospered under —constitutional assaults. Early in 1957 the Supreme Court struck down a Michigan statute that defined obscenity as material having a "deleterious influence upon youth." "Surely," said Justice Frankfurter, "this is to burn the house to roast the pig." But the effect of the decision was simply to make one of the *Hicklin* modifications, acknowledged in most states, compulsory in all. A few months later, the Supreme Court held that state and federal anti-obscenity laws that spoke in general terms were valid. Affirming a pair of criminal convictions, the Court sustained both the Comstock Law and one of its statehouse nephews, an act of the California legislature. The second paring down of *Hicklin* was given sanction: judgments could not rest on isolated passages. With these familiar caveats, however, a solid majority ruled that anti-obscenity statutes could stand against the First Amendment guaranties.

The Court set out a definition of obscenity that incorporated the two limits upon *Hicklin*, suggested that frames of reference may change in time, and substituted the word "prurient" for "lustful." It added, among other things, that the decision merely confirmed the existing judicial view of the subject. One of the other things was to become important, but at the time it drew no attention. The opinion, handed down in the famous *Roth* case, was widely accepted as one that gave constitutional approval to the established law of obscenity.

One day in the spring of 1959, Rosset asked whether I would like to try a case for him. (He had not been a client; we knew each other mainly from the tennis court.) What case? I asked. *Lady Chatterley*, he said. I said yes. That was the last easy answer.

To begin with, there was a question of strategy. As I have said, the overriding issue up to this time was whether the book

was "lustful"—that is, sexually exciting. *Lady Chatterley* had a
famous author, but literary achievement had been assigned a
minor role in obscenity cases. At first, courts had not even lis-
tened to statements about the quality of a book; a book did not
deprave or corrupt any the less for being artful.* When they
began to allow critics to testify, they did so only because the
testimony might demonstrate that the book was not really sexy.
And not all courts regarded evidence of literary merit as aiding
the defense. Right up to 1966, some judges denounced good
writing on the ground that it made a pernicious book all the
more effective: well-written obscenity was the worst kind.

But by the 1950's most courts were willing to hold (usually in
connection with a "classic") that sufficient literary quality could
drown out a certain amount of lustfulness. If there was great
enough merit, and little enough sex, the court might decide that
the reader's reaction would be intellectual or aesthetic, and not,
as Father Gardiner put it, a "genital commotion." †

Thus the law recognized two kinds of books: literature,
which produces cortical responses, or in any case emotional responses from somewhere above the belt, and pornography,
which gets you in the groin. The categories were treated as mutually exclusive.

The categories were not, in my opinion, mutually exclusive.
A book might do both; it might be a work of art and at the same
time stir sexual response. Stated this way, the point sounds reasonable—to some (at the time when this will be read) even self-
evident. But to state it this way would mean I was undertaking
the defense of something the courts had always condemned.
"Do you suggest," I could hear the judges asking, "that pornography is not to be suppressed?"

The modifications of the *Hicklin* rule were no help. The
complaint was not what *Lady Chatterley's Lover* would do to

---

* As late as 1920, H. L. Mencken wrote: "Unluckily, all the decisions
are against admitting critical opinion in evidence. The Act was drawn up
by Comstock, and it is a very deft piece of work."

† Harold C. Gardiner, S.J., who has been among other things literary
editor of *America*, is a highly gifted advocate on the side of censorship. The
phrase appears in his *Moral Principles Towards a Definition of the Obscene*,
in the periodical *Law and Contemporary Problems* (volume 20).

children, but what it would do to adults. The *Ulysses* decision, though it was a tribute to the boldness of the publishers and the advocacy of Morris Ernst, actually confirmed the *Hicklin* test. Both the trial court and the appellate court were able to conclude that *Ulysses* was not really lustful. Judge Augustus Hand, for the court of appeals, reached the result by way of the whole-book rule: "The erotic passages," he said, "are submerged in the book as a whole and have little resultant effect." The whole-book rule was hardly a barrier to the pursuers of *Lady Chatterley*. Judge Woolsey found that the sex in the book repelled rather than attracted; it was "emetic, not aphrodisiac." The implication, of course, is that the book was not likely to promote sin. Nausea is not immoral.*

This would not work with *Lady Chatterley*. To be sure, Lawrence put a lot in his novel besides the sex. But sex was its theme, and the presentation of the theme involved the specific description of sexual experience. The "erotic passages" took up much more of the book than those in *Ulysses*. Indeed, if impact as well as extent was considered, it was the nonsexual passages that might be deemed isolated. Nor could Lawrence's descriptions be said to make sex unattractive. What Mellors and Connie were up to sounded pretty good. Certainly not emetic and, to most people, probably aphrodisiac.

Perhaps I was skeptical of the utility of the *Ulysses* formulas because I disliked them. *Lady Chatterley's Lover* would undoubtedly excite many of its readers. I did not want to deny it. I did not want to argue that because the book had literary quality it was not lustful. I wanted to argue that because it had literary quality it should not be suppressed, and that it did not matter

---

* Woolsey got the publicity, but Hand produced a better opinion. Augustus was the cousin of the more famous, but not judicially abler, Learned Hand. The latter, whose opinions contain some of the best prose America has produced, achieved enormous prestige as a judge which might more appropriately have been accorded him as a writer and a philosopher of the law. Learned Hand was extraordinarily creative, but he was better at contributing ideas than at choosing between competing ideas presented to him, and the primary function of a judge is to judge. (One who has both sound judgment and an original, creative mind is a great judge; Holmes and Brandeis are examples.)

that it was lustful. Although no court had said such a thing, and despite the fact that most courts had said the contrary, I thought I had authority for the position. The authority was very high—the United States Supreme Court. The difficulty was that the case I proposed to use as a precedent was generally regarded as a precedent pointing the other way. It was the *Roth* case.

On the face of it, the strategy was risky. We would be conceding the point that until then had determined the outcome of obscenity cases. But the publisher was willing to take the chance. "Appeal to sexual interest," our brief stated, "does not create obscenity."

I suggest that Rosset is owed a debt of gratitude—or, if you happen to be on the other side of the fundamental issue, a deep reproach. It is one thing for a lawyer to gamble on a novel theory. If he is presenting what he believes to be the law, or what the law ought to be, a defeat may hurt, but the hurt will be soothed by the thought that it was a good venture and that the theory proposed may someday become the law. The publisher is in a different position. He is usually, and naturally, interested in selling his book, not in altering the shape of legal doctrine.

Moreover, more than money was at stake. There is a saying around the criminal courts: "The lawyer always goes home." Though the *Lady Chatterley* case started as a contest about whether the book might be mailed, there was a better than even chance that an adverse decision would touch off criminal prosecutions. The lawyer always goes home; the client may not. One who publishes a book held to be obscene may indeed go to jail.

Samuel Roth did. And paradoxically, it was his case on which I was relying.

Aspects
of the Law *

I SAID THAT THE CASE I PROPOSED TO USE AS A
precedent was generally regarded as a precedent pointing the
other way. Some readers may want to know what a precedent is,
exactly, and how a lawyer uses one.

The kind of questioning a lawyer usually hears is less patient:
What good are precedents? Are they not the dead hand of the
past? Could not simple fairness, understood by all, settle our
disputes? The law's detractors feel that justice and the law are
counterposed. They speak of "technicalities," a useless and ridiculous word—useless because some factors ought to affect decisions and others ought not, and the epithet will not reduce the
force of the former or serve to delimit the latter; ridiculous because it implies that technique may be dispensed with and a
complicated mechanism yet be made to work. These critics ask,
with an air of keen-mind-cutting-through-to-essentials, why the
courts cannot decide each case according to what is right.

The principle to which they object is called *stare decisis* ("to
stand by decided matters"). The words suggest a fixedness that

---

* I must warn the reader that part of this chapter represents a highly
personal view of the law, and that if he is interested in the jurisprudence
involved, he ought not to stop with this short and undocumented description.

the principle in action does not have. *Stare decisis* means that issues once resolved ought to stay that way unless there is an extraordinary reason to change them. But in many fields of law (apart from simple points rarely litigated), the resolution of the issue—which, generalized, is a rule—is more a tendency than an absolute.

Rules of law are, in their essence, rules of degree. Cases of the same degree occur only rarely; Parmenides is present, but Heraclitus dominates. You cannot, because the water flows, enter the same stream twice. Even if all the testimony and all the documents in the matter at bar were precisely the same as those in the precedent cited, the two cases would not be the same. In the time between, the world would have changed. The world as it exists when the case is tried itself is a fact in the case.

A rigid insistence on repeating earlier decisions is in reality a denial of the principle. A true devotion to precedent may require different results in situations superficially similar. *Stare decisis* is hardly rule by rote; it is rather a gravitation toward the legal experience of the past. Allowance having been made for change in circumstance, it demands that courts should try to decide things now as they decided them before—subject always to the capacity for modification that is part of each living cell of the law. Courts are naturally influenced by what seems just in the specific human situations before them, but they have no authority to decide each case solely according to what seems just, and they rarely—very rarely—make a rule that is entirely new. Indeed in some fields of law, where it is especially important that there be freedom to act in reliance on a given legal fundament, courts will not wander from what is established; they wait for legislatures to make the move. And throughout the law, the courts are not likely to change their ways very much at a time.

There are several reasons why they are not:

(1) *Stare decisis* is an anticorruption device. If courts are not bound by external rules, if they are not called upon to explain their decisions in terms of precedent, corruption is made easier. "What is right" in a particular case too readily becomes what is right for the particular judge or his friends. There should be a

single set of laws for rich and poor alike; that much is easy. There should also be one set of laws for those who helped the judge get on the bench and those who opposed, for those who have good stock-market information to give the judge and those who don't, for the political clubhouse and the rest of the neighborhood, for the organized group and the unattached private citizen. *Stare decisis* does not insure this. But it makes it complicated and awkward for the judge to be dishonest. His decision must appear consistent with what has been done in the past, and more than an appearance of consistency is necessary to avoid reversal on appeal. A system in which he was bound only to achieve a "just result" would be a breeze for the crooked judge. There are considerations, he would tell you, that are not immediately apparent; one must not be too technical.

(2) More broadly—whether or not what stands in the way is corruption—fairness demands that people in similar situations should be treated in a similar way.

(3) Society implies order, and order implies not only a uniform application of law at any moment, but also a strong continuity from moment to moment. There must be a given pattern for each instant in time, and the pattern must hold still—reasonably still—as time goes by. It is important to know in advance the legal consequences of one's actions, and private ethics do not afford a solid basis of prediction. There are many conflicts between individuals in which ethics are quite neutral, and even some in which they may argue a result different from the law's. The rules that resolve these conflicts express a judgment as to what works best, and most closely approximates justice, in a sufficiently large number of situations—sufficiently large so that future situations can be assimilated to that judgment, without a contest and a victory and defeat on each occasion. A general solution will not do ideal justice in all the cases of its class, but lacking general solutions, individuals and institutions in a complex society are left uncertain as to how to act. The rules provide a structure, and plans are made in reliance on the structure. Nothing in the heavens ordains, for example, that a contract for the sale of real estate must be written and signed, but the economy will not function if in one season the courts demand the writing and in the next they do not. Indeed, sometimes the good

of society requires more urgently that there be a rule than that the rule be good. It may be argued that cars should be driven on the left of the road rather than the right; the point does not seem important. But it is very important that they keep to one side or the other, and that the rule not be subject to frequent change.

(4) There is a practical utility in *stare decisis* that is not confined to the law. Habit has its defects, but it is economical. The search for precedent goes on everywhere: in the business office, when a difficult question comes up, we head for the files; how was it handled the last time? The law is not involved; there is no external compulsion. But we know that last time thought and effort went into the problem, and it seems a good idea to have the benefit of that thought and effort now. The past has banked its wisdom, and it is foolish not to draw on it.

And so the law adheres to the past. If there is no fitting precedent because the circumstances are so very different, a new principle may be announced, but more often an old one is modified to suit. Ordinarily, the circumstances being sufficiently similar, the court calls on earlier cases to justify its decision. Sometimes there are several that seem pertinent, but they differ among themselves; the precedents are said to be in conflict, and courts look for "the weight of authority." The more evenly distributed the weight, the greater the freedom that the court enjoys (or grumbles about). If there is no conflict among the precedents and they seem to forbid the decision that the present court thinks right, the court's first effort is to find distinguishing features; it will try to show that what are said to be opposing precedents do not in fact oppose the present solution.

Occasionally time and events, or simply further thought, demand that a precedent (or even a line of precedents) be overruled—that is, held to be wrong or so inappropriate to new conditions that it must be explicitly discarded. (Overruling can be done only by the court from which the precedent came, never by lower courts, which can disapprove but not reject.) But when this happens, the court may find that its new decision is in better harmony with the past. The judges remark that the precedent was itself inconsistent with older cases; it is treated as a nonreproductive mutation, a mistake in the ontogeny of the law. In the rare situation where the distinctions are not impressive enough, or the weight of authority is too heavy to yield to subtle shifting, or there is no sounder ancient tradition to go by, and yet the court is convinced that the precedent will not serve —then the opinion will allow, with a nearly audible sigh, that if the cited case cannot be squared with the present decision, then the cited case must be regarded as overruled. This does not happen often. The lawyer as advocate should not count on its happening at all. He had better try to show that what he is asking— no matter how fresh or strange it may at first appear—will, considered thoroughly, be found to fit the structure of the law, and not be out of keeping, really, with earlier judicial ideas.

Although historically it is the conservatism of the courts that has excited most of the complaints, we currently have a Supreme Court attacked for what are called its innovations. The complaints about adherence to precedent come traditionally from the left; the cry against the present Court comes roughly from the right. The Justices are accused of disregarding rules of law, abandoning standards, inviting chaos and—the ultimate in flouting authority—going Communist. And Congress expresses its legal learning by denying to the Justices a raise in pay that it grants to other government employees.

The congressional anguish (and that of some sections of the American Bar Association, for another respectable example) is not in fact what it is said to be. There is no real mourning for *stare decisis*. There is only a wail of frustration from those who do not like the Bill of Rights, did not really know it was there, and would certainly have voted against it in 1787. The wailing is not for a lost principle, but for distasteful results.

For three quarters of a century following the Civil War, Supreme Court majorities could not seem to find the Bill of Rights, except when property or income needed protection.*

---

* A judicial utterance that is cited to epitomize the attitude is that of federal judge Josiah Van Orsdel, who in 1922 held a women's minimum-wage law unconstitutional, a decision subsequently affirmed by the Supreme Court. A half-sentence of his has more than once been quoted (in derogation) by liberals:

Less myopic, the current bench is abused for decisions that enforce constitutional liberties other than the liberty to make money. But this is hardly a departure from the principle of *stare decisis*. What the Court has done in the last decade—on separation of church and state, on civil rights, on censorship—is in its legal essence conservative. The Court insists on adhering to an old document too long ignored.

Stare decisis does not stand in the way of needed change, but it almost never permits a gap in the continuum. The origin of the change can usually be found in decisions which themselves did not make the change, or did not make it unequivocally. The law cannot be picked up at one point and set down again at another point far away. It can only be nudged along. Sometimes, however, it can be given a pretty good nudge.

It should be remembered that of the three fundamental principles which underlie government, and for which government exists, the protection of life, liberty and property, the chief of these is property; . . .

Although this pretty well indicates the tendency of the Supreme Court majorities during the period mentioned, the selection is unfair to Judge Van Orsdel; the rest of the sentence is this:

not that any amount of property is more valuable than the life or liberty of the citizen, but the history of civilization proves that, when the citizen is deprived of the free use and enjoyment of his property, anarchy and revolution follow, and life and liberty are without protection.

The judge's values were decent—not what the first half of the sentence, standing alone, would imply. But his fears were unfounded: anarchy did not follow when the courts, some time later, sustained new minimum-wage laws, along with much other legislation that "deprived [the citizen] of the free use and enjoyment of his property." Civilization did not disappear. Neither did the institution of property; all that happened was that more people got more of it.

It is arguable that the courts' concern for property rights during the period, and their striking down of legislation that would hamper free enterprise, were in the long run beneficial—that a growing America needed that degree of economic wildness (despite the attendant brutality) to achieve economic strength, and ultimately to spread its wealth over nine tenths of its people. The Bill of Rights, however, will not be fulfilled so long as the other tenth is robbed.

That is the teleology and the effect of precedents. Now I will speak about their anatomy and habitat. Precedents consist of what courts do, and of what courts say—the former more than the latter. They are found in the printed reports of cases (although in earlier times, when reporting was unofficial and unsystematic, they were often found only in the memories of judges and lawyers). In general, the things courts do are called decisions, orders and judgments, and the reasons they give for what they do are called opinions.*

The function of an opinion is to let the community know what the law is and to justify the court's action to the parties. A simple summary of the facts of the case and of the result would tell us a good deal, but it would not tell us enough. We need to know which facts the court deemed significant, the precedents it looked to, the meaning found in statutory language, the weight ascribed to contentions of counsel. The court's statement of these things is important principally for the aid it gives us in foreseeing what will happen in future cases. It is important also because having to make the statement will reveal the weakness

---

* A little more legal vocabulary, for present and future use: A trial is a way of ascertaining facts; it employs as fact-finding devices the examination and cross-examination of witnesses and the study of physical evidence, most prominently documents. The law to be applied is determined by the judge, after hearing (or reading) argument. (A brief is simply an argument written out.) If there is no jury, the judge determines the facts as well. A verdict is a jury's doing; a judge's determination is a decision. A motion is a party's request that something be done in the course of the litigation; the judge's response to the request is also a decision. So is an upper court's affirmance or reversal on appeal. The final exercise of judicial power on behalf of one party or the other is a judgment—an acquittal or a conviction in a criminal case, a dismissal or the granting of relief (an award of money or a decree controlling conduct) in a civil case. An intermediate exercise of the power is an order.

In many cases there is no opinion. Frequently the dispute is not as to the law but only as to the facts, and there is less need for an opinion. But even where there is an issue of law, and even where the case goes up on appeal, it may be decided without opinion, or with a very brief opinion—a proper timesaver when the reasons for the result are clear enough.

of the incompetent court and impose a restraint on the corrupt one. And finally, justice owes the losing side an explanation.

An opinion should deal explicitly with the contentions it rejects; if there is a plausible argument left unrebutted, the opinion is a failure. But this kind of failure occurs with an unfortunate frequency; it is bad for the law and unfair to the litigant. When the case is looked to as a precedent, its meaning will not be clear; the facts may suggest an approach and a possible solution that the opinion unaccountably ignores.

The failure is due to several things. One is the fact that most judges are overworked; they simply do not always have the time to write a well-reasoned rejection of a well-reasoned argument. Another is honest incompetence; the judge has a feeling that a certain decision should be reached but is not able to deal with the barriers that seem to stand in the way. A third is part of the general problem of judicial corruption; if he is unable to refute the arguments of the side that he wants to rule against, the dishonest judge simply disregards them.

To write a really good opinion, a judge must be gifted, both in analytical reasoning and in the use of language. These talents are not the same as those involved in reaching the right result. Good judgment may be found in one who has no large capacity either for legal analysis or for the use of language. But a good opinion, since it must state the reasons for the result, requires something beyond the ability to arrive at it. (A judge who lacks the necessary abilities may nevertheless be able to put his name to a good opinion if the lawyer for the winning side has given him a good brief. This is an area where plagiarism is not only lawful, but keenly desired by the victim.)

Corruption does not mean only the little black bag. It means anything that induces the judge, consciously, to make a ruling different from what an objective view would recommend. There is also unconscious corruption. For example, a highly respected New York judge of some years back: impeccably honest in the ordinary sense, he had worked his way up from the ghetto, and was unduly respectful toward prominent Wall Street lawyers and unduly receptive to their arguments. Another judge of the same background might have a prejudice the other way. I distinguish between conscious and unconscious corruption because innocent biases are not so much an evil as a difficulty.

Some of the worst opinions in legal history—considering the eminence from which they issued—were written by a judge who was neither corrupt nor incompetent. He was a Chief Justice of the United States Supreme Court. His name was Edward Douglass White, and he was on the bench from 1894 to 1921. White was a good man—"an untiring worker . . . courageous and kind to young practitioners," a judge of "gracious demeanor and democratic simplicity of manner." He maintained this demeanor in spite of a curious physical disability.* But in a position where elegance is highly desirable and lucidity a basic requirement, White never seemed to be able to find the right words. (He was known as a linguist, but apparently English was not among the languages that made his reputation.)

White had a formula he used when it was a little too difficult to refute an opposing point. Having arrived at the conclusion he considered correct and finding the way to it blocked by an argument from the losing side (or by the lower court whose decision was being reversed), White responded by simply dismissing the argument. He would describe the issue that was posed and then say: "To state the question is to answer it."

One of the Justices while White was Chief was John J. Clarke. Clarke's tenure was notable for several things: the fact that it was very short, the fact that it ended because he resigned to work for world peace, his sometimes wavering membership in a triumvirate of dissenters (the others being the more celebrated Holmes and Brandeis), and his outstanding ability. (Where the Bill of Rights was concerned, he was zealous on fair trial, less than zealous on free speech.) Relatively obscure among Supreme Court Justices, he should be famous, if for nothing else, then for one great phrase.

It was delivered in an antitrust case decided in 1920, the year

---

* This was ". . . a nervous affliction which prevented him from writing unless he pressed the first finger of his right hand against the right side of his nose and held his pen between his second finger and his thumb. In order to write in this position he would lower his face until his nose almost brushed his paper. If by some accident his finger slipped off his nose the pen would fly out of his hand."

Harding was elected. The majority, speaking through Clarke, held that a group of companies acting in concert might consti- tute an illegal monopoly even though they controlled only part of an industry. (The opinion, for a time obscured, later emerged as a pillar of New Deal antitrust policy.) Chief Justice White, along with two other Justices, dissented. We may assume that in keeping with the Court's routine, the prevailing and dissenting views were advanced at the Justices' conferences, and the usual judicial arguments took place in chambers.

One of the important sections of Clarke's opinion begins:

Accepting the risk of obscuring the obvious by discussing it . . .

This, it is fair to say, was addressed directly to White. Clarke apparently could take no more of the Chief's bland and mad- dening rejection of good argument. But his tight phrase has a significance that goes far beyond any criticism of one Justice. It is a lovely comment on one of the principal failures of intellect —the dismissal of the difficult or the complicated, or the merely unwelcome, by the device of calling its contrary plain or clear or obvious.*

While a good judicial opinion, being both a work of logic and a work of art, is rare, most judicial opinions have some value. But not all parts of an opinion have equal value. In the citing of precedent, a distinction is made between "holding" and "dictum." A holding is the result reached on the facts presented, taken together with the reasoning on which the result is based. The ordinary use of the word to designate a statement of belief —"We hold these truths to be self-evident"—is not the use here. A court's holding has to do not so much with what it says as with what it does.

Anything in the opinion not necessary to the result is called dictum. The full phrase is *obiter dictum*—literally, a thing said by the way. A holding is a binding precedent; a dictum is not. A dictum may be influential, depending on the level from which it

---

* Compare John Calvin, answering the point that his division of man- kind into the Elect and the Damned was inconsistent with Christian prin- ciples of equality and brotherhood: "I stop not to notice those fanatics who pretend that grace is offered equally and promiscuously to all."

comes, the reputation of the particular judge, and the intrinsic merit of the statement. But no court is obliged to follow the talk, as distinguished from the action, of an earlier decision.

The earliest example I have found of an opinion containing both holding and dictum is in Numbers, Chapter Twenty-seven. Zelophedad had died, leaving five daughters and no sons. There was some general sentiment to the effect that women could not inherit land, and so the five daughters went to Moses and petitioned for a judgment that they were entitled to an inheritance. Moses apparently felt that the law was not settled and passed the case on up. "And Moses brought their cause before the Lord. And the Lord spake unto Moses, saying, '. . . thou shalt cause the inheritance of their father to pass unto them.'"

The Lord went further, however, and gave Moses a whole set of rules: if there was no son, the land of the deceased should go to daughters; if no daughter either, then to the brethren of the deceased; if no brethren, then to his father's brethren; and if no sons, daughters or brethren, then to "his kinsman that is next to him of his family." (Lawyers will recognize a startling resemblance to contemporary intestacy statutes, statutes that govern the passing of property when there is no will.)

The Lord's decree that the daughters of Zelophedad should have an inheritance was the holding of the case in the narrowest sense of the term. His statement that, in general, where there were no sons, daughters should inherit, was a holding in the broader sense—the principle on which the judgment was based. What the Lord said about brothers, uncles and next of kin, however, was dictum; there was no such case before the Lord. In this instance, though, the distinction between holding and dictum would be thoroughly blurred; the Lord was sitting not merely as Judge but also as Legislative Assembly.

The stress on holding is basic to our empirical, adversary kind of law. A court is charged only with deciding the issues before it. The contest between advocates is expected to produce the relevant facts, precedents and policies. But the advocates are interested, ordinarily, only in winning the case in which they are engaged. Matters that do not affect the outcome will not be presented with the full energies of counsel. Except on questions that the court is bound to resolve in order to dispose of the case, there is not that intense and combative exploration on which the law relies. Nor is there, on the part of the court, the sobering responsibility for decision that tends to exclude high-sounding vacuities.

In raising holding high above dictum, the law, as usual, reflects a human universal; our actions are more significant than our explanations. The Wall Street customer is more interested in what his broker buys for himself than in what his broker recommends. There is high philosophy in the gambler's "Put your money where your mouth is." It states, in seven words, a fundamental of Anglo-American jurisprudence.*

I have been talking of the vital principle of the law—precedent—and how it is used. The substance on which the principle works is of two kinds: the common law, and statutes. "Common law" may be misleading. It was not named for any egalitarian characteristic. It was derived from tradition and custom, and the word "common" was used to distinguish between custom merely local and custom common to all of England, and between custom prevailing within special groups (merchants, for example) and custom prevailing among Englishmen generally. The theory was that the courts were merely giving effect to existing usage and practice. The law had always been the law. "The memory of man," say the old opinions, "runneth not to the contrary."

To some extent, the theory reflected reality; the common law did embody usage and practice. But to an extent at least equal, the common law embodied the judges' ideas of what the law ought to be—usage considered desirable and practice considered

---

* The restriction of precedential significance to what is before the court has the effect of excluding points that could have been made but were not —even if the point should have been obvious. A court may go beyond what counsel have presented, and decide the case for reasons that counsel have not thought of, but judges are not obliged to develop original arguments, and rarely do. The power of a precedent is circumscribed not only by its facts, but by the points of law that were put before the court.

correct. Moreover, the custom was not always clear, and sometimes there was really no custom at all. Unless history stood still, situations would arise that were not part of any tradition. Then the courts had to adapt a tradition, or invent one. As time went on, they invoked broader and broader concepts of what the immemorial common law was (or rather must have been). The ultimate development was a complete system of *a priori* propositions and deductions therefrom, as in Sir William Blackstone's *Commentaries.*

The living law—the law applied by the courts as distinguished from the law as it was described in treatises—was never really at home in Blackstone's house of intellect; human experience is too varied, and (corruption aside) the judges usually had common sense enough to render decisions that would answer human needs. Outside Blackstone's *Commentaries* and inside the courts, there was at least as strong a compulsion to mold the proposition to fit the case as there was to decide the case by applying the proposition. But whatever elements entered into it—the influence of custom and tradition, the attraction of a snug closed *a priori* system, the desire to make rules beneficial to society, the impulse to do right in the specific case (along with the inducements to do wrong)—the common law was in fact made by judges, subject always to the constraint imposed by *stare decisis.*

The other source of the law at first seems quite different. Statutes are written rules that come from legislative bodies— Congress, Parliament, state legislatures, constitutional conventions, in earlier times the King. Here it appears that the rules are not gradually constructed from the inductive combining of decisions, but rather are instantaneously decreed in abstract statements that have a fixed and crystalline nature. It is an appearance only. Legislation, in our legal system, has the same agile, pliant quality that we see in the common law.

Judicial lawmaking is perhaps more apparent where the common law is concerned, but judges also make law where cases are governed by statute. The best of legislation does not apply with a clean clarity to all situations, and the many statutes that are less than well drafted stand in deep need of construction. If the language of a statute, in its application to a particular case, is capable of two or more competing meanings, the court in choosing one of them becomes something more than a translator.

Deciding how far a court should go to resolve statutory contradictions or to fill statutory blanks is part of the judicial art, and each time a court does this it is creating a precedent. Thus where statutes are concerned, *stare decisis* also has its role to play, and the formation of law is again in large measure inductive.

The United States Constitution is in a sense a statute—a written instrument created by a legislative body. (The British Constitution, unwritten, may be considered part of the common law.) Like other statutes, it needs judicial interpretation. There are important differences, however. What is a vice in an ordinary statute may be a virtue in a constitution. A statute should deal as precisely as possible with its subject. People affected should know where they stand, and if changing times make it work badly or experience shows it was a poor idea to begin with, repeal or amendment is relatively easy. A constitution, however, is meant to last. Highly specific provisions would involve a damaging rigidity. The part of the Constitution with which we are concerned, the Bill of Rights, would, if it were an ordinary piece of legislation, be impossibly vague. But as a general statement of the freedom and dignity of individuals, a shield against the overwhelming power of government, it is magnificent—magnificently lofty and magnificently practical.

Our rights being stated in such broad terms, the role of the courts as interpreters must be large. What might be a trespass upon legislative power when a court deals with an Act of Congress becomes a necessary exercise of responsibility when the court deals with the Constitution.

The judges are not merely interpreters; they are the final interpreters. They can nullify action taken by other branches of government on the ground that it conflicts with the Constitution, even though the other branch furiously disagrees. (This is the "doctrine of judicial review.") That judges should have such power is by no means self-evident; British judges, for example, do not have it, and the Constitution does not prescribe it. The

Supreme Court bestowed the power upon itself, and lower courts have followed suit. This happened in 1803, under the leadership of John Marshall. The Constitution declares itself the supreme law of the land. From this Marshall argued that when legislation inconsistent with the Constitution appears to govern a case, the Court has no choice but to strike down the legislation. The same analysis would apply to actions of the President.

Marshall had substantial opposition. It was argued that the judiciary had no more right to pass on the validity of the actions of the legislative and executive branches than did Congress or the President to pass on the validity of judicial decisions. Each branch had its own duty to support the Constitution; each official took the same oath to do so. Thomas Jefferson and Andrew Jackson, among others, vigorously attacked Marshall's pronouncement; their views are well known. Not so well known, and perhaps a bit surprising, especially because of what seems to be its late date, is the opposition of Abraham Lincoln. In his first inaugural address, Lincoln said that while the Court's rulings on constitutional issues should bind the parties in specific cases, such rulings should have no permanent generalized effect. Otherwise, "the people will have ceased to be their own rulers." Lincoln's attitude is less surprising when we note that the Supreme Court, after its 1803 decision, did not upset any federal legislation until 1857. Then, in the *Dred Scott* case, the Court nullified the Missouri Compromise and helped to bring on the Civil War, a use of the assumed power that would hardly recommend it to Lincoln.

Marshall's theory prevailed, but objections continued for a long time. In the 1930's many people felt that the doctrine of judicial review was standing in the way of the country's efforts to save itself from ruin. Today Marshall seems to have been vindicated, but maybe we were just lucky: for the past quarter-century most of the Justices have been men of extraordinary ability and high ideals. The members of the Court are appointed, not elected, and appointed for life, and so they are beyond the direct control of the people. It is not inconceivable that someday most of them will be men of low ideals or little ability, and either of these possibilities could be disastrous. Yet the process of constitutional amendment gives us a residue of control, and so do political processes less direct, as Franklin Roosevelt demonstrated with his threat to pack the bench. The plan was not enacted, but its objective was achieved; the Court's attitude toward social and economic legislation changed appreciably. (Another political appeal, without Presidential sponsorship, and thus far unsuccessful, has been taken from the decisions of the Court of the 1960's—the "Impeach Warren" appeal.)

Despite the distinguished opposition, leaving the last constitutional word to the Supreme Court seems to be the wisest way to deal with a question that has no thoroughly satisfactory answer. In the long run, law-imbued Justices are more likely to adhere to fundamental principles of liberty than jumpy congressmen or action-minded Presidents.

It was this power of the courts to undo statutes that was invoked in the defense of *Lady Chatterley*, *Tropic of Cancer* and *Fanny Hill*. The defense in each case was that the anti-obscenity statute the government sought to use, as applied to the particular book, was unconstitutional—that the First Amendment, properly interpreted, stood in the way. The interpretation I urged would constitute a rule as to the meaning of the Amendment and I would be asked to cite the precedent on which my proposed rule was based.

Now, before we get down to cases, a final few didactic paragraphs.

I said, and passed it by quickly, that what our courts do, more than what they say, produces rules of law. It is not the courts' business (it could be, under a different legal system) to invent and proclaim abstract rules. Instead, they create principles through their decisions, and while invention is often involved, it must work on the materials of the past. Courts may properly make general statements only as they are appropriate to the occasion, and nothing qualifies as an occasion except a specific dispute between litigants.

Sometimes the distinction between judicial action and utterance is extreme. There may be no clear statement of principle—

there may even be conflicting pronouncements in the cases —yet the decisions themselves will have a hidden consistency; a silent rule of law will lie ready for articulation.* More often, of course, the rule is explicit, if not always well stated. But it usually needs the molding and the definition that is gained only when a number of decisions are considered together; the process is essentially inductive.

Once in a while a single case can supply the rule. The court must be high enough, the case as presented must cut a sharp issue, and the court must resolve the issue with a statement of law that makes a snug fit with the facts. But even here it is not the statement alone that constitutes the law; whatever appears in the opinion gets form and color from the particular case.

We arrive now at the last and most difficult question: how do we separate the gratuitous from the necessary, the dictum from the holding? What besides the naked result itself may be considered part of the precedent? One reason for the difficulty is that opinions are not always clear. Sometimes there are simple lapses in logic or ambiguities in expression. Sometimes, on more complicated issues, there may be lines of thought so tangled that

---

* This was impressed on me very early, at the beginning of my second year in law school, when I was writing something for a law review. It was in the field that is called, rather charmingly, the law of conflict of laws— which has to do with choosing the law to govern a transaction that has roots in several states, where the different states would treat the transaction differently. The particular question related to a living donor's trust and the restrictive rules that sometimes invalidate such a trust. The beneficiaries may live in one state, while the trustee administers the trust in a second, the property is located in a third, and the donor himself is a resident of a fourth. There was a jumble of contradictory opinions; calling on "established principles," some courts picked one state, some another. But I was struck by the fact that in every case the court picked a state whose laws would make the trust valid. The judges, it seemed, were worried about the children for whose support the trusts had been set up, and while they could not quite bring themselves to say that this determined their decisions, it was the plain meaning of what they had done, and they could be counted on to do it again, no matter what the legal theory might be.

There are not many situations in which a rule is so well hidden or so clear once it is uncovered, but the caricature illustrates an important feature of our judicial system.

it is hard to see which line runs unbroken from the question to the answer. But even assuming a reasonable clarity, there is frequently no sure way to define the precedent.

Rules of law may be stated in varying degrees of generalization. The particular set of facts on which decision has been made can be described in different degrees of abstraction; the case can fit into smaller or larger concentric patterns. In order to ascertain the principle a decision stands for—to mark the precedent it constitutes—it is necessary to select a pattern of the right size and shape. The selection, I would say, depends on what is sufficient for the purposes of precedent, the purposes I discussed early in this chapter. The pattern should not be so large as to foreclose the flexibility the law ought to have. It should not be so small that we end with an impractical complexity of tiny rules.

Without postponing too long the story I propose to tell, I cannot now go farther with this aspect of the law. Let me simply say that opinion-as-precedent can be a plastic thing in the hands of lawyers and judges. It is open to the advocate to contend, despite what the court said, that a generalization of only a certain breadth was needed to produce the cited decision. He may argue that some of the opinion is the bone and muscle that support the result, and all the rest is fat. He may even argue that the court has not stated the true support of its decision, or stated it only casually—that there is a neglected proposition which is necessary to the result, a proposition to be deemed implicit in the court's reasoning and therefore in its holding. Something scarcely mentioned by the court may be an essential part of the precedent.

The Roth *Case*

TWO CHAPTERS AGO I SAID THE *ROTH* CASE WAS generally regarded as a defeat for civil libertarians, and that nevertheless it was the lever with which I hoped to open the mails to *Lady Chatterley.* The *Roth* case was actually two cases.

Samuel Roth, who had earlier lent his name to less-celebrated obscenity litigation, was a man of considerable culture. Some of the material he sold was trash; some of it was unquestionably literature. (Roth's previous convictions involved, among other things, *Ulysses* and Schnitzler's *Reigen.*) His own view (expressed to me in conversation some time after he got out of jail) was that reading is itself a great good, that any kind of reading is better than no reading and that some people will read only rather low material, which he was willing to supply. In the case that gave him immortality, Roth was prosecuted in the federal courts of New York under the Comstock Act. At about the same time, a man named Alberts, whose list had none of the occasional quality that Roth's had, was prosecuted under state law in California. Each was convicted, and their convictions were affirmed by intermediate appellate courts. The Supreme Court heard the cases together in the spring of 1957, and decided them that June. The Court wrote one set of opinions for both cases, which became known as the *Roth* opinions. (It is not known whether Alberts found this objectionable.)

The appeals had reached Washington in attenuated form. The lawyers for each defendant asked the Court to rule on only one question—whether the anti-obscenity statute under which he was prosecuted was unconstitutional "on its face." That is, they did not argue that the specific publications could not be suppressed; they argued that the statutes were altogether void. Hence every Justice but one treated the cases as presenting a broad, totally abstract issue: may the government ever punish the publication of obscene writing? The Court ruled that it might, and upheld both the federal and the state statutes.

Five members of the Court joined in an opinion written by Mr. Justice Brennan. (Frankfurter, Clark, Burton and Whittaker were with him.) Chief Justice Warren added a vote in favor of affirmance, but for different reasons. Mr. Justice Harlan concurred on Alberts' conviction but dissented on Roth's. Mr. Justice Douglas and Mr. Justice Black dissented in both cases, in an opinion written by Douglas. The split was thus six to three on Roth's conviction and seven to two on Alberts', fairly formidable majorities for the modern Supreme Court.*

To all the Justices the main question was a First Amendment question. The Brennan majority saw it as "whether obscenity is utterance within the area of protected speech and press." They held that it was not. (They also rejected certain contentions based on other constitutional provisions; the only one worth noting was that obscenity was impossible to define and therefore the statutes were too vague, which they disposed of by saying "the Constitution does not require impossible standards"

---

* In strict usage, living members of the Court are referred to as "Mr. Justice," while the dead are honored by dropping the "Mr."

There is no difference of any consequence between the titles "judge" and "justice." Their official use is governed by the statute establishing the particular court. While the members of the United States Supreme Court are called justices, so are the members of the New York Supreme Court, which is supreme only in the sense that it is that state's most important court of original jurisdiction. Those of the highest New York court—the Court of Appeals—are called judges. And the lowliest judicial officer in most states is the justice of the peace.

A court of original jurisdiction is one where cases start, as distinguished from a court that reviews decisions (an appellate court). It is sometimes called a trial court, although as often as not cases end without a trial.

and "when measured by common understanding and practices" these statutes were definite enough.)

The ground of the Douglas-Black dissent was that the First Amendment, cast in absolute terms, excludes laws that make expression illegal. The government may regulate only conduct, Douglas said, and speech and writing may be suppressed only when they amount to conduct, or are "so closely brigaded with illegal action as to be an inseparable part of it." Since anti-obscenity statutes impinge upon speech and writing as such, these two Justices would have held the statutes unconstitutional.

Harlan distinguished between federal and state laws. He took a narrow view of what the federal government could do—that is, a liberal view of what might be published. On the other hand, he felt that state governments should be given great latitude in dealing with obscenity. The tastes and needs of different communities vary, he argued, and it is a feature of our political system that state legislatures should be permitted to experiment. Hence he would have reversed Roth's conviction, but he agreed that Alberts' should be affirmed.

None of the other Justices recognized a federal-state distinction. The First Amendment, and the other nine amendments of the Bill of Rights, were designed as a protection against the new, suspect central government that a great many Americans did not want at all. The Fourteenth Amendment, on the other hand, was adopted after the Civil War, when people (the people who won, that is) were worried about what state governments might do. It does not spell out the safeguards of the Bill of Rights, but it forbids the states to deprive any person of life, liberty or property without due process of law, and over the years the Court has decided that "due process" includes a number of the assurances originally demanded of the federal government. Free speech is among them. Harlan, however, felt that the guaranties did not operate with the same force where the states were concerned.

The Chief Justice also stood alone, upon a very different ground. Ordinarily the Court considers only questions that the litigants raise, and here the sole defense was that the statutes were totally, in all circumstances, invalid. If one arrived at the conclusion that on some occasion they might have valid use, that would defeat the defense. But Warren went farther: he believed the courts should focus not on the kind of book being sold, but on the kind of person who sold it. As to *Roth* and *Alberts*:

> The defendants in both these cases were engaged in the business of purveying textual or graphic matter openly advertised to appeal to the erotic interest of their customers. They were plainly engaged in the commercial exploitation of the morbid and shameful craving for materials with prurient effect. I believe that the state and federal governments can constitutionally punish such conduct.

For the litigation that followed, all the *Roth* opinions were important, but by far the most important was Brennan's. Since it spoke for five Justices, it was the opinion of the Court, and it thus drew the contours of the precedent.

Because it was crucial to the cases that came later, the reader should first see the opinion on his own, without comment from me. It is reprinted below, excluding only citations, footnotes (except one that has had particular importance) and a few paragraphs that can be omitted without jeopardy to sense or balance.

> The dispositive question is whether obscenity is utterance within the area of protected speech and press. Although this is the first time the question has been squarely presented to this Court, either under the First Amendment or under the Fourteenth Amendment, expressions found in numerous opinions indicate that this Court has always assumed that obscenity is not protected by the freedoms of speech and press. . . .
>
> The guaranties of freedom of expression in effect in ten of the fourteen states which by 1792 had ratified the Constitution, gave no absolute protection for every utterance. Thirteen of the fourteen states provided for the prosecution of libel, and all of those states made either blasphemy or profanity, or both, statutory crimes. As early as 1712, Massachusetts made it criminal to publish "any filthy, obscene or profane song, pamphlet, libel or mock sermon" in imitation or mimicking of religious services. Thus, profanity and obscenity were related offenses.
>
> In light of this history, it is apparent that the unconditional phrasing of the First Amendment was not intended to

protect every utterance. This phrasing did not prevent this Court from concluding that libelous utterances are not within the area of constitutionally protected speech. At the time of the adoption of the First Amendment, obscenity law was not as fully developed as libel law, but there is sufficiently contemporaneous evidence to show that obscenity, too, was outside the protection intended for speech and press.

The protection given speech and press was fashioned to assure unfettered interchange of ideas for the bringing about of political and social changes desired by the people. . . .

All ideas having even the slightest redeeming social importance—unorthodox ideas, controversial ideas, even ideas hateful to the prevailing climate of opinion—have the full protection of the guaranties, unless excludable because they encroach upon the limited area of more important interests. But implicit in the history of the First Amendment is the rejection of obscenity as utterly without redeeming social importance. This rejection for that reason is mirrored in the universal judgment that obscenity should be restrained, reflected in the international agreement of over fifty nations, in the obscenity laws of all of the forty-eight states, and in the twenty obscenity laws enacted by the Congress from 1842 to 1956. This is the same judgment expressed by this Court in *Chaplinsky* v. *New Hampshire:*

> There are certain well-defined and narrowly limited classes of speech, the prevention and punishment of which have never been thought to raise any constitutional problem. *These include the lewd and obscene. . . . It has been well observed that such utterances are no essential part of any exposition of ideas, and are of such slight social value as a step to truth that any benefit that may be derived from them is clearly outweighed by the social interest in order and morality. . . .* (Emphasis added.)

We hold that obscenity is not within the area of constitutionally protected speech or press.

It is strenuously urged that these obscenity statutes offend the constitutional guaranties because they punish incitation to impure sexual *thoughts,* not shown to be related to any overt antisocial conduct which is or may be incited in the persons stimulated to such *thoughts.* In *Roth,* the trial judge instructed the jury: "The words 'obscene, lewd and lascivious' as used in the law, signify that form of immorality which has relation to sexual impurity and has a tendency to excite lustful *thoughts*." (Emphasis added.) In *Alberts*, the trial judge applied the test laid down in *People* v. *Wepplo*, namely, whether the material has "a substantial tendency to deprave or corrupt its readers by inciting lascivious *thoughts* or arousing lustful desires." (Emphasis added.) It is insisted that the constitutional guaranties are violated because convictions may be had without proof either that obscene material will perceptibly create a clear and present danger of antisocial conduct, or will probably induce its recipients to such conduct. But, in light of our holding that obscenity is not protected speech, the complete answer to this argument is in the holding of this Court in *Beauharnais* v. *Illinois*:

> Libelous utterances not being within the area of constitutionally protected speech, it is unnecessary, either for us or for the state courts, to consider the issues behind the phrase "clear and present danger." Certainly no one would contend that obscene speech, for example, may be punished only upon a showing of such circumstances. Libel, as we have seen, is in the same class.

However, sex and obscenity are not synonymous. Obscene material is material which deals with sex in a manner appealing to prurient interest.* . . .

* I.e., material having a tendency to excite lustful thoughts. *Webster's New International Dictionary* (unabridged, 2d ed., 1949) defines *prurient*, in pertinent part, as follows: ". . . Itching; longing; uneasy with desire or longing; of persons, having itching, morbid or lascivious longings; of desire, curiosity or propensity, lewd. . . ."
Pruriency is defined, in pertinent part, as follows: ". . . Quality of being prurient; lascivious desire or thought. . . ."
We perceive no significant difference between the meaning of obscenity developed in the case law and the definition of the A.L.I., Model Penal Code: ". . . A thing is obscene if, considered as a whole, its predominant appeal is to prurient interest, i.e., a shameful or morbid interest in nudity, sex or excretion, and if it goes substantially beyond customary limits of candor in description or representation of such matters. . . ."

The early leading standard of obscenity allowed material to be judged merely by the effect of an isolated excerpt upon particularly susceptible persons. *Regina* v. *Hicklin*. Some American courts adopted this standard, but later decisions have rejected it and substituted this test: whether to the average person, applying contemporary community standards, the dominant theme of the material taken as a whole appeals to prurient interest. The *Hicklin* test, judging obscenity by the effect of isolated passages upon the most susceptible persons, might well encompass material legitimately treating with sex, and so it must be rejected as unconstitutionally restrictive of the freedoms of speech and press. On the other hand, the substituted standard provides safeguards adequate to withstand the charge of constitutional infirmity.

Both trial courts below sufficiently followed the proper standard. Both courts used the proper definition of obscenity. . . .

The *Roth* case was hailed as a victory by those bent on suppression. There had been attacks on the Comstock Act and on a typical state law, and the attacks had been repulsed. The favorite arguments of those who opposed censorship—that obscenity was impossible to define and that there was no demonstrable connection between exposure to it and antisocial behavior—had been explicitly rejected. There was some stately language about the importance of the First Amendment guaranties, but obscenity, the Court held, lay outside those guaranties.* Obscenity was given an elaborate definition—the prurient-interest formula—which the opinion said was only a summary of what most courts had already been saying. The two unpalatable elements of the *Hicklin* rule were no longer accepted. But otherwise the old law apparently remained intact. It might indeed be said that *Roth* had strengthened it. The intellectual minority was not going to have its way; the tastes of the avant-garde would not disrupt the restraints on publication that a majority morality required.

There was reason for the censors' satisfaction. Most students, including those who would have liked to see a change, agreed with this interpretation of the case. There are internal inconsist-

---

* A paragraph calling for "ceaseless vigilance" to protect "material which does not treat sex in a manner appealing to prurient interest" was omitted from the reprint above for the same reason that it has been so widely quoted: it is a resounding statement of high principle that all sides can subscribe to.

encies in the *Roth* opinion; one encounters items that simply do not fit. But on the face of it, the most plausible summary seems to be this:

> The question is whether obscenity is protected by the First Amendment. It is not. This is demonstrated by the following: (1) The Court has always assumed that obscenity is not protected. (2) The First Amendment guaranties are not absolute; thirteen of the fourteen states that ratified the Constitution provided for the prosecution of criminal libel, and all fourteen made either blasphemy or profanity, or both, statutory crimes. (3) Statutes and decisions "sufficiently contemporaneous" with the ratification of the Constitution indicate that obscenity was among the exceptions to the guaranties. And this is fitting, because obscenity is utterly without redeeming social importance. Accordingly, "we hold that obscenity is not within the area of constitutionally protected speech or press." Now we go on to define obscenity. It does not mean simply material dealing with sex. "The standards for judging obscenity" must safeguard "material which does not treat sex in a manner appealing to prurient interest"— "i.e.," says the footnote, "material having a tendency to excite lustful thoughts." The *Hicklin* rule has been liberalized to this extent: "Later decisions have . . . substituted this test: whether to the average person, applying contemporary community standards, the dominant theme of the material taken as a whole appeals to prurient interest."

Lady Chatterley could not, of course, survive this reading. Obscenity is not protected by the First Amendment, and obscenity is defined by the prurient-interest test, which is set forth in the carefully constructed sentence that forms the climax of the opinion. It is a test that emphasizes the average man and community standards, and despite the mitigation of *Hicklin*, still turns on lustfulness. Social importance is mentioned, and literary merit might be a form of social importance, but the reference has the sound of an incidental comment, not a test. It merely confirms the reasonableness of excluding obscenity from the protection of the First Amendment, a conclusion arrived at by other routes.

You will recall, however, that an opinion is not in itself a precedent. The precedent is the holding: the decision together with the reasoning on which the decision is based. The rest is dicta—persuasive perhaps, and influential especially when the Supreme Court is speaking, but not binding upon future courts.

The simple answer of *Roth* to the simple question raised is clear enough: anti-obscenity statutes are not, in general, forbidden by the First Amendment. But that cannot be the entire holding; the conclusion is not self-evident, and in future cases courts would look to the reasons that supported it.

The reasons that the *Roth* majority stressed were not good. It was true that the Supreme Court "had always assumed that obscenity is not protected," but assumptions are not law; certain older courts had always assumed that heresy required burning. The statements on which Brennan relied came from opinions that had nothing to do with obscenity. They were offhand remarks, tossed out when obscenity was not in issue. *Dicta* so *obiter* cannot constitute precedent.

The other reasons offered rest on constitutional history. But there is no specific evidence of the attitude toward obscenity of those who framed the First Amendment. Brennan's historical argument is all inference, and the inference is unwarranted.

That the laws of the ratifying states provided punishment for libel, blasphemy and profanity does not prove that the people were willing to give the federal government such power. Profanity in any event is a special case; a common use of it is the insult hurled in a charged social situation. It is close to action— the word "hurl" is indicative—something that may be restrained in the interest of peacekeeping. We cannot suppose that those who wrote the Bill of Rights would have agreed that a book should be censored because it contained profane statements. And the hypothesis becomes ludicrous when we consider blasphemy. The founding fathers were not seventeenth-century theocratic sectarians. They were eighteenth-century students of John Locke, divided on many points but united in a rational libertarian philosophy.*

---

* When we speak of the attitudes of 1787, we must remember that it was the new central government that people were worried about, and that many of them viewed encroachments by state governments quite differently. The point is not affected, however. By the time of *Roth*, the Fourteenth Amendment had been held to incorporate most of the Bill of Rights (as I

It is certain that the Supreme Court, at the time when it decided *Roth*, would not have sanctioned the suppression of a book on the ground that it was profane or blasphemous. Yet if these colonial exceptions to freedom of speech were no longer tolerable, how did their terminated existence justify present-day punishment for obscenity? As for criminal libel, prosecutions have been so rare in our history that it may be questioned whether it is part of our law at all.

Brennan's history ends in anachronism. The opinion cites statutes and decisions as supplying "sufficiently contemporaneous evidence"—an odd concept—of the meaning of the First Amendment. None of them was in fact contemporaneous with the adoption of the Amendment. Their dates range from 1800 to 1843. But it would not matter if these statutes and decisions had more fiting dates. Even if something were part of the law in 1787, it does not follow that the framers of the Constitution meant it to remain part of the law. By its terms the Bill of Rights seeks to preserve certain features of Anglo-American law and to reject others, and to guard against certain practices governments had been known to engage in, whether or not pursuant to law. It is incongruous, even grotesque, to argue that whatever existed in colonial law was enshrined in a document that gave legal form to a rebellion.

The assumption and the history, then, prove nothing. The First Amendment speaks of freedom; it does not speak of preserving patterns of sexual behavior. Some other reason must be found for the Court's conclusion.

Fasten onto the language of the Amendment: Congress shall make "no law abridging the freedom of speech and of the press." This is one of the plainer statements in the Bill of Rights; it is not like "due process of law" or "unreasonable search." The language appears to be unequivocal. So if there is something that seems to be speech or press and yet may be pro-

---

mentioned a few pages ago), and the free-speech guaranty applied with equal force to state and federal governments. Thus, whatever might be said about the view of the guaranty in 1787 is thoroughly applicable even though it is a state law rather than a federal law that we are concerned with.

hibited, the phenomenon must be accounted for. The Court's declared reasons do not account for it.

We can agree with Brennan that those who framed the First Amendment, when they used the words "freedom of speech or of the press," did not intend to embrace every utterance. There are recognized exclusions from the guaranty; obscenity, the *Roth* decision tells us, is one of them. But why is obscenity not protected? Let us consider Brennan's statement about social importance. In form an adventitious aside, it could be something more. Parts of the opinion dressed as holding may be dicta; this ragged dictum may be holding. Obscenity can be thought of as utterance of so little value that it does not amount to "speech" or "writing" within the meaning of the First Amendment. It can reasonably be said that the majesty of an organic charter of government was not intended to protect every insignificant mouthing, every worthless scrap of paper. The contrary can be said too, but the matter is at least arguable.

In a situation like this the advocate is entitled to urge that the opinion be given a free translation. The interpretative summary that appeared a few pages back adheres as closely as possible to the language and structure of the opinion, but it is oversimplified in order to give consistency to a judicial statement that cannot count consistency among its virtues. If the opinion were in fact consistent and its reasoning strong, there would be no chance of getting a lower court to depart from its ostensible meaning. But here we have an opinion woven largely of dubious history and non sequiturs, and almost hidden among them, a thread of solid meaning. The precedent, one may argue, does not lie in the weaknesses of *Roth*; it lies in its strength.

If the Court's statement about social importance contains the true support of the decision, another step may be taken. Utter lack of social importance, it is said, justifies anti-obscenity laws. Then is that not a defining test of obscenity, so far as the Constitution is concerned? If there is speech that may be suppressed only because it has no value, then it is only speech wanting in value that may be suppressed. "The mark of suppressible obscenity," said my briefs, "inheres in the constitutional justification of the suppressive legislation."

The trouble was that no one agreed with me.

An important decision—particularly a decision on a question that the Supreme Court had never ruled on before—draws comment and discussion in legal publications. *Roth*, naturally, drew a great deal. The principal legal publications are treatises written by academics or expert practitioners, legal encyclopedias, and scholarly journals put out by the law schools and bar associations. They are treated by the courts as secondary authorities, in no way binding but frequently cited, and relied on where judicial precedents are divided or unclear.*

Instead of being able to draw on these secondary authorities for support, I found them solidly arrayed against me. The initial comments in legal periodicals all agreed that the Court's prurient-interest formula was now the constitutional definition of obscenity, and made no suggestion that any other definition might exist. As time went on, and the views of important legal writers appeared, this was confirmed. Dean Lockhart and Professor McClure of the Minnesota Law School were probably the leading commentators on the law of obscenity. A 1954 article of theirs had been cited in *Roth*, both by the majority and by the dissenting Douglas. Reexamining the subject in 1960 in the light of *Roth*, they treated the decision as one that established the prurient-interest test as the single definition of obscenity. Although they felt there ought to be a constitutional right to introduce evidence of social value, they regarded such a development as something that might occur in the future, and were "not sanguine about it." And even as a possible future develop-

---

* The *Restatements* issued by the American Law Institute, which do not fit any of these categories, are particularly influential. Written by committees of distinguished judges, practitioners and professors of law, they attempt to state what the law is or ought to be. The footnote in the *Roth* opinion cites one of them.

It is a matter of some interest that in the United States the best legal journals—and the best ones are very good indeed—are completely edited and managed (and to some extent written) by law-school students. These are the "law reviews." In no other profession are the authoritative periodicals of research and comment put in the hands of apprentices.

ment, admitting evidence is not at all the same as allowing it to control the situation.

In 1961 Professor Paul of the University of Pennsylvania Law School and Professor Schwartz of the University of California Law School published a very good book on Post Office banning. They too found that the *Roth* case had established the prurient-interest test as the sole definition of obscenity. Moreover, wrote the authors, the test "was only a new verbalization—although apparently a better wording—of the old traditional tests. . . ."

Writing as late as 1964, Albert B. Gerber, a lawyer prominent in the defense of obscenity cases, summarized the decision entirely in terms of prurient interest, "which," he said, "the Court defined to be 'material having a tendency to excite lustful thoughts.' "

These authorities were on the side of freedom and would be inclined to interpret *Roth* as liberally as possible. Yet they all accepted the average-man community-standards prurient-interest formula as the only test established by the opinion, and none of them suggested that social value could in itself save a book. Certainly those on the other side would not read the case the way I read it. "The exponents of censorship hailed the decision," Dean Lockhart said, "seeing in it an end to this foolishness about constitutional protection for material related to sex." Father Gardiner, a particularly eloquent and sophisticated exponent of censorship, wrote that the prurient-interest test had been "canonized." *

Perhaps the most interesting evidence of the outlandishness of my position came from the American Book Publishers Council, the trade organization of the book-publishing industry. The Council issues an excellent *Freedom-To-Read Bulletin*. In 1963, when I had been urging the value theory upon the courts for more than four years, and had actually got some of them to accept it, the *Bulletin* said:

> Some judges—and a good many laymen—have proceeded on the assumption that, in substance, the Court held that

---

* The only published indication of any agreement with my point of view came after the *Lady Chatterley* case had been decided, from Professor Harry Kalven of the University of Chicago Law School.

publications having any redeeming social importance could not be obscene, and therefore were entitled to the protection of the First Amendment. Others, carefully tracing Justice Brennan's reasoning through a complex maze of opinion, notes and footnotes, believe that the majority view is that all ideas and writings having the slightest social importance are entitled to the protection of the First Amendment *unless* they are obscene and therefore beyond the pale of constitutional protection.

The implication, of course, is that the analysis described in the second sentence is correct: that social importance is pertinent only where a book is not obscene. But if a book is not obscene, that is the end of the matter; there is no need for a saving standard. Social importance, the *Bulletin* was really saying, has no meaning as a legal concept.

The Council's natural bias is toward freedom of expression. The fact that its *Bulletin* made this statement in the fall of 1963 throws a cold bleak light on the loneliness of the position I occupied in the spring of 1959.

£ady Chatterley:

the Trial

THE FIRST TROUBLE THAT CAME OUT OF GROVE'S publication of *Lady Chatterley's Lover* was not with the Post Office. It was with the police. The news came to us indirectly. A deputy chief in charge of the Washington vice squad had heard the book was on sale. He telephoned Brentano's, we were informed, and asked whether it was true. The clerk said it was. The deputy chief told him to get a copy, turn to a particular page and read the page aloud over the phone. The Brentano man complied. What he read had no sex in it; it probably had to do with conditions in the colliery. The vice-squad leader did not have the Grove edition; he must have had (for law-enforcement purposes) a European edition that had got by Customs.

The press reported that the deputy chief was considering seizure of the book and criminal prosecution. We sued him, asking for a declaratory judgment that the book was not obscene.* The

---

* A suit for declaratory judgment is a very young form of legal action, about a half-century old. The idea is that it may be well to have a dispute decided before anybody gets hurt. The court is asked to state the rights of the parties—that is, to describe the legal situation—rather than to award money or issue a command (though the court may sometimes grant an injunction at the same time).

suit remained dormant while the Post Office action went forward in New York, and when that was ended, the matter was settled for Washington too.

On April 30, 1959, two days after the Washington suit was filed, Robert K. Christenberry, formerly chairman of the Boxing Commission and candidate for mayor, and now postmaster of the City of New York, took a hand. He ordered the interception of twenty-four cartons of the book that Grove had mailed. Christenberry asked the Post Office Department in Washington for instructions. The book had been banned from the mails some thirty years earlier, and the department saw no reason to change its mind. A few days after the seizure Grove heard about it informally, and a few days after that got an official notice. The notice set a trial for May 14.

The circumstances of the *Lady Chatterley* trial presented some special difficulties (apart from that basic difficulty, the state of the law). One difficulty was that there was not much time to prepare. Successful trial lawyers have often said that thorough preparation is the key to success. The event in the courtroom is interesting and sometimes exciting, but the outcome is more often a product of the drudgery that preceded it.

I had not been retained by Grove Press until close to the time when the Post Office acted, and then we had to move fast. If the distribution of a book is interrupted, it may never recover, and the longer the interruption the greater the loss. That the publisher welcomes a banning is one of the myths of cynicism. A new work can conceivably benefit from the publicity, partly because people might not otherwise hear of it, and partly because of the hankering to read what we are told we mustn't. But whether the publicity is worth the litigation depends on how much of each there is, and experience shows that the cost of the latter is likely to exceed the value of the former. In any event *Lady Chatterley's Lover* was not a new work; it was already well known, and well known as something forbidden. Moreover, its copyright status was at best doubtful, and other publishers might be thinking about competing editions. It was therefore important to the publisher that things go forward quickly, and at every point we pressed for an early hearing. A consequence was that there was considerably less than the usual period to do the basic research, plan the strategy, find witnesses and draft the legal papers.

There was a compensating advantage, however. I would be free of the nagging doubt about whether everything has been done that should be done. If the preparation had not been sufficient, I could assure myself it was the result of circumstance, not of sloth. And a great deal of ground was covered under the beneficent whip of time.

The other difficulty had to do not so much with the history of the matter as with the history of me. I had never tried a case before. I had been to court, of course, but always for the argument of appeals and motions, and a trial is something quite different.* The most obvious difference is in the examination and cross-examination of witnesses, but this, I discovered, is a craft less arcane than one might think. Trial procedures were more of a problem—or would have been if I had not had the advice of my partner, George Zolotar, and Morton Yohalem, the Washington attorney who worked with me in the case. Both belong to a tiny elite: superb all-around lawyers. Finally, I had no experience with the operation of the rules of evidence. But here, as usual, the law makes sense, and the "technical" rules are a product of the realities that ought to govern the case.

At least, this was the way things struck me at the time. If there are some who would disagree, let them think of these comments as a reflection, if not of the facts, then of a mood. Having a matter this important for my first trial was a little scary, but I thought I could handle it, and if Barney Rosset was willing to take a chance, why so was I.

The trial took place within the Post Office Department. The Post Office and other government agencies are part of the executive branch, but they also have legislative and judicial powers. Their legislative powers are exercised when they issue regula-

---

* Nonlawyers whose view of the law comes mainly from plays, films and television may think of the word "trial" as covering everything (or nearly everything) that happens in court. Actually, it is just one of several stages in litigation; its purpose is to establish the facts. Civil litigation is often concluded without there ever having been a trial.

tions, their judicial powers when they decide how the regulations apply to disputed situations. The agency's decisions are
subject to review in the courts, but the scope of that review is a
much litigated question. It became a crucial question later in
the *Chatterley* case.

Departmental trials differ very little from those in the regular
courts. The man who presides is not called judge, and does not
wear robes, but he acts like a judge. In the time of the New
Deal, there was loud complaint about the powers of the administrative agencies, and the anti-Roosevelt newspapers (that is to
say, almost all the newspapers) were fond of saying that the
agencies played the triple role of judge, jury and prosecutor. To
an extent the criticism was warranted (the Administrative Procedure Act of 1946 was designed to meet some of it), but the
combination of functions cannot be altogether avoided. The
courts would be glutted to the point of paralysis if they had to
make all the decisions that are involved in the complicated economic regulation that modern society requires. And the system
does not work badly. Comparing it with the dispensation of justice in some of the lower state courts, there is certainly less corruption in the federal administrative tribunals, and probably
more judicial ability.

The Post Office functionary who acts as judge is called "Judicial Officer." In this case it was Charles D. Ablard. Though he
was an employee of the department, there was no question
about his fairness. He reached a strange result—or rather,
strangely failed to reach a result—but this was not due to any
lack of integrity. Nor was there any question about his ability;
he knew his subject, and he ran the trial well.

Grove had sold book-club rights to Readers' Subscription,
and Readers' Subscription was sending out circulars. Their circulars, as well as Grove's books, were impounded by the Post
Office, and they received notice of a hearing on the same date.
The two proceedings were joined. Readers' Subscription was
represented by Paul, Weiss, Rifkind, Wharton and Garrison,
one of the best of the large New York law firms, and Jay Topkis
and Arthur B. Frommer of that firm appeared for them.

Our adversary was the general counsel of the Post Office
Department. (The Postmaster General himself, Arthur E. Sum-

merfield, retained a theoretically judicial posture.) Saul J. Mindel and J. Carroll Schueler appeared for the general counsel.
The case was tried mostly by Mindel on the one side and me on
the other.

On the day of the trial, we began by asking for a temporary
lifting of the ban while the case was being decided. A good
many copies had been distributed before the Post Office took
action. If the book should ultimately be held mailable, we argued, the imposition of the ban would have caused a serious
financial loss to the publisher. If, on the other hand, the book
should ultimately be held obscene, the beast was already at large.
I reminded Ablard that while the Postmaster General might have
made up his mind, the Judicial Officer must regard the question
as yet to be decided, else he was not judicial. Mindel replied that
in the opinion of the general counsel the book was obscene and
to send it through the mails was a crime; the Post Office had to
rely on the opinion of its own general counsel, at least until
there had been a full hearing. Ablard seemed impressed with
Mindel's argument, and about to deny our motion. So I
suggested that the ruling be postponed until the end of the trial.
Our hope was that after he had heard the whole case, Ablard
might be more favorably disposed and raise the ban while he
worked on his decision.

Topkis joined in our motion and made another of his own—
to dismiss the entire proceeding. He had several grounds, the
principal one being that the Postmaster General lacked authority to impose a ban.* This brought up an old unsettled question.
The Comstock Act had neglected to give the Postmaster General explicit power to exclude books from the mails. All the
postal banning had been based on a power that was implied.
The Act made it a crime to employ the mails to distribute obscenity, and the Post Office had taken the position that it could

---

* Topkis also contended that there could not be suppression without a
jury trial and that the Post Office proceeding was invalid because it was
against a book rather than a person. At the time, as it happened, these two
contentions were being presented to the United States Supreme Court in
an attack on a New York obscenity statute. The Court rejected them and
upheld the New York statute, in a decision announced on the day before
Lady Chatterley moved into the federal district court.

not permit itself to participate in a crime. Mindel argued that Topkis's points had already been rejected by the courts. The decisions he cited were district court decisions, however, and so far as the United States Supreme Court was concerned, the question was an open one. It still is.

It was an interesting question, but not to me. The objective, as I saw it, was not simply to beat the Post Office. It was to establish the right to publish this book, and even beyond that to shrink the scope of anti-obscenity laws. This would not be accomplished by a decision that sheared the Postmaster General of his asserted authority; there were other, more drastic, governmental powers at the service of censorship. (In the somewhat different situation in which the book club found itself, Topkis' attack was well conceived.)

A strategy directed toward what one presumed to think good for society coincided with a strategy directed to what was good for my client. If the federal courts decided in our favor on the one ground we were urging—if *Lady Chatterley's Lover* was held entitled to the protection of the First Amendment—that would probably be the end of all attempts to suppress the book, under any statute, state or federal. But if we won on the ground that the Post Office had no power to do what it did, then there would be no ruling on the legality of Grove's publishing the book. The federal government could proceed under the criminal sections of the Comstock Act, and each state could invoke its own anti-obscenity law. Having defeated the Postmaster General, I could proudly present to my client the prospect of criminal trial.

Rosset and I had discussed these matters, and there was no disagreement between us. Our defense was based solely on the assertion that the publication of the book came within the guaranties of the First Amendment. For forensic purposes, we called attention to the shaky foundation on which the Post Office's assumption of power rested, but we did not ask for a ruling that the power did not exist. Nor did we raise other points that might have challenged the propriety of the proceeding.

Ablard denied Topkis's motion to dismiss the suit and deferred his ruling on my motion for a temporary lifting of the ban. Mindel now made his opening statement.

MR. MINDEL: . . . The Post Office Department is not, of course, acting as a censor when it administers the mailability statute. It exercises no prior restraint. The book has already been printed and distributed, and it is not until it is deposited in the mails for delivery by employees of the postal service that the question is raised as to its decency within the terms of the statute. . . .

We do not contend that Lawrence is a writer without standing or that his efforts in *Lady Chatterley's Lover* lack any literary merit. Neither do we say that the Post Office Department is to set itself up as a clearing house to determine what is good literature and what is not. Rather, it is our position that whatever literary merit may be found in the unexpurgated edition, it is outweighed by the obscenity; that the dominant effect of the book, taken as a whole, is one which appeals to prurient interests. The courts hold that we must attempt to strike a balance, and that if the obscenity is dominant, the book may not be mailed even though possessing some literary, scientific or other merits. The addition of the filthy and obscene terms, repeated freely and frequently throughout the book, together with the repetitious discussions and descriptions of the sex act, upset the balance, so that the literary merit is submerged and outweighed by the obscenity.

This charge is made with regard to the effect of the book on the average member of the community, and not upon a particular class, much more sophisticated than the average, which may become so immersed in its admiration of the author's technical skill in this book and his other works that it overlooks the end to which that skill is applied; that is, the extremely graphic and detailed portrayal of a woman's sex experiences with a variety of men before and during her marriage. A literary critic, a book reviewer, may enter his plea that *Lady Chatterley's Lover* should not be barred, but in doing so he merely expresses his personal opinion in the matter. He can speak only for himself and not for the community at large. . . .

This was a well-prepared opening statement, an excellent summary of the then generally accepted view of the law. It left no room for the idea that literary merit alone could save a book. It conceded the *Ulysses* principle that if there was enough literary merit, and little enough sex, the obscenity might be "submerged and outweighed." The concession cost the Post Office nothing; indeed, in stressing the converse implications of the *Ulysses* case, Mindel showed that it was actually a precedent against *Lady Chatterley*.

Mindel had begun by disclaiming the role of censor. The word "censorship" has at least two meanings.* Broadly, it refers to any kind of suppression of speech or writing. More narrowly, it refers only to the kind of suppression that operates in advance of publication. In the eighteenth century, after the revolutions had put an end to licensing in England, the accepted doctrine was that no prior restraint on freedom of speech was valid, while no subsequent punishment for having spoken was invalid. The doctrine is no longer accepted—in either branch—but the phrase "prior restraint" still has some talismanic effect. I shall point out in a later chapter why I think there is no reason to regard it as more deadening than any other method of enforcing obscenity legislation. But so long as the courts viewed it as something particularly drastic, and so long as the words carried their historical burden of bad connotation, I would try to show that the postal ban was a prior restraint. If the Post Office officials felt uncomfortable with the badge of censor, I wanted to pin it on them. So I based my opening statement on Mindel's disclaimer:

> MR. REMBAR: My brother has said that there is no censorship involved here. The Post Office, he claims, is not acting as a censor. He says that the publisher is perfectly free to manufacture the book, have it bound, pay royalties, do everything but get it to the public.
>
> I confess I don't understand the difference between that and censorship. A censor does not act until he sees what you are ready to offer to the public. That is exactly what is hap-

---

* Etymologically, the word yields little. "In ancient Rome, dating from about 443 B.C., the censors were two officials appointed to preside over the *census* or the registration of citizens for the purpose of determining the duties they owed to the community." (McCormick and MacInnes, *Versions of Censorship*.) The idea of governmental restraint on expression antedated the *census*, which thus provides not the source of censorship but merely the source of its name.

pening here, unless our motion is granted. If our motion is granted, all questions of censorship are out of the case. If our motion is granted, there is no issue of prior restraint. But if it is denied, we are dealing with censorship in its most powerful, most obnoxious form.

The rest of the statement had to do with my version of the *Roth* case.

The Post Office then put in its proof. Mindel simply offered the book itself and our stipulation that it had been mailed. This was the traditional case for the prosecution: the judges or the jury could see for themselves that the book was obscene.

It was then my turn to submit evidence in defense, or try to. The first witness was Barney Rosset. There were the usual preliminary questions, and then:

Q. About how long has Grove been in existence?

A. About ten years.

Q. About how many works have been published by Grove during that period?

A. Over three hundred books have been published.

Q. Would you name some of the authors whose works have been published by Grove?

MR. SCHUELER: Objection. I fail to see any relevancy of what books Mr. Rosset has published in his position of president of Grove Press—I would like at this time to have some sort of an offer of what this testimony is supposed to elicit. I fail to see where we can gain anything by the testimony of the publisher of this book.

MR. REMBAR: I will tell you what this question is intended to elicit. The conduct of the publisher is one of the elements that the courts have held relevant in a proceeding of this kind; not merely the book itself, but what kind of publisher is involved, what kind of audience does he aim at, what channels of distribution does he use, what business is he in. All of these things have been stressed over and over again in the cases.

THE JUDICIAL OFFICER: Are you relying on the concurring opinion of Chief Justice Warren in *Roth?*

MR. REMBAR: I am relying on that opinion, among others.

At the moment, I could not have named the others, but the Chief Justice's comments were good enough for Ablard, on this question anyway, and Rosset was allowed to tick off some Grove authors.

Having explored the character of the publisher, I now sought to explore the character of the particular publishing venture:

> Q. Could you describe briefly the steps taken in connection with the publication of the book which is the subject of this proceeding?
>
> MR. MINDEL: May we have a continuing objection to this line of questioning as being irrelevant, incompetent and immaterial and does not go to the issues in deciding whether the book is obscene? *
>
> THE JUDICIAL OFFICER: What is the purpose of the question, Mr. Rembar? I am not sure I understand the question.
>
> MR. REMBAR: This publication—the publication of this book in its present form—is, in our view, an important public service. It has made a substantial contribution to American culture. Very great pains were taken in this publication to secure the authentic manuscript, to have it reviewed by scholars, to sound out the opinion of critics and scholars in the field as to whether it ought to be published. All these things, I believe, are highly relevant. . . .
>
> THE JUDICIAL OFFICER: The objection is overruled.
>
> A. I contacted Mark Schorer, professor of English at the

---

* Competence has to do with the general reliability of certain kinds of evidence. For example, an interested party's description of his conversation with a man now dead is usually not competent; dead men tell no tales, and the witness will not feel the spur to truth that the threat of contradiction carries.

Relevance means what it means in ordinary usage. The court will not admit evidence that is beside the point. For one thing, it is a distraction, and may confuse the issues. For another, it is important that the time of the court not be wasted.

Frequently, both the competence and the relevance of what is offered as evidence is questionable. We then hear the opposing attorney say that it is "incompetent, irrelevant and immaterial." "Immaterial" adds nothing to "irrelevant." (There is some fine conceptual distinction, but lawyers cannot seem to remember what it is. It makes a pleasant parlor game, or rather office game, to ask trial lawyers to cite an example of something that is material but not relevant, or relevant but not material.) Added to the asserted lack of competence, they give us the incantation, which is standard —not only in courtroom drama, but in real courtrooms—and has its source in our deep fondness for trinities and the rhythms of magic.

University of California, an acknowledged expert on the writings of D. H. Lawrence. Professor Schorer went to New Mexico, where he examined the original manuscript of the book. . . . In addition to that, I wrote letters to a group of people, amongst whom were Jacques Barzun, dean of Faculties of Columbia University; to Archibald MacLeish, former Librarian of Congress; to Harvey Breit, at that time an editor of the *New York Times Book Review*, and various other people. Upon getting their confirming opinions to my own, that it was a great book and a significant book, we proceeded with the publication.

Q. Up to the time when the Post Office imposed its ban, what sort of distribution did Grove engage in?

A. We engaged in the distribution normal to the book-publishing industry. We sell the books to the known, acknowledged and usual sources, which are mainly bookstores in the leading cities of this country.

Q. What sort of promotion and advertising was taken on by Grove in connection with this book?

A. We consulted with the advertising agency with whom we always work, and by a mutual decision we used a kind of advertising which we felt was proper to this book, advertising which would in no way lead to sales if people were looking for something of a purely titillating intent.

The testimony I had been drawing from Rosset was, I thought, important in any obscenity case, and especially important in this one. At the time, Grove Press was young, small and struggling, hardly known outside the literary world and altogether different from the prominent publicly held company it has since become. The judges who would eventually be deciding this case might never have heard of Grove. I wanted to show that this was no fly-by-night trying to cash in on one big dirty book. It would be good to associate the company with some of the respected giants of publishing.

Q. Who is your advertising agency?

A. Sussman & Sugar, Inc.

Q. Do they represent other publishing firms besides yours?

A. Yes.

Q. Can you name some of them?

A. Among the firms they represent are Random House, Harvard University Press, Simon & Schuster, Cambridge University Press.

Q. I show you a folder containing certain papers and ask you what the papers are that are contained in the folder.

A. These are clippings from the magazines and newspapers in which we placed our advertisements. These are the actual advertisements themselves.

Q. Are these representative of all the advertisements that you placed?

A. As far as I know, I believe that these are all of them.

MR. REMBAR: I offer this file in evidence.

Later in the trial I offered Grove's circular. Naturally, it had some good things to say about the book. There was an objection:

> MR. SCHUELER: We object to the introduction of this exhibit on the ground that it is a self-serving document. The best evidence is the individual who wrote the letter. Further, on the ground that it is not relevant; and again, on our continuing objection to testimony elicited from this witness bearing on his intent in depositing the book.

The second of Schueler's objections was based on the "best evidence rule," which states that where documentary evidence is used, it must be the original, unless the original is unavailable; in a suit on a contract, for example, the signed document itself must be produced, and not an unsigned carbon. But the rule has to do with the use of a document as evidence of what it says— the physical contract, for example, being merely proof of a legally enforceable understanding of the parties.

> MR. REMBAR: I think the question of best evidence is irrelevant. This isn't offered as evidence of something else. This is offered as showing the dignified and restrained way in which this book was presented and as showing that booksellers were never at any time incited to sell this book on the basis of the reputation which it had gathered in some circles because of the fact that it was subject to ban.
>
> THE JUDICIAL OFFICER: The method of distribution is a relevant question. As far as the best evidence goes, this witness who identified it and the witness who signed this letter is

on the stand. I don't think that objection is at all well taken.
As far as the method of distribution, I think Mr. Mindel will
concur that in other proceedings, the government has shown
methods of distribution in an effort to prove their case. I
don't know why the mailer here can't show a method of distribution in order to prove his.

* * *

Q. (by Mr. Rembar): Mr. Rosset, apart from the profit
motive—which we will of course stipulate that a corporation
engaged in private enterprise is interested in—what was the
intent and motive of Grove Press, Inc., in publishing this
book?

Mindel and Schueler both objected.

MR. REMBAR: I rely on the opinion of Chief Justice Warren—concurring, it is true, but not disputed by the majority,
and expressive, I submit, of various lower-court opinions on
the subject—that the conduct of the publisher is a relevant
matter.

Ablard ruled that Rosset might answer the question, and Rosset's answer, which we will come to later, was excellent.

The facts regarding the book's advertising had a legal use beyond indicating the character of publisher and its venture.*
They provided an indication of what the public found acceptable—the "community standards" of the prurient-interest
formula:

Q. (by Mr. Rembar): Can you tell me the publications in
which that advertising appeared?

A. Some of them were the *New York Herald Tribune;*
the *New York Times; The New Yorker* magazine; *Saturday
Review* magazine.

* * *

Q. Did any of these newspapers and magazines to which
you refer refuse to take advertising for this book?

---

* The attention I was giving to the manner of publication, to the advertising and distribution of the book, and to the publisher's behavior generally
may be puzzling to readers who have heard that the 1966 Supreme Court
decision in the *Ginzburg* case was pure judicial creation—that the Court,
in concentrating on the way the publisher sold his books, had sprung a
brand-new legal theory on an unsuspecting bar.

MR. MINDEL: Objected to as calling for a self-serving statement on the part of this witness.

MR. REMBAR: That is a matter of fact, if I may say so.

MR. MINDEL: How would he prove it?

MR. REMBAR: He is the president of the company which attempted to place the advertising. He is the man most likely to hear if there was any objection.

THE JUDICIAL OFFICER: What was the nature of your question?

MR. REMBAR: Did any of the magazines or newspapers to which the advertising was submitted raise any objection to carrying it?

MR. MINDEL: I think here he is attempting to go beyond a factual statement by the witness as to where he attempted to place his advertisements, to bring in another element going perhaps to community acceptance, which I think is outside the scope of any testimony by this witness. I object on that ground.

MR. REMBAR: Are you suggesting that someone could better testify as to the question I just asked?

MR. MINDEL: I am suggesting that the question is improper.

MR. REMBAR: Are you questioning its relevancy?

MR. MINDEL: Yes.

THE JUDICIAL OFFICER: What is the relevancy?

MR. REMBAR: My brother is saying that the question of community acceptance is irrelevant.

MR. MINDEL: I question its competency.

MR. REMBAR: If you are questioning its competency, you are suggesting that Mr. Rosset is not in a position to say whether Grove Press received any objection to its advertising.

MR. MINDEL: I am questioning the competency of the testimony for the purpose indicated. That is, to attempt to prove community standards.

*   *   *

THE JUDICIAL OFFICER: I don't see where the question of competency comes into play here. It looks to me like a question of relevancy. This witness is certainly competent to testify as to what matters were brought to his attention as the publisher. . . . What is the purpose of the testimony?

MR. REMBAR: The purpose of the testimony is to show acceptance according to community standards, and we have other evidence to offer along those lines. . . .

MR. MINDEL: The *Roth* case—

THE JUDICIAL OFFICER: Just a minute. Let Mr. Rembar elaborate on what part of *Roth* he is relying on.

MR. REMBAR: On page 489, the Court puts the question as whether, to the average person, applying contemporary standards, the dominant theme of the material taken as a whole appeals to prurient interest. Now contemporary community standards means standards right now, not in 1896,* and newspapers are important reflectors of public opinion and important molders of public opinion. The reception they give to a particular book, I believe, is highly relevant to the question of what the applicable community standards are.

MR. MINDEL: That requirement, of course, was asserted there to apply to community standards, but the question now before you is whether a witness can give assistance in determining what the standards are.

THE JUDICIAL OFFICER: I will overrule your objection.†

Mindel had evidently assumed I asked the question in order to show community acceptance of the book—at least at a certain level of the community—and had also assumed I was trying to show that there had been not one rejection of the advertising. The first assumption was correct, but the second was not. And I had another purpose:

Q. The question is whether any of the publications had rejected your submission of advertising.

A. When we originally placed the advertisements, no publication rejected it.

Q. What do you mean by originally?

---

* Schueler had previously cited a Supreme Court case that was unfamiliar to me but that I was reasonably sure was not recent. I interrupted to ask its date: 1896, he said.

† The reader will note, in this exchange, that for the second time I referred to counsel on the other side as "my brother." This somewhat archaic form of reference is still occasionally heard, and I favor it. Lawyers are, of course, brethren at the bar. But if that fraternal notion is rejected by the reader as patently unrealistic, the term remains appropriate: a lawyer may properly call his opponent "brother" in the sense that Hemingway's Old Man called the fish he killed his brother.

A. We have been refused the right to place a second advertisement by one publication. Others have accepted continuing advertisements.

The other purpose was to show the chilling effect of a Post Office ban. The fact that initially everybody accepted the advertising might tell us something about community standards. The fact that one magazine later changed its mind told us something else: that we were dealing with a far-reaching censorship, not just with mail-carrying.

Q. On what ground did they refuse?
A. This publication refused it on the ground that they had been warned by the Post Office Department that if they accepted advertising, their publication might be seized. Therefore, they did not wish to take the chance.
Q. They had already accepted and published advertising previous to that?
A. They had already accepted and published the advertising, yes.

I then offered book reviews in evidence.

THE JUDICIAL OFFICER: Is there any objection by the government?
MR. MINDEL: There is objection along the lines previously entered to evidence looking to prove or attempting to prove community acceptance. I read to you from *People* v. *Wepplo*, Superior Court of California, where again a book was involved in prosecution and the court said: "The jury were competent to decide the question of the character of the book without resort to these adventitious aids. If the book sold by the defendants was in fact obscene, judged by its contents, it would not become any less so because other book dealers were selling it or the public library had copies of it or literary critics praised it as a work of literary merit or because other books equally bad were being openly sold." Of course, my present objection is to the one part about the literary critics. It is on that basis that I ground my objection that this is immaterial.
THE JUDICIAL OFFICER: What did Judge Woolsey have to say about that?
MR. REMBAR: He went rather far in this respect. He asked a couple of friends of his, who he thought were qualified as

literary people, to give him their opinion. Then Judge Hand, in the circuit court, refers to the reputation of the work in the estimation of approved critics.

* * *

THE JUDICIAL OFFICER: Relying on the decisions in the *Ulysses* case both in the trial court and the Court of Appeals, the objection is overruled and the reviews are accepted into evidence as Grove Press Exhibit Number 2.

* * *

MR. REMBAR: Our next two offers of evidence are the news articles and the editorials and other expressions of journalistic opinion which attended the publication of this book and the events since its publication.

THE JUDICIAL OFFICER: By events, you mean the events occurring in the Post Office Department which led up to this proceeding?

MR. REMBAR: And certain other things as well. Our position, again, is that the newspapers reflect community standards and have a powerful effect on community standards and that they form very strong evidence of what those community standards are.

MR. MINDEL: I make my objection very strenuously. Here we see, I think, the opening even further of this avenue of approach, attempting to prove community standards. Certainly, the newspapers' comments cannot be accepted as proof of community standards. . . . It is just opening it wide open to take in anything, to try to show, through testimony and through documentary evidence, what the community standards are, which just can't be done in this fashion.

* * *

THE JUDICIAL OFFICER: How does this prove community standards? That is my problem.

MR. REMBAR: As I said before, I think the Judicial Officer can take judicial notice of the well-known fact that newspapers reflect public opinion. . . .* I think that the newspapers, having greeted this as a major literary event and having reported efforts to suppress it with some distaste, have shown

---

* Applying the doctrine of "judicial notice," a court may accept certain things as true without their having been proven under the rules of evidence. These are ordinarily matters of common knowledge, or matters which, if not commonly known, can be determined from sources that are not subject to serious question: thus, for example, the dates on which the moon is full.

that these important voices of public opinion have a certain view toward this book. I think that view is relevant. I find it hard to see why the Post Office Department, which presumably is protecting the public and not its own mailmen, are not interested in finding out what the public thinks about it.

MR. MINDEL: We, of course, have the greatest respect for the press of the United States. However, you cannot have any outside agency or group of people usurping the function of the law-enforcement officials. The courts have very clearly stated that the function is within the hands and decision of the court to make this determination and it cannot just blithely take these articles and say, "These people think it is all right; therefore, as a matter of law, it cannot be wrong." These editorial writers are not lawyers. . . . They would be usurping, as I say, the right of the Judicial Officer or any other tribunal if all they would do is to come in with these articles from newspapers and magazines and what have you and say, "Here you are. These are the articles. You have no recourse. You must find as these articles indicate." . . .

MR. REMBAR: He says that the writers of the editorials are not qualified to say what the law is. We are not offering this as evidence of the law. Naturally, the law is something which has to be interpreted and applied by the Judicial Officer. They are evidence of how the book is received, what the community at large thinks about it. There may be arguments as to the weight to be given to that evidence, but I submit that in the light of the *Ulysses* case and the *Roth* case, there can be no doubt that the evidence, for whatever it is worth, is admissible.

THE JUDICIAL OFFICER: This seems like a propitious time to take a luncheon recess.

My argument could have been rebutted, at least partially. Newspaper editorials do constitute some evidence of community standards, but it is evidence that reflects a bias against restraints on expression. Newspapers have a special interest in freedom of the press, and they are therefore, in this regard, flawed mirrors of community standards. Editorial pages that are conservative on most matters are often liberal on matters of censorship. But it was up to my opponents, not to me, to point this out.

When Ablard made his rulings on the evidence, he admitted the reviews but excluded the editorials and news items. At the same time, he denied Mindel's motion to strike the oral testimony that went to the same subject. I thought the rulings were inconsistent. It made little practical difference, however: when an offer of documentary evidence is rejected, the evidence nevertheless becomes part of the record; otherwise, the reviewing court would not be able to tell whether the ruling was correct. Accordingly, if the Post Office decision went against us and we went into court to challenge it, the judge would have the editorials and the news items before him. (As it turned out, the federal court later held that all of this evidence should have been admitted.)

After the noon recess Malcolm Cowley came to the stand. Testimony is ordinarily confined to simple statements of fact, answers to questions like "Who?" "When?" "Where?" "What happened?" Some things, however, are generally agreed to be not matters of fact but matters of opinion. The law handles this by allowing opinions to be stated by people qualified because they are expert in the field. Thus in a suit for personal injuries, the amount recovered depends on the extent and severity of the injuries, and physicians are the experts. To take a quite different example, the estate tax is levied on the value of the property a man leaves his heirs. When the estate consists of cash, or securities traded on the stock market, value is a matter of fact. But when it consists of real estate or jewelry or paintings, or a going business, value is a matter of opinion.* Here again there are people highly qualified—real estate brokers, jewelers, art dealers, financial analysts—and their opinions are admissible evidence. It was such precedents that I cited when our opponents challenged my use of witnesses to analyze and appraise a book.

But whether a witness is expert enough to break the general rule that witnesses may state only fact, not opinion, is itself a matter of proof, and the process is called "qualification." That

---

* The current lively market in paintings, and their use as a medium of investment, almost moves them out of this category and into that of marketable securities. This particular cultural renascence, of course, owes more to the Internal Revenue Code and its golden infant, the capital gain, than it does to any increase in our aesthetic sensibilities.

is, it must be established that the witness is especially learned or experienced in a particular field. Cowley's examination began with qualifying questions:

Q. Will you tell us your occupation, Mr. Cowley?

A. I am a literary critic and historian. I have been working in that field for forty years, writing for newspapers, magazines and writing books. I have made somewhat of a specialty of the folkways of readers and writers; that is, my last book, *The Literary Situation*, was more or less a book of literary sociology rather than criticism. I made a study of the changing values of public acceptance during the last forty years.

* * *

Q. Will you enumerate some of your honors and achievements?

A. For three years I was president of the National Institute of Arts and Letters. I have been visiting professor at many universities; most recently at Stanford University this spring, visiting professor of English. I am at present the literary adviser to the Viking Press.

Q. Are you acquainted with the works of D. H. Lawrence?

A. I am.

Q. Would you give us your estimate of the position he occupies in English literature?

MR. MINDEL: I object.

THE WITNESS: He is generally—

THE JUDICIAL OFFICER: Just a moment. There is an objection.

MR. MINDEL: I make the objection to this line of testimony on the part of the witness, which gets us once more to the question of expert testimony on the issue here, which is, of course, to decide whether this book is obscene. The cases which have heretofore been cited in favor of the idea receiving the publisher's views of literary critics are limited to that. I think Judge Learned Hand makes it very clear, in the case of *United States* v. *Levine*, which is the one case that has been referred to so often in this proceeding—

MR. REMBAR: By you; not by us. We have not referred to that case.

MR. SCHUELER: I will read the language. He says, "On the other hand, it is reasonable to allow in evidence published reviews of qualified critics—quite another thing, incidentally, from expert witnesses at the trial—for such evidence does not lead far afield and is rationally helpful, though in the end it is the jury who must declare what the standards must be." * In other words, the end here is that the Judicial Officer is the one who must declare what the standards should be. . . .

MR. REMBAR: If I might suggest, sir, in the interest of getting this hearing over with and permitting these witnesses, who have been kind enough to devote their time to this, to go back to their regular occupations, could we elicit the testimony, subject to a motion to strike?

My thought in urging that the testimony be heard first and the argument heard later—that the testimony be admitted subject to a motion to strike—was that it would be helpful to have the Judicial Officer hear what Cowley had to say, even if he might later conclude it was not legally relevant. Moreover, like the exhibits Ablard held inadmissible, testimony once given is part of the physical record, and the reviewing court would see it even if Ablard eventually granted the motion to strike. Mindel, of course, was aware of this.

MR. MINDEL: We would stipulate, of course, as we have in our opening statement made clear, that there is literary merit in this book. If that will be the testimony of the witness, then, of course, we have conceded that this is so.

THE JUDICIAL OFFICER: What is the purpose of the testimony? Is it any different than that which was produced through the testimony of the printed reviews and comments of the book?

At this point I wanted to question Cowley about two things—the literary and hortative ends toward which Lawrence aimed his novel, and the increasing frankness of current literature. I

---

* The *Levine* case had been cited only once, in a portion of the transcript that has been omitted. Mindel's "so often" was the natural error of a lawyer who has been thinking a good deal about a case he intends to rely on. The position taken in Learned Hand's opinion, that while book reviews were admissible, oral testimony on literary value was not, was the reverse of what my opponents in other cases urged. No one after Mindel cited Hand's peculiar preference—understandable perhaps in his home but peculiar in court—for printed critical opinion over live critics subject to cross-examination.

cited the *Roth* community-standards-average-person-prurient-interest formula (apart from the not yet established social-value test) as justification for both. The testimony on current literature would be relevant to contemporary community standards; as to testimony about Lawrence's intent, I argued that what an author set out to accomplish showed what he was appealing to, and therefore had something to do with the dominant appeal of his book. In the cases that were to follow, I altered my position; I argued that while there could be testimony on community standards, no witness could help the court on the appeal-to-prurient-interest part of the formula.

There were several reasons. One was simply further thought on the fascinating puzzle of what the *Roth* standards meant and how they were to be applied. Objective evidence can be presented on the current state of community standards, but appeal to prurient interest is thoroughly subjective. There could be evidence on it only if an extensive survey were conducted among the readers of the particular book—a project hardly practicable and never undertaken. No individual witness can offer anything more than his individual reaction, and the reaction of one person tells us nothing.

The other reasons were less analytical. Exploring this particular area—the author's purpose and intent—would help with *Chatterley* but hurt us with *Fanny Hill*; Cowley and Kazin testified that Lawrence was deeply serious, and had no thought of titillation, something that could not very well be said of Cleland. As a practical matter, the advocate's choice was fairly simple: only our side was calling witnesses in this case, and so the more the witnesses were permitted to say, the better. After *Lady Chatterley*, prosecuting attorneys also began to use witnesses, and had plenty of them who were ready to state that *Tropic* and *Fanny* appealed, predominantly if not entirely, to prurient interest. Had the more sophisticated analysis I finally arrived at been helpful in the trial of *Lady Chatterley*, I might have arrived at it sooner.

But even if the proposition that value alone could save a book was just starting on its way, literary testimony for more limited purposes had become generally admissible in the time since Mencken wrote his lament. (The important question for the cases that were now beginning was not whether the court should listen to critics, but what it should do with what it heard.) So I offered a second reason for allowing Cowley to speak about Lawrence's intent: the writer's purposes are pertinent to a critical analysis of his work, and are therefore a proper part of literary testimony.

THE JUDICIAL OFFICER: I think the best way to handle this particular problem at this time is Mr. Rembar's suggestion. If we let this witness testify without constant interruption, at the conclusion of his testimony—I am assuming, Mr. Rembar, you will confine yourself to the purpose which you have stated in calling the witness and not go afield—

MR. REMBAR: Yes sir.

THE JUDICIAL OFFICER: Confine yourself to that. [Then to Mr. Mindel:] At the conclusion of his testimony you may move to strike any, all or part.

Q. (by Mr. Rembar): You mentioned that you were, among other things, a literary sociologist. Can you explain what that term means?

A. I mean that I have made a study at various times of what the standards of the public are, what sort of books they admire, what sort of books they condemn, and a study of the lives of writers themselves to see under what conditions they produced their books.

Q. Are you familiar with the works of D. H. Lawrence?

A. I am.

Q. Can you tell us about the place he occupies in English literature?

A. Very briefly, he is considered to be the most significant English novelist after Joseph Conrad.

Q. Are literary critics and literary historians in general in agreement with this estimate?

A. We are in such agreement on that point that eight hundred books have been written about D. H. Lawrence.

Q. Are you able to discern in the works of D. H. Lawrence any sort of consistent social or moral philosophy?

A. There is a consistent social and moral philosophy which, if you try to sum it up in one word, would call for the word "naturalness." He believes that body and mind should not be separate; that, on a ground partly attributable to the artificial conditions of a mechanical age, we have separated thinking from the body too much, and that a return to the natural human being is essentially a solution. . . .

Q. Are these ideas expressed in the book which is the subject of these proceedings?

A. They are very strongly expressed. It was his last novel, and he was trying to sum up in a way what he had said before in *Lady Chatterley's Lover*.

Q. Would you say that the description of sexual encounters in this book is germane to the expression of these ideas?

A. It is entirely germane. It is almost at the heart of it, because he is trying to advocate in the book sexual fulfillment in marriage. That is the purpose of the description of the sexual acts throughout.

Q. Counsel has referred to certain language in the book. Is there any language in the book which you would say was extrinsic to these purposes?

A. There is no language in the book that is extrinsic to the purpose. Lawrence wrote the book three times, as is stated in the preface. The first version, which has already been published here, was without the bad words which you find in the third version. Lawrence felt strongly, according to his diaries and records, that he had not got across what he was trying to say. And so for his artistic and moral purpose, he introduced these words into the third version and manuscript.

Q. For how many years, Mr. Cowley, have you been a student of the English and American novel?

A. Forty years.

Q. Over this period of time, have you observed any change in the manner of recounting sexual episodes?

MR. MINDEL: I object. I believe this is getting beyond the original purpose of the testimony as discussed and as referred to earlier by Mr. Rembar.

MR. REMBAR: I find that this testimony, when it is uninterrupted, is quite illuminating.

MR. MINDEL: I don't think I need be remonstrated for interrupting with what I think is a proper objection. The original purpose as stated by counsel was to attempt to show the motive of the author. Here apparently he is going beyond that to get whatever comments the witness has to make as to the general changes in literature over the many years that he

has just referred to, which is, as I say, going beyond the originally stated purpose.

MR. REMBAR: I mentioned two purposes: one was the intent of the author; the other was the literary context in which
the book appears. I mentioned those two purposes. They are
both subject to attack on the motion to strike. I would like to
get this testimony over with and leave our legal argument for
a more appropriate time.

THE JUDICIAL OFFICER: I think we can permit it. . . .

A. If I might divide my answer to that question into two
parts, the first part will be the standards of morality expressed
in literature and also in magazines, and the second part
would be the language itself. There has been a great change
in both respects. I do not find anything in *Lady Chatterley's
Lover* that essentially I can't find in the *Ladies' Home Journal.* This is in substance, sir. In substance, it is what marriage
counselors are telling the counselees five days a week as a result of various forces, including Freudian psychology and
great worries about repressions and perversions. This sort of
idea of fulfillment in the marriage state has become enormously common.

Q. Enormously common, did you say?

A. Common, yes. It is almost universal. To my amaze-
ment, as I say, I find it in articles in the *Ladies' Home Journal,* for example.

The second part, in view of language, there are a certain
number of short Anglo-Saxon words for bodily functions that
were regarded until World War I as being wholly part of a
secret language of men, comparable to the secret language of
men that the anthropologists have found in the South Pacific
tribes. These words were used in the smoking room, in the
bar room, in the barbershop, but no woman was supposed to
know them unless she was an utterly degraded woman. After
World War I, women increasingly demanded admission to
what had been the sacred places of men, the smoking room,
the bar room, the barbershop even, and demanded knowledge of the secret language of men. So that there came one
word after another in one novel after another. Some literary
historian should follow the fate of these four-letter words,
when they first appeared, which of the first words appeared in
Hemingway's *Farewell to Arms* in 1929, which of the words
first appeared here in *Ulysses,* when it was introduced in

1931; which of the words appeared in, let us say, *The Naked and the Dead, From Here to Eternity* and, more lately, *By Love Possessed.*

At the present time there is not one word printed in *Lady Chatterley's Lover* that has not heretofore appeared in a reputable work of fiction. There is no more secret language of males. That has been abolished.

As I was about to turn Cowley over to his cross-examiner, it occurred to me that a man's accomplishments sound even better coming from someone else.

Q. (by Mr. Rembar): One last question, Mr. Cowley. Do you know Mr. Kazin?

A. I do.

Q. Could you tell us briefly a little about his standing in the field of literature?

MR. MINDEL: I object. For one thing, there is no identification of Mr. Kazin. Furthermore, it seems to me that this is getting, again, into the area of inadmissible testimony, as to the standing of this third person, whoever he might be.

MR. REMBAR: This is Mr. Alfred Kazin, who sits here (indicating).

MR. MINDEL: Then he should speak for himself.

MR. REMBAR: You can qualify a witness by other means than by his own statements.

THE JUDICIAL OFFICER: You want to qualify your second, or your third, witness?

MR. REMBAR: Yes. If anything, that is better qualification than by the witness's own words.

THE JUDICIAL OFFICER: For that purpose, do you have any objection? It seems to be unique, but I am not sure it is erroneous.

It was unique so far as I was concerned too, but so was most of what was going on.

Q. My question refers to Mr. Kazin's standing as a literary critic and a literary historian.

A. Mr. Kazin was literary editor of *The New Republic* for the period in the 1940's. He did a very distinguished job there. He wrote a book—

MR. MINDEL: I don't think the answer is responsive.

THE WITNESS: I am trying to tell you what Mr. Kazin did. It is in answer to the question.

MR. REMBAR: Mr. Mindel, we don't have a jury here. What are you worried about? Let him say what he has to say. Let him finish his observation.

THE JUDICIAL OFFICER: Are you withdrawing your objection?

MR. MINDEL: No, I don't.

THE JUDICIAL OFFICER: State it.

MR. MINDEL: I have stated it. I don't think it is responsive to the question. I don't especially appreciate the personal comments of counsel. Neither one of us is acting for a jury.

MR. REMBAR: All right. Apparently I was misunderstood. I in no way meant to imply that you were performing for a jury, Mr. Mindel. All I meant to suggest was that where you have a hearing before a judge sitting without a jury, or an administrative hearing officer, you don't have the same necessity for cutting off testimony as you do when you are before a jury. I certainly meant nothing beyond that. I am awfully sorry if it sounded that way.

MR. MINDEL: I appreciate the instruction of counsel.

Q. (by Mr. Rembar): Would you proceed with your answer, Mr. Cowley?

A. Mr. Kazin was literary editor of *The New Republic* in 1940; was author of a book at that time, a history of American literature since 1885, called *On Native Ground,* which was very favorably received. Since then he has written two other books, also praised very highly. He has been a contributor to many magazines for a long time, to *The New Yorker* in their book-review section. He later was a contributor, a steady contributor, to the book-review section of *The Reporter.* He has lately been a full professor at Amherst College. His standing in the literary community is high.

Cowley's cross-examination was a splendid confrontation. Mindel, a very good lawyer, was tough and incisive. Cowley was blandly resistant—pleasant, even benign—and just as tough. His healthy pink complexion, his handsome white hair and mustache, even his hearing aid, all seemed to preclude notions of wickedness; if a man like this approved, how could the book be prurient?

Mindel began with what was to become a repeated theme in the prosecution of these cases: literary people could not speak for the average man who was the central figure of *Roth*. I had expected something of this sort and had discussed the possibility with Cowley.

> Q. Would you agree that your literary background far exceeds that of the average person in the community?
> A. Possibly, yes.
> Q. Would you agree that as a literary critic, Mr. Cowley, when you read a book you look for certain things by way of the art and technique of the author that the average member of the community might not look for in reading a book?
> A. Yes.
> Q. As a matter of fact, do I state it correctly when I say that this is the most important consideration in your mind when you read a book?
> A. Not necessarily, because I am also a publisher's adviser and I have to be able to guess what the public will think.

Mindel dropped the subject and went to the matter of the bad language:

> Q. You have just said, as I understand, that you would not say that he may use any words in any way, that there is some point at which you would cut him off; that is, in your opinion as a literary critic?
> A. Yes.
> Q. But in this book, do you agree that he has used all of these words, that he has used them in relation to sex relations and to excretory functions, and such things, and that is not the point at which you would cut him off?
> A. Not this particular author at this particular point, with this particular purpose in mind.
> Q. You would say, then, Mr. Cowley, that because an author has standing, because he has skill, it does not mean that he shall proceed without restriction?
> A. Once again, I would have to say that depends. It would hurt my standing as a philosopher, sir, but all these things become terribly relative when you get down to cases. But I think when a writer is as distinguished as D. H. Lawrence, when he is as serious in his purpose as D. H. Lawrence was

from the beginning to the end of his career, he should be allowed a great deal of latitude.

Q. You are considering the book with relation to the man who wrote the book?

A. Yes.

Q. In other words, you are excusing him because you think well of him; do I understand your argument?

A. No sir, I don't say that because I think well of him. There are writers who are men of distinction and men of conviction and they deserve a great deal more liberty than third-rate talents without any real conviction.

Cowley's answers remind us how long a way the law traveled in the next seven years. Cowley felt strongly enough about freedom of expression to appear as a witness—something not undertaken lightly—yet he was impelled to say that the degree of freedom we were advocating should be reserved for men of Lawrence's caliber. On this approach, less-gifted writers, however serious, might be denied the use of certain words. Moreover, Cowley's testimony involved a reliance on "public acceptance" that would leave it open to the prosecution to argue that the public disapproved.

It is sometimes difficult to keep in mind how radical a change has taken place since 1959—a change both in the law and in general attitudes. At the date of the *Lady Chatterley* trial, most people felt that the mere use of the evil words, to the extent that Lawrence used them, was enough to warrant suppression of the book. For purposes of winning the *Lady Chatterley* case, with an author so eminent, Cowley's relativistic approach was perhaps the best one. But today not even the most eager prosecutor would make the argument that bad language, in whatever quantity, can alone condemn a book.

Mindel then set a small trap:

Q. Would you agree that Lawrence as an author was obsessed by the problems of sex?

A. "Obsessed," sir, isn't quite the word. It was a central part of his doctrine that there should be a healthy sexual relationship between men and women, or let me say between man and woman, because he did not believe in promiscuity.

* * *

Q. Would you disagree with this language I quoted to
you about being obsessed about the problems of sex if I tell
you I was quoting from the *Encyclopaedia Britannica?*

Up to this moment Mindel had not indicated that he was quoting.

A. Yes, because "obsessed" is usually taken to mean a
neurotic interest, an unhealthy interest. I would disagree with
the *Encyclopaedia Britannica*. I would say his thought was
very much concentrated on the subject of sex relationships,
but I would not call it an obsession in the sense of a neurotic
compulsion.

Q. Does your disagreement with this article indicate a
lack of unanimity in your profession with regard to Lawrence?

We had not covered the *Encyclopaedia Britannica* in our preparation, and collision with so weighty an authority could be damaging. I thought I had better rouse myself.*

MR. REMBAR: May I say this? We don't know what article
he is talking about or what it says.

MR. MINDEL: This is an article which appeared in the *Encyclopaedia Britannica*, 1952. Part of it, after reviewing his various works, says that Lawrence, who died of consumption—

THE JUDICIAL OFFICER: Just a moment. Do you want to
identify that?

MR. MINDEL: This is just a typewritten copy.

THE JUDICIAL OFFICER: It is not authenticated though,
Mr. Mindel. In all the exhibits the respondent has offered
today, there has been some effort at authentication other
than just a statement of counsel.

MR. MINDEL: If you feel it is necessary, I will offer it as an
exhibit.

MR. REMBAR: I will object to its acceptance.

---

* Judith Crist, who reported the trial for the *Herald Tribune*, told me
afterward that my usual posture, when I was not on my feet, was a deep
slump in my chair, arms over the sides and knuckles scraping the floor. I
was surprised. I thought I was eager and attentive. She said the contrast
when I rose to make an objection lent emphasis to what I had to say. It
was, in her opinion, an effective courtroom technique. If it had been deliberate, I would have been flattered.

MR. MINDEL: How can you object to the acceptance of an article from the *Britannica* when you have gotten in articles from all over the world?

THE JUDICIAL OFFICER: That is your typewritten copy though. There is a substantial difference as far as identification.

MR. MINDEL: A comparison could be made for verification with the *Britannica*.

MR. REMBAR: I must strenuously object. I don't even know if that is what it says in the *Britannica*.

There was a conference at the bench, and after examining what Mindel was reading from, I stipulated that the excerpt as a whole might be received in evidence. Cowley then proceeded to answer the question about unanimity.

A. There is no author of the last fifty years, there is no author of the last two hundred years, about whom the literary profession is unanimous. I can only give you a consensus, a majority, a pretty overwhelming opinion of the majority about Lawrence.

Q. Have you ever canvassed the field of your profession with regard to this question?

A. No sir. I can only report the reading of reviews about Lawrence, the reading of books about Lawrence, of which I have said there have been something more than eight hundred. In fact, the presence of the article in the *Encyclopaedia Britannica* is proof that the *Encyclopaedia Britannica* considers him important.

The fuss had given Cowley time to consider, and his answers were excellent.

Mindel then attacked Cowley's thesis that Lawrence was engaged, essentially, in marriage counseling. He succeeded in establishing that not one of the sexual acts in the book involved a lawfully wedded couple,

Q. . . . How does that fit into your concept that this carries out fulfillment, sexual fulfillment, in marriage?

A. Sir, I will have to explain that the whole book is directed toward what doesn't happen in the book, but toward which all the hopes of the characters are directed. The marriage, and the lasting marriage with children, of Lady Chatterley and Oliver Mellors.

Q. You are directing your thoughts, then, to something which happens after you finish reading 350 pages of this book?

A. Yes sir.

Q. That is the fulfillment that we have to speculate about?

A. Yes. But that is the aim, and it is the feeling all through the book that there should be no merely promiscuous intercourse among people, but that a man and woman are destined for each other and can satisfy and fulfill each other in the marriage relationship.

Q. How do you fit into that her relations with the character Michaelis?

A. Very unhappy. Her relations with Michaelis are very unhappy, and almost repulsive, and so depicted by the author. That is the promiscuity that Lawrence feels makes people unhappy.

Q. Your last comment was that the relationship that she had with this Michaelis was evidence of promiscuity?

A. That was promiscuity, and it was unhappy.

Q. Do you define promiscuity there as the extramarital status of the relationship?

A. Relationships without love.

Q. Isn't it a fact that for a while she thought she was in love with Michaelis?

A. She did, and then she found she wasn't.

Q. So there was, such as it was, a feeling of love; nevertheless you think that was promiscuous?

A. That was, as Lawrence regarded it, promiscuity, a sort of intellectual relationship that he thundered against.

Q. That was an intellectual relationship between her and Michaelis?

A. A relationship in which the actual emotional relation of the two people is partly subordinated to a sort of intellectual dillydallying, and how he despised the intellectuals through the book. An exclamation point comes after that.

Q. Also a question mark.

Mindel had covered unacceptable words and unacceptable ideas. Now he moved to unacceptable events. With the thoroughness of a good legal draftsman, he referred to the "minute detail" with which Lawrence described "the sexual relationship and the emotions which were felt by the parties prior to, during and after the act." At another point, Mindel asked Cowley "whether it is a complete description; in other words, from the beginning to the end of it, there is no doubt left in the mind of the reader. . . ." And:

> Q. Would you agree that he probably omitted no detail in the description of the act, that it could not be made more graphic?

It seemed to me an appropriate time to call attention to the rules governing expert testimony:

> MR. REMBAR: I don't know that Mr. Cowley is qualified in this area.

The place where the trial was held was much larger than the ordinary courtroom, and it was filled. When it had calmed down (with some prodding from the Judicial Officer), Mindel got back to the dirty words. Cowley felt that Lawrence was really not adept at using them. Then Mindel raised a question that would come up often in these cases: did the author *have* to use such language?

> Q. Is it your feeling, Mr. Cowley, that it is vital and indispensable to this sort of a description to use these so-called four-letter words, as they are used in this book?
> A. It was vital to Lawrence. It was vital to Lawrence to use them. It wouldn't have been vital to another writer; but to his purpose of trying to remove sentimentality from the sexual act and at the same time reveal passion and tenderness —the original title of this book, you know, was *Tenderness.*
> Q. I couldn't hear you.
> A. The original title of the third version of *Lady Chatterley's Lover* was *Tenderness.*
> Q. I understand that. Yes sir. You say his purpose was to remove sentimentality?
> A. To remove sentimentality and leave passion and tenderness. There is a distinction there between sentimentality and passion, or tenderness.
> Q. Do you make a distinction between tenderness and sentimentality?
> A. Sentimentality in this case would be a false sort of

emotion. He thought he could accomplish this by using what seemed to him the absolutely hard, definite Anglo-Saxon words for physical function. To make it perhaps easier for you, I am not entirely sure it worked. I will be honest, as a literary critic. I am not entirely sure that the use of the four-letter words produced exactly the effect he wanted. But he was trying very hard for this particular effect and couldn't find any other way of doing it.

Q. Are you saying, then, that the author did not accomplish his purpose?

A. No author ever accomplishes his full purpose. I am not sure it couldn't have been done in another way, but I know that Lawrence couldn't have done it in any other way.

Q. Because he has a peculiar technique, then, do you say it is proper for him to do it?

A. We are getting far away from the subject. I am tempted to get off here. If Lawrence had been one of these boys, a young man who grew up in bar rooms telling dirty jokes, he couldn't have written the book in that way. He had a positive revulsion for dirty jokes, for any sort of leering about sex, for any sort of pruriency, to use that awful word. When he finally came to write about these things, he used the dirty words in a way that nobody who was used to using the dirty words would use them. Only a clean-minded man and not a prurient one could have written that way. My apologies, sir, for this, but it is a very interesting psychological point.

Mindel employed a device that was to become *de rigueur* for prosecutors in these cases, the device of embarrassment. He referred to Cowley's statement that men no longer had their secret language:

Q. Does that mean, then, they are commonplace in the social language of today's American family, or whatever polite society means?

A. It doesn't mean that, but it means you can hear them in plays and you can read them in novels, and sometimes hear them in language of co-eds.

Q. Why do you select co-eds?

A. Because I am familiar with co-eds.

Q. Have you read various reviews that have appeared in the newspapers of this book?

A. I have.

Q. Have you found in any of them these four-letter words that are in the book itself?

A. No. The newspapers do not print those words.

Q. Would you be inclined during your testimony on the stand at this meeting to use those four-letter words to make more pungent or more clear your testimony on the book?

A. I don't like this new fashion of using those four-letter words all over the place. I would rather keep them for the secret language of men. I am very much against the abolition of the smoking room and the bar room.

Q. How secret is it when it is published in the book which the publisher hopes to sell to millions of people?

A. I am just reporting what is happening to the customs of society. Society is accepting these words in places where they were formerly not accepted.

Q. Are you a member of society?

A. Society in general? I hope that everybody in this room, sir, is a member of society.

Q. Do you say that all of us accept those words for use in common conversation?

A. I say that society in general is accepting them in a way that it never accepted them before.

Q. And yet you would be terribly reluctant to use it here, wouldn't you?

A. But not to read them or not to hear them in the theater.

MR. MINDEL: May the record show the witness answered yes to the last question? The witness nodded his head, which I think was an affirmative.

MR. REMBAR: He added, "Not to read them, or to hear them in the theater."

This was a point I had discussed with our witnesses: what is considered unacceptable in one medium of expression need not be unacceptable in another.

Mindel brought up Cowley's comments about tenderness and found a passage in the book to worry him with. It was the passage that ends:

Though a little frightened, she let him have his way, and the reckless shameless sensuality shook her to her foundation, stripped her to the very last and made a different woman of her. It was really love.

Here again, I thought, a diversion might be beneficial.

MR. REMBAR: May I interject? I must object to this line of questioning. I think it is thoroughly well settled that a book cannot be judged on the basis of individual passages. Mr. Cowley has testified what the dominant themes and ideas in the book are. If there is a single incident which shows the other side of it, it in no way contradicts Mr. Cowley's previous testimony.

THE JUDICIAL OFFICER: Do you want to reply to that objection?

MR. MINDEL: I agree that the book must be judged as a whole. We have said that all along. Yet if . . . a witness says that a book is designed to show the tenderness of the marital relationship and I can take these different parts of the book and show that it is quite the opposite, I think that is a legitimate question. I have completed, however, my question on that point.

THE JUDICIAL OFFICER: Since you have completed it, I won't bother to rule on it.

Mindel took up the matter of expurgation:

Q. Is it your feeling, Mr. Cowley, that the unexpurgated book is a better literary work than the expurgated, which has circulated for so many years?

A. I think it is much better. As Archibald MacLeish says in the introduction, it is not obscene at all, but where they expurgate the book, it becomes suggestive in those passages, those passages where something is left out. The unexpurgated book is not suggestive at all.

Q. You think that suggestiveness is worse than the outright, complete, uninhibited picture of the scene?

A. I do.

Q. If one stands outside the door of a room and the door is shut and one hears certain sounds and words being said behind the door, it might be the suggestiveness of a sexual encounter. You can envisage that situation, the possibility, can you not?

A. I can.

Q. Then the door is opened and you see the parties in the

sexual act right before you. Do you say that the closed-door situation is less desirable and less stimulating and less offensive, possibly, than the open door, where you see the parties in the act?

MR. REMBAR: I must object, because the Supreme Court has drawn a very clear distinction between conduct which may be offensive to the public taste, and literature.

THE JUDICIAL OFFICER [addressing Mindel]: I think you are going pretty far afield on cross-examination. I hate to restrict you, because, as I said before, I let Mr. Rembar go pretty far on direct. I think that type of question is going pretty far afield.

MR. MINDEL: You do not think it is a proper question in view of the reference to suggestiveness?

MR. REMBAR: Of a book?

THE JUDICIAL OFFICER: I think Mr. Rembar has a good point. I don't think your hypothetical question is quite on the point.

At this moment Frommer, for the book club, joined in:

MR. FROMMER: I object to the entire line of questioning on the ground the complainant has not laid any foundation whatever for the assertion that *Lady Chatterley's Lover* contains a graphic, explicit and anatomical description of the sex act. In fact, it does not.

Mindel was delighted.

MR. MINDEL: Do you want us to read from the book and convince you of it?

MR. FROMMER: If you will be able to point out one such passage to the hearing examiner, I will appreciate that.

I signaled to Frommer that I thought the challenge to Mindel on this point would not help us, and he retrieved the situation nicely. The episode dissolved in a fortunate confusion:

MR. MINDEL: I will be very glad to point out many. I don't think we need do it here.

THE JUDICIAL OFFICER: We are either going to do it here or nowhere.

MR. REMBAR [to the Judicial Officer]: I take it you are going to read the book.

THE JUDICIAL OFFICER: Yes.
MR. FROMMER: Then I will withdraw my objection.

There was still *my* objection—that the law did not treat writing and conduct the same way.

MR. MINDEL: Read back my previous question, please.

The open-door question was reread.

MR. MINDEL: I withdraw the question.

Cowley's cross-examination ended a little while later. After cross-examination, the attorney who called the witness can question him again (on "redirect") to clarify or expand his answers. I felt there was no need of it here, except for one point. I handed Cowley the passage from the *Encyclopaedia Britannica* that Mindel had quoted:

Q. (by Mr. Rembar): In connection with the encyclopaedia article, would you please read this. (Short pause.) When Mr. Mindel asked you about the word "obsessed," it was not in the context of what you have just read. In that context, would you say that the word means preoccupied, or would you say it means neurotically involved?
A. In this context, it means preoccupied.
MR. REMBAR: That is all.

Alfred Kazin now came to the stand. His own statement of qualification, added to what Cowley had already said about him, was impressive. I put a general question to him:

Q. You heard Mr. Cowley testify to a change in the range of tolerance in the general reading public over the past thirty years. Do you agree or disagree with what Mr. Cowley had to say on that?

My question involved, more or less consciously, two things that were to become important to us, both in this case and in the cases that followed. One was "range of tolerance." Judge Bryan, who would hear the *Lady Chatterley* case when it got to the federal district court, had recently presided over a criminal trial for obscenity. I was unaware of it, but in his charge to the jury he had several times used the phrase "limits of tolerance." When I took "range of tolerance" into the federal courts, I luckily found a receptive audience.

The other was "general reading public." In our brief, which I wrote after the trial—there had not been time to prepare one in advance—I argued that if books are to be judged by community standards, they should be the standards of those who read them, rather than the standards of the population at large. The relevant community, I said, was the community of readers, whose libraries should not be selected for them by nonreaders.

At the time, these things were far from fully thought out. To an extent I was learning from my own questions, as well as from the answers, and the two phrases were not so much chosen as voiced. Mindel objected.

> THE JUDICIAL OFFICER: Is this testimony any different from that which was elicited from Mr. Cowley?
>
> MR. REMBAR: The testimony may be different. I don't know what Mr. Kazin is going to say. The questions are the same type.

After argument Ablard allowed the question.

> A. I agree entirely with Mr. Cowley. I think, as a literary historian who studied very closely literary trends, literary changes in taste, and above all the relationship of the public to literature, I have been struck by the increasing tolerance and increasing acceptance of wider and wider areas of human experience discussed in literature.
>
> Q. You said you are a particular student of public response?
>
> A. Yes. One of my special interests, like Mr. Cowley's, has been what one may call the trends of literary taste, what the public has responded to, what it has bought, what it has cared for mostly.

Kazin then gave us an illuminating, concise review of the American novels of the past decade. I found myself listening for the pleasure of it.

What Cowley and Kazin had to say about increasing frankness in the treatment of sex, and decreasing restraint in the use of forbidden words, was true. The difficulty, which we would

surely meet in our opponents' briefs, was the matter of degree.
None of the books that our witnesses mentioned was so much
concerned with sex, or so graphically concerned with it, as *Lady
Chatterley's Lover*. If appeal to sexual interest were the test,
these comparisons were not going to save the book. It would be
necessary to argue that when the Supreme Court used the
phrase "prurient interest," it must have had something different
in mind. I tried to develop the point through Kazin's testimony
and certain exhibits:

Q. (by Mr. Rembar): Mr. Kazin, in your study of the
relation between literature and the public, have you observed
any increase, in our culture generally, in attempts to appeal,
not to prurient interest, but to sexual interest?
A. Yes indeed, I have, and I have observed it both as an
editor in a publishing house, as a critic of contemporary
books and as a professor in various American colleges. . . .

We had brought to court some recent issues of *Life*, *Look* and
The Saturday Evening Post, together with a cigarette-advertis-
ing poster that I had seen at a lunch counter and obtained from
the manager (at the cost of a half-puzzled, half-disapproving
stare). Each contained a photograph likely to produce a sexual
response in the average man.

Q. (by Mr. Rembar): In this issue of *Life*, Mr. Kazin, I
would like you to address yourself to page 104.
MR. MINDEL: I object to any questions on the contents of
any of these magazines.
MR. REMBAR: I haven't asked a question yet.
MR. MINDEL: Obviously you are going to ask him a question.
MR. REMBAR: Reserve your objection until I do. . . . I
would like the record to show I am calling attention to page
104 of the issue of *Life*, page 70 and 71 of the issue of *Look*,
the cover of *The Saturday Evening Post*, and to this poster
advertising L & M cigarettes, which is displayed.
I propose to ask Mr. Kazin whether these are representative of an appeal to sexual interest which permeates our culture today. . . . I am not saying that they are prurient. I am
saying quite the contrary, that they are not. I want to have
the record show that there is a difference between appeal to

prurient interest and appeal to sexual interest, that appeal to
sexual interest is something which is widely, commonly accepted. . . .

MR. MINDEL: I would object to the introduction of these
exhibits or any testimony on these exhibits as going way and
far beyond the scope of this case. It has no relevancy to the
matters before you, and that is, the issue of obscenity of *Lady
Chatterley's Lover*. . . .

MR. REMBAR: In counsel's cross-examination of Mr. Cowley, he drew repeated attention to the fact that this book
deals with sex. . . .

MR. MINDEL: . . . I am sure you do not contend there is
any similarity between the content of *Lady Chatterley's
Lover* with regard to sexual interest and the type of material
they have in these magazines.

MR. REMBAR: If my brother would agree to confine his
cross-examination to matters of prurience and eliminate all
references to matters of sexual interest generally, I could
agree with his argument, but he has not done that.

Ablard refused to accept the exhibits. As my statement indicated, it was not my purpose to show there were other things
being published that were "just as bad." When we went to the
district court, the attorneys for the book club offered a stack of
girlie magazines. We stuck with *Life, Look* and *The Saturday
Evening Post*. To call attention to the currency of trash—to the
availability of other publications of which a court might disapprove—would, in the eyes of the disapproving court, prove nothing except that the government does not have time to prosecute
everything that ought to be prosecuted. But if *Life, Look* and
The Saturday Evening Post, which no one would think of as
"prurient," had material that excited sexual reaction, then material that appealed to prurient interest must be something else,
and the circulation figures of these periodicals said a good deal
about community standards. I was not trying to show what lay
at the edge of public tolerance (or beyond) but what lay right in
the middle of it.

The demonstration through evidence was not required; the
courts could take judicial notice of the fact. But it makes a
difference whether a judge has merely an oh-sure sort of accord
with the abstract proposition that there is a lot of sexual stimu-

lation around, or whether he has some provoking examples on
his desk. Confronted with published material of unquestioned
respectability and unquestionable sexual interest, he might be
compelled to seek another meaning for the word "prurient."

We left that subject and went to the author's intent. Here
Kazin got us into rather deep water.

> Q. Mr. Kazin, would you please tell us what you conceive
> to be the aims and intent of D. H. Lawrence in this book and
> whether the passages that have been referred to as objection-
> able are relevant and germane to those aims and that intent?
>
> A. To answer the question, in my opinion, Lawrence was
> a deeply and naturally religious writer who was concerned
> wholly with giving man in our industrial and mechanical pe-
> riod a new sense of consecration for his life. For him, sex, far
> from being an obsession in the clinical sense, was a symbol of
> this path toward imaginative freedom.
>
> MR. MINDEL: I didn't get that.

Neither would most people. The judges who later read the
record undoubtedly understood the point Kazin was making,
but either they rejected it, or they were not sufficiently impressed. In any event, they mentioned nothing about religion in
their highly literate descriptions of the book. Kazin took it farther:

> *Lady Chatterley's Lover,* in that sense, is an entirely religious
> novel, and he worked it over and over again three times in
> order to convey perfectly that seriousness of purpose.

One might question the validity of using the word "religious" to
express what Kazin had to say about Lawrence. I question it. It
is really a form of advocacy. Many of our leading critics—social
as well as literary—like to take familiar words and turn them to
unfamiliar uses. Some old connotations are carried over, some
new ones are added, and the critic gains one or both of two
things: an easy downhill start over deceptively familiar ground,
and the shock value that comes from the combination of elements ordinarily kept separate (religion and dirty words, for example). The end is not discovery but persuasion, not so much
ultimate illumination as the arresting of attention. A clear statement, as distinguished from an intriguing statement, would

require the use of a new word for the differing concept, or at
least a warning to the reader that his present understanding of
the word is to be put aside.

But whatever might have been the validity of the point on a
critical or pedagogical level, it was bad for the practical purposes
of the case. Most judges would be likely to regard the statement
as strained, if not bizarre, and to the extent they might distrust
the academic world, even question its good faith. I thought of
trying to show through further questions that the word "religious" was being used in a special sense. But I did not know
where Kazin, warming to his subject, might go. As things stood,
this was a rather short statement in a long stretch of testimony.
I decided to let ill enough alone.

We moved to the forbidden words:

Q. Is there any such language in this book which you have
not seen in reputable and publicly accepted novels of the last
several decades?

MR. MINDEL: Objection as to reputable. It is again an
opinion by this witness. What are these books he is talking
about, anyway? By whose standards are they reputable?

MR. REMBAR: Published by reputable publishers and
suffering no prohibition from the mails. Is that [a long, hard
"that"] sufficiently definite?

THE JUDICIAL OFFICER: Do you have any objection to that
as phrased?

MR. MINDEL: If this witness knows which books have not
been banned from the mails, if he can testify as to that.
Would you ask your witness whether he is familiar with all
the books that have been banned?

MR. REMBAR: That is not the question. I asked him
whether these words have been found in books which have
not been banned.

MR. MINDEL: That's right. I understand that. If he knows
of books which have not been banned in which these words
are found, he can answer the question. He doesn't have to
know of every single book that has been published. If he
knew of every single book that has been published, he might
be able to—

THE JUDICIAL OFFICER: I think the question is clear. He
can answer it.

THE WITNESS: I know of a book which has not been banned and in which each one of these words occur.

Here, I felt, Mindel was making a mistake. His objections were overruled, and the very fact that he was making objections gave the testimony a significance that intrinsically it did not merit. As I have mentioned, the extent to which Lawrence used the language, and the context in which he used it, made *Lady Chatterley* quite different from the contemporary novels to which Kazin was referring. The Post Office could have pointed this out in its brief or summation, without flattering the statement by working so hard to keep it out of the record.

On cross-examination, Mindel went immediately to Kazin's use of the word "religious." My wondering whether I should ask Kazin to expound his views became academic. Mindel was asking him to. I could only hope that the exposition would help rather than hurt. It helped. As a matter of fact, Mindel himself assisted, by suggesting a contrast with the word "ecclesiastical":

Q. You used the term before—"religious novel." You said this is a religious novel, an entirely religious novel. I think you will recognize that that would not be a term ordinarily attached by the layman to a book of this sort, thinking of religion in the ecclesiastical sense. I ask you, when you used that term, if you attached some significance to it that the layman wouldn't ordinarily intend.

A. I believe that the words "religious" and "ecclesiastical" are not synonomous for all persons. . . . Literary historians and critics generally agree that ever since the Renaissance a great deal of what has been most valuable in Western literature and art has expressed a private or personal religious purpose rather than an ecclesiastical one, that the same ideas and nobility found in the medieval world directly attached to the Church is found in many poems, plays, works of art, by individuals who had no ecclesiastical adherence. Lawrence in all his works is notably the English novelist of the twentieth century who most personifies that tradition . . . and by "religious," I mean specifically a desire to get closer to a greater source of being than is found in society itself. For Lawrence, you see, every true, deep tenderness of people was in itself a form of communion. . . .

Q. Do you mean to say—and I am asking this for clarification for me and perhaps others—that these relationships between the characters of this book were for the purpose of spirituality, and that that was the effect of these relationships, these various sex engagements?

A. These meetings were not for the purpose of spirituality, but the point that Lawrence made was that in the deep love relationship of sex, there is a great spiritual value which is tantamount to the spiritual value people have always sought for from life. Lawrence is hardly alone in this.

In his opening statement, Mindel had relied heavily on the Learned Hand opinion which contained the frequently cited statement about the "critical point in the compromise between candor and shame." Hand, it seemed to me, was referring to social standards of decorum; Mindel, however, turned the word to a different use.

Q. Is there any contradiction in your mind between shamelessness and spirituality?

A. I don't think Lawrence is ever shameless.

Q. Do you think Connie was ever shameless?

A. I think she had experiences which surprised her.

Q. Do you think she was ever shameless?

A. From whose point of view?

Q. Her own.

A. No, I don't.

Q. May I draw your attention to page 298, where she says, "In the short summer night she learnt so much. She would have thought a woman would have died of shame. Instead of which, the shame died," which I think means the same thing, that she was shameless.

A. Mr. Mindel, when you use the word "shameless," I mean by it, and I suspect that you would mean by it, that which is shameless to everybody. A murder is shameless. An unprovoked assault is shameless. But one's own shame, which is sort of a creation of one's moral attitude, can drop away very easily. It is a normal biological growth for people, especially for girls. It is hardly considered shameless in the same sense as is said by Lawrence.

Q. What do you think she said here?

A. What Lawrence says, that she was shamed, that she lost that part of her repressiveness and inhibitedness.

Mindel went to another passage in the book. Frommer objected:

MR. FROMMER: . . . I suggest we have gone far enough in this picking and choosing of stray sentences and paragraphs in the book.

THE JUDICIAL OFFICER: I have been waiting for someone to object to that. I think you are absolutely right. By doing this, we are doing the very thing that the courts have been most unanimous on since *Ulysses*, that we can't pick and choose.

The reason Ablard had been kept waiting was that I saw nothing to gain by objecting, and something to lose. The basis for objection—the whole-book rule—was obvious, and might well have worked, in view of the prestige and liberal aura that the rule had by this time developed. But if I were the judge, I would have upheld Mindel on this point. Where a witness makes a general statement about a book, his cross-examiner should be allowed to cite chapter and verse in testing his statement. This is altogether consistent with the proposition that ultimately the book must be considered as a whole. But quite apart from the propriety of the questions, Kazin's answers were strengthening our case. There is no point in spiking a line of cross-examination that is producing beneficial testimony.

Mindel turned to a different subject. He had set a little trap for Cowley. He also had one for Kazin:

Q. From your study of Lawrence, would you say that he felt that these words he used were obscene?

A. No.

* * *

Q. (by Mr. Mindel): I have before me a volume called *Sex, Literature and Censorship* by D. H. Lawrence. Are you familiar with this?

A. Yes.

Q. I have it open to page 120, which is the article in here called "Apropos of *Lady Chatterley's Lover*." This, as I understand, was written by Lawrence, commenting upon his own book. . . . He says: "And these notes, which I write now almost two years after the novel was finished, are not intended to explain or expound anything: only to give the emotional beliefs which perhaps are necessary as a background to the book. It is so obviously a book written in defiance of convention that perhaps some reason should be offered for the attitude of defiance: Since the silly desire to *épater le bourgeois*, to bewilder the commonplace person, is not worth entertaining, if I used a taboo word, there is a reason. We shall never free the phallic realty from 'uplift' taint until we give it its own phallic language and use the obscene words." That is his language.

MR. REMBAR: What is the question?

THE JUDICIAL OFFICER: What is the question?

THE WITNESS: What is the question?

Win, place and show.

MR. MINDEL: I am asking the witness whether he wishes to change his answer as to his opinion of whether Lawrence felt that the words that he used were obscene, which, of course, goes to the testimony that has been permitted with respect to the motive of the author.

THE JUDICIAL OFFICER: You may answer.

THE WITNESS: Lawrence did not believe that his use of these words was obscene. He believed that these words were generally regarded as obscene.

MR. REMBAR: I should like to object to this line of questioning on the ground that it confuses two concepts. One is the idea of "obscene words" as meaning words which are suffering from some sort of taboo or other. The other is the use of the word "obscene" as employed in this statute to make certain works nonmailable. . . .

THE JUDICIAL OFFICER: Your theory being even if he admitted the specific words were obscene, it would be of no moment to this case?

MR. REMBAR: Yes sir.

THE JUDICIAL OFFICER: Do you agree with that fundamental idea, Mr. Mindel?

He did not. But Ablard did.

THE JUDICIAL OFFICER [to Mindel]: . . . I really think your question is irrelevant.

Mindel had thought of another way of making things difficult for the witness:

Q. Would you agree the sexual incidents are the most forceful parts?

A. Among the most forceful, yes. I would agree.

Q. Therefore, would it not be a natural part of a literary review to quote some of that, to exemplify for the reader of the literary review the forcefulness of the writing that the reviewer is speaking of, in the same way as if he wanted to illustrate the poetry of another book?

A. No, it wouldn't, because no critic who knows his job and wants to represent the book he admires as clearly as possible to his audience is going to take something which is likely to be misunderstood by an audience. He would want to quote passages which are strictly coherent. I have written a long essay on this book for *Atlantic Monthly*. I have quoted many passages in it, not among them the sex passages. . . .

Q. You included none of the four-letter words in your article?

A. I saw no reason to.

Q. Do you think it would have been published had you?

A. I saw no reason to.

Q. Would you answer my question?

Mindel was right; Kazin was ducking the question. I thought that I had better intervene.

MR. REMBAR: That calls for a conclusion of law and also a conclusion as to what the editors of the magazine would do. I don't think Mr. Kazin can speak on this subject.

MR. MINDEL: This witness has spoken very broadly about the attitudes of editors, writers and publishers and everybody else involved in this business of creative literature. He certainly ought to have some idea of what the publisher of this magazine would consider as acceptable.

Mindel's response to my objection was a good one; my objection was not valid, and he had shown why. But at this point Ablard interposed some questions of his own, and the exchanges wandered away from the question Mindel had asked. This gave me an opportunity to make a point I wanted to make, in the course of supporting my objection. I held up the poster that had not been accepted as evidence; a picture of a fine girl in a fine bathing suit (1959 was, in the United States, slightly pre-bikini).

MR. REMBAR: In this line of questioning, my opponent has equated appeal to sexual interest with the use of these words. I think that is the main weakness of the government's case. I think the use of these words, if anything, dampens sexual interest. So far as taking words out of context goes—I use this not in an effort to get it into the record, but just by way of illustration—if you took a particular square inch of this picture—

MR. MINDEL: I object.

This was an odd inversion. Mindel was the questioner at this point, cross-examining Kazin, and what was being considered was my objection to his question.

MR. REMBAR: —and published it, I dare say it would be obscene. The picture as a whole is not.

MR. MINDEL: I would like to make a special point in saying, as I tried to make very clear in the outset of my opening statement, that our opinion of this book is not based on the four-letter words alone. There are many extensive descriptions of sex acts in here, and of course you take the book as a whole, which is colored, necessarily by its parts. . . .

THE JUDICIAL OFFICER: I think I am going to sustain the objection [that is, my objection to Mindel's question]. The witness has already elaborated sufficiently his reasons in not including these portions in his own review.

Ablard had—understandably, considering how much had happened meanwhile—forgotten what the last question was. It was not why Kazin had not used the sexual passages in his review, but whether *The Atlantic Monthly* would have published the review if he had.

Mindel then asked Kazin whether the novel itself could be published serially in magazines. The question produced a three-way conflict.

MR. FROMMER: That is a totally unfair question, because that question assumes that Mr. Kazin has to testify about the estimates that an editor must make as to what legal proceedings could be brought against him, such as a Post Office legal proceeding. If it were put, Would these editors publish this work absent the fear of legal prosecution? then I think it would be an acceptable question and would relate to community standards, to morality and to obscenity.

*   *   *

MR. MINDEL: The witness has testified and given every indication that this is within the area of public acceptance.

MR. REMBAR: As a book.

MR. FROMMER: As a book.

MR. MINDEL: Therefore I asked the question that I did.

MR. FROMMER: I submit the question is objectionable unless the witness is asked, Is this book within the area of public acceptance disregarding the threat of legal prosecution?

THE JUDICIAL OFFICER: That doesn't phrase the question as you mentioned it either. The question deals with publication in a serial form, which is in effect not abiding by the whole-book rule.

MR. REMBAR: I think we know in different media there may be different standards.

My statement had the ring of assurance that only ignorance can provide. The proposition that I so glibly said "we know" was not a rule of law. But it seemed to me a sound approach, and I was to urge it upon the Supreme Court six years later, when I was a little better educated.

The medium here is publication in a volume. I think while my questions related to the general cultural level of acceptance of sexual material, you don't impeach the answers or the witness by asking specifically whether this book would be published in some other medium.

THE JUDICIAL OFFICER: You would concede then—and you don't have to answer this, because you are not on the stand—that the actual basic part of this book, the story itself, if published in another medium, might possibly be obscene?

MR. REMBAR: It might possibly. I don't think it should be read as a Saturday-morning program on the radio, for example.

MR. FROMMER: Readers' Subscription have not so conceded.

MR. MINDEL: What was the concession?

MR. REMBAR: The concession was that I would not think it proper for this book to be read on the radio Saturday mornings.

MR. MINDEL: Why Saturday mornings?

MR. REMBAR: Because that is when children listen.

MR. MINDEL: How about Saturday evening?

MR. REMBAR: You heard my concession.

THE JUDICIAL OFFICER: I proposed the question. It is my fault for initiating this line of questioning.

MR. MINDEL: May I have just one moment here?

THE JUDICIAL OFFICER: All right.

(Short pause.)

MR. REMBAR: Was there a ruling on this question about serialization? I objected to the question. Has it been withdrawn?

THE JUDICIAL OFFICER: It was either withdrawn—

MR. MINDEL: I thought you ruled on it.

THE JUDICIAL OFFICER: I think what I said was that in view of what the witness had said about the taking out of specific parts, I thought he sufficiently elaborated on it.

MR. MINDEL: May I frame the question the way Mr. Frommer suggested? He would not object to it.

MR. REMBAR: But I object to it very seriously. I do not think that what might happen if this book were offered for publication in magazines, newspapers, or anywhere else, has any relevancy. The question before the Judicial Officer is whether this volume, this specific volume, is entitled to mailing privileges.

THE JUDICIAL OFFICER: I do think we are getting pretty far afield.

Schueler entered the contest, with the aim of exploiting the divergence between Frommer and me:

MR. SCHUELER: Could we establish one thing for the record at this time, whether this is a consolidation, as I believe it to be, with co-counsel?

THE JUDICIAL OFFICER: It is a consolidated hearing. But since each of these gentlemen is representing separate clients and separate respondents in these proceedings, there is a possibility that they might not both agree on every question that is propounded. This is the first time there has been any divergence of opinion. I think that is a remarkably good record.

That particular record wasn't quite as good as Ablard thought.

Do you have any more questions?

MR. MINDEL: Does this resolve this part of it?

MR. FROMMER: There is no question on the record.

MR. MINDEL: I started to offer one.

MR. REMBAR: And I objected to the question. You started to take a statement that Mr. Frommer made and put it in the form of a question. . . .

MR. MINDEL: I am trying to take advantage of Mr. Frommer's concession here. The question is whether Mr. Kazin, the witness, believes that a magazine would be likely to publish this book in serial form absent any fears of legal action that might result.

MR. REMBAR: I object to it on the ground it is extremely hypothetical and that it is irrelevant to the consideration of whether this volume is entitled to mailing privileges.

THE JUDICIAL OFFICER: A lot of other issues have been raised. What is the purpose of the question?

MR. MINDEL: It gets back to the testimony by this witness that developed on direct examination as to the acceptance of such matters by the general public.

THE JUDICIAL OFFICER: I think your question is improper. I will sustain the objection. It is immaterial for those purposes which you have just stated.

MR. MINDEL: I think now we have completed our cross-examination.

Rosset's testimony had been interrupted so that Cowley and Kazin would not be kept waiting too long. He was recalled to the stand to complete it, and it was at this point I asked the question about his motive in publishing the book:

A. Without being redundant, I would just like to say that along with Mr. Cowley and Mr. Kazin, I consider *Lady Chatterley's Lover* to be a great book and a significant part of the heritage of the English-speaking people. As a publisher in a free marketplace, I am also looking for stimulating, challenging, possibly profitable opportunities to publish good books. I stand by this book and every other book that we have brought out.

When *Lady Chatterley's Lover* was published [that is, first printed], the publishers of its day evidently felt unable or afraid to risk any possible legal consequences in publishing

it. The book was never published officially in this country.
Lawrence died and the book sort of went into the backwash
of history. It certainly has been available in this country all
these years in what is known as under-the-counter market. It
is openly and legally distributed in Europe—in English and
in foreign languages.

Rosset meant on the Continent. In fact, however, only in some
Continental countries was the book free of ban, and even this
proved little, since in those countries it was in a language that
their "average person" could not read. In England there was no
attempt to publish *Lady Chatterley* until after the decision here.

But somehow or other nothing happened to have the book
brought here. It occurred to me, and I am sure it occurred to
many other publishers, that since the book was written in
1928 the emotional maturity of the American people has un-
dergone a great change. We have heard a good deal of testimony about that today. It occurred to me that it would be
incomprehensible if this book were published today that the
public would be shocked, offended or would raise any outcry
against it; but rather they would welcome it as the republish-
ing, the bringing back to life, of one of our great masterpieces, and therefore I went ahead and published it. Thus far,
all of my anticipated feelings have been rewarded with what I
expected to happen as having happened, with the exception
of this hearing.

This was self-serving, of course, and argumentative, but awfully
good. I believe that Rosset's statement impressed the Judicial
Officer. It certainly impressed me. It may even have impressed
Mindel and Schueler.

The next half-hour or so was devoted to matters that concerned Readers' Subscription alone. For purposes of proof, the
Post Office lawyers had asked that a few copies of the book-club
circulars be received in evidence as samples representative of the
entire mailing. The book-club lawyers had agreed.

Arthur Rosenthal, president of Readers' Subscription, took

the stand and described the club and how it operated. His own bearing—the tone of his testimony—was the best evidence, I thought, of the club's quality. Frommer then sought to show that its membership was made up of mature, educated readers. Schueler and Mindel objected. Ablard drew attention to something about the samples that might create an issue as to the composition of the mailing list, and therefore make Frommer's questions relevant:

> THE JUDICIAL OFFICER: . . . the exhibit which you [the Post Office attorneys] sought to introduce here and which was introduced is addressed to one Mary Ann McFarland of the Girls' Latin School in Chicago, Illinois.
> MR. MINDEL: How does that disprove what we are saying?
> THE JUDICIAL OFFICER: It raises in my mind the question that possibly Readers' Subscription is disseminating this to ninth-grade students.
> MR. MINDEL: I think if anyone is hoisted, it is the mailer by his own petard.
> THE JUDICIAL OFFICER: It may be, but that is now in evidence. I think in view of the fact that this—right on the face of it at least—indicates to me that his mailing list may be somewhat suspect, that counsel should now be able to go into this.

While this was going on, Rosset and I had a quiet conference. It might be that Mary Ann was not a student. We had somebody make a telephone call to Chicago. The call produced the information that she was indeed not a student. She was the registrar of the school, age over forty. We passed the information on to Frommer, whose questioning of Rosenthal had been proceeding meanwhile. Frommer tried to get the information into the record through the witness he had on the stand.

> MR. SCHUELER: Objection. This is hearsay evidence. . . . In addition to that, this is only representative of twenty thousand. . . . We selected at random from twenty thousand. It was stipulated this was representative of twenty-thousand-odd circulars.
> MR. FROMMER: I shall reserve this questioning for another witness who actually made the phone call.

After a pause, Schueler and Mindel gave up:

> MR. MINDEL: We will concede the next witness will testify
> the call was made to the school and he got the information
> indicated here for it by counsel.

This concluded the testimony. There was some closing argument, and the trial was over. It had all taken place in one day, a
day that began early and ended late but went fast.

ℒady Chatterley:

the Federal Courts

ABLARD HAD INDICATED THAT OUR APPLICATION
to hold off the ban while the case was pending was not within
his jurisdiction. So the next day, May 15, 1959, we made the
same application, in writing, to Postmaster General Summerfield. The Postmaster General took a week to decide that we
ought not to have this temporary provisional relief.

On May 28 Ablard issued an "order." It set forth his decision
that he was not going to make a decision:

> The book at issue, which is the unexpurgated version, has for
> many years been held to be nonmailable by the Post Office
> Department and nonimportable by the Bureau of Customs
> of the Department of the Treasury. To hold the book to be
> mailable matter would require a reversal of rulings of long
> standing by the department and cast doubt on the rulings of
> a coordinate executive department. This proceeding is there-
> fore referred to the Postmaster General for final departmen-
> tal decision. . . .

We did not know how long Summerfield would take, now that
he had the whole case to decide. So we renewed the application
to suspend the ban, by a letter on May 29 and again by telegram
on June 5. Nobody answered. Though there was still no final

ruling that the book was obscene, we felt that we were now entitled to go to court.

There is no prescribed procedure for judicial review of a Post Office ban. Ordinarily the legislation under which an agency acts gives the person aggrieved an explicit right to challenge the action in court. When a book is seized by Customs, the statute goes so far as to put the burden of bringing suit on the government; if the importer demands his book, the government must either turn it over to him or start a forfeiture suit in the federal court. The only way to question a Post Office ruling, however, is to invoke the court's general power as a court of equity.*

Even where a statute provides for judicial review, a court usually will not stir until the administrative process has been completed. One must first exhaust the possibilities of winning within the agency. Since the Post Office Department had not yet made its final determination, this presented a problem. We would try to solve it by calling on the principle that justice delayed is justice denied. The department had banned the book from the mails for a month, while it was making up its departmental mind about whether the book ought to be banned. This, we felt, was in itself a cause for complaint and made the case ripe for the courts.

On June 10 we sued Christenberry, a more or less innocent bystander. Summerfield was calling the shots, but it was Chris-

---

* That is, the inherent power possessed by a modern court by reason of its double ancestry—the ancient common law courts and the courts of chancery, or equity. The best-known exercise of equity jurisdiction is the injunction. The Appendix gives a few further details.

We are dealing here with questions that lawyers usually call "procedural." The word "procedural" is used in contrast to the word "substantive" to mark a fundamental legal classification; the rules that define relationships and govern conduct (the substantive law) are separated from the rules that determine how disputes are heard and decided (the procedural law). The phrase "on the merits" (which the reader will see once in a while) has a meaning close to "substantive"; it generally refers to the ultimate question to be decided, as distinguished from questions which, though perhaps important, are procedural or preliminary. "On the merits," however, is a relative term; it sometimes refers not to the final question, but simply to a question one stage deeper than the one with which it is being compared.

tenberry who was holding the books, and who was therefore inflicting the immediate legal injury (if there was a legal injury). We filed suit in the federal district court in New York.*

Our suit asked that the book be declared not obscene and that Christenberry be directed to forward the mail. At the same time we moved for preliminary injunction, a process by which a defendant is ordered to do something, or refrain from doing something, while a lawsuit is pending—the final relief, or the denial of it, to await the outcome of a trial. Here the trial had already been held; the judge would have the record of it before him, and he would grant or deny a preliminary injunction on the same basis that he would grant or deny the final injunction. The preliminary motion, therefore, would decide the whole case.†

The day after we filed, the Postmaster General gave us his decision. This was coincidence; it would no doubt have been

---

* The district courts are federal courts of original jurisdiction—that is, courts in which cases start. Apart from some specialized tribunals (such as the Court of Claims, which hears money claims against the federal government, and the Tax Court, which decides controversies between the taxpayer and the Internal Revenue Service), the district courts handle all federal cases, with two exceptions: a few that go directly into a court of appeals and those over which the Supreme Court has original jurisdiction (such as suits in which two states are opponents). Between the district courts and the Supreme Court is a set of appellate courts called courts of appeals. There are eleven of them; ten hear appeals from groups of district courts called "circuits," and the eleventh from the District of Columbia. (There are enough cases in the District of Columbia to keep an appellate court busy, because a large proportion of the litigation that concerns the federal government comes up there.)

The word "circuit" goes back to the time when travel was difficult. Either the litigants, with their lawyers and their witnesses, had to go a great distance to get to where the court sat, or the court had to go to where the trouble was. Since it was easier for one person to travel than for a group, the judges obligingly rode from place to place.

† The government cross-moved for summary judgment, a procedural device designed to end the entire litigation without a trial; it can be used where (as here) the facts are not in dispute. The motion for summary judgment had no effect on the outcome; it merely permitted the district court to formally wind up the case. It did, however, have an effect on the title of our brief, which to avoid inordinate length, bore a sorcerer's caption: "Brief on Motion and Cross-Motion."

announced on that day anyway. The problem of an uncompleted administrative process was solved. The decision was definitive.

Summerfield cited three cases—*Roth, Ulysses* and *Besig*—and the greatest of these, judging by his opinion, was *Besig*. That was the 1953 case in which a federal court of appeals had refused to allow copies of Henry Miller's *Tropics* to be brought into the United States. Half of Summerfield's opinion was devoted to quotations from *Besig*. Relying on them, and on the conventional reading of *Roth*, he concluded:

> The contemporary community standards are not such that this book should be allowed to be transmitted in the mails.
>
> The book is replete with descriptions in minute detail of sexual acts engaged in or discussed by the book's principal characters. These descriptions utilize filthy, offensive and degrading words and terms. Any literary merit the book may have is far outweighed by the pornographic and smutty passages and words, so that the book, taken as a whole, is an obscene and filthy work. . . .

Summerfield's action at least solved our procedural problem; the suits could no longer be said to be premature.

Both Grove Press and Readers' Subscription went to court. Jay Topkis appeared for Readers' Subscription. Christenberry was represented by S. Hazard Gillespie, Jr., United States Attorney for the Southern District of New York; Robert J. Ward was his principal assistant. Gillespie was a former partner in the huge law firm of David, Polk, Wardwell, Sunderland & Kiendl, and the only lawyer in the case listed in the *Social Register*. He occupied what is probably the third most important legal post in the country. Because of the quantity and significance of the federal litigation that comes up in New York City, the United States Attorney for this district has a responsibility exceeded only by that of the United States Attorney General and the Solicitor General.

The cases were scheduled to be heard by Frederick van Pelt Bryan, a judge who combined intellect with a hard courtroom sense. Motions are regularly heard on a "motion day," which, in a busy court, may involve the calling of a hundred of them and the argument of twenty or thirty.* When it is known that the argument will take a good deal of time, however, or where there is more than ordinary public interest, a special date may be set, and that was done here.

There was a meeting in Judge Bryan's chambers to fix the date and settle some procedural arrangements. At the meeting I made a request that was labeled, justifiably, unusual. Grove Press and Readers' Subscription had begun their suits on the same day and made similar motions, which would be heard and decided together. In such situations the two cases are usually known by the title of the case that is listed first. (Thus the opinions in the *Roth* and *Alberts* cases are called the *Roth* opinions.) The book club's complaint reached the clerk's office a few hours before ours, and the cases were listed in that order. But I thought it might be valuable to Grove to have the case known by its name and I asked that the sequence be reversed. I argued that Grove was entitled to this because it was in essence Grove's venture. The attorney for the book club objected. Bryan considered for a moment, smiled a judicial smile and granted the request. "Your client is the father," he said, "and he wants to give the baby his name. Right?" (The question of legitimacy was reserved.)

The argument I would advance—in this case and in those to follow—was based on the Constitution. I would ask the court to pay little attention to what had been said to be obscene or not obscene under the various statutes. No matter what Congress or the state legislatures had meant to do, the First Amendment necessarily confined their enactments in narrow straits. But this did not require a ruling that the statutes themselves were null and void. Just two years earlier, in the *Roth* case, the Supreme

---

* A judge's handling of a motion day is revealing. Bryan presided over the turmoil with a mixture of tough discipline and high courtesy that is worth watching. I recommend visiting the federal court on such a day; it will give the nonlawyer a notion of the difficulties that inhere in the administration of the law, and how they are sometimes made to yield to character and talent.

Court had held that anti-obscenity laws were not, on their face, unconstitutional. Over a period of time the Court may change its position, but there was no reason to expect it to change its position on so stark a point so soon. Moreover, apart from the nearness in time, it is a doubtful thesis that these statutes have no legitimate application at all. In the legislative junk pile that constitutes our anti-obscenity law, certain valid public interests may lie hidden or distorted.

Hence I would argue not that the Comstock Act as a whole was invalid, but that the First Amendment forbade its application to the book I was defending—principally because, in that same *Roth* case, the Court had held (whether or not it was immediately apparent) that the Amendment protected any writing not utterly worthless.

But the idea that literary merit could save a book was not the whole of our defense; we would not rest on this long-shot version of what the Supreme Court really meant but failed to say. I could also build an argument on the prurient-interest formula: that it was not simply *Hicklin* renovated—it was a new kind of test, by whose terms *Lady Chatterley* was not obscene; "prurient" meant something special, and a normal sexual interest was not prurience. Judicial acceptance of this would take us beyond a narrow, okay-this-time victory; it would not produce as much of a change in the law as the value theory, but it would help.

Acceptance would not come easily. A persuasive argument could be made (and was) that lustfulness was still the key. The Brennan opinion said the prurient-interest test was no different from that adopted by "later decisions." Though the decisions cited were themselves inconsistent, a distillation produced the *Hicklin* test modified only by the whole-book rule. Moreover, there was Brennan's footnote, appended to his first mention of prurient interest: "i.e., material having a tendency to excite lustful thoughts."

And the phrases "average person" and "contemporary community standards" were too prominent in the carefully constructed sentence that formed the climax of the opinion, prominent and poisonous. They appeared to make restraints on publication a matter of majority preference. The Supreme Court, my opponents kept pointing out, had put the whole question of obscenity where it belonged—in the hands of that embodiment of the community, the jury. The average man can tell us what kind of talk is considered dirty around the neighborhood saloon or the country club.

Now it is a fact that literary values are of small consequence to most people. Eliminating material obviously read for other reasons—textbooks, manuals of instruction, astrologies, financial statements—the number of adults who read books is small. If we also eliminate books used solely for entertainment, sexual or other, the number is smaller still. (I do not deprecate entertainment, but those who look for nothing else cannot be counted in the number who would read *Chatterley* for the qualities that critics cherish.)

An outstanding best-seller among books taken seriously as literature will have, in all editions, perhaps a million and a half buyers. The various editions of *Lady Chatterley's Lover* that came out in 1959 and '60 sold over six million copies. The average man, it was pretty clear, was buying because it was a dirty book.

Changes have taken place in the past decade, but even at the present time, the kind of writing that Lawrence did in *Chatterley* is simply not acceptable by community standards. One might like to read the book, but this is not the same as saying one favored its publication. The community often tolerates private indulgence while it refuses public recognition. Consider the even-handed approval, during Prohibition, of the man who took a drink, and of the prosecutor who jailed the gangster that supplied it. If, in 1959, there had been a ballot on whether *Lady Chatterley's Lover* should be openly published, the vote, in my judgment, would have run about nine-to-one against. My odds might be slightly off—either way—but in any case it is quite clear that the proponents of publication would have lost quite handsomely.

Remember that the intellectual minority does not constitute the community, and tends to have a distorted view of these things. With deep apologies to my readers, I must suggest that many of them will not have a full appreciation of how the community as a whole feels about the issues with which this book is concerned. Intellectuals suffer from the disadvantage of talking to each other. They are apt to work together, to go to each other's parties, and to read each other's writing. A parochial view is hard to avoid.

There was a striking example of this in the incredulous dismay felt by almost all intellectuals at the Supreme Court's decisions of March 1966; though they cleared *Fanny Hill*, they affirmed prison sentences for Ralph Ginzburg and Edward Mishkin. It had been assumed, by people who wanted it so, that censorship for obscenity was just about ended. There was no such assumption on the part of the general public, which greeted the decisions—except for the unfortunate one that protected *Fanny Hill*—with gratification. On both sides, the reactions were inappropriate. The fact was that the Supreme Court took a long step toward freedom. Misapprehension as to where the Court stood before it took the step caused most of the confusion. Misapprehension as to the effect of the decisions caused the rest.

So the phrase "average person" created severe problems for us. So did "contemporary community standards," a concept which owed a great deal to a much-cited opinion of Learned Hand. The opinion, written in 1913, came precisely halfway between the *Hicklin* decision and the *Chatterley* trial. At that date *Hicklin* had, in its particular field, undone the American Revolution, successfully colonizing our law of obscenity. Hand was deciding a criminal case based on the mailing of a novel called *Hagar Revelly*. The defendant demurred to the indictment (that is, argued that it should be dismissed without trial) on the ground that the book was not obscene. Hand overruled the demurrer; he held that the defendant must stand trial, and that the question of obscenity must go to the jury, to be decided in accordance with the *Hicklin* rule. Having recognized the sovereignty of the rule, he then protested it.

This sometimes happens in the lower courts, when a judge feels that the precedents express an unfortunate view of the law, but are clear and cannot be distinguished away. Thus the strong-minded Hand, not yet an appellate judge, could properly criticize the rule he was constrained to follow, and propose that it be changed. But the change he proposed, though it seemed to be on the side of freedom, in fact was not.

Hicklin, he pointed out, required us "to reduce our treatment of sex to the standard of a child's library in the supposed interest of a salacious few. . . ." (Forty-four years later, in the case of the Michigan statute, the Supreme Court agreed.) Hand questioned "whether in the end men will regard that as obscene which is honestly relevant to the adequate expression of innocent ideas. . . ." (The relevance of the form of expression to the writer's theme also became important in later cases—though Hand's statement, robbed of meaning by his insertion of "innocent," was itself of no use.) But Hand's main criticism is one that ultimately works against freedom. Times change, he said: ". . . the rule as laid down, however consonant it may be with mid-Victorian morals, does not seem to me to answer to the understanding and morality of the present time. . . . If there be no abstract definition, such as I have suggested, should not the word 'obscene' be allowed to indicate the present critical point in the compromise between candor and shame at which the community may have arrived here and now?"

It is, of course, true that times change, and true that rules of law change with them. It is legitimate, and often effective, for the defender of a book to point this out. But the concept should be used as a one-way valve. The flow should never be the other way. In the last one hundred years, majority notions of what is proper have moved in the direction of freedom, and so defenders of books might cite the trend of history. But for two hundred years prior to that the trend was quite the opposite. Seventeenth-century dramatists and eighteenth-century novelists would have had a tough time in the late nineteenth century.

When we are asserting First Amendment guaranties, the temper of the times is an ally we dare not trust. It is an unexceptionable proposition that 1868 concepts of morality should not have governed the right to publish in 1913, but neither should the concepts of morality of 1913. Nor, I was to argue, should the moral concepts of 1959 govern the *Chatterley* case. Hand's corollary is pernicious. A freedom to express what conforms to prevailing standards is not the freedom the First Amendment contemplates. The "compromise between candor and shame at which the community may have arrived here and now" would perhaps allow a writer in 1913 to say more than he could have said in 1868. But the First Amendment is a cheap thing if all it provides is the assurance that one may say what a current majority is willing to hear.

Hand's words, voiced as a plea for a more liberal standard, were often used against us. (Mindel had used them in this case.) They were cited as confirming the meaning and the overriding importance of Brennan's reference to "contemporary community standards." The meaning they were said to confirm was that general community sentiment, not the preferences of a minority composed of literary people, should determine the outcome.

In attempting to deal with the average-person community-standards prurient-interest formula, I proposed, to begin with, that it had two branches. The Brennan footnote, which started with the reference to lustfulness, ended with something more helpful; it cited a statement of the American Law Institute:

> A thing is obscene if, considered as a whole, its predominant appeal is to prurient interest, i.e., a shameful or morbid interest in nudity, sex, or excretion, and if it goes substantially beyond customary limits of candor in description or representations of such matters.

From this I argued that the formula required both that the book have a certain kind of appeal and that its expression exceed the bounds of current candor. There were, I was saying, two independent tests—prurient interest and social value—and the former was itself a double test.

This breakdown turned out to be useful in court. With the social-value argument it gave us three separate opportunities to save the book. But (apart from the value theory) the main contest was on the meaning of "prurient interest," "average person" and "contemporary community standards," whether they added up to one criterion or two. What I said they meant may be summarized by quoting a few paragraphs from one of my briefs:

> When this Court, in *Roth*, formulated the prurient-interest test, it was not engaged in the simple exercise of synonym-swapping. Most earlier efforts to give meaning to the term "obscene" had ended by doing no more than replacing one epithet with another. "Obscene" was defined as "lewd,"

"lewd" as "lascivious," "lascivious" as "libidinous," "libidinous" as "licentious" and "licentious" as "lustful." "Immoral," "improper" and "impure" were tried, along with "indecent," "filthy" and "vulgar." The succeeding definitions had different trim, but no functional change, and the troublesome vagueness persisted.

In the last decade, however, it has been held that the matter must be considered in a constitutional context, and in that context *Roth* dispelled a great deal of the vagueness. The Court chose a word that had not been prominent in earlier formulas—the word "prurient." It was a word whose peculiar connotations set it apart from its predecessors. The choice, of course, was not mere rhetoric. The purpose, we suggest, was to make it clear that the *Hicklin* test and its derivatives were no longer the law, and to define more narrowly and with greater depth the characteristic that must be found in the material upon which anti-obscenity statutes may operate.

The fact that a publication might appeal to the sexual interest of the reader, or might create a sexual response in him —the fact that the publication might, under the older definitions, be called lustful—would not satisfy the new and narrower prurient-interest test. The etymological source of "prurient" is a word that means "itching," and its present-day connotations include "dirty," "nasty," "morbid," "unwholesome". . . .

The Court's narrow definition of the material that might be proscribed conformed with—indeed was required by—the realities of our culture. A legislative attempt to do away with books on the ground that they may be sexually stimulating becomes ludicrous when viewed against what we see around us. . . . [A novel], no matter how much devoted to the act of sex, can hardly add to the constant sexual prodding with which our environment assails us. Apart from the evidence offered, the Court may take judicial notice of the fact that our advertising, our motion pictures, our television and our journalism are in large measure calculated to produce sexual thoughts and reactions. We live in a sea of sexual provocation. . . .

Nor do the references, in the prurient-interest formula, to "the average person" and to "contemporary community standards" imply a broader brush of condemnation. The

theme of the portion of the *Roth* opinion in which the prurient-interest test is stated is the final rejection of the *Hicklin*
rule. *Hicklin* had notorious weaknesses: (a) it stressed isolated excerpts of the book in question; (b) it judged those
excerpts by their effect on the particularly susceptible, and
(c) it looked to fixed concepts of propriety, regardless of
time, place and circumstances. The courts that refused to follow *Hicklin*, as the *Roth* opinion says, (a) considered the
book as a whole, (b) judged it according to its effect upon
the normal adult rather than upon the particularly susceptible, and (c) stressed current mores and reading habits as distinguished from the notions of propriety entertained by British judges of the mid-nineteenth century. This Court's use of
the term "average person" was designed to remedy the second weakness of the *Hicklin* rule, and the use of the term
"contemporary community standards" was designed to remedy the third.

The "average person" is the subject whose responses are
involved; he is not the arbiter whose views on publication are
to decide the constitutional question. The Court's repudia-
tion of the *Hicklin* doctrine did not permit its replacement
with a rule by which an "average" notion of what is objectionable should control the freedom to write and be read.
Such a rule would forbid dissent in matters of taste, and
would impose a tyranny no less repugnant to the constitutional guaranties than that imposed by *Hicklin*. . . .

The negation of the *Hicklin* test expressed in the phrases
"average person" and "contemporary community standards"
does not mean that the rights guaranteed by the First
Amendment are to be determined by conducting a Gallup
Poll among the population at large. The phrases were not
meant to limit writers and publishers to the average person's
conception of the kind of writing that ought to be published,
or to limit a minority of readers to the kind of reading that a
majority might think good for them. Where a statute purports to control general publication, the reference to "the average person" excludes as criteria the possible responses and
attitudes of special elements of the population. (A less intru-
sive statute, which might, for example, regulate sales to children, is to be distinguished from a statute that suppresses
publication altogether.) The reference to "contemporary
community standards" fixes attention on the historic fact

that standards change. The Court was not seeking to chain creative minds to the dead center of convention at a given moment in time.

This exegesis might leave the prurient-interest formula very little room in which to operate. Attacked from other points of view, by lawyers whose problem was not a lustful book but a book objectionable on other grounds, the test might be still further narrowed. But what might happen in other kinds of cases was not exactly a pressing problem. All the court had to consider in our case was whether the test was narrow enough to exclude *Lady Chatterley* from the area of the obscene.

This then was the legal basis of the defense of *Lady Chatterley*: a highly restrictive interpretation of what the Supreme Court meant by its prurient-interest formula, plus another, independent test that I hoped the judges could discern in *Roth*. The novel might arouse lust, but, I would contend, it was not the nasty kind of thing that could be called prurient, and in any event it had value far beyond the modicum of social importance that would invoke the protection of the First Amendment. Once, working on an early brief in the case, I drew two circles that overlapped just slightly. I marked one "prurient," the other "utterly worthless." The small pointed ellipse formed by their intersection represented what might be constitutionally suppressed. *Lady Chatterley's Lover* did not come within it. If the book was in the circle marked "prurient," I proposed to argue, it was surely not in the part of it that was also circumscribed by the circle marked "utterly worthless."

Suppressible obscenity

❧

One might think that the outcome of the case would depend on whether the Postmaster General was right or wrong. It was not that simple. There was an antecedent issue: how far might the court go in questioning the Postmaster General's ruling? The court might disagree with Summerfield on whether *Lady*

Chatterley's Lover was obscene, yet refuse to upset his decision.

When a court reviews the decision of an administrative agency, there is almost always a presumption that the agency was right. This reflects, and intensifies, the presumption that attends appellate review of a trial court's decision.

A trial court resolves the disputed issues of fact, and, the facts fixed, it then determines how they are to be dealt with under the law. On appeal, the traditional theory is that the questions of law may be considered afresh but that findings of fact are to be let alone. The historical function of the appellate court is to correct errors of law. (This is subject to the caveat that the boundary between law and fact is a shifting one. Depending on social and individual needs, a question of fact in one case may become a question of law in another.) An appellate court may be influenced by what the court below thought about the law, but unless it has a high regard for the particular judge, it is ordinarily no more influenced by his opinion than by the arguments of counsel. The lower court's resolution of questions of fact, however, stands on quite another footing. The trier of the facts sees the witnesses, hears how they tell their stories, observes their demeanor and is therefore in a better position to get at the truth than a reviewing court, which has only a paper record.*

Where administrative action is concerned, judicial review is usually more limited than in an appeal from one court to another.† The agencies are specialists in particular areas of economic activity. They make daily decisions about the application

---

* The theory has been modified in the course of time. The conceptual basis of the modification is that a trial court commits a kind of legal error when it makes a finding of fact without evidence to support it. Modern statutes give appellate courts varying degrees of power. Some courts can reverse if the findings are "clearly erroneous"; some need only decide that the findings are "against the weight of the evidence"; some still work under the old standard of "no supporting evidence." Whatever the formula, appellate courts usually reverse on the facts when they think it pretty clear that the court below was wrong, and not when, though they might disagree, they think the question close.

† The term "judicial review" usually has the broad meaning ascribed to it here. It also has a special, and different, meaning: the testing of legislative and executive action for constitutionality—the "doctrine of judicial review" mentioned in an earlier chapter.

of their statutes and develop an expertise that a court, dealing as it must with the whole of the law, cannot possibly match. The Securities and Exchange Commission is much more familiar with what goes on in the stock market than is the average judge. The National Labor Relations Board knows more than he does about collective-bargaining agreements. The Civil Aeronautics Board knows more about air traffic, and the Federal Communications Commission about television and radio broadcasting. Moreover, the disputes that come before the agencies frequently involve huge and intricate fact patterns. If the courts started from scratch each time—if they had to make all the findings of fact themselves—the judicial system would be instantly overloaded, and brought to a sticky halt.

Hence the reluctance to upset findings of fact is even stronger in the review of agency determinations than in appellate review. The court may feel compelled to go along with the agency's findings even when it regards them as quite dubious. Moreover, beyond this reluctance to alter findings of fact, there is a general disinclination to upset the agency's judgment of what ought to be done about the facts.

The concept goes by several names—administrative discretion, agency finality, the presumption of administrative regularity. In practical terms, it means that in many cases a judge who would have decided things differently if the case had been in his court from the beginning will nevertheless refuse to disturb the decision. He will set it aside only if he is convinced that it was altogether arbitrary and unreasonable, or that the situation is the exceptional one to which the rule favoring the agency is simply inappropriate.

At the time of the *Lady Chatterley* case, the rule was operating with particular vigor where Post Office bans were in issue. Walter Gellhorn, one of the leading authorities on administrative law (and a perceptive and witty writer on the subject of censorship), said, "Judges tend to sustain an exclusionary postal ruling so long as it lies within the outermost fringes of debatable soundness." In the circuit in which our case was brought, the court of appeals, refusing to disturb a Post Office ban, had recently declared that "judicial review channeled within the confines of a plea for an injunction should not be overextensive." (The statement was made in a case involving, of all people, Samuel Roth.)

So getting the federal courts to reverse Summerfield required something more than getting them to disagree with Summerfield. They had to disagree so violently they would be willing to override the customary presumption. Or they had to be persuaded that despite the precedents, there should be no such presumption in this kind of case. I aimed at both.

The argument fell naturally into two parts: one on the scope of review, the other on whether the book was obscene. Logically scope of review came first; the limits of what the court is able to do should be explored before the court sets about doing it. Logic and advocacy, however, often follow different paths. A judge persuaded on the merits is apt to treat procedural questions in a way that will allow him to get to the merits. If the judge got the feeling that Summerfield ought to be reversed, his inhibitions about reversing an administrative agency would tend to subside. I took up the book and let scope of review wait.

The law of obscenity was not new to Bryan. He had recently presided over a criminal trial under the Comstock Law, and soon after we began he showed that he was quite familiar with *Roth*. I talked about the decision anyway; I was going to offer an interpretation that Bryan had not heard before. After summarizing the facts of our case and touching lightly on those of *Roth*, I went straight to the value theory. Bryan saw a difficulty almost immediately; there was troubling language in the very paragraph on which my thesis was based:

MR. REMBAR: . . . In the *Roth* case the majority undertook to define obscenity in two ways. At one point early in the opinion the Court says what obscenity is not. Later on it says what it can be.

In the first place, the Court says, you can't have obscenity where you have a work that has ideas of even the slightest social importance.

THE COURT: Wait a minute. Are you quite sure that the majority said that?

MR. REMBAR: I believe so, your Honor, but we have the case here, and I think that is the best way to find out.

THE COURT: I think it is. As I recall that language, it says,

> "All ideas having even the slightest redeeming social impor-
> tance—unorthodox ideas, controversial ideas," et cetera—
> "have the full protection of the guaranties—"

Here the judge, whose rich baritone ordinarily filled a courtroom
quite comfortably, enlarged it somewhat:

> "unless excludable because they encroach upon the limited
> area of more important interests."

The "unless" language might be read as negating my argument
—that is, the Supreme Court might have been saying no more
than that the First Amendment protects expression of social importance unless there is some good reason it should not be protected. Or, translated into our particular subject matter, that a
work of literary value would be entitled to the protection of the
Amendment unless it happened to conflict with society's interest in forbidding the publication of obscene material. The sentence may have been only a spot of rhetoric.

If it was more than rhetoric, the "unless" clause would have
to be seen as a narrow exception, not a broad reservation that
effectively neutralized the first part of the sentence. A list of
decisions was appended, in a footnote, to the language Bryan
was stressing. Very often a statement that would be ambiguous
standing alone gains specific content from the precedents the
court cites in support of it.

MR. REMBAR: . . . The Court explains that sentence by
citing a long string of cases. When you read those cases, you
see that each one of them involves not a book, not writing in
itself, but some form of conduct, or else the direct and immediate influencing of conduct.

If I may refer to a few of them, the Court cites the *Harriss*
case. That had to do with the disclosure provisions of the
Federal Lobbying Act. It cites *Breard* v. *Alexandria*, and that
had to do with a municipal ordinance prohibiting peddlers
from calling upon private residences without invitation. It
cites *Teamsters* v. *Hanke*, which is an injunction against
picketing. It cites *Kovacs* v. *Cooper*, which was a municipal
ordinance prohibiting sound trucks emitting loud and raucous noises. It cites *Prince* v. *Massachusetts*, which involved a
state statute prohibiting newspaper sale on the streets by mi-

nors; *Labor Board* v. *Virginia,* which involved the coercion by
an employer under the National Labor Relations Act; *Cox* v.
New Hampshire, which involved a state statute requiring a
license for parade. It cites *Schenck* v. *United States,* which
contains the famous Holmes opinion having to do with in-
ducement to evade the wartime draft, where Holmes got the
majority to accept the "clear and present danger" rule.

THE COURT: I know it.

MR. REMBAR: All of these cases have to do with specific
kinds of conduct that a statute seeks to prohibit. They do not
have to do with writing in itself.

Though the decisions of the footnote were all freedom-of-speech
decisions, a discernible red thread ran through them, quite
different from the blue one that ran through the kind of case we
were presenting to Bryan. The *Roth* majority was saying, I suggested, that "expression brigaded with conduct" could be prohibited altogether, even though it had social importance, if it
collided with something else more important. But expression di-
vorced from conduct—of which books are an example—could
be prohibited only if it was "utterly without social importance."
Bryan seemed satisfied with the explanation.

There was another problem in the *Roth* statement. It spoke
of "ideas." It said nothing about literary merit, or about any
other kind of artistic merit. The struggles from which the First
Amendment emerged involved expository writing, not fiction,
and primarily writing that dealt with political conflicts. If the
Amendment was to guarantee freedom to the artist, it had to be
stretched beyond its historical antecedents. The Amendment
needed less stretching here than it would in later cases. *Chatterley* may fairly be described as a novel of ideas. Still, it was not a
pamphlet denouncing the divine right of kings. I continued:

We feel that there is a social importance in a book which
has merely literary value, and that that should be added to
what the Supreme Court here says is entitled to the guaranties. However, we don't have to go that far, because . . .
whether you agree with Lawrence or not, he had something
to preach to the public. He inveighed against sex without
love. He preached against the mechanization of the lives of
individuals that he felt came from the increasing industrialization of society. He was waving a banner in favor of an hon-

est approach to emotional and sexual problems, as against a
hypocritical one.

Finally, he was, it seems to me, arguing very strongly that
the approach to sex should be wholesome, natural, healthy
—and not morbid or, to use the Supreme Court's word, prurient.

That brings us to the second definition in the *Roth*
case. . . .

I was sliding into my interpretation of the prurient-interest
formula, and I made my argument that the Supreme Court used
the word "prurient" to designate a special, morbid kind of sexual interest. Bryan seemed receptive to that much, but then he
asked me to take the average man and community standards
into account:

> I wish for the moment that you would take those three
> concepts and put them together for me as far as your view is
> concerned and see how you can evolve for me, as far as the
> plaintiff contends here, a consistent pattern of what they
> mean when they are all put together.
>
> MR. REMBAR: The part of the majority opinion to which
> your Honor alludes is a part that comes after—

I would not let go of the point that the reference to social importance was the most significant part of the opinion.

> —the Court's affirmative statement of what obscenity means
> under the Constitution, and it is brought in in this way: the
> Court refers to what was the most celebrated case in the field
> until recent years, *Queen* v. *Hicklin*. It was a case decided in
> 1868, and it announced a rule which had certain notorious
> weaknesses. . . .
>
> The Supreme Court here is rejecting that rule, and saying
> that a good many courts already have rejected it. . . .
>
> As to the average person, I want to say a few more words. I
> don't think that Mr. Justice Brennan in the *Roth* case was
> asking us to go out and take a Gallup Poll among readers.
> This is not a matter of voting. . . . If among 170,000,000
> people 90,000,000 thought the book was bad, while 80,000,-
> 000 thought it was perfectly all right, I don't think that Mr.
> Justice Brennan means that that book should be banned. If
> that were the case, it would make dissent in matters of that
> kind impossible.

THE COURT: Isn't the key to that, Mr. Rembar, found in the additional phrase, which as I say I interpret at least to mean "does not exceed the outer limits of tolerance of the community" or "the outer limits of tolerance imposed by the standards of the community in these present times"? In other words, isn't that an additional protection and must not that be read in conjunction with this other test in order to afford the maximum protection given by the Constitution to the reading public generally?

MR. REMBAR: That is a point which is stressed in our brief. We feel that both those elements are implicit in the *Roth* test.

Bryan's point was not the same as the one I had been making; it was an additional argument, which I had not yet come to. I felt that a better glove for the average-person nettle was furnished by my explanation (the rejection of *Hicklin*) than by his (the outer limits of community tolerance). But I was grateful for agreement on the underlying proposition that the language of the prurient-interest formula, for whatever reason, was not to be taken literally.

We moved to Ablard's rejection of some of the evidence I had offered:

THE COURT: It is your contention that the failure to consider any so-called extraneous evidence was error in itself on the part of the Post Office Department?

MR. REMBAR: Some of the evidence was admitted, your Honor, some was rejected. It is our contention that it was error to reject what was rejected, but it is also our contention that on the basis of what was admitted, this book has been shown to fall outside the scope of Section 1461.*

Bryan was using the hearing in the way a hearing should be used. He came prepared. He had evidently read the record and read at least parts of the briefs, and he was familiar with the principal precedents. Frequently judges have their first exposure to the issues at the oral argument, which may then be a waste of time; they merely listen to a recitation of what they would get more quickly by reading the briefs. Bryan, in contrast, could de-

---

* The United States Code designation for the central provision of the Comstock Law.

vote the day in court to an exploration of the points—there were plenty of them—that seemed most troublesome. He was a vigorous participant, not a passive auditor. He asked about the Post Office's procedure.

MR. REMBAR: . . . Grove Press is not urging, as an independent ground for your Honor's decision, the lack of authority of the Post Office generally.

THE COURT: I may say, Mr. Rembar, whether they are urging it or not, I am very seriously concerned with the question of whether the Postmaster General has any authority at all under the statutes in this situation. I hope you briefed that question.

MR. REMBAR: We did, your Honor.

THE COURT: Good.

MR. REMBAR: However, we should like your Honor to consider the question of whether this book is obscene. We feel it is not obscene. Therefore we do not press procedural points here, or points of Post Office authority.

Now it was time to attack the presumption with which the government was trying to support the Post Office finding of obscenity. I said the courts that set the precedents on review of postal bans had not been confronted with the claim that the First Amendment was involved; that after *Roth* the question of obscenity could not be regarded as a question of fact but must be regarded as a question of constitutional law, and that the judges, not the postmasters, were the constitutional-law experts. Ablard, who was the trier of the facts, I added, had made no decision, while Summerfield, who made the decision, had not been present at the trial.

Bryan, of course, knew a great deal about judicial review of administrative action. The argument became even more of a colloquy. The Postmaster General, I said, might be an expert on moving the mail, but he was not an expert on literary matters, or on the law of obscenity. What, then, Bryan asked, were the standards of judicial review I would apply?

MR. REMBAR: . . . the standards here are the standards of a trial *de novo*,* because there is nothing here which should

---

* A consideration of the case then starts all over from the beginning, as though there had been no prior proceedings.

influence this court's judgment, and the entire record which Mr. Summerfield had before him is now before your Honor. It is not a matter of your being unable to see the witnesses who testified, because he wasn't able to either.

THE COURT: What do you say I must apply?

MR. REMBAR: You must consider the book and the surrounding circumstances, all of which are in the record and referred to in our brief; and against the book, in this context, you must apply the rule of the *Roth* case. . . .

THE COURT: What weight do you say I must give to the decision of the Postmaster General?

MR. REMBAR: Zero.

THE COURT: In other words, you say it is my function to decide this question *de novo* here?

MR. REMBAR: Yes sir. We say that on the basis of this record it is up to you to decide whether D. H. Lawrence was an author or a pornographer.

I ended my argument there. Bryan said he would hear from counsel for Readers' Subscription.

Topkis, a fluent advocate, began with a sympathetic description of the book club, and then made a telling point about the haphazard effect of the Post Office ban: a good many of Grove's books had gone through the mails before the ban was imposed, and Grove had shipped by truck as well, but the book club distributed only through the mails and had been stopped before it began. Hence, Topkis argued, there was discrimination against his client; the Post Office was preventing it from selling a book that people could buy elsewhere. Next Topkis attacked Ablard's exclusion of evidence:

MR. TOPKIS: . . . I say it is absurd. I say if the community-standards test means anything, then evidence is admissible as to what are community standards. How are archeologists a few centuries hence going to find out what the standards have been in this time? They are going to look at the newspapers. They are certainly not going to look at the collected papers of Arthur Summerfield.

Topkis sought to add his collection of girlie magazines to the record:

MR. TOPKIS: . . . I would hand up to your Honor an affidavit with some supporting exhibits. . . . Your Honor will see that this is a collection of magazines, all of which are today accepted for mailing by the Post Office Department of the United States.

THE COURT: I am not awfully impressed by that argument, frankly. The fact that the Post Office Department lets some pretty rough stuff get by and does not do anything about it does not seem to me to be very much evidence. I do assume this is rough stuff. I haven't read it, and I don't know, but I assume you wouldn't hand it up unless it was.

MR. TOPKIS: You are so right, your Honor.

THE COURT: However, it does not seem to me to be relevant. I will take it for what it may be worth, but frankly, it does not impress me very much.

Bryan asked Topkis about *Roth* v. *Goldman*, the case in which the court of appeals had said postal bans should rarely be upset—the same court of appeals that would review Bryan's decision in this case. Topkis was in a position to speak with authority:

MR. TOPKIS: I had the pleasure of clerking for Judge Frank [one of the judges who decided *Roth* v. *Goldman*] that year and remember that case well. I would suggest that the court there uttered the usual language—

THE COURT: You are dealing with what must be called hard-core pornography.

MR. TOPKIS: That was my point. It was in that case that the judge writing the *per curiam* opinion said there is no merit in this work to excite us to consider the record carefully; this is a piece of smut; so we will follow the usual rule of administrative finality." However, the case at bar is not that case. The case at bar concerns a book of conceded literary merit by a great author. So I would suggest first that the suggestion in the *Roth* [v. *Goldman*] case of a rule of administrative finality was ill considered for reasons I shall suggest in a moment. . . .

Topkis then quoted a Supreme Court case in which Chief Justice Hughes said that "when a constitutional issue is presented, it is the duty of each and every court to decide the facts, to apply the constitutional doctrine for itself."

Bryan again asked about the Post Office power to ban. I had tried to draw the court's attention away from this question;

Topkis did his best to get the court to rule on it. The divergence was due at least in part to the differing situations of our respective clients; it may also have been due to differences in the temperament and style of the two lawyers.

It was now the government's turn. Gillespie began by describing the steps that had led to the lawsuit.* Next he undertook to clear up what might have been read as an inconsistency in the Postmaster General's findings. Bryan accepted the explanation but made a comment indicating that our protests about the department's leisurely meandering to a decision (while it refused to lift the ban) may have had some effect:

> THE COURT: It is a little sloppily done; let us put it that way. After all, he had from May 8 to June 11 to do it less sloppily.

On the scope of judicial review, Gillespie said that the Postmaster General had most certainly considered the facts. He stated the basic principle of law (which we contended was inapplicable):

> that even though the court might well have reached a conclusion contrary to the Postmaster, it may not substitute its own views if there is substantial evidence to support his findings of fact. . . .

and:

> the extent to which your Honor can go in going behind that decision is extremely limited.

He had cases that seemed to establish the principle.

On the question whether *Lady Chatterley's Lover* was an ob-

---

* Gillespie's synopsis of the trial was fair enough, except for what seemed to me a totally inadequate summary of the testimony given by Cowley and Kazin:

> MR. GILLESPIE: Suffice it to say that both of these gentlemen, Cowley and Kazin, who are critics of substantial standing in their fields, testified that the book, in their opinion, does not tend to excite lustful thoughts in the reader.

This was not important, but it surprised me. It was a kind of advocacy that is common enough, but ordinarily among lesser lawyers. It was probably a slip, and I decided to ignore it. The record would speak for itself.

scene book, Gillespie took the traditional view—that testimony as to literary value might have some relevance, but that the presence of literary value could certainly not be a controlling factor. He cited the *Ulysses* case as one that supported the Post Office position (and in this, as I have indicated in an earlier chapter, I think Gillespie was right):

> So much for the tests. Where did that leave Postmaster Summerfield in considering *Lady Chatterley's Lover?* Are the erotic passages submerged in the book as a whole so as to have little resultant effect, as Judge [Augustus] Hand said? We submit that the Postmaster General had basis for concluding otherwise and that the erotic passages far outweigh whatever literary merit the book may have.

Gillespie described the book. Like the Post Office lawyers, he emphasized the immorality of the central character ("you have what, in common parlance, is a tramp. . . ."). But for him the vice of the book had a special color. He apparently disapproved not only Lady Chatterley's adultery but also her choice of a lover. He had little regard for Mellors; he could not remember the man's profession, and called him a "caretaker" instead of a gamekeeper. Considering Gillespie's thorough familiarity with other details of the book, the small inaccuracy could not have been due to a lack of diligence. It seemed to stem, rather, from a poor opinion of, and consequent inattention to, this low-class fellow. Lady Chatterley was, after all, a Lady, and one might have thought that if she were going to go outside her marriage, she need not have gone that far out. Her first companion in adultery had at least been one of her own class.

This was probably fantasy on my part, the ruminations of a lawyer who must sit still while his opponent speaks. Yet Gillespie several times described the book as one involving deterioration, the decline of Lady Chatterley. He even cited Vergil: "And we follow her progress down the slide—'*Facilis descenus Averni*,' as Vergil, I think, described it." One wondered whether the deterioration was not more social than moral. The Post Office lawyers had emphasized that Connie Chatterley was immoral from the start, and Gillespie himself had mentioned the early transgressions. What, then, was the decline?

Gillespie willingly conceded that testimony about literary value had some relevance. Indeed, he admired Lawrence's talent, and his admiration at times amounted to enthusiasm:

MR. GILLESPIE: The great argument that has been made here by these gentlemen is that this man was a literary master, that since Conrad he is the outstanding English author. One of these things that this man was able to describe and, by golly—I beg your pardon—he certainly could describe, and I would submit that his descriptions are as good as anything that could be done with the same matter on film.

The bearing of this excellence, however, was that it made it all the more necessary to ban the book. Gillespie subscribed to the well-written-obscenity-is-the-worst-kind doctrine. He read aloud one of the love scenes in the book. He read it well, and looking up, addressed the court:

MR. GILLESPIE: . . . I say to you where you find passages of that type spread through a book which literally describes the decline of a woman of this nature, your Honor is faced with a very serious problem.

Gillespie ended by arguing that the Post Office had the power to ban.

There were, in my view, weaknesses in Gillespie's argument, but overall it struck me as persuasive. He said, in the course of it, ". . . I am as interested in protecting the rights under the First Amendment as anyone else is," and there was no question but that the statement was sincere. Gillespie was a person of evident culture who knew and appreciated literature. The mantle of the censor simply did not fit him. Despite his concern for First Amendment freedoms, however, he felt that a line had to be drawn, and that it had to be drawn somewhere on the near side of *Lady Chatterley's Lover*. And the fact that he was concerned made his argument all the more telling.

My reply took off from Gillespie's citation of Vergil. I mentioned another Latin author, one who might easily have run into trouble with Postmaster General Summerfield, but one whose suppression, I suggested, the courts would not countenance.

THE COURT: Now I will hear from Mr. Rembar.

MR. REMBAR: I would like to comment on Mr. Gillespie's perspicacity in citing Vergil rather than Ovid. The works of the latter certainly show a wide range of community tolerance.

Bryan had a nice comment:

THE COURT: So does Vergil, if you are familiar with your Vergil.

MR. REMBAR: Not as familiar as your Honor.

THE COURT: There is a lady named Dido, as I remember.

I returned to *Roth* v. *Goldman*, the case on which the government was relying so heavily to restrict the court's review of Summerfield's decision. Topkis had said the case was not comparable because it involved hard-core pornography. I was not comfortable with that distinction. The point, it seemed to me, was whether the Postmaster General was to be given a head start, and not where the particular starting line might be located. There was a better reason to ignore *Roth* v. *Goldman*:

that decision cannot bind the court in any way because it was a decision, prior to the *Roth* case, in which no constitutional point was raised or considered. I say this not merely on the basis of the published opinion; I have gone through the record. There was simply no constitutional issue in that case.

This being so, the principle for which we were contending—that no deference is due an administrative determination of a constitutional question—was not tested by *Roth* v. *Goldman*. It was decided before *United States* v. *Roth*, at a time when nothing was involved in such cases except what Congress, in passing the Comstock Act, meant by "obscene."

I concluded by both denying and demurring to Gillespie's allegation that the Lady was a tramp. It was not true, and even if it were, an author could not be confined to writing about characters that the Post Office approved. Bryan agreed:

THE COURT: Whether she was or not does not make any difference. If she was a professional prostitute, it wouldn't make any difference.

MR. REMBAR: What I wish to emphasize is not only that it cannot control the case, but that it indicates the point of view that the Postmaster General brought to this case. . . .

Topkis's reply dwelt, eloquently, on the moral quality of the book—a note on which I would just as soon we had not concluded. (Although I admired his skill, I had misgivings about tethering literary freedom to high-mindedness.)

Judge Bryan closed the hearing with some courteous remarks and a suggestion that additional briefs be filed by both sides. It was a complicated case.

The decision was announced on July 21. It gave summary judgment in our favor. Christenberry was permanently enjoined "from denying the mails to this book or to the circular announcing its availability."

The opinion was long and well written—half of it devoted to scope of review, half to the question of obscenity. The first half was a struggle. The precedents were the other way, and it was especially difficult for a district court to avoid the effect of a court of appeals decision in its own circuit. Bryan managed. He accepted our argument that in this case he was faced with a question of constitutional law, not a question of practical administration, and he could therefore consider the case *de novo*. On the obscenity issue itself, Bryan went no farther than he felt he had to go. The value theory was not tested. He was able to decide the book was not obscene by the prurient-interest rule—that is, the prurient-interest rule as he now construed it. Although early in the hearing he had defined "prurient" as "having a tendency to arouse lustful thoughts," by the end of the case he accepted my much narrower interpretation of the Supreme Court's language. His opinion referred to:

prurient interest—that is to say, shameful or morbid interest in sex.

While the opinion made no explicit use of the value theory, a good part of it was devoted to the value of the book. Our brief had said, "The book is in large measure polemical," and had argued that the descriptions and language to which the Postmaster General objected were relevant to the presentation of Lawrence's ideas. Bryan wrote:

> The book is almost as much a polemic as a novel.
>
> *   *   *
>
> These passages and this language understandably will shock the sensitive-minded. Be that as it may, these passages are relevant to the plot and to the development of the characters and of their lives as Lawrence unfolds them.

Bryan made something new of the "submerge" test. With a deft sleight of hand, he turned it around so fast one might think it was the same old test. The court of appeals had said *Ulysses* was not obscene because the rest of the book submerged the sex. Bryan said *Lady Chatterley's Lover* was not obscene because the sex failed to submerge the rest of the book:

> Nor do these passages and this language submerge the dominant theme so as to make the book obscene even if they could be considered and found to be obscene in isolation.

The opinion also stated that the book did not go beyond "the contemporary standards of the community and the limits of its tolerance." This was shown, it said, by the reactions to the book in the newspapers (whose exclusion by Ablard it held to be error) and by the increasing frankness of contemporary novels. Here both Bryan and I were on shaky ground. The essence of the matter was that contemporary community standards ought not fix the boundaries of artistic freedom. They should be constitutionally relevant only to free us from the thickets of the past.

I would have liked Bryan to agree with me that the Supreme Court's reference to contemporary community standards and to the average person had little significance except as a rejection of the *Hicklin* rule. For the present case, though, he did not need to. Bryan accepted my argument that the prurient-interest test was itself a double test—that both morbid sexual appeal and a violation of the community standards were required; he had probably reached that conclusion before the hearing. Accordingly, once he decided *Chatterley* did not have the interdicted appeal, anything he had to say on community standards was surplus.

If he had accepted my entire exegesis of the prurient-interest test, and even if he had gone farther and accepted the value test as well, Bryan would not have been violating the principle of *stare decisis*. They represented a construction of the *Roth* opinion, not a denial of it. But they involved a wide departure from prior norms, and the decision itself was departure enough. *Lady Chatterley* had been by common consent obscene, and the very fact that a judge sanctioned its publication would advance the law regardless of his reasoning. Unusual interpretations of the Supreme Court's language, even if ultimately sound, can invite reversal. Bryan may have felt he could make his decision more secure if he did not confront the Supreme Court with the most distant implications of *Roth*.

I am describing what the silent part of his thinking might have been. It is all conjecture. But it is natural for a court of original jurisdiction, in stating its reasons, to suffer some compulsion to speak the language of the higher court.

The government appealed. The court of appeals was on vacation, and would not hear the case until the following fall; meanwhile the book could be distributed. So Gillespie applied for a stay, an order that would allow the Post Office ban to remain in effect until the appeal had been decided. There was argument before three judges called back for the purpose. The stay was denied.

The appeal itself was heard in December, by Charles Clark, former dean of Yale Law School, Sterry Waterman of St. Johnsbury, Vermont, and Leonard Moore of Brooklyn. (Clark, now dead, was in my view one of the half dozen great judges that our country has produced—a statement that may appear extreme to most lawyers, but one I would be pleased to debate.)

There is no official record of an appellate argument, and usually (except in the Supreme Court) no unofficial record.

Court stenographers are employed not to preserve the eloquence of counsel, but to preserve the facts. On this appeal, however, the oral argument pretty much paralleled the briefs.*

The government's brief argued hard that the courts should have little to say about how the Post Office is run: "The cases are legion" in which juries, who determine only fact and not law, have been given the job of deciding whether a book is obscene. If obscenity is a question of fact in a court, it must also be a question of fact when the trial takes place within an agency. (The conclusion was correct if the premise was sound, and judging by the cases that preceded this, the premise was sound.) The brief taxed Judge Bryan with inconsistency:

> Shortly before he decided the instant case, Judge Bryan in a criminal prosecution under Section 1461, recognized that obscenity was a question of fact by charging the jury in the following language:
>> The question of fact as to whether a book is of such a character as to stir such impure sexual impulses and arouse lustful passions or whether it exceeds the limit of tolerance by current standards is a question of fact and must be determined by you alone. . . .

The brief then urged that anyway the Postmaster General was unquestionably right in regarding *Chatterley* as obscene. It referred to the "four-letter words which are liberally sprinkled throughout the dialogue" and the "detailed descriptions of the male and female genital organs, the sex act and the internal and external sensation they produce. . . ." It therefore followed that:

> the basic justification for the Postmaster General's conclusion that *Lady Chatterley's Lover* is obscene lies in the fact that

---

* The courts of appeals have more work than three judges can handle. Hence they have a larger number of judges (the number varies in the circuits; the second circuit has nine), and individual appeals are heard by panels of three. It is different in the Supreme Court, where each of the Justices, unless illness or other special circumstance prevents him from participating, works on each case. The outcome in a court of appeals may depend upon which of the judges happen to be sitting.

the individual words, the individual paragraphs and the individual scenes cannot find refuge, as the cases say, in an otherwise high-minded overall exposition, for this overall exposition could not be lower. In expounding a theme approving promiscuous sexual relations both before and in the state of matrimony, the publisher has lost the right to defend the individual paragraphs as part of a wholesome literary masterpiece.

The government had Lawrence himself write the conclusion. Their brief ended with three passages from the book which, they stated, "clearly transcend the bounds of decency and appeal to the prurient interest."

"Perhaps," said my brief,

these individual passages can be considered obscene out of context—as, for example, when quoted in a legal brief—but this, under the law, is irrelevant. . . . There is no authority whatever for appellant's effort to damn the book with individual passages, and then to ask whether there are other things in the book that can rescue it from condemnation.

That is, there was no such authority that survived *Roth*, in which the Justices, when they "rejected the *Hicklin* test, meant what they said."

Appellant next compounds the error by setting up a test based on the morality of the author's ideas. What standard of morality is to be used is not clear; it is not even clear that the Postmaster General's concepts of morality coincide with those of counsel here. From a constitutional point of view, however, it is not necessary to inquire. In the *Roth* opinion the Supreme Court spoke of the right to advocate ideas, "unorthodox ideas, controversial ideas, even ideas hateful to the prevailing climate of opinion." More recently, the Supreme Court has held unconstitutional a statute that authorized the censorship of a motion picture on the very basis that appellant uses here.

The reference was to *Kingsley Pictures* v. *Regents*, in which the Supreme Court's decision had come down on the day before our argument in the district court. The decision had a limited utility. Although it involved a motion picture based on *Lady Chatterley's Lover*, the issues were altogether different from those in our case. There was no contention that the film contained indecent scenes or objectionable language. Justice Frankfurter remarked that it would not even "have offended Victorian moral sensibilities." The New York Regents (a licensing authority) had refused to allow the film to be shown on the specific—and ridiculous—ground that "the theme is the presentation of adultery as a desirable, acceptable and proper pattern of behavior." Since the only justification offered for their censorship was that the picture advocated a disapproved idea, the Regents were running blindly, head on, into the barriers of the First Amendment. It was perhaps the easiest case to decide that the Supreme Court had had in a long time, and resulted in an unusual unanimity. Its significance for our purposes was that it magnified the fault in one of the links of Gillespie's chain of reasoning: his argument that the objectionable descriptions and language could not "find refuge" in the "central idea" of the book because the central idea was itself "immoral."

The brief continued:

Appellant quite frankly gives us the corollaries of his argument. The position would be different, appellant tells us, if Lawrence's moral views coincided with those of the writers of the brief. The "individual passages" might be defended, if the theme of the book were "wholesome"—that is, a theme to which counsel (or, presumably, the Postmaster General) could subscribe. Or, put another way, a work advocating the Postmaster General's moral precepts would be admitted to the mails even though it were written in the language to which he objects.

The lengths to which censorship takes us are glimpsed again in the last full paragraph on page 33 of appellant's brief, where it is said that the work "would not have suffered" if particular scenes were not done "so vividly," and where complaint is made of "repetition" in the writing. This may or may not be valid literary criticism; it is hardly legal argument.

On scope of review, I said that administrative agencies working on economic problems or resolving their own housekeeping problems could not furnish precedents on issues of personal liberty:

> Viewed as a matter of the coherent administration of government under the Constitution, it is strange indeed that an appointed official, chosen for his success in political management* and presumably also for his ability to manage the business of carrying the mails, should ex officio have the power to determine what literature the American public may see and what it may not. . . .
>
> The Post Office, of course, like other agencies has its own expertise. Administrative determinations by the department in matters where it has special competence, and where no question of constitutional law is involved, may very well be accorded weight by the courts. These would be matters relating to the department's essential function—the transmission of the mails—and to situations which might impair or otherwise affect the discharge of that function. The Post Office, for example, is expert on how mail should be addressed, on how material should be packaged, and on what substances may or may not be safely carried, and on certain aspects of the classification of mail. But the Post Office has no special competence on literature, freedom of speech and constitutional law.

On March 25, 1960, nearly four months after the case was argued, the court of appeals affirmed. The main opinion was written by Clark; Waterman joined him. Moore wrote a separate concurring opinion.

Clark agreed that the Postmaster General's decision was "fully reviewable":

> Although this conclusion is vigorously attacked by the government, it is difficult to see why it is not sound, particularly as reinforced by the constitutional overtones implicit in the

---

* The reference was to the tradition, since violated but honored at the time, that the office of Postmaster General is to be filled by the manager of the successful Presidential campaign.

issue. There can be no doubt that in large areas of postal activity involving the delivery of the mail the Post Office Department exercises discretion not to be controlled by courts. But to determine whether a work of art or literature is obscene has little, if anything, to do with the expedition or efficiency with which the mails are dispatched. And here it is clear that no question of evidence was involved. In fact the departmental officials considered only the novel itself against the background of the statute and declined to consider the expert opinion proffered by the plaintiffs. The question was thus one starkly of law. Moreover, the plaintiffs raised the constitutional issue of freedom of expression, Judge Bryan ruled upon it below, and it can hardly be escaped in this class of cases. . . .

Clark spoke about the difficulty of dealing with obscenity cases:

And we need have no illusions but that a large business is done in exploiting "hard-core pornography" for money's sake. In general this trash is easily recognized, with its repetitive emphasis (usually illustrated) upon purely physical action without character or plot development; and even if its direct connection with crime or incitement to juvenile or other delinquency is not proven—as many now assert—it cannot arouse sympathy because of its essentially repulsive, as well as fraudulent, character. It is when we come to more genuine works of literature that troublesome issues arise.

Clark, like Bryan, was not ready to take the step of giving social value independent status as a test of obscenity. He did, however, put great stress on the literary value of the book. Indeed, the basis for his conclusion on the question of obscenity was a small essay in literary appreciation:

By now the story of the novel is well known. . . . But of course the story is a small part of the work. Actually, the book is a polemic against three things which Lawrence hated: the crass industrialization of the English Midlands, the British caste system and inhibited sex relations between man and woman. . . . The rationale he seeks to establish is thus one surely arguable and open to a writer. And if the aristocratic, but frustrated, heroine is to be taught naturalness in self-

expression by her husband's servant, the plot line is rather
clearly indicated. . . .
Obviously a writer can employ various means to achieve the
effect he has in mind, and so probably Lawrence could have
omitted some of the passages found "smutty" by the Postmaster General and yet have produced an effective work of
literature. But clearly it would not have been the book he
planned, because for what he had in mind his selection was
most effective, as the agitation and success of the book over
the years have proven. In these sex descriptions showing how
his aristocratic, but frustrated, lady achieved fulfillment and
naturalness in her life, he also writes with power and indeed
with a moving tenderness which is compelling, once our age-
long inhibitions against sex revelations in print have been
passed. . . .
   The same is true of the so-called four-letter words found
particularly objectionable by the Postmaster General. These
appear in the latter portion of the book in the mouth of the
gamekeeper in his tutelage of the lady in naturalness and are
accepted by her as such. . . . In short, all these passages to
which the Postmaster General takes exception—in bulk only
a portion of the book—are subordinate, but highly useful,
elements to the development of the author's central purpose.
And that is not prurient. . . .

Moore, in concurring, made it plain that he believed the
book should not be published. But judges are expected to
follow a precedent set by an upper court, whether or not
they approve of it, and when it is clear, they have no choice.
What made Moore's concurrence so striking an example of
true judicial performance was that the meaning of *Roth*
was thoroughly arguable. If he had kneaded the precedent
to fit the result he preferred, he could not have been called
wrong. But he was evidently convinced that *Roth*, objectively considered, required a judgment in favor of *Lady
Chatterley.*
Most of his opinion was devoted to the reasons—they
were good ones—why he disliked the decision he felt compelled to make:

The Supreme Court (not the Postmaster General) chose the
test of "contemporary community standards" and "appealing

to prurient interest." But what "community" and what is "prurient interest"? And is a single judge or a group of judges in any one restricted geographic district all knowing as to community standards? At least the Postmaster General by virtue of his office and his staff of inspectors in every state of the union is mindful of the type of questionable material found in the mails and the reaction thereto of each community. . . .

Stating that it was correct, under *Roth*, to admit evidence on community standards, Judge Moore continued:

Whether such an approach would satisfy those who, marching under the banner of freedom and tolerance, are themselves often the most intolerant of the views of others, I do not know. Surely this minority group which preaches freedom of the press without restraint would probably not be willing to honor "contemporary community standards" if these differed from their own.

I agreed with Moore that "contemporary community standards" made a bad test, and was doing my best to disarm it. (But meanwhile I was trying to make it work for us, rather than against us.)

Then there is the doctrine of the "book as a whole." In other words, if out of some four hundred pages there were three or four pages which clearly are in the "obscene" category, they constitute merely a *de minimis* one percent and hence the good overwhelms the bad. The very proposal of such a principle should suffice to demonstrate its impracticability as a test of whether the statute has been violated, because obscenity could then parade abroad under the protective cloak of a quantity of innocuous pages.

"However," Moore concluded, drily substituting a word, "this case must be decided in accordance with contemporary judicial standards, and therefore I reluctantly concur." *

---

* In an obscenity case decided three years later, involving quite different issues, Judge Moore took a somewhat more relaxed view of *Lady Chatterley's Lover*. His opinion contained the following footnote:

Only for the true sportsman has the book been properly reviewed and appreciated. In *Field & Stream*, November 1959, appeared the following "Book Review":

There were intimations that the Post Office Department was eager to take the case higher, but the final decision on government appeals to the Supreme Court is made by the Solicitor General. He apparently felt that the unanimous conclusion of four respected federal judges was enough. So did the enforcement officials of all the states. There were no more prosecutions.

Although written many years ago, *Lady Chatterley's Lover* has just been reissued by Grove Press, and this fictional account of the day-by-day life of an English gamekeeper is still of considerable interest to outdoor-minded readers, as it contains many passages on pheasant raising, the apprehending of poachers, ways to control vermin, and other chores and duties of the professional gamekeeper. Unfortunately one is obliged to wade through many pages of extraneous material in order to discover and savor these sidelights on the management of a Midlands shooting estate, and in this reviewer's opinion this book cannot take the place of J. R. *Miller's Practical Gamekeeping.*

£ady Chatterley:

Postscript

THE RIGHT TO PUBLISH *LADY CHATTERLEY'S Lover* having been established in the United States, Penguin Books decided to try it in England. The predictable prosecution followed, and the scarcely less predictable result. After the United States had honored Great Britain by permitting one of its most important writers to be published, a patriotic British jury could hardly deny him publication at home. It is the prophet, not the novelist, who must forego honor in his own country, and in any case the rule does not apply to dead prophets. D. H. Lawrence was a British National Monument. What went on in the Old Bailey was not so much a trial as an unveiling.

There is a report of the British case called *The Trial of Lady Chatterley*, edited by C. H. Rolph (and published by Penguin, a company enterprising enough to find a profit in adversity and to make two books grow where before there had been hardly one). Rolph found it "safe to say . . . that there was never the smallest likelihood that [the jury] would agree on a verdict of 'Guilty'. . . ."

In anticipation of the litigation, Sir Allen Lane, Penguin's head, asked for copies of our briefs and the record of our case. We sent them, but if they furnished the text, the British trial was low parody. Our trial took one day; theirs took five. We called two witnesses (other than the publisher); the Penguin defense called thirty-five (and announced that there were another thirty-five suited up and ready to take the field). Our two witnesses were presented as established critics, qualified to give expert testimony on literary matters. Their list of witnesses included—in addition to established critics—four clergymen, a lady who edited fashion magazines and "women's pages," a witness "best known to most of the jurors, no doubt, as an outstanding television personality," the headmaster of a boys' school and the classics mistress of a girls' school, the members of Parliament who drafted the obscenity statute under which the prosecution was brought, and one witness whose qualifications were that she was young, bright, female and a Roman Catholic (qualifications that would recommend her for a number of things, but not for giving testimony in a censorship case).

Our witnesses were called to supply evidence that would help the court decide whether the book had value. This was also a function of the British witnesses, but they were not so confined. Primarily, it seemed, they were called to render opinions on whether the book ought to be published—the witnesses thus acting as lobbyists to a jury sitting as a legislature. In effect, the jurors were asked not to perform their traditional task of applying the law (as explained by the judge) to the facts as they saw them, but rather to determine what the law ought to be.

None of this is *ad hominem*. The chief defense counsel, Gerald Gardiner, was one of the most brilliant barristers in England, and he capped a distinguished career at the bar by becoming Lord High Chancellor.* Mervyn Griffith-Jones, who repre-

---

* The Lord High Chancellor is the first judicial officer of the United Kingdom. As a matter of protocol, he takes precedence immediately after the archbishop of Canterbury, who himself follows only the royal family. The Lord High Chancellor presides over the highest courts of the United Kingdom and the Commonwealth, but that is not all he does. The law imposes many duties on him. He is in charge of the administration of the British judicial system, being responsible for the selection of High Court judges, county court judges and justices of the peace (except in the County Palatine of Lancaster). He is the Chief Judge of the House of Lords when it sits as the final court of appeal in the British judicial system; he is also Speaker of the House of Lords when it sits as a legislative body. He acts

sented the Crown, had a considerable reputation before the *Chatterley* trial, and he went on to make other headlines prosecuting Dr. Stephen Ward in the Profumo scandal (thus, for reasons explained in a later chapter, indirectly contributing to our defense of *Fanny Hill*). Eventually he became Common Serjeant of the City of London.*

My criticism is surely not of counsel, nor of the outstanding solicitors, Rubinstein, Nash & Company, who organized the defense. I do believe, however, that the question whether *Lady Chatterley's Lover* might be openly published was decided on better grounds in America than in England. One reason, I think, was the existence of the United States Constitution. Another was the willingness of the American publisher to stake the case on the issue of freedom and to relinquish whatever other legal argument or tactic might give him a victory.

Other factors that made the two cases different were the nature of the British anti-obscenity statute and the presence of a jury. The statute was a compromise and had the characteristically bad features of a compromise. The trial by jury opened the way to all the antics and irrelevancies that are perhaps tolerable in ordinary private litigation, but seem violently incongruous where what is involved is a fundamental question of freedom. And there was nothing beyond the jury's verdict. The judge's

---

as the formal medium of communication between sovereign and Parliament. He is a member of the Cabinet, Custodian of the Great Seal and the Keeper of the Queen's Conscience. It is not merely murder, but treason, to kill the Lord Chancellor at a time when he is performing his duties. (This seems not at all consistent with the British concept of fair play; the Lord Chancellor's duties being so great and so numerous, it is difficult to come upon him at any other time.) One is not surprised that in *Who's Who*, Gerald Gardiner listed as his after-hours pastimes only two items, and that one of them was "law reform."

* One might wonder why a distinguished barrister should wish to turn to a military career, noncommissioned at that, and one with such a pejorative designation. But for those not given to bemusement, "serjeant" is a judicial as well as military term, and signifies higher rank in the British courts than in the American army. Here it refers to the second highest judicial post in the City of London.

lengthy charge was not illuminating, and there being an acquittal, there was no appeal. There was thus no thoughtful examination of whether the book came within the words Parliament had chosen or, if there was some doubt about the words, whether some basic principle of law should affect their meaning.

Having said that counsel were not to blame, let me continue with what I found so disappointing in the goings-on in the Old Bailey. The prosecution became an attack not on *Lady Chatterley's Lover,* but on Lady Chatterley. This was to some extent what Gillespie had sought to do in our case, but the American courts responded that a writer must be free to portray any kind of character. "If she were a professional prostitute," Judge Bryan said, "it wouldn't make any difference."

The British judge apparently did not share this view; in any case, he did not intervene either to save the lady's honor or to declare it irrelevant. In defense of the prosecution, it appears that it may have been pushed into this kind of attack; its opposition concentrated on *Lady Chatterley's* elevated morality. Griffith-Jones's opening address dealt with matters more germane to freedom of expression. By the end of the trial, however, he declared the issue to be whether the ideas in the book conformed to the prevailing mores. In closing, apparently confident that the jury would share his incredulity, he stated:

> The book is said to be in support of marriage. If you accept that, if you think that that is a realistic view of this book, so be it, members of the jury. Then it is not obscene. . . .

The defense was grounded on (a) associations with religion and respectability and (b) the weight of numbers. The witnesses were not so much offering evidence as putting prestige into the claim that the book was innocent. They were not only celebrated (some of them for accomplishments in fields other than literature); they were virtuous people, as the defense established through testimony, with children and good war records. And there were so many of them.

With the issue drawn in those terms, the prosecution could have made quite a battle of it. There surely were personages who disapproved of the book. (The trial judge himself was one; he was plainly unhappy with the verdict.) The prosecutor could have had forty churchmen there to match the four for the defense, and a hundred clear-eyed twenty-one-year-olds (Protestant as well as Catholic and, with luck, a Jew or two) to counter the defense's little miss. There were surely some television personalities in the United Kingdom who would have been willing to testify against sin.*

Griffith-Jones evidently felt that the book itself, plus eloquence, would do the job. But at several points his rhetoric gave aid and comfort to the defense. The most spectacular item of this sort was in his opening address. "Is it," he asked the nine men and three women of the jury, "a book that you would even wish your wife or your servants to read?"

Did Griffith-Jones know that the members of the jury had servants? (Three, at least, had no wives.) If any were not rich enough to afford servants, would there not be some resentment toward the apparently well-heeled barrister who addressed them? And what would be the effect if one of the jurors was himself (or herself) a servant? †

To some extent the question may have been a slip—that is, Griffith-Jones may have regretted the particular formulation—but it came from an attitude firmly fixed. At the end of the trial, commenting on some of the defense testimony, he asked the jury, "Do you think that that is how the girls working in the factory are going to read this book . . . ?" ‡

---

* Lest it be thought there is jingoism in this, let me note immediately that it would be fatiguing to count the American television personalities who would have leaped at the chance to please their sponsors, and fatten their Neilsons, by taking a fearless stand against sin.

† Griffith-Jones had a background that is a prerequisite for (although it cannot fully explain) the question. He was a product of Eton and Cambridge, an officer of the Coldstream Guards, and a member of a number of clubs, including the Marylebone Cricket Club, Pratt's and White's. White's, founded in 1693, was clogged with dukes and had an eighteen-year waiting list for membership. Pratt's has been described as resembling any "New Yorker cartoon of a typical English club"; its waiting time, nevertheless, was only ten years. Gardiner was a product of Harrow and Oxford, and he too was an officer of the Coldstream Guards, but he seemed to have established a somewhat closer touch with the rest of the population.

‡ Another item of interest in Griffith-Jones's opening address was his informing the jury that there were thirteen episodes of sexual intercourse

And so the trial became a contest between a prosecution saying the ideas and the principal character in the book were immoral, and a defense saying the book was a righteous one and look at all these respectable and/or famous people who think that *Lady Chatterley* is good for you.

Alfred Kazin had testified that Lawrence had an essentially religious approach. Here again the British trial was caricature. Kazin had kept his point well within the bounds of literary analysis; his statement had to do with literary, not ethical, values. Not so the witnesses in the Old Bailey; they testified in moral and theological terms that *Lady Chatterley's Lover* was "highly virtuous" and "puritanical," that in it "sex is taken . . . as a basis for a holy life."

That there are ideas in a book is fundamental. But that they are high-minded ideas is not. We had defended *Lady Chatterley* not on the ground that it promoted morality, but rather that it presented a view on the subject. A less acceptable view would also justify publication, or even one thoroughly deplorable. The fact that a book is on the side of the angels should never be crucial. Else we may find ourselves suppressing the devil's proposals, the precise negation of freedom of speech.

While the jury was being turned into a legislature, legislators were moonlighting as expert witnesses. Witnesses are supposed to supply evidence or qualified opinion, not legal advice to the court. Yet the defense called Roy Jenkins and Norman St. John-Stevas, members of Parliament, to testify that their Act was not intended to apply to the book on trial. It was as though the Post Office had called Anthony Comstock to testify that in his judgment *Lady Chatterley's Lover* was obscene under the Comstock Act. Separation of powers is not so prominent a feature of the British political system as it is of ours. British law nevertheless posits a clear distinction between legislative and judicial function; the House of Lords knows when it is sitting as a legislative body and when it is sitting as a court of justice.

Legislators enact laws; courts expound them. The legislators'

---

in the book and that the only variations among them were "the time and the *locus in quo,* the place where it happened." The jury no doubt appreciated the translation, but they may have sensed an ambiguity.

job is done when they have passed the statute, which from that point on should lead an emancipated life. Citizens are entitled to take legislators at their word, and to rely on the statute as it is written. Government becomes silly when members of Parliament are permitted to come along later and shape the statute by testifying, "What we meant to say was . . ." *

Granted that the separation of powers is less marked in British constitutional theory than in American, some separation there must be. Suppose the *Lady Chatterley* prosecution had called three or four MP's to testify the other way. Would there have ultimately been another counting of heads, this time in the Old Bailey rather than in the Houses of Parliament?

The defense was properly interested in winning its case. But the judge, it would seem, could have managed things better. He gave every indication that he would have preferred a verdict of guilty, yet he permitted the defense to do things he could easily have prevented. The explanation, I think, is that though the judge disagreed deeply with the defense in his feeling about the book, he saw the issue in the same light they did; their approach, if not their objective, appealed to him. He was not, in this instance, concentrating on principles of freedom; he was against the book and the witnesses were for it, and in his mind, the report suggests, that was pretty much all there was to the case.

The British defense was thus permitted to do precisely the kind of thing that those on the side of suppression attempted to do (and for the most part were prevented from doing) in our cases—to influence judges and juries with irrelevant testimony, or with the mere presence of witnesses whose testimony could not possibly be relevant. In London the defense called a headmaster of a boys' school and a classics mistress of a girls' school; in New York a Post Office hint that *Lady Chatterley* was offered to schoolgirls was firmly rejected. In London clergymen were brought to court to say *Lady Chatterley* ought to be published,

---

* This is quite different from the use of "legislative history"—recorded statements made in legislative debate or committee hearings. Such materials are often referred to as an aid in interpreting statutes, but they are contemporaneous expressions of intent, regularly recorded, not individual afterthoughts.

and were allowed to say it; in New York, later on, clergymen were brought to court to say *Fanny Hill* ought to be suppressed, and had their testimony rigorously confined to the literary aspects of the book.

The judge may also have felt that the new Obscene Publications Act constrained him to let the trial take its course. He may have felt so constrained, but he should not have. The sponsors of the Act, intending to liberalize the law, had run into strong opposition. The result was a rather strange hybrid. It retained some of the worst features of the old *Hicklin* rule, making the primary question whether the book would "tend to deprave and corrupt persons likely to read it." But it added a saving clause: there was to be no conviction

> if it is proved that publication of the article in question is justified as being for the public good on the ground that it is in the interests of science, literature, art, or learning, or other objects of general concern.

The initial provision is a relative of the prurient-interest test— more precisely, an ancestor. As to the saving clause, there is a general principle of interpretation, no less in British law than in American, that catch-all language takes its meaning from the more specific items that accompany it. The "objects of general concern" were "science, literature, art or learning" and the like. The Act need not have been read as connecting the right to publish with the moral stance of the publication. The proper issue, in Great Britain as in the United States, was whether *Lady Chatterley's Lover* is "justified" (Parliament's word) because it communicates ideas and because it is literature.

Instead the issue was morality, and the question of freedom was thoroughly obscured.

Perhaps I am expressing a peculiarly American view. I do not think so. There are the many prosecutors here, and the Citizens for Decent Literature, to evidence the fact that I do not speak for an American consensus.

We have a First Amendment and the British do not, but one might have expected something closer to the Amendment's ideals in the country from whose traditions and philosophies it was most directly derived. And while the judge in the Old Bailey was permitting witnesses to expound the law, there were at least two celebrated Englishmen—Mill and Milton—who, had the writ run far enough to reach them, could have testified that the view I express is not a novel one in England.

Don't Laugh

I HAVE JUST NAMED, SO THAT BRITONS SHOULD not feel lonely, the Citizens for Decent Literature and the many American prosecutors who were quick to stamp out crime (as embodied in books). I could have named others—the Motion Picture Association of America, for example.

Some of our liberal judges, appalled at the prospect that courts might become boards of censorship, have suggested that groups outside the government might do the job. The First Amendment's injunction that "Congress shall make no law" abridging free expression would then be literally obeyed, while organizations of private citizens could use moral suasion, and communications media could set voluntary rules of restraint for themselves.

It is a poor suggestion. This kind of moral suasion is in reality economic pressure. Collective self-censorship never pursues principle; it flees in fear. In both instances—whether the orders come from outside groups or from within the industry—money, not the First Amendment, determines issues of free speech.

The Motion Picture Association of America is the trade association of the industry. It was established early in the 1920's, when movie people first got scared. Hollywood was offending public morality—that is, sexual morality—and the companies decided that some self-policing was required. The MPAA has outgrown its origins, and has other, beneficial functions (for example, settling competing claims to the use of a particular title). But it is still best known as a house detective, and it performs this function by enforcing a Production Code. The organization was originally called the Hays Office, after the first president of the MPAA, Will Hays. Later it was called the Johnston Office, after Eric Johnston.

Under the code, seals of approval are granted or withheld. Between the date I speak of, 1959, and the date this chapter is written, 1966, both the operation of the code and the significance of the seal have grown feeble. But at the time, the operation was rigorous and the seal highly significant. Major distributors refused to handle films that did not have the seal. There was no legal compulsion, but they abided by the code.

Even the most daring of them could not sustain rebellion. On two occasions United Artists had distributed films without the seal. Understanding its maverick role, it separated itself from the herd, for a while. It resigned but came back later and, a forgiven prodigal, again conformed.

United Artists had, however, made money on its two adventures. Then why did the companies attach so much importance to the seal? Partly it was a matter of noblesse oblige or, as it is sometimes called, combination in restraint of trade. One company might do well with a code-breaking film, but if other companies followed its lead, the original advantage would be canceled out, and all of them would end, competitively, where they started, and have a lot of trouble besides. Believing that in the long run this would cost them money, they felt honor-bound.

Apart from such general considerations, there were difficulties for the individual film that lacked the seal (the UA recusancy notwithstanding). There were still many states and municipalities that had official film censors, and to these people the seal was a cue. The military would not allow such a picture to be shown at its installations, and this is a considerable source of revenue. And private film-censorship bodies—the Legion of Decency was the most important—were influenced by the seal, or rather would be strongly influenced by its absence. In the most pragmatic sense, the function of the code administration was not so much to interpose its own objections, as to assist the motion picture companies in avoiding the condemnation of groups outside the industry.

The ultimate sanction was boycott. Any single picture without the seal might do well, but if an organized group such as the Legion punished the exhibitor by boycotting his theater for a period of time (regardless of what happened to be playing), the exhibitor would eventually have to fold. So exhibitors avoided condemned pictures. The exhibitors were the customers of the distributors, and the distributors controlled the studios.

In 1959 there was a story going around that was grisly but heartening. In the fall of that year, after the *Lady Chatterley* trial, there was a code case that was grisly but—ultimately, and in some measure—heartening.

You will remember the story. It had various forms. A wounded warrior is found in the jungle, pinned to the ground by a spear through his side, fevered, thirst-racked. "Does it hurt?" his rescuers ask. "Only when I laugh," he answers.

The story was funny and horrible, its horror redeemed intrinsically by the note of fortitude-in-adversity. The case was funny and horrible, its horror redeemed only by its consequences.

The picture that made the case was *Happy Anniversary*. It was based on the Joseph Fields–Jerome Chodorov play called *Anniversary Waltz*. The stars were David Niven and Mitzi Gaynor. It was a clever little film about husband-and-wife problems. This husband and wife, it transpired, had lived together before they were married. Their problems were created, indirectly, by this historic fact. So were our problems with the code.

The code administrator was Geoffrey Shurlock. He and his staff were cultured and intelligent, but bound by the code, and they informed the producers that changes had to be made. (This despite the fact that the couple had been married for thirteen years and the illicit relationship was not pictured, being a distant, if not dim, memory.) There were negotiations that ended in confusion, and the seal was withheld.

If a producer or distributor was not willing to accept the administrator's decision, recourse might be had to a board of appeal. The board was huge. It consisted of the heads of the major motion picture companies, plus the heads of the theater chains, and some independent producers. (At the hearing, it was easy to distinguish the independent producers from the other board members; the independents wore their topcoats without putting their arms in the sleeves.) It was very seldom that the board disagreed with the administrator.*

Both the producers and the distributor, which was United Artists, appealed. Seymour Peyser, then general counsel of United Artists, suggested that I represent the producer and we work together on the case.

I hadn't been to the movies very much for quite a while, and in order to give me an idea of the prevailing standards of acceptability, Peyser arranged for the screening of some current films. Six, he thought, would constitute an adequate sample. The hearing was coming on so quickly that we had to see all of them in two days. Six movies in two days is a lot.

Most of the half dozen—all of which had the seal—ladled out large helpings of cheap sex. At the hearing we said so, avoiding the word "cheap" in deference to their production budgets. Since the heads of the studios that had produced the films were members of the board, our argument was tactless, but there is no tactful way of dealing with a judge who has a vested interest. The sex in *Happy Anniversary*, we maintained, was charming, the lines were witty and the net effect was healthy. In several of the movies we had just seen, the sex was tawdry, the lines were cliché-ridden and the net effect was pestilential.

The code administrator made a vigorous argument in response. Most of the examples of sexual frankness in the films we cited, he said, took place between married couples; in my client's film, he told the all-too-comprehending judges, the man and

---

* The original administrator had been Joseph Breen. It was under Breen that the code was construed to require that in any scene involving a man and a woman on a bed, the man must have at least one foot on the floor. This has given rise to scholarly dispute over whether the appropriate legal antecedent is to be found in the pool hall or the boarding house—the regulation on awkward cue-ball position or the rule-of-fairness at the dinner table.

woman were not married when they first went to the hotel. To the extent that the other films involved sex between couples who were not married, in each instance and without equivocation they came to a bad end.

The advocate scans his bench for reactions. This was an unusually large tribunal, and the waves of sagely nodding heads induced a slight seasickness. My client's picture, the administrator continued, treated these things lightly, and it was quite apparent that David Niven and Mitzi Gaynor would live happily ever after, despite their transgression.

The argument was lucid. In the pictures that had the seal, whenever sex was consummated between persons unmarried, the audience was assured that the wages of sin is death, or at least a terrible glumness. *Happy Anniversary*, on the other hand, was exactly what its title implied.

My reply argument was brief. The board, I suggested, was being asked to elevate the tag line of a current joke to the status of a rule of law. They all knew the joke, I said. The effect of a decision against my client would be a solemn proclamation that it only hurts when you laugh.

The matter ended in a compromise. The board retreated from its position, somewhat. There would not have to be retribution. Repentance would be enough. The picture would get the seal if it added an expression of regret that the premarital abomination had ever taken place.

Making a change at this late date presented technical problems. The producers, however, offered a practical suggestion that the board accepted. The suggestion was that a wild line be used. A wild line is dialogue that appears on the sound track when there is no one speaking on the screen; it may be delivered by a character off camera, or it may be the unspoken thought of a character shown. At one point in the picture, when things are going badly, David Niven is sitting sad and silent. The wild line would be inserted here. It would read: "I never should have taken Alice to that hotel room before we were married. I don't know what I could have been thinking of."

Niven was in South America, and the picture was scheduled to be released before he got back. It was therefore agreed that another actor should speak the line, which would be dubbed into the film for the initial showings. After Niven returned, he would redo the line. His voice would then be redubbed, and used in the film for the rest of the run. The seal was bestowed, and *Happy Anniversary* went into the theaters.

The result was not exactly what the board anticipated. The actor who read the line failed to get the necessary note of remorse into his voice. Instead, he sounded sweetly sentimental and nostalgic, but a bit puzzled. It was as though he were trying very hard to remember exactly what it was that he had in mind when he took the girl to the hotel. In terms of audience response, the addition turned out to be one of the high points of the film.

Niven provided a brilliant sequel when he returned. He firmly refused to read the line. He said the picture was in no sense dirty and therefore it needed no change. He would not be party to anything that implied he had acted in a dirty picture.

The redemption, as I say, lay in the consequences. Since a decision totally in our favor would have involved an acknowledgment that the code standards were rotten, we could at best gain a compromise. The compromise, however, hardly furthered the aims of the code. In fact, the case made the censors look ridiculous—perhaps even to themselves. The enduring consequence was some small effect on MPAA policy. The organization became more liberal, which in this context simply means more sensible. *Happy Anniversary,* I am told (by an unimpeachable source that I have no inclination to impeach), made a contribution to the change.

A final note on the movie industry before we return to the books. In our respective activities Peyser and I (he more than I) had dealt with members of a special group of motion picture people—producers and distributors and unclassifiable general entrepreneurs in the field. They were mainly Central European or Mediterranean in origin, not all of them Hungarian. They were men of great shrewdness, esoteric business ethics and assorted accents. (One of them was particularly charming in his speech. He apparently had no native language. He spoke five or six fluently, each with a heavy accent.) We had noted an initial difficulty in communication with these businessmen; there seemed to be too many misunderstandings.

The difficulty, we had each come to appreciate, was not a matter of accent, and certainly there was no lack of fluency. In any language their vocabulary would be arcane. It was not that the words themselves were strange; it was that the meanings assigned to them differed from common usage.

Peyser and I prepared a glossary that would help in the negotiations. The four principal nouns that came into their business conversations were:

(1) liar
(2) crook
(3) a seven-letter word
(4) a ten-letter word.

The meanings, once grasped, were fixed and clear. A liar is somebody who remembers something that you wish had not happened. A crook is somebody who cannot remember something that you wish had happened. A seven-letter word is somebody who owes you money. A ten-letter word is somebody to whom you owe money.

Once familiar with these and a few other items of basic vocabulary, you can deal quite efficiently with the group.*

---

* Following the decisions discussed elsewhere in this book, four-letter words are apparently now permissible. No court, however, has yet spoken specifically on the subject of seven-letter words and ten-letter words, and it is out of a solicitous regard for the indemnity which the writer of this book has given to his publisher that the substitutions above are used.

Tropical

Storm

THE PUBLICATION OF *TROPIC OF CANCER* CAUSED
far more trouble for Grove Press than did the publication of
Lady Chatterley's Lover. And this, peculiarly, was the result
of the fact that the legal situation was so much improved.

Grove Press put *Tropic* out in 1961, the year after the *Lady
Chatterley* litigation ended. The federal agencies, with the
Chatterley opinions now part of the law, came to the intramural
conclusion that *Tropic* was not obscene in the constitutional
sense. Customs lifted its ban, which had been sustained in a
high federal court only eight years earlier, and the Post Office
permitted the book to be mailed. Both actions were apparently
taken on advice from the Department of Justice. This meant
there would be no Post Office case, no Customs case, and no
federal criminal prosecution in which the question of *Tropic's*
obscenity might be litigated.*

---

* At about the same time, a federal district judge in New York had indicated, although in the most *obiter* of *dicta*, that he thought the book was
not obscene. A copy published abroad had been seized by Customs at Idle-
wild Airport, which lay within the jurisdiction of the federal court for the
Eastern District of New York. The lady who imported the book brought
suit for injunction in Manhattan, in the Southern District of New York.
When there is a contest over a Customs seizure, federal law provides a

One reason why we had pushed so hard and so fast in the *Lady Chatterley* situation—why we felt it worthwhile to sacrifice full-scale preparation to gain an early trial—was the guess that it might stall other litigation. With a fine fat federal case going, local prosecutors might hold off to see how it came out. It was a good guess. While the Post Office proceeding was under way, the state courts stayed quiet; when it was over, the federal ruling, a pronouncement of constitutional rights, ended whatever dreams of prosecution state officials may have been cuddling.

But with *Tropic of Cancer* there was no federal case—nothing to distract eager local district attorneys, nothing with which those less eager could put off importuning citizens. Legal action in state courts started soon after the book was published. The volume of litigation increased when the paperback came out. Eventually there were over sixty cases, some of them civil suits, most of them criminal. Grove Press strained to defend, or help defend, each of the prosecuted booksellers.

To some extent Grove's defense of those who sold its books was voluntary; to some extent it was a contractual obligation. In hardcover distribution, there is ordinarily no elaborate arrangement between the publisher and those who sell its books to the public. The major paperback houses, however, give their wholesalers, and the wholesalers' customers, an indemnity—that is, they promise to pay any expenses resulting from an encounter with the law. In turn, they get an indemnity from the hardcover publisher, who thus bears the ultimate responsibility (unless the author can make it good, something that was not expected of Miller).

The timing of the paperback was not a matter of choice.

special legal action, which the statute requires to be brought in the district of the port of entry. The injunction suit therefore seemed superfluous, and in any event it was in the wrong district. Judge Thomas F. Murphy (who, *obiter*, had been the prosecutor of Alger Hiss) threw it out. His decision rested on the jurisdictional point, but in the course of his opinion he made his comment on the book. The question of obscenity was never reached because the Department of Justice meanwhile made its view known to Customs, which thereupon abandoned its hoary routine of seizing *Tropic of Cancer* and let the importer have her book.

Grove would have been happy to continue with the hardcover, on which there is much more profit per copy, until the legal issue was settled. But a few months after the hardcover was published, one of the smaller paperback houses, without Miller's authorization, decided to bring out its own edition. A paperback would pretty much put an end to the hardcover sales. A lot of people were willing to pay seven and a half dollars for the Grove book, if it were the only one available; not many would be if they could get practically the same thing for seventy-five cents. (Paperback publication of important books is usually postponed, by contract, for a year or more.)

The chances of preventing paperback competition lay somewhere between poor and nonexistent. The copyright status of *Tropic* was at best clouded. It had first been published in Paris by Obelisk Press. Obelisk and its successor, Olympia Press, brought out works of widely varying quality, ranging from junk to books by Miller, Durrell, Nabokov, Donleavy and Burroughs. But most of what they produced was for a special market: Americans and Englishmen traveling in France. (The best-known Olympia line is called *The Traveller's Companion.*) Maurice Girodias, the proprietor, once described himself as "an active and conscious pornographer." Indeed, he was part of a pornographic dynasty—Obelisk had been his father's imprint—and Anglo-American anti-obscenity laws were its economic lifeblood. It was a short-lived dynasty, ending in the cataclysm that swept away most of the Anglo-American anti-obscenity structure.*

---

* During this period France became more restrictive in its policies, hoarding gold (consonant with French tradition) and cracking down on obscenity (not altogether consonant with French tradition, at least as understood abroad). Girodias got into a lot of trouble with the De Gaulle government (not for taking money from foreigners). He was prosecuted in the criminal courts, and two of his companies—in addition to publishing books, he ran a splendid restaurant—were enmeshed in insolvency proceedings. The restaurant was lost; the publishing company survived—intellect, in this odd instance, perhaps outdoing appetite. But things were tough. Early in 1965, Girodias announced that he would leave France. Meanwhile, the United States, losing its gold, and facing a balance-of-payments problem, had begun to encourage a reverse tourism. And our anti-obscenity restrictions had been receding: the *Chatterley* and *Tropic* cases had been decided, and *Fanny Hill* seemed to have a fair chance of surviving. I mentioned to

Until the *Chatterley* decision, it was hardly conceivable that these books would ever come out in the United States, and so Obelisk-Olympia paid little attention to the formalities of our copyright law. But I had a theory under which *Tropic* might nevertheless have copyright protection, and we presented it to the lawyer for the intruding paperback. It created sufficient doubt to cause a compromise. Grove paid certain costs that the prospective competitor had incurred and the competing edition was abandoned.

This avoided the immediate threat, but it was obvious that other publishers would see an opportunity to ride Grove's coat-tails up and over the censorship battle. Grove's only recourse was to arrange for a paperback edition itself before somebody else did.

The paperback increased the fury. It provoked, for example, a great roil of police action in Chicago and its suburbs, where the hardcover had been selling peacefully in department stores and bookshops. Paperbacks usually arouse the censorious more than hardcover books. The proposition was sometimes over-stated; some commentators had declared that anti-obscenity action was confined almost entirely to paperbacks. The overstate-ment is shown by the three cases this book deals with; in each, the legal battle was well under way before there was any paper-back edition. But in general the proposition is valid; these cases were exceptional, involving books that were notorious before they were published.

The very fact that Grove had put out a paperback would weigh against it in court—whichever edition might be involved —at least with some judges and some juries. The problem in advocacy was to explain the reprint without sounding guilty about it. From one of our briefs:

> Ordinarily, for economic reasons alone, Grove would have preferred to have continued its hardcover sale. However, the only way to preserve Grove's and Henry Miller's position was

---

Girodias (at a cocktail party, of course, not in my office) that perhaps he ought to move to the United States, publish books by French authors that would lead to prosecution if they were published in France, and sell them to French tourists traveling in the United States.

to publish a Grove paperback edition. The foregoing is offered by way of background; Grove makes no apologies for offering an acknowledged literary classic to the American public at a reasonable price.

Those urging suppression announce, as the reason for their more vigorous pursuit of paperbacks, that the lower price makes the evil material available to minors. A concern for the young is valid, but the distinction between hardcover and softcover books is not realistic, ignoring as it does the economic facts of teen-age life in the time of prosperity during which these books were published. The purchasing power of the allowance-and-baby-sitting set of the 1960's was a large enough factor in the economy to rate a lead article in the *Wall Street Journal,* and the content of radio programs demonstrated that advertisers regarded the market of minors as large and rich. If no paperback edition was available, the hardcover was not beyond adolescent reach, especially since group purchase plans were ideally suited to the purposes the censors had in mind. A teen-ager bent on destruction of his moral fiber was not likely to be balked by the price of the fiber-eating literature.

But in any event the asserted reason is an inadequate explanation of the censor's objectives. It is not *pais* but *demos* that he seeks to save. There is an inverted snobbism at work. The mass of men needs protection; let the wealthy and the highly educated be damned. The aristocracy, even if it is only an intellectual aristocracy, has traditionally been accorded a special morality.

The economics of the period dulled the distinction; the mass of men could afford to buy the hardcover if there was no reprint. But the distinction could become real enough if we should have another Depression. By concentrating on paperbacks, the censors might create a condition in which the one third of the nation that was ill fed, ill housed and ill clothed would at the same time have its prurient interest insufficiently appealed to.

Yet it is even more than a matter of protecting the common man against a prurience that the elite may be permitted to enjoy. The censor's motivation goes deeper, into a longing to preserve the common man from the ravages of intellect. The intellectual enemy is a small minority, and in any case it is a minority that cannot be saved from its own devil.

Sex in literature provided the field on which the struggles recounted in this book took place, but the war was wider. The true censor has objectives beyond the masking of the erotic and the indecent. The end in view is an established principle of suppression, available anywhere in the world of the mind.

There had been, and still are, four main methods by which censorship for obscenity is imposed. One is the judicial enforcement of anti-obscenity laws—through criminal prosecution, through injunction or through administrative action reviewable in the courts. Another is an official's publicly proclaimed readiness to go to court if the book is sold. A third is police pressure on individual booksellers and their suppliers. A fourth is pressure by groups outside the government, which takes the form of organized recommendation to book-buyers or moviegoers, or even a boycott of the bookseller or theater.*

The fourth method involves the power of government only indirectly, and it has rarely been challenged in court.† The third method, quite apart from whether the particular book is obscene, has been held an invasion of First Amendment guaranties. The second may or may not be, depending on circumstances.

---

* Administrative suppression without immediate judicial review—censorship in the narrowest sense and originally its principal form—has just about disappeared. The Post Office, since the time of *Chatterley*, has gradually abandoned its use of the ban, and instead recommends criminal prosecution to the Department of Justice. So far as motion pictures are concerned, there are very few licensing agencies still in existence; at the date of writing there are only two state boards (in Maryland and Illinois) and less than a half-dozen municipal boards. Under a 1965 Supreme Court decision, these agencies must act through the courts, and cannot suppress films on their own.

† It does, however, involve the government to this extent: the boycott is premised on our economic system, which depends on the law; the boycott weapon is the dollar, which the law has established and maintains. On this basis it might be argued that the First Amendment can be invoked.

The first—court actions in which the question of obscenity is fought out—is certainly not objectionable as it is normally employed. But it was not normally employed against *Tropic of Cancer*. Instead of one case there were sixty. The cash and energy required to fight the battle sixty times over, or even twenty or ten times over, could bankrupt a publisher. Even if he survived, his enthusiasm for braving the censors would be sharply diminished, especially when he was weighing a deserving manuscript of small commercial appeal. Ultimate vindication would not matter. A difference in degree made a difference in kind, and there was now a fifth method: censorship by multiplicity of litigation. The forces of suppression had come upon a good thing.

I have been asked whether the situation was conspiratorial— whether this huge storm of litigation was masterminded. I do not think so; I think it was a true storm, not a production. There was a certain amount of coordination: district attorneys are in touch with each other and have meetings where matters of common interest are discussed. There was also, no doubt, some coordination among local pressure groups that had national affiliations. But I saw nothing that reflected a high degree of centralized organization—no deliberate, unified effort to get Grove Press or Henry Miller. On the contrary, what I saw simply reflected the fact, apparent in connection with each of the books I defended, that most people who gave attention to the matter were against its publication. It cannot be stressed too often that it was the United States Constitution that saved these books, and not the will of the people.

Thus there was born, more or less accidentally, as is the way with bastards, a new weapon of suppression. It was highly effective, and the law provided no procedural answer to it. In one state where a number of prosecutions were taking place within a single federal district, we tried to get a federal court to intervene and decide the issue of obscenity itself. But the doctrine that one court will not interfere with another stood in the way. This is a developing field of law, but it has not developed—and certainly had not developed at the time—to the point of affording a solution.

It was a procedural perversion. The courts were being used to effect a victory for suppression through the very existence of judicial proceedings. The solution had to come not from changes in procedure, but from changes in the substantive law. That is, the definition of obscenity had to be so narrowed, and the shelter afforded by the First Amendment so broadened, that most district attorneys would not want to bring action. It was not a matter of changing the form of obscenity litigation; it was a matter of expanding the right to publish.

However accidental the discovery of litigation-in-itself as an instrument of censorship may have been, the censors were quick to appreciate its utility. It continued to be used, after the *Tropic* litigation was over, in other cases—sometimes even when the prosecutors knew they must eventually be defeated. In December of 1964 the Chicago *Daily News* reported:

> Assistant State's Attorney Daniel J. Leahy said: "We're well aware of the decisions lately of the supreme courts. We do not agree with them as a whole or any part of them."

The import, of course, was that the attorney's version of the law, and not that of the highest courts, ought to determine whether a book should be prosecuted.

A congressman made the tactic even more explicit. In March of 1965, the *Hollywood Reporter*, a motion picture trade paper, contained the following:

> Representative Dowdy advocated getting local authorities to prosecute sellers of nudie magazines and other offensive publications and exhibitors of films they believe obscene, even if it is known that under Supreme Court interpretations of law no convictions can be gained. Dowdy said in this way exhibitors and others would simply give up because the receipts would be less than the expense.

Commencing or continuing prosecution in these circumstances is of course improper. The stirring up of unfounded litigation constitutes the ancient offense of barratry (a word, incidentally, that also signifies the deliberate sinking of a ship in order to steal its cargo). But such efforts and advice would not last long or amount to much. Eventually the law takes hold.

The development of the new weapon did not mean the familiar ones were neglected. In large areas of the United States *Tropic of Cancer* was unavailable, quite apart from any case that might be pending. The book simply wasn't around. Many wholesalers refused to handle it. In some instances the reasons were obscure. In some they were known.

Take Rhode Island. True, it is a small state. Yet one would think it would need more than the efforts of a single official to see to it that not a copy of the *Tropic* paperback was sold there. But one man did it: Attorney General J. Joseph Nugent. Grove's record of copies shipped, under the Rhode Island entry, bears the number "3380." The record of copies returned, under the Rhode Island entry, bears the number "3380." The state, like forty-eight others, had anti-obscenity laws that could have been invoked, but Nugent was not going to fall into that trap. A judge might think the book ought not to be suppressed; going to court can be a risky business. Instead Nugent got in touch with local wholesalers, and they agreed—voluntarily, it was said —not to distribute the book. Then the attorney general made an announcement: *Tropic of Cancer* was banned from sale in the State of Rhode Island.

In Maryland, County Manager Mason Butcher ordered the book removed from a public library. A cardholder who felt that libraries ought to be run by librarians went to court, but County Judge Ralph G. Shure agreed with what Butcher had done, and set an example of deference toward other branches of government that might shame certain aggressive judges (such as those of the United States Supreme Court). "I also commend the county manager," said the judge, "for banning this book from public distribution immediately upon notice, rather than waiting for the courts to determine whether or not it is obscene."

Virginia, the state that gave us Thomas Jefferson, James Madison and George Mason (an ancestor of Manager Mason Butcher?), had a flurry of nonjudicial bans. The Roanoke superintendent of police, it was true, had read only parts of the book, but, he pointed out, he did not act before he consulted the local commonwealth attorney. According to the Roanoke *Times*, the commonwealth attorney "said he had not read the book at all but that he had heard that it is considered obscene by some people." In Norfolk, another enforcement attorney apparently considered it unnecessary even to arrive at an opinion of the book's obscenity. The book is "objectionable, if not obscene," he declared. Local distributors were quick to respond. The *Virginian-Pilot* reported that one of them said, "All they would have to do is hint to me that they were dissatisfied and they would get my fullest cooperation." Virginia seemed to be outgrowing Jefferson. "Eternal vigilance is the price of liberty" was fading fast, and "You can't fight City Hall" was coming on strong.

Amarillo, Texas, suitably, brought a sheriff into the script. Not content with ordering the books to leave town before sun-up, he arrested them on their way out. The local distributor had agreed to an injunction, and five thousand copies were at a freight depot, ready to be shipped back. At this point The Law of the Panhandle seized them.

In Mishawaka, Indiana, Chief of Police Bolerjack, acting without a court order or even a search warrant, took forty-one copies of the book. He told the local press he gave the bookstores no receipt: "All I did was shoplift."

In Maine the Bangor *News* stated that the local wholesaler agreed not to distribute *Tropic* after he consulted the chief of police and the county attorney. He was informed that "they don't think the novel is the type of literature they'd like to see on sale."

A San Diego wholesaler returned *Tropic* without putting it out at all. The return was announced not by the wholesaler but by the local chief of police. The chief told the *San Diego Union* that the wholesaler had acted "on his own initiative." As to whether he had read the book, the chief said he started it but was unable to finish it; he could not go on "because it was too obscene." Conversation around San Diego police stations is apparently exceptional.

Georgia had a State Literature Commission, a lovely title for a board of censors. The commission branded *Tropic* obscene, and most Georgia booksellers gave in; three who did not were arrested.

The Chicago suburbs presented a busy scene of police censorship. Pretrial examinations made a judicial record of it. For example, a police sergeant in Mount Prospect informed his chief that a driver for a wholesaler had told him about "a book entitled *Tropic of Cancer*, which he [the driver] thought was an obscene book." The chief and the sergeant went around to a store where a package of books, still unopened, had been delivered. The sergeant, the chief testified, "pulled the book out, and I stood there for four or five minutes and thumbed through the book from page to page." The chief then visited six drugstores in Mount Prospect and suggested to the man in charge of each that he look at *Tropic*. "Did you call his attention to any particular pages?" asked Elmer Gertz, our Chicago attorney. "Page five, yes," answered the chief. He then made a series of phone calls to the police in other suburbs. The Skokie acting chief described the Skokie procedure: "We would go to these vendors in town, and we would ask them to remove the books from the shelves." "Were you acting on the basis of any ordinance or statute?" asked Gertz. "No, sir," answered the acting chief.

These are examples, not an exhaustive list. In some places the book was confiscated. In others retailers heeded advice from the police and returned their stock, or the wholesalers took the hint. The result was that in large areas of the country, without any judicial determination of obscenity, *Tropic* disappeared from the stores, or never appeared at all.

Grove could very probably have obtained injunctions against the officials involved—if not always in the lower courts, then almost certainly in the higher courts. This would not be interfering with litigation already pending; it would only be restraining out-of-court censorship. But Grove could not afford that many more lawsuits. We sought one such injunction in Chicago, but the aim was not so much to stop the unlawful police activities there as to get a ruling on obscenity that we might use as a precedent elsewhere. Gertz handled the case with great skill and breathtaking thoroughness, and the judge decided *Tropic* was not obscene. But it turned out to be only one more lower-court decision, and when the first high state court to consider the matter reviewed what had happened up to then, it merely paired the Chicago decision with one in Philadelphia that had gone the other way. The Chicago case then crept a painful

course through the Illinois appellate courts that came to an end
only after the United States Supreme Court, in another case, had
ruled on the book.

I have been describing situations where pressure by public
officials was exercised openly and the facts were known. There
were other situations where the reasons for *Tropic*'s disappear-
ance were unclear but where it seemed that police pressure was
being applied in ways less overt. The paperback edition was particularly vulnerable to such pressure. Publishers sell hardcover
books directly to bookstores and through book jobbers. Paperback distribution—which has been going on for only a few
decades—has an altogether different system. The books go to the
newsstand or drugstore through magazine distributors called
"wholesalers." When paperback publication started in this
country, the natural outlets were not bookstores, but newsstands. Newsstands were supplied by these wholesalers, who
thereupon got into the book business. There are approximately
eight hundred such firms in the United States.

If enforcement officials tell a wholesaler, on the quiet, not to
handle a certain book, they are likely to be obeyed. The profit
on any particular title is hardly worth the ill will of the police.
There were cities in which whip and jockstrap one-shots were
left on the stands undisturbed, while the wholesaler declined to
distribute *Tropic of Cancer* on the ground that it would get him
in trouble. Sometimes he would not even allow that this was the
reason; he would indulge in the comfort of sanctimony and assert that as a matter of principle he would not handle such a
book.

It is not plausible that the coexistence of freedom for trash
and repression for good writing was a matter of chance. Express or implied, the understanding was that some publications
for whose sale the wholesaler might otherwise be prosecuted
could safely be sold, if he stayed away from others designated
as critical. Famous underground books would always be able
to make the critical list. Newer, less celebrated books that were
seriously written and seriously received were also vulnerable;
nothing infuriates the vigilante so much as the combination
of sex and intellect. So far as the trash was concerned, it was in
some cities subject to periodic crackdowns (after each of which

it would reappear in the racks) but for the most part it was not bothered.

Thus, in many places suppression occurred without benefit of judiciary. But ultimately the question whether the book could circulate would depend on judicial decision. "Ultimately," however, was to be a long time coming.

I did not conduct the trial of any of the *Tropic* cases. I argued two of the appeals, but apart from that, the very number of the lawsuits kept me in the office, trying to help the various trial attorneys around the country. I made a few trips to sore-spots to give counsel to counsel; otherwise, it was a matter of telephone calls and correspondence. Two brilliant lawyers, Shad Polier and Steven Tulin, joined me in this staff work.

The cases varied, of course, but they shared the central issue. I wrote a basic brief, distributed to all of our attorneys, which contained among other things the essential arguments I made in the *Lady Chatterley* case: the restrictive reading of the *Roth* prurient-interest test, and the notion that social value constituted a separate, independent test.* As to prurience, the difficulty was that, for most people, if *Tropic* had no prurient appeal, it had no appeal at all. Some critics had said the book was an affirmation, an essentially healthy book that showed Henry Miller's love of life. But the life it depicted—to the average man and the average judge—was hardly lovable. And this time the Supreme Court's substitute for "lustful" was not going to help. I had argued in the *Chatterley* case that the root of "prurient" was a word meaning "itch," and its connotations "nasty" and "unwholesome." On that etymology, the very first paragraphs of *Tropic* got us in trouble.

In analyzing the objectives of anti-obscenity legislation, I

---

* The brief also undertook an analysis of what, I submitted, were the underlying objectives of our anti-obscenity laws. If a judge found the precedents inconsistent or unenlightening, he might, I hoped, wonder just why he should be asked to enjoin the publication of a book or to send a man to jail for selling it. (I do not list these objectives here; they come up in the discussion of the oral arguments.)

urged that offensiveness in a book was too trivial a reason to limit First Amendment guaranties. But not many judges were ready to be that analytical. For most the reaction was likely to be revulsion (or uncomfortable attraction), and for some—if the decision were to be made in terms of prurience—there would be a direct and unbreakable connection between reaction and decision.

The best chance lay in the value test. In addition to what our expert witnesses would say, there was an impressive mass of published material attesting to the importance of Henry Miller and his most famous work. Moreover, from a more general point of view, a recognition of social value as an independent constitutional criterion was the best thing that could come out of the litigation. And so that was the main emphasis of the broadcast brief.

On motions, evidence is ordinarily presented through affidavits—written statements sworn to be true—and this was the way our evidence on value was presented. (Affidavits are not used at trials, except for certain limited purposes, because the affiant is not present to be cross-examined, or if he is, he can give his evidence orally.) They are usually prepared by lawyers; the affiant (the person who makes the affidavit) adopts the language as his own by swearing to it. But these affiants, being writers by profession, wrote their affidavits themselves, and did not take kindly to changes; and in the main the affidavits required no changes.

One, however, went through an unusual editing process. It was the affidavit of the poet and critic John Ciardi. Ciardi, who lived in Metuchen, New Jersey, brought a draft to my office. I discussed some changes with him, and then had to leave for an appointment. He rewrote parts of it while I was out, and was gone by the time I got back and saw the revised draft. It was excellent, a beautifully written statement about "the role of the serious artist in a free nation," the meaning of *Tropic of Cancer*, and the value of the book. ("The violence of Miller's mockery, moreover, is indispensable to the moral stature of *Tropic of Cancer*. Only as he mocks the false can he praise his dream of what men should be.") But there was one small thing that might do large damage to our case. The final paragraph was this:

Such a book must not be removed from the memories of civilized men. It is both an essential admonishment and an essential exhortation. It is moreover a valiant and true work of art. To remove such a book from the experience of mature and reasonable readers on the grounds that immature and prurient readers may be either offended or excited by it, is an assault upon an artistic integrity. It is a denial of freedom on the queasy grounds that men are not fit for freedom. It is to say that the least of men shall dictate the diet of the best.

What bothered me was the last sentence. The judges could easily find a note of snobbery in it, and it would not matter that it was unintended. They might view the affidavit as arguing that *Tropic of Cancer* should be exempt from anti-obscenity laws for the benefit of an elite. This was not only likely to irritate a judge; it also flew in the face of the "average person" and "community standards" concepts. The court might well say, with some satisfaction as well as firmness, that the law was designed to serve the interests of the population at large, and was not concerned with catering to the desires of the self-chosen "best."

We had already imposed on Ciardi, who had devoted his time and his talent to a matter in which he had no direct personal interest. I felt that he would not like to see his work of art (for the affidavit was indeed a work of art) mauled by another hand, and at the same time I hesitated to ask him to come into New York again for another conference and some further writing. But if I could think of a change small enough so that it would require little discussion and slight enough so that it would not disrupt the flow of his language, he might agree to the change by telephone.

I called and inquired whether he would allow me to change a single letter. A single letter? he asked. Yes, I said: I would like to change the first letter of the last word in the affidavit from a *b* to an *r*. Ciardi approved the substitution, and the affidavit in final form made the censors, rather than the readers, the outsiders.

Tropical

Clearing

THE FIRST TRIAL OF *TROPIC* TOOK PLACE IN Boston, in September 1961. It antedated my participation in the matter, and I made no contribution to it. It was tried by Ephraim London, who had handled the outstanding motion picture obscenity cases, and handled this case with his accustomed competence. It was a civil action, under a special Massachusetts statute, tried before a judge sitting without a jury. The judge decided against the book, an outcome in no way attributable to London's painstaking defense; the transcript strongly suggests that no amount of testimony or argument could have changed the judge's mind.

The defense witnesses included three distinguished figures from the universities: Mark Schorer of California (who had written the introduction to *Lady Chatterley's Lover* and was shortly to publish his superb study of Sinclair Lewis), Harry Moore of Southern Illinois, and Harry Levin of Harvard. Their testimony, together with the wealth of published material on *Tropic* and its author, built a record that would form a solid basis for the value argument on appeal.*

---

* The witnesses on literary value in the cases dealt with in this book frequently differed among themselves, some finding considerably more value

A curious shadow was cast in the Massachusetts trial. At one point, London was attempting to elicit testimony on Grove's standing as a publisher. The judge questioned the relevance of the testimony. Then came the following exchange:

> MR. LONDON: I think it is relevant to show this is not a publisher of cheap pornographic books. I think it's relevant to show that the list of books is one of exceedingly high quality.
>
> THE COURT: Well, do you mean that the publisher, let us say, like Putnam, if he published—Putnam's, I assume that is a good publishing house—
>
> MR. LONDON: I would agree.
>
> THE COURT: If Putnam published a book, it would not be obscene, but if XYZ published the same book it might be obscene?

It was approximately two years later that Putnam found itself in the same court, trying to establish that it was not a pornographer. The judge in the *Tropic* case might have picked Random House or Harper or, closer to home, Houghton Mifflin or Little Brown, but the example of respectability that came to his mind was the future publisher of *Fanny Hill*.

The trial also produced a charming three-way interchange among court, counsel and witness. The introduction for the Grove edition of *Tropic* was a reprinted essay by Karl Shapiro. It began:

> I call Henry Miller the greatest living author because I think he is. I do not call him a poet because he has never written a poem; he even dislikes poetry, I think. But everything he has written is a poem in the best as well as in the

---

than others. I treated this as something that helped rather than hurt our position. The differences of opinion, I argued, lent credibility to the testimony, and if the value theory was accepted at all, it would sustain books of moderate merit as well as those thought to be masterpieces. In the Massachusetts *Tropic* case, however, the disparity amounted almost to a War of the Two Harrys. Professor Moore testified that the book had "very high literary value" and that Miller had "very high, very great talent, yes sir." Professor Levin, on the other hand, gave an unembellished "yes" to the question whether the book had literary value; pressed for further comment, he said that Miller had "considerable talent as a very special sort of writer, not, I may say, the kind of writer I personally prefer. . . ."

broadest sense of the word. Secondly, I do not call him a writer, but an author. The writer is the fly in the ointment of modern letters; Miller has waged ceaseless war against writers. . . .

It was an interesting idea, but in none of the cases did any lawyer or witness refer to it; it had no obvious effect one way or the other on the legal issues. It did not escape the Boston judge, however. When Harry Moore was on the stand, London asked whether the book had literary value:

> A. Oh, I think it has very high literary value. I think that it is splendidly written in an age when not many things are splendidly written. In current American literature, for example, we have only a few people who have—you can put this word in quotes—"written."
> THE COURT: What's the word?
> THE WITNESS: "Written." We use the word "style," but that sounds a little too artificial and decorative.
> THE COURT: What was the word?
> THE WITNESS: "Written."

Counsel lent a hand:

> MR. LONDON: Past tense of "write."
> THE COURT: I was just wondering what the difference is when you say, "It's written"—the word "written" instead of "style."
> MR. LONDON: Your Honor, he just indicated that was in quotes.
> THE WITNESS: I put it in quotes. The word was first used in this sense by one of the greatest critics in the world, the famous poet and critic T. S. Eliot, who used the word thus about 1936 or '7 in his introduction to Djuna Barnes's book *Nightwood*, and it was also used some years later, just at the end of the war, by Edmund Wilson in an article in *The New Yorker*.
> THE COURT: Do you differentiate, Mr. Moore, between "written" and "writer"?
> THE WITNESS: Well, sir, Edmund Wilson, when he used the word in this sense, in quotes, was speaking of Somerset Maugham, and he said he could not read Somerset Maugham's books because they weren't written.

THE COURT: That doesn't tell me much. I don't want to really get trained to deliver the course.

THE WITNESS: Well, sir—

THE COURT: All I had in mind is that the man who wrote a foreword of this book, Karl Shapiro, doesn't like the word "writer" and he calls him "author."

The appeal was my job. Massachusetts has only one appellate level. (Some states, like the federal government, have two—New York, New Jersey, Illinois and California, for example. The theory is that none but cases of general importance will filter through the intermediate level, so that the highest court will act chiefly to resolve conflicts among the lower courts and to announce and define the law.)* The Supreme Judicial Court of Massachusetts has a long tradition of judicial excellence. It was, however, the court that just seventeen years earlier had found Lillian Smith's *Strange Fruit* too sexy, and fifteen years before that, had held *An American Tragedy* obscene. There had been changes in personnel, of course, but the tradition was there (along with the precedents), and two of the judges to whom I would make my argument had been on the bench that ruled against *Strange Fruit*. I felt confident about how *Tropic* would do in the United States Supreme Court, but not at all confident about how it would do here.

We wanted badly to win in Massachusetts. A victory in the first high state court to consider the book would give us an advantage in the cases pending in other states, especially if the victory came in this court, with its general reputation for legal ability and its particular reputation for making "Banned in Boston" part of our language. Moreover, it would be helpful, when we got to Washington, to get there a winner. It is always a little easier for an appellate court to affirm than to reverse, even as independent and individualistic a group of judges as those of the Supreme Court.

Yet I wanted more than a victory in the Massachusetts court.

---

* The highest state court is the final arbiter of the law unless a matter of federal jurisdiction—such as a federal constitutional question—is involved.

I wanted two other things. One—though at this point it might have been too much to hope for—was an explicit acceptance of the social-value theory. The *Lady Chatterley* opinions had not given us that. The other was a victory on such terms that our opponents could take the case to the Supreme Court.

Putting a case before the Supreme Court at an early date might make all the difference to Grove. Only a decision there could end the mass of litigation. If the Supreme Court held that the First Amendment protected the book, no court could suppress it, whatever the state law might appear to be. If it held the contrary, that too would end the litigation, and probably put Grove out of business; the imposition of fines in the many prosecutions and the cutting off of sales, added to the expense already incurred, would be too much. But if all the cases and their costs went on too long, it might not matter—so far as Grove's continued existence was concerned—whether there was an ultimate victory or an ultimate defeat.

It is not every state-court case that the Supreme Court will review, or that it is permitted to review. The Court's jurisdiction is defined in Article III of the Constitution and in supplementary Acts of Congress. The statute dealing with the Court's appellate jurisdiction goes back to the Act of 1789, passed by the first Congress that met under the Constitution. (The Bill of Rights was adopted later; our First Amendment question would go to the Supreme Court by virtue of a statute that antedated the Amendment.) The Act provides that state-court judgments may be reviewed by the Supreme Court only where the validity of a treaty or a federal statute is in question, or where the validity of a state statute is challenged as conflicting with federal law (constitutional or statutory), or where some other federal right (constitutional or statutory) is put in issue. If we lost in Massachusetts, there would be no question about our coming within the Act; the decision would necessarily involve a denial of our federal constitutional claim. But, as I say, we did not want to lose. And if we won, the Supreme Court's jurisdiction would depend on the nature of the Massachusetts decision. If Massachusetts decided in our favor because the book was not obscene under its statute, or because the constitution of the commonwealth protected its publication, or because the trial court had committed error under Massachusetts law, there would be nothing for the Supreme Court to review. Unless we won on a pure and rigorous federal ground, the attorney general would have nothing to complain to the Supreme Court about. So I abandoned some defenses.

At the trial, London had urged the First Amendment, of course, but he had also urged that the book was not obscene under the traditional concepts of obscenity, that it did not come within the condemnation of the Massachusetts statute, and that its suppression would violate the guaranties of the Massachusetts constitution. We jettisoned these additional arguments. "We do not," my brief stated, "contend that the [Massachusetts] statute has an effect any narrower than the First Amendment allows it. We concede that the statute covers all material that is obscene in the constitutional sense. We waive all objections to the proceedings below and to the judgment based thereon." By lightening ship, we perhaps reduced the chances of winning the case, but we increased the chances of reaching the Supreme Court if we did win it.

Under the Massachusetts statute, the plaintiff is the attorney general of the commonwealth. The action is against the book itself, and the publisher may, if he wishes, intervene. The attorney general was Edward J. McCormack, Jr., a member of a politically powerful family; his uncle was the Speaker of the House of Representatives. These connections, together with McCormack's ability and attractive personality, promised a bright political future. He had the misfortune, however, to collide with a member of an even more important Massachusetts family. At about the time of the *Tropic of Cancer* appeal, he was contesting the Democratic nomination for the United States Senate with Edward Kennedy, a circumstance that eventually cost Grove Press a lot of money.

The Supreme Judicial Court has seven members, of whom five ordinarily hear each case. When we rose to argue the *Tropic* appeal, however, all seven filed in. This was unusual. William Homans, the Massachusetts lawyer who was local counsel for us (and who nevertheless was soon thereafter elected to the Massachusetts legislature), told me that this was the first time in his experience that he had known the court to bring all its members to the bench. Either the justices felt that the case was particularly important, or they felt that it was particularly difficult, or both. (It could not be they were there because they all wanted to read the book. *Fanny Hill*, perhaps; *Tropic of Cancer*, no.)

Representing the appellant, I spoke first. The legal issue, I said, had changed since the time when this court considered *An American Tragedy* and *Strange Fruit*, and attention must now be focused on the guaranties of the First Amendment. I then submitted my interpretation of the *Roth* case. My principal emphasis, for reasons already mentioned, was on the social-value theory, but since it was at this date no more than that—a theory —I devoted a large part of my argument to the prurient-interest test. Here my confining "prurient" to what was nasty, which worked very nicely for *Lady Chatterley's Lover*, worked less nicely, as I have said, for *Tropic of Cancer*. The trial judge had found *Tropic* "filthy, disgusting, nauseating and"—showing a fine flair for anticlimax—"offensive to good taste." Miller's concentration on lice, turds and the clap made it a bit difficult to put him in a category with Lawrence. Our opponents pressed the point in their brief. They cited the *Roth* footnote associating prurient interest with a "shameful or morbid interest," and contended that *Tropic of Cancer* came precisely within the definition.

But there was more that could be said about the prurient-interest test. (It was an almost inexhaustible source of hermeneutics.) When the Supreme Court referred to morbidity and shamefulness, I argued, it had in mind not subject matter, but the attitude of the reader as induced by the writer. Certainly the Court did not intend to exclude any part of life from the range of topics an author might write about; literature cannot be limited to the pleasant and the wholesome. Brennan, I contended, was referring to a morbid and shameful treatment, something altogether different from the treatment of a morbid or shameful subject. Miller described events and thoughts that the bench might think degraded, but he dealt with them as a serious artist, not a hack exploiting book-buyers' guilty urges.

I cited, as precedent, Chapter Thirty-eight of Genesis. It is ancient literature of great beauty. It is also the source of the word "onanism." The story has contrasting themes of vitality and morbidity. For much of the chapter, morbidity is the essence—death, and the defeat of birth through a perversion of sex. Nevertheless, Chapter Thirty-eight, apart from its religious meaning, is quite clearly literature, not obscenity. *Tropic of Cancer*, I said, also combined vitality and morbidity, and also was literature, not obscenity.

The assistant attorney general who argued the appeal emphasized the "average person" and the "contemporary community standards" language of the *Roth* opinion: maybe a few intellectuals could see literary merit in the book, but the vast majority of people could see nothing in it but filth. Watching the judges while my opponent was speaking, I had the impression that some of them, perhaps most of them, shared this view. If winning depended on finding four justices of the seven who liked the book, we could not win the case. We would have to find four who agreed that a book highly regarded by a respectable number of respectable critics was assured protection, even though the justices might thoroughly dislike it.

In my reply I sought to emphasize that this was indeed the meaning of *Roth*; if the law had suppressed what most people had rejected, our cultural store would be sparsely stocked. I needed an example of disapproved art that had later gained general acceptance, and the notes on the back of a record album popped into mind. I mentioned the raging abuse that attended the initial performance of Beethoven's First Symphony. When the argument was over, a distinguished-looking man, a stranger to me, came up and made some courteous comments. The reference to Beethoven's First Symphony he thought was particularly apt, because I knew, didn't I, that three of the seven justices were accomplished musicians, and two of them were trustees of the Boston Symphony? It would have been gratifying to be able to say that I knew—that my preparation was just that thorough, and my argument thoughtfully tailored to the interests of the individual judge. On the other hand, it was gratifying to be that lucky.

The argument was heard in the middle of May 1962. At the end of June, when the Massachusetts court had not yet acted, the United States Supreme Court made a decision that I felt might help us. It was in a case called *Manual Enterprises* v. *Day*,

Postmaster General. There was a new administration in Washington, and, naturally, a new Postmaster General. He had excluded some magazines from the mail, and the lower federal courts had upheld the ban. The Supreme Court reversed by a vote of six to one. Two Justices did not participate. Frankfurter was ill, and White so newly appointed that he took no part in the decision. Clark was the dissenter.

Black concurred in the reversal without giving his reasons. He had stated his "absolute" interpretation of the First Amendment on other occasions, and could fairly assume it was known. Brennan, Warren and Douglas based their concurrence on a point we had renounced in the *Chatterley* case—that there was no statutory authority for the Post Office assumption of power to exclude books from the mails.

Harlan also wrote an opinion for reversal, in which Stewart joined. They ignored the question of Post Office power, and held that the magazines were not obscene. The opinion established—or confirmed, depending on how one reads the *Roth* case—a test of "patent offensiveness." As he explained it, to be condemned under this test, publications had to be "so offensive on their face as to affront current community standards of decency." I had argued in *Chatterley* that the prurient-interest formula required the fulfillment of two conditions: the kind of appeal the Supreme Court had in mind, plus a wide transgression of contemporary limits of candor. "Patent offensiveness" could be considered merely an elucidation of the second condition, but Harlan treated it as an additional test. He was given the duty of announcing the judgment of the Court (Supreme Court judgments are customarily announced from the bench by one of the Justices, usually by the writer of the prevailing opinion), and in the official reports of the Court's cases his opinion appears first. It has thus been given a certain weight that a two-judge opinion would not ordinarily have.*

---

* Possibly the reasons for the prominence that the Court gave it were these: of the seven Justices, two (Black and Clark) went their individual ways, and of the five remaining, three took a position which would upset a long-established practice of the Post Office. The Chief Justice may have felt that this position should not be regarded as "the opinion of the Court"— since it represented such a departure—unless a majority joined in it.

Harlan's opinion was helpful to us, for reasons that will appear shortly, even though the test of patent offensiveness would seem to be one that *Tropic of Cancer* could flunk easily enough. But while I cited it in support of our argument, I would have been obliged to concede, if pressed, that the opinion was unrealistic. (Nobody pressed.) It described the publications involved in the decision as follows:

> Petitioners are three corporations respectively engaged in publishing magazines entitled *MANual, Trim* and *Grecian Guild Pictorial*. . . . The magazines consist largely of photographs of nude, or near-nude, male models and give the names of each model and the photographer, together with the address of the latter.

As Clark, dissenting, added, some of the advertisements:

> captioned a picture of a nude or scantily attired young man with the legend "perfectly proportioned, handsome, male models, age 18–26. . . . Finally, each magazine specifically endorsed its listed photographers and requested its readers to support them by purchasing their products.

Quite apart from the question whether the First Amendment protects advertising of this kind, one may find Harlan's appraisal of the publications a bit strange. The main point of his opinion was that the magazines were not offensive to the general reader: they might have a special, even prurient interest for homosexuals, but for others they had no particular meaning. "It is only material whose indecency is self-demonstrating," said the Justice, that the anti-obscenity laws can begin to reach. Apparently he felt that the significance of the models and the addresses was beyond the comprehension of the general reader.

I do not think that I have used the word "unrealistic" unfairly. Moreover, if there is any justification at all for applying anti-obscenity legislation to printed materials, it lies in the effect the materials may have on the conduct or welfare of those who read them. Harlan's rationale involved the proposition that the magazines spoke a secret language only homosexuals could understand, a corollary of the broader proposition that the world is divided neatly into heterosexuals (large group) and homosexuals (small group). He apparently did not consider the effect of the magazines on young men of unformed and ambivalent character.*

But whatever the weaknesses in Harlan's opinion, its reasoning helped my theory of the *Roth* case, indirectly but substantially. For one thing, it supported the point that the prurient-interest test was itself a double test. For another, and much more important, it could be argued that Harlan's opinion opened a passage for the entry of an independent social-value theory. The primary argument against the value theory was that *Roth* appeared to set up a single definition of obscenity—the prurient-interest definition. Harlan said nothing about social value, but he did say that it was a mistake to think that *Roth* established prurient interest as the only test. Even though, on analysis, his new formulation might be merely an expatiation of one aspect of the prurient-interest test, Harlan presented it as something separate and distinct, and his presentation was quite inconsistent with the generally accepted simplistic view of *Roth*. I sent a long letter to the Supreme Judicial Court saying so.†

In the middle of July the Supreme Judicial Court announced its decision. By a four-to-three vote it reversed the trial judge and became the first high court to hold that *Tropic of Cancer* might lawfully be published in the United States. We were, of course, happy about the decision; it was only nine years earlier that a federal court of appeals had unanimously declared the book obscene. But we were even happier about the opinion of the court. Written by Justice R. Ammi Cutter, it gave explicit recognition to the social-value test—the first judicial opinion to do so. Said Cutter:

> We think, in the light of the decisions reviewed above, that the First Amendment protects material which has value because of ideas, news or artistic, literary or scientific attri-

---

* This is not to say (or deny) that the magazines should have been suppressed.

† After the prescribed series of appellant's brief, respondent's answering brief and appellant's reply (and the oral argument), no further statements by counsel are ordinarily permitted. There are exceptions to this rule, and one occurs when a decision that seems to have bearing on the case comes down after the date of argument. A letter to the court is the usual procedure.

butes. . . . We conclude, therefore . . . that with respect to material designed for general circulation, only predominantly "hard-core" pornography, without redeeming social significance, is obscene in the constitutional sense.

I had been arguing for three years that the Brennan opinion in *Roth* meant that if a book had literary value, it could not be suppressed, whether or not it might be obscene by other tests. But Brennan, as I have conceded, hadn't quite said so. Cutter now had. A court sitting on Beacon Hill, of all places, was the first to give unequivocal sanction to a constitutional theory that made a radical change in the law of censorship.

Cutter went on to apply the test to *Tropic of Cancer*, adding emphasis to the court's decision by expressing his distaste for the book:

It is not the function of judges to serve as arbiters of taste or to say that an author must regard vulgarity as unnecessary to his portrayal of particular scenes or characters or to establish particular ideas. Within broad limits each writer, attempting to be a literary artist, is entitled to determine such matters for himself, even if the result is as dull, dreary and offensive as the writer of this opinion finds almost all of *Tropic*.

Competent critics assert, and we conclude, that *Tropic* has serious purpose, even if many will find that purpose obscure. There can be no doubt that a significant segment of the literary world has long regarded the book as of literary importance. . . . We think that the book must be accepted as a conscious effort to create a work of literary art and as having significance, which prevents treating it as hard-core pornography.

Chief Justice Wilkins and two others said that they "could not join in the foregoing opinion." They filed a concise dissent that described the *Roth* case as "too dim a beacon by which to guess a course."

The majority opinion was what we had hoped for in another aspect as well. It was pitched precisely on the narrow ground that we had urged:

The [appellants] concede that the statute covers all material that is obscene in the constitutional sense. . . . We rest our decision squarely on the First Amendment, so that if review of our decision is sought, there may be no doubt that this case has been decided solely upon the federal issue.

The case was now in a perfect posture for Massachusetts to carry it to the Supreme Court. Moreover, the dissenters had taken the position that if a book such as this were to be granted protection, Washington should have the responsibility. Thus the attorney general not merely had an opportunity to go to the Supreme Court; he was being prodded on up by the highest court of his state. And as a practical political matter, it appeared to be the wisest thing for him to do. In the eyes of those who objected to such books he would be doing everything possible to preserve Massachusetts from Henry Miller, while those on the other side could not fairly criticize him for seeking a nationwide resolution. It looked as though we were going to be able to end all the *Tropic* litigation at a relatively early date.

The Supreme Court allows ninety days in which to appeal. A good part of the ninety days went by, and no notice of appeal was filed. The Massachusetts senatorial primary took place. Kennedy won, by an unexpectedly wide margin. We imagined that the primary campaign had been keeping McCormack busy and he would now get moving on the appeal. But nothing happened. As the period drew to a close, we became uneasy and made inquiries. We were told, by someone who was in a position to know, that there would be no appeal. Our informant gave us this explanation: McCormack had not merely lost the primary; he had taken a terrible trouncing. Granted that his opponent was the President's brother, one would have thought the popular attorney general would have at least made a close race of it. Apparently McCormack had thought so too. As our informant put it, the vote left him in a state of shock. Traumatized, he did nothing about the appeal. The Massachusetts *Tropic of Cancer* case ended in Massachusetts.*

---

* The question whether to appeal lay entirely in the attorney general's discretion, and there might, of course, have been good reasons for not taking the case higher, apart from any temporary loss of appetite for contention. (Letting the time expire was obviously not an oversight.) But in the light of the factors that favored appeal—viewed from both sides of the issue— the explanation we heard was plausible.

In any event, McCormack recovered, and four years later became the

Meanwhile, in New Jersey, we took our troubles to a three-judge federal court. New Jersey was the state that had the most arrests and the most prosecutions. We asked the federal court to stop what was going on in the state courts, and to give us a decision on whether the book was obscene. The effort was pretty much unprecedented at the time, and these three federal judges, at least, were not ready for it. They held that they ought not to interfere with proceedings in the state courts and hence there was no need for them to render a ruling on the book. They indicated, however, that they thought it obscene, and they appeared to be particularly moved by a quotation that Grove had put in its paperback edition. The opinion began:

> This is a suit to enjoin certain New Jersey law enforcement authorities from proceeding under the law of that state against a book titled *Tropic of Cancer*. The principal plaintiff is the book's publisher, who advertises its book on the cover page of same as ". . . an unbridled obscenity, which it is." We do not reach the question of whether that deliberate statement is true, because, as will appear, in its present status the controversy is clearly an issue for the State of New Jersey to resolve.

The use of the word "deliberate" is interesting. One could agree that there was nothing absent-minded in the way Grove prepared its covers, but they were quite decorous, a refreshing change from most paperbacks, and the *Tropic* cover was no exception. In any case, the statement to which the court referred was not on the cover; it was on an inside page containing some descriptive material about the book and its author (including his election to the American Institute of Arts and Letters) and some quotations from reviews. The language to which the court referred was from *Life* magazine, and the quotation as it appeared in the book was: "*Tropic* will be defended by critics as

---

Democratic nominee for Governor, running in the same election as another Massachusetts attorney general with whom we litigated. Edward Brooke, who brought the action against *Fanny Hill*, was the Republican candidate for the United States Senate. Brooke won and McCormack lost, the voters of Massachusetts thus manifesting a preference for Henry Miller over John Cleland.

an explosive corrosive Whitmanesque masterpiece (which it is) and attacked as an unbridled obscenity (which it is)." The court, following the best traditions of theater and motion picture advertising, evidently felt that part of the sentence was enough.*

The case was not a good one to take to the Supreme Court, because it might be decided on the thorny question of whether a federal court should interfere with state-court proceedings. Grove could very well lose on that point, and have the expense of a Supreme Court appeal, without getting a decision on whether the book itself was entitled to protection. And even if the Supreme Court should decide that in these circumstances a federal court ought to act, Grove might still have no ruling on its book; the result could be simply a federally imposed limitation on the number of New Jersey state prosecutions. We had to wait for another case like the one in Massachusetts, a case where the question of obscenity was unavoidably involved, to come up through the state courts.

The three-judge federal court announced its decision a couple of weeks after the Massachusetts decision. Earlier in that same year, 1962, there had been some decisions in various lower state courts. In Philadelphia a judge had held the book obscene. In Chicago a judge had held it not obscene (in the case described earlier). In California there had been two jury trials; in one there was a guilty verdict, in the other an acquittal. (The acquitting jury, however, let the press know that the book was obscene and they had acquitted merely because they felt the particular bookseller was innocent.)

The Philadelphia trial was notable for what is perhaps the most local evaluation of a novel that has ever been made. The Reverend William Vaughn Ischie, Jr., a priest of the Episcopal

---

* We may speculate on whether if the quotation had been on the cover as the court said it was, and had as prominent a place on the cover as the court gave it in its opinion, and had been cut down and taken out of context in the way in which the court had cut it down and taken it out of context, there would have been an instance of "pandering," in the sense in which the term became important in the *Ginzburg* case four years later.

Church, called as a witness by the Commonwealth of Pennsylvania, made the following statement:

> I see nothing in this book which would be of any value to help correct any of the evils or any of the problems facing Philadelphia, or that would be constructive in solving any of these difficulties.*

The Philadelphia trial was also notable for turning up a witness who said he was sexually aroused by the book. (The standard statement by those opposing the book was that it provoked reactions in other people.) On cross-examination by the bookseller's attorney, Dr. Austin Joseph App, associate professor of English at LaSalle College, gave this testimony:

> Q. When you read the book, did you find that you were excited to lustful thoughts?
> A. Yes, yes. I read these pages. I wouldn't be allowed in any court in this country to—nobody can, unless he is ninety years old, one foot in the grave, and T.B. besides.
> Q. This book aroused you?
> A. Certainly it did. It would arouse you too. The pages I mentioned, that I said were suggestive, and I meant not just page 91. Some pages are so revolting that if you were civilized you would be so disgusted—you might not want to vomit, or might not want to kiss somebody, but there are some pages that I couldn't even mention—the delicate way he speaks of stroking—I couldn't in any court in the land read that.
> Q. That aroused you?
> A. That aroused you, yes. Don't think because I'm a teacher that I'm not human.
> Q. At this point, why did you continue reading?
> THE COURT: Now, look.
> A. I am a professional critic. I am the founder of a magazine on criticism. One book isn't going to drive me into sin.
> Q. Right.

The Los Angeles trial also had some interesting witnesses for the prosecution. One was the novelist Leon Uris. Another was Dr. Frank Baxter, the academician and television personality (Los

---

* Rivaling in parochialism a Yiddish newspaper's review of Norman Mailer's *The Naked and the Dead* that began: "This is a story of two Jewish boys. . . ."

Angeles thus providing a cracked-mirror image of the Old Bailey). Baxter delivered the following expert opinion:

> If this book depicts the private life of the average citizen of Los Angeles, I welcome with great joy the hydrogen bomb.*

That summer three employees of a bookstore in Syracuse, New York, went on trial. (One being named Fritch, the name of the case was *People* v. *Fritch*.) A jury found them guilty. An intermediate court reversed, and the district attorney took the case to the highest court of the state, the Court of Appeals.

There were three Roman Catholics among the seven judges of the Court of Appeals, and on the argument I added a new authority to the ones I had been citing—Saint Thomas Aquinas. Aquinas wrote that it is not every sin that the government ought to punish. The secular law, he reasoned, deals with relationships between people; it regulates a man's actions toward his fellowmen. There is another kind of evil that occurs within the individual himself and is to be dealt with by the church, not by the government. Private sin is different from public crime, and only the latter lies in the province of man-made law.

I could concede that in the eyes of many people the experience of reading *Tropic of Cancer*—the salacious pleasure that might be gotten from it—was evil enough. (Considering the judges' comments on the book in the course of the argument, it was plain that the concession cost nothing.) But, as Aquinas said, it was not an evil with which the machinery of government is designed to deal.

It appeared that the only Thomists on this bench were Judge Dye, a Presbyterian, Judge Fuld, a Jew, and Judge Van Voohris, an Episcopalian. They dissented. The New York court, like the Massachusetts court, split four to three; only this time there were four votes against the book.

During the argument, Chief Judge Desmond made it clear that he was not impressed by the fact that many critics and scholars gave Henry Miller a high place among twentieth-cen-

---

* "As quoted in "Witchcraft and Obscenity," by Stanley Fleishman, *Wilson Library Bulletin* (April 1965).

tury writers. Just because some people regarded Miller as a major talent, did that mean he should be permitted to publish pornography?

I responded that conceivably Miller might decide to become a commercial pornographer and write utterly worthless trash of the degree of prurience and offensiveness that forfeits the protection of the First Amendment. At the moment, however, the court was considering not trash, but *Tropic of Cancer*, a work of merit and importance. Judge Desmond remained unimpressed.

The principal opinion for the majority was written by Judge Scileppi.* Desmond filed a concurring opinion that was eloquent in its denunciation of the book.† A few years earlier he had written a concurring opinion in a case that went the other way. The case involved a magazine called *Gent*, whose title would have been more descriptive had it been plural. Judge Stanley Fuld, who was one of the dissenters in the *Tropic* case, had delivered the principal opinion, which in some re-

---

* Judge Scileppi's opinion contained this statement:

In the exercise of our duty to make an independent constitutional appraisal, we have read the book carefully and conclude that it is nothing more than a compilation of a series of sordid narrations dealing with sex in a manner designed to appeal to the prurient interest.

To this was appended the following footnote:

Obscene and filthy passages are to be found on the following pages in the hard-cover edition: 4, 5, 6, 7, 16, 18, 20, 24, 25, 28, 32, 36, 39, 40, 42, 43, 44, 45, 46, 47, 52, 53, 54, 56, 58, 59, 60, 62, 73, 80, 85, 87, 89, 92, 97, 100, 101, 102, 103, 104, 105, 107, 111, 112, 113, 114, 115, 116, 117, 118, 120, 121, 122, 123, 124, 126, 127, 134, 135, 139, 140, 141, 142, 144, 145, 146, 156, 159, 160, 171, 172, 175, 188, 190, 193, 202, 203, 207, 215, 216, 217, 220, 225, 229, 230, 231, 232, 233, 234, 235, 236, 237, 238, 239, 246, 247, 248, 249, 250, 256, 257, 258, 259, 272, 273, 274, 282, 283, 288, 289, 290, 291 and 292.

† Judge Burke concurred in both the Scileppi and the Desmond opinions. Judge Foster concurred only in the Desmond opinion. Judges Dye, Fuld and Van Voohris were very strong in their dissents. Fuld accepted the proposition that *Roth* had established an independent social-value test, and stated it firmly: ". . . a book . . . may be stamped as obscene, and beyond the pale of constitutional protection, only if it is 'utterly without redeeming social importance' and only if its 'dominant theme' is an appeal to 'prurient interest.' . . ."

spects went farther in support of freedom of expression than any previous high-court opinion. Desmond did not quite go along with Fuld, but his concurrence was liberal in its own right. He apparently had second thoughts, however, and in the *Tropic* and *Fanny Hill* cases he voted for suppression, writing opinions markedly different in tone from the one he had written earlier. Of *Tropic of Cancer*, he said:

> From first to last page it is a filthy, cynical, disgusting narrative of sordid amours. Not only is there in it no word or suggestion of the romantic, sentimental, poetic or spiritual aspects of the sex relation, but it is not even bawdy sex or comic sex or sex described with vulgar good humor. No glory, no beauty, no stars—just mud. . . .

Desmond, a man of high intelligence, saw no humor in *Tropic*. In contrast, many of the literary people on whose evaluation we relied mentioned humor as one of its main merits. Harold Pinter considered *Tropic* in essence a comic novel, "a fine comic novel."

On this point, while I disagree with both, I think Desmond's appraisal is no worse than Pinter's. The comedy in the book is essentially comic relief. The impulse to laugh comes principally from the context in which the jokes are made. The atmosphere is very much like that of the classroom. There is no response to humor so easily induced as that of the cramped and aching students; given the circumstances, almost any change in subject gives pleasure, and a little wit goes a long way. The reaction of the reader of *Tropic*, I think, is much the same.*

---

* Pinter's appraisal was made not in a trial but in a three-way conversation which sticks in my memory not so much for its content as for the motoring adventure that followed it. When Rosset and I left the New York City bar at which the conversation took place, he offered me a lift in his Isetta, a small soap bubble of a car. We turned left off Central Park South onto a busy Seventh Avenue and ran out of gas in the middle of it. One advantage of the Isetta is that in such circumstances the embarrassment does not last long; we picked the car up and carried it over to the curb. Then we met an unexpected difficulty: none of the several garages in the neighborhood would sell us a can of gas. It was something about our having to supply the container ourselves, and a special kind of container; we could only begin to guess at what dark politico-economic forces were at work. Baffled and annoyed, we walked back to the Isetta, which was

But though the majority said that the book was obscene, they did not reinstate the conviction. There was another issue in the case. The Supreme Court had held, in 1959, that one may not be convicted of selling an obscene book unless *scienter* is proved. *Scienter* is an ancient term in the criminal law; it means, roughly, an awareness of what one is doing, and for many kinds of prohibited conduct—not all—there is no crime unless the awareness exists. To support a conviction for selling an obscene book, it must be shown that the bookseller knew what the book contained; otherwise, said the Supreme Court, there would be an undue restraint on circulation, a restraint that would impair First Amendment guaranties.

The ruling was thoroughly practical. Without it, to make sure that he would stay out of jail, a bookseller would have to read all the books he sold, and if he were uncertain about any of them, consult a lawyer. His possible profit on a given title would never be worth the cost of a legal opinion or even the time of reading the book. He would solve his problem by refusing to sell anything that looked or sounded dubious, or that somebody might tell him was dubious. There could then be untrammeled circulation only of those books that survived the bookseller's own blunderbuss censorship.

In the Syracuse case, the district attorney's proof of *scienter* seemed to be inadequate. From Grove's point of view, this was an obfuscating issue, but with a criminal conviction at stake, we made every argument that might win. Here the majority agreed with us, and sent the case back for retrial on the matter of *scienter*. It made a happy ending for the defendants; the district attorney gave up. But it meant that once again a case came to an end before it could reach the Supreme Court. The judgment was in our favor, and you cannot appeal from a victory just because you are dissatisfied with the way you got it. Moreover, the Supreme Court will ordinarily hear appeals only from judgments

---

parked just outside a drugstore. From somewhere between us there came an idea. (Working together on these cases had induced habits of collaborative thought.) We went into the drugstore, bought four cans of cigarette-lighter fluid, poured the contents into the gas tank, started the car and drove off.

that are final, and this one was not final; it contemplated a further trial.

At about the same time, two cases were working their way through the California courts. One was the Los Angeles criminal case. The other was a civil action in which a bookseller and his customer, in a suit against the Los Angeles city attorney, asked for a declaratory judgment that *Tropic* was not obscene. The criminal case ended, so far as the California courts were concerned, with an affirmance of the conviction at an intermediate appellate level. The United States Supreme Court agreed to review the case. Shortly afterward, the declaratory judgment action arrived at the highest court of California and produced a result both good and bad.

The good part was the court's acceptance of the social-value theory. The California anti-obscenity statute had been recently amended, and liberals in the legislature managed to incorporate a value test in the statute itself. (It is a fair assumption that most of the legislators did not know what they were doing.) But the California Supreme Court did not rest the decision solely on the statute. Judge Tobriner, who wrote for a unanimous court, said that even if the state law did not have its special language, the decision would be the same, because the book was protected by the First Amendment, and this was because the book was not utterly without redeeming social importance. Here was a precedent to add to the one given us by the Massachusetts majority. The highest courts of two states had now lent their authority to the proposition that *Roth* established an independent value test.

The bad part was that the decision kept the California cases out of the United States Supreme Court. The plaintiff bookseller could not appeal because he had won. The defendant city attorney could not appeal because the decision was based not only on the Constitution but also on the statute. If the highest court in California said the book violated no California law, there was no federal question for the Supreme Court to review. For the same reason, the criminal case lost its jurisdictional footing. Since it was declared to be the law of the state that *Tropic* was not obscene, the Supreme Court, without saying a word about the book, simply vacated the judgment of conviction and sent the case back to California.

Several weeks earlier there had been a decision in the highest court of Wisconsin. Here we had our third four-to-three vote, this time in favor of the book. The Wisconsin majority gave some support to the value test—support not nearly as positive as that in Massachusetts and California, but at least hinted at. Wisconsin officials made no move to take the case farther.

New York, California and Wisconsin all acted in the middle of 1963, about a year after Massachusetts. The courts of last resort in four states had now ruled on the book, and there was still nothing on the Supreme Court docket. There was, however, some highly respectable authority for the social-value theory; we were no longer confined to a subterranean reading of the *Roth* opinion.

The Illinois Supreme Court was later to decide unanimously against the book, creating an almost perfect symmetry. Illinois balanced California, and in each of the other three states there were four-to-three decisions, two in our favor and one against. When *Tropic of Cancer* finally reached the United States Supreme Court, we were leading in high-court decisions by the margin of one judge's vote.

The storm did not end with a great thunder and lightning and a sequence of bright skies. It ended with a small discordant noise, an echo of another case.

The Supreme Court acted on a Florida judgment. It was an improbable candidate for Supreme Court review: the constitutional issue seemed to have been waived in the course of the proceedings, and the judgment—by an intermediate, not the highest, court of Florida—had been based solely on the meaning of the local statute. Grove consulted an outside firm of Florida attorneys, known to be expert in constitutional matters, on the chance of getting to Washington. The advice received, well reasoned and well supported by precedent, was that there was almost no chance, because, the constitutional question being out of the case, the Supreme Court had no jurisdiction. But the Court gave us a welcome surprise and agreed to take the case. And disposed of it in the same breath.

There were neither briefs nor argument in the Supreme

Court. The ruling was made on the papers filed in connection with the petition for certiorari.* The Florida judgment was summarily reversed. The decision and the fact that the Court was accepting the case were announced simultaneously.

Four of the nine Justices did not deal with the merits at all. They merely stated that certiorari should not have been granted. They did not give their reasons; reasons are not given for the denial of certiorari. But it was doubtful that the four deemed the publication of *Tropic* unworthy of consideration. The Court at the time was taking other obscenity cases; there was wide public interest in *Tropic*; there were closely divided decisions in the state courts; an enormous amount of litigation was awaiting word from on high; and whether *Tropic* might be published involved an important constitutional issue (or would, in a proper procedural setting). With such good reasons for granting certiorari, it is a fair guess that the four Justices who voted to deny it did so because they believed (as did the Florida lawyers consulted) that in this particular case the constitutional issue had disappeared along the way.

The five Justices who did deal with the merits all voted to reverse, but they wrote no opinions. Instead, each of the five announced he was reversing for the reasons he gave in another case decided the same day. The other case was *Jacobellis* v. *Ohio*, which dealt not with a book but with a motion picture. After hearing argument once in *Jacobellis*, the Court had scheduled a second argument to treat some points insufficiently explored. Meanwhile the petition for certiorari in the Florida *Tropic* case came up.

The picture was *The Lovers*, which, as one of the Justices pointed out, was really quite innocuous.† But the Court, revers-

---

* Certiorari is one of two methods by which the Supreme Court reviews the decisions of lower courts; the other is appeal, the statute making specific use of the generic term. Certiorari is a direction to the court below to send up the case (*volumus certiorari*—"we wish [the record] to be certified"). It is a discretionary exercise of jurisdiction, while appeal is available, in described situations, as a matter of right. In either instance, of course, the Supreme Court must have jurisdiction, which is given it only in the classes of cases prescribed in Article III of the Constitution.

† Mr. Justice Goldberg: ". . . the love scene deemed objectionable is so

ing the state court conviction by a six-to-three vote, used the occasion to publish its various ideas on the law of obscenity. Black and Douglas adhered to their view that expression may never be banned. Stewart advanced the proposition that only hard-core pornography may be suppressed; he applied the proposition to the case before him by saying that while perhaps he could not define hard-core pornography, he knew it when he saw it, and this film was not it. Brennan wrote an opinion for reversal which I will get to in a moment. Goldberg joined in the Brennan opinion and also wrote a concurring opinion of his own. White concurred in the reversal but wrote no opinion.

Chief Justice Warren voted the other way and developed something new—a proposed rule that in an obscenity case the Supreme Court should affirm the lower-court decision whenever there is "sufficient evidence" to support it. He defined sufficient as more than "any" but less than "substantial." Since he could not say "that the courts below acted with intemperance or without sufficient evidence," he dissented. (It is hard to see how the Warren rule could ever lead to a different result; there is always some evidence of obscenity in an obscenity case that reaches the Supreme Court.) Clark joined Warren. Harlan also dissented, on the ground he had taken in *Roth*—that the states should be left pretty much alone in their handling of the subject.

The Brennan opinion, fortunately, got the most attention. It came first in the official reports, as had the Harlan opinion in *Manual Enterprises*. This was probably because it was clear the rest of the Court would not accept the Black-Douglas view, and because the only other opinion on the majority's side that had the adherence of more than one Justice was Brennan's.* What

---

fragmentary and fleeting that only a censor's alert would make an audience conscious that something 'questionable' is being portrayed. Except for this rapid sequence, the film concerns itself with the history of an ill-matched and unhappy marriage—a familiar subject in old and new novels and in current television soap operas."

 * To become "the opinion of the court," an opinion must ordinarily be joined in by a majority of the judges (as was Brennan's in *Roth*). An opinion by fewer than a majority may nevertheless have particular significance: because of the fixed positions held by other members of the court, it may exert a controlling leverage in subsequent cases. There has been a

he wrote was excellent from our point of view. It made the value test explicit. And it gained force from the fact that it was written by the Justice who had spoken for the majority in *Roth*. Brennan cited the Massachusetts and California *Tropic* cases and stated:

> We would reiterate, however, our recognition in *Roth* that obscenity is excluded from the constitutional protection only because it is "utterly without redeeming social importance," and that "[t]he portrayal of sex, e.g., in art, literature and scientific works, is not itself sufficient reason to deny material the constitutional protection of freedom of speech and press." It follows that material dealing with sex in a manner that advocates ideas, or that has literary or scientific or artistic value or any other form of social importance, may not be branded as obscenity and denied the constitutional protection. Nor may the constitutional status of the material be made to turn on a "weighing" of its social importance against its prurient appeal, for a work cannot be proscribed unless it is "utterly" without social importance.

This could hardly have been better. Brennan was accepting our argument that the presence of value in itself invoked the protection of the First Amendment, and saying, in effect, "This is what I meant all the while."

The difficulty was that it represented the view of only two Justices. It was not the opinion of the Court. And by the time the Court would find occasion to rule on another obscenity case, one of the two would no longer be there; Goldberg took another job. But in any event, for their several reasons, five Justices had decided that *Tropic of Cancer* was not obscene, and except for a flickering afterglow, Grove's litigious travail was over.

In Illinois, the highest court of the state retrieved its opinion, expunged it and complied with the Supreme Court's decision. But the Illinois court did not stop there; it carried compliance to a point that made it the Till Eulenspiegel of appellate courts.

---

tendency, however, among some courts and some lawyers, to regard the opinion that appears first in the report of the case as entitled to special consideration simply for that reason. I do not think this is sound, but it increased the usefulness of the Harlan opinion in *Manual Enterprises* and the Brennan opinion in *Jacobellis*.

On the day it had decided against *Tropic*, the court had also affirmed a conviction of Lenny Bruce. The Supreme Court action did not necessarily affect the Bruce conviction; nevertheless, the Illinois court changed its decision there as well. Six of the seven judges joined in a new opinion in which they repeated their condemnation of Bruce and then made an elaborate bow in the direction of Washington. They treated the Brennan opinion as the opinion of the Court, and decided it meant that if any part of a performance had any value the anti-obscenity law could not operate. Although the conviction of Bruce, in my estimate, would have been reversed if the case had reached the Supreme Court, the Illinois judges were going quite beyond anything Brennan had said. Their leftist deviation led their most liberal colleague to complain. He concurred in the reversal of Bruce's conviction, but wrote a special opinion protesting the majority's formulation of the rule.

The Supreme Court had given the drama an amusingly flat ending. The outcome was expected, but so was a treatment of the issue somewhat less casual, somewhat more direct. *Tropic of Cancer* was saved on a review that had no briefs, no argument, and not even an opinion that the book could call its own—by a decision from which nearly half the bench held aloof.

But in the Supreme Court's action that day there was a significant gain for the value theory. The high state judges who had accepted the theory—the majority in Massachusetts, the minority in New York, the entire bench (with some help from a local statute) in California—were now joined by two members of the Supreme Court. And though one of them was not long for the Court, the other, who now gave explicit statement to the value test, had been the author of the *Roth* opinion.

Tropic
---
of Brooklyn

THERE WAS ONE *TROPIC* CASE THAT MADE NO
law, had no trial, never went beyond a minor criminal court and
deserves special mention. It deserves special mention because it
was the only case in which Henry Miller was a defendant.

Miller was prosecuted in Brooklyn, his own home town. Taking a local-boy-makes-bad view of the affair, a Brooklyn grand
jury recommended criminal action. Barney Rosset and Grove
Press were also defendants, along with three wholesalers.

The grand jury acted in the summer of 1962, having pondered the matter for eight months. It suggested that the defendants be prosecuted under Section 1141 of the New York Penal
Code, by what is called an information. An information is a
formal charge presented to the court by the district attorney.
Ordinarily the business of the grand jury is to return indictments. It can, however, recommend prosecution where indictment is not a prerequisite.* Violation of the New York anti-

---

* New York, like other states and the federal government, makes indictment by grand jury a prerequisite to prosecution for "a capital or other
infamous crime." This means, roughly, a violation that carries a sentence
of more than one year. Certain minor offenses can be prosecuted without
either indictment or information, on the complaint of an individual, who
is most often a police officer but may be a private citizen.

obscenity law is a misdemeanor rather than a felony, and indictment is not necessary. But this does not mean that the violation is not serious. The word "misdemeanor" may suggest such things as smoking in the subway and spitting on the sidewalk, but it covers a wide range of offenses, and the penalty for transgressing the New York anti-obscenity law, apart from fines, can be up to three years in jail.

In this case the information was rather peculiar. The language of criminal pleading, and the rococo architecture of Section 1141 itself, combined to create something which to the lay eye must be a sort of lawyer's fantasy, and which even to the lawyer may seem a little exotic. The first count of the information alleged that:

> The defendants, on or about and between January 1, 1961, and June 30, 1962, in the County of Kings, unlawfully sold, loaned, gave away, distributed, showed and transmuted and offered to sell, lend, give away, distribute, show and transmute, and had in their possession with intent to sell, lend, distribute, give away, show and transmute, and advertised, and offered for loan, gift, sale and distribution, a certain obscene, lewd, lascivious, filthy, indecent, sadistic, masochistic and disgusting book, and written and printed matter entitled Henry Miller, *Tropic of Cancer* and bearing on its cover the legends "A Black Cat Book 95¢"; "This Is the Complete Unexpurgated Grove Press Edition Originally Published at $7.50," which book and printed matter was copyrighted in 1961 by Grove Press, Inc., and is captioned "First Black Cat Edition 1961—Third Printing—Manufactured in the United States of America," and which book and printed matter depicts and represents acts and scenes wherein the sexual organs of both male persons and female persons are portrayed and described in manners connoting sex degeneracy and sex perversion, and which acts, scenes and descriptions were of such a pornographic character as tend to incite lecherous thoughts and desires; and the defendants designed, copied, drew, printed, uttered and published, and manufactured and prepared said book and printed matter, and wrote, printed, published and uttered, and caused to be written, printed, published and uttered, an advertisement and notice giving information, directly and indirectly, stating and purporting so to do, where, how, and whom, and by what means and what

purports to be, the said obscene, lewd, lascivious, filthy, disgusting and indecent book and printed matter can be purchased, obtained and had.

The special quality of the document came mainly from the wording of the statute and the strict requirements of specificity in criminal pleading. But there was something else. When several persons have been involved in a crime, the charge is often made in two counts. One count alleges that they have done the forbidden deed, the other that they entered into a conspiracy to do it; the conspiracy itself is treated as a separate crime. The double charge was made in the *Tropic* case, with bizarre results.

Conspiracy, despite its romantic and sinister connotations, is merely an agreement to engage in prohibited conduct, followed by some step taken to give effect to the agreement. Assuming the sale of *Tropic* was illegal, there was indeed a conspiracy here. The publishing contract made by Miller and Rosset, followed by the business dealings between Grove and the three wholesalers, provided all the elements of the crime, if the object in view—the sale of *Tropic*—violated the statute.

The trouble was that the information took in too much time and territory. Its second count alleged that the defendants "unlawfully and corruptly conspired, combined, confederated and agreed together to commit the crime," and went on to say:

It was the plan of the said conspiracy that the said book and printed matter was to be prepared and authored by the defendant Henry Miller and was to depict and represent acts and scenes wherein the sexual organs of both male persons and female persons were to be portrayed and described in manners connoting sex degeneracy and sex perversion and were to be of such a pornographic character as would tend to incite lecherous thoughts and desires.

It was part of the plan of the said conspiracy that the defendants Grove Press, Inc., and Barney Rosset were to print, publish and utter the said book and printed matter while the defendant Imperial News Co., Inc., Brooklyn News Co., Inc., Pacific News Co., Inc., were to act as distributors of the said book and printed matter.

It was part of the plan of the said conspiracy that the defendants were to design, copy, draw, print, utter and publish and manufacture and prepare said book and printed matter.

THE END OF OBSCENITY

It was part of the plan of the said conspiracy that the defendants were to write, print, publish and utter, and cause to be written, printed, published and uttered, an advertisement and notice giving information, directly and indirectly, stating and purporting so to do, where, how and whom and by what means and what purports to be, the said obscene, lewd, lascivious, filthy, disgusting and indecent book and printed matter, can be purchased, obtained and had.

The information charged, properly, that both the direct violation of Section 1141, and the conspiracy to violate the section, took place "on or about and between January 1, 1961, and June 30, 1962." But the conspiracy was alleged to include a plot to "prepare and author" the book, which was in fact prepared and authored in the early 1930's. Giving the People of the State of New York the benefit of the doubt and extending the period covered by the information accordingly, there was still a problem. At the time the conspiracy was undertaken, as in the course of the proceedings I managed to point out, the principal corporate defendant was not yet in existence, and one of the two individual defendants, Barney Rosset, was twelve years old. With the author in Paris and the publisher in a Chicago grade school, proof of the conspiracy as charged would have presented an impressive case of international juvenile delinquency.

The tanglefoot conspiracy count was a product of the kind of rush that occurs in a busy law office. It might give us some psychological advantage in the litigation, but it was not likely to have much effect on the ultimate result. As a matter of fact, the district attorney himself and his assistants in the case were highly competent lawyers, thoroughly sensitive to the problems of freedom that were involved in a prosecution they felt obliged to handle. They were intent on holding the author and the publisher responsible for any violation that might exist, and they felt strongly that Henry Miller should himself appear as a defendant, but they were gentlemanly throughout, and quite willing to avoid any unnecessary expense or unpleasantness.

The district attorney, Edward Silver, did not press for an early trial. He had a sensible concern for the efficiency of his office, and saw no point in using the time of his staff, and of a busy court, on the difficult trial of a question that would in any

event be decided elsewhere. If a higher court held the book obscene, conviction in the Brooklyn case would be automatic; if it
held the contrary, conviction would be impossible.

Meanwhile, the procedures of the criminal law went forward.
We had to plead to the information, and there was the question
of bail. I went to court on these matters, to a court I had never
appeared in before and had visited only once or twice. It was the
successor to the old Magistrate's Court, now a division of the
New York City Criminal Court; its business consists of minor
cases and preliminary aspects of cases that will be tried elsewhere. Each time I saw it in action, I was struck by the contrast
with courts as we generally think of them. The difference is
enormous, and disheartening. This is poor man's law; we have
not yet achieved democracy in the dispensation of justice.

The session at which we said "not guilty" was one that dealt
with a miscellany. Pleas were taken. Decisions were made on
whether the accused should be held for grand jury action. Bail
was set. There were some brief trials. Probation reports were
heard. Sentences were imposed. The courtroom was crowded,
with constant flow and eddy of patrolmen, detectives, lawyers,
courtroom attendants, district attorney's men, complainants,
people freshly arrested, and people brought in from jail. Conferences—or maybe merely conversations—were going on between
lawyers and defendants, police officers and assistant district attorneys, attendants and the judge, and people who seemed to be
just passing the time of day. The entrance to the courtroom was
a pair of swinging doors, and they banged back and forth like a
corner saloon on Saturday night. Among the constitutional
guaranties being violated was that of public trial. The public was
there all right, but it could not witness the trial; the noise made
what was going on at the bench inaudible to all but the participants. The woodwork was scarred. The plaster was peeling. It
was a huge and grimy bargain basement of the law—or, rather, a
huge stationary pushcart—and some of the goods were shoddy
and most of the bargains illusory.

The defendants seemed generally to be petty thieves, drunks,
wife beaters, husband beaters and people who had engaged in
simple extramarital violence, plus a publisher. The judge worked
on his feet, pacing back and forth and handing out justice right

and left, probably with what was, under the circumstances, a good deal of accuracy. But the circumstances were wretched, and they made real justice impossible. The concept of considered judicial review of the law and the facts, as presented by carefully prepared adversaries, was alien to this courtroom.*

When our case came up, the district attorney asked that Rosset be held in bail of five hundred dollars, a modest request. I argued that there should be no bail at all; if Rosset were intent on fleeing, leaving behind his publishing company and his house, another five hundred dollars was not going to stop him. The judge agreed, and Rosset was released on his own parole.

After a while, we arranged a procedure with the district attorney that would save both sides the time and expense of a full-scale trial. A written statement of the facts (which were really not in dispute) would be submitted to the court. The case against the wholesalers was dismissed, and the case against Henry Miller severed—that is, reserved for separate prosecution. The allegations of conspiracy were dropped.

Meanwhile, a stately dance had taken place, in which the district attorney and Henry Miller were transcontinental partners. Grove, Rosset and the wholesalers had appeared in the case voluntarily. Miller had not appeared, either legally or physically. The court issued a warrant for his arrest. A warrant is effective only within the jurisdictional limits of the court that issues it. This was a New York court, and Miller was in California. (The fact that Miller had once lived in Brooklyn had nothing to do, legally, with his being prosecuted there. Crimes are prosecuted where they are committed, and in this instance the crime was the distribution and sale of the book in Brooklyn.) Though the district attorney's office extended a polite invitation—even going so far as to offer to pay his travel expenses—Miller apparently felt no inclination to visit old haunts. As time went on, the invitation was repeated, with increasing vigor, but Miller had be-

---

* A principal reason is that there is too much for the law to do in a large city, with the legal manpower that is available. People who are disturbed about the increase in crime might contemplate the effect of an increase in the fairness and dignity with which the criminal law is administered. But it would take some money, and frequently the people most disturbed about crime are the people most disturbed about taxes.

come a homebody. The prosecution then threatened to have
him extradited. Neither the district attorney nor I knew for sure
whether extradition would work.*

The procedure requires both administrative and judicial action. The governor of the extraditing state must make a request,
and the state in which the fugitive is found decides whether to
honor it. If the governor of the second state agrees to the extradition, the fugitive can nevertheless contest its propriety in the
courts of that state. While the Brooklyn case was pending, the
California Supreme Court had held *Tropic* was not obscene
under California law. When extradition is sought for conduct
that does not constitute a crime in the harboring state, there is
a good chance he will not be sent back. But there was no assurance that this would happen.†

Letting the threat of extradition hang, the district attorney
proceeded against Grove and Rosset. The statement of facts was
prepared in the spring of 1964, with the thought that it would
be submitted to the court after its summer vacation. Then, in
June, came the Supreme Court decision on *Tropic*, and in July
the New York Court of Appeals sustained *Fanny Hill*. Though
the Albany judges had arrived at their various conclusions about
Fanny Hill before the Supreme Court's decision was handed
down, the majority took note of it and mentioned that their
own 1963 ruling on *Tropic* was now overruled. That disposed of
the Brooklyn case; the district attorney agreed to its dismissal.

---

* One day while this was going on, Miller and I talked on the phone.
After we had finished with whatever it was that had to be discussed, Miller
asked, "Tell me, how is all this going to come out?" The New York Court
of Appeals has held the book obscene, the score on the various trials around
the country was pretty bad, and Miller's extradition was a hovering possibility. I felt sure, though, that when a case got to the Supreme Court, the
decision would be in our favor. "There'll be a lot of trouble along the way,"
I answered, "but it will end right." "Isn't that interesting," said Miller,
quite serious "that's just what my astrologer told me."

† At one point it was suggested that we sue in New York to prevent it.
The chances that a court would entertain such an action were so remote
that the most likely outcome would be to stir the district attorney to action
when perhaps he contemplated none. The only aspect of the proposed suit
that appealed to me was its title; since it was up to the governor to make
the request for extradition, the name of the case would be *Henry Miller* v.
Nelson Rockefeller.

Aspects
of the Lawyer

THE LITIGATING LAWYER IS A MERCENARY, ONE of the few remaining examples of the hired combatant. His premise is hostility. There are rules within which he must ply his trade, but assuming the court is honest, they are not difficult to enforce, and therefore not difficult to abide by. The rules observed, the hostility is socially approved, indeed demanded.

Almost all our occupations are competitive, of course, but in most callings the battle is waged darkly and with guilt. The approved mode is constructive cooperation, and reasonableness toward those with whom one deals. Though the standard is not always honored, the standard creates the guilt. Even salesmen and advertisers shrink from denouncing a rival product; they prefer to dwell upon the values of their own. The courtroom lawyer, on the other hand, spends half his time exposing the fallacies of his brother at the bar, an exercise in scorn and damage. If he is cordial, we understand that it is only good manners. His aggressions conform to moral premise, and need not smolder. He is therefore courtly out of court—after working hours a generally amiable person.

The ethic is the ethic of the mercenary, and it is very sound. The lawyer does not have to take a case he does not favor. But once he takes it, there are no internal conflicts. His duty is clear:

within the rules, he is expected to do everything possible to serve his client's cause. This loyalty need not be thought a virtue. It is an ethical good in the classic, rather than the Christian, sense. It is something that is good here and now for the man who has it.

Mercenary as an adjective and mercenary as a noun express two different—in some respects contradictory—concepts. The adjective implies that the chief motive is money. For the soldier of fortune, however, the chief motive is fighting. The professional soldier, if he has real ability, could make more money doing something else. The same is true of the courtroom lawyer, who, on the average, gets less for his time than the lawyer who stays in his office; if the fees matched the effort, most litigation would cost too much for the size of the stake. This is one reason so many suits are settled out of court—a resolution economically desirable but ethically and psychologically deplorable. The just cause should not be compromised. The good fight should not be left in the dressing room.

The need for combativeness arises from the fact that our legal system is an adversary system, the hypothesis being that contention forces out the truth. This presupposes partisanship and bias; since the partisans are opposed, the thrashing and wrangling sends the facts to the surface. The judge and jury will have everything before them—or if not everything, then much more than there would be without the competition. The judge must be relatively passive; the highly partial lawyers have the responsibility of giving the court the evidence, the authorities and the reasoning.

Unlike some mercenaries, a lawyer always wants to win. He need not handle every matter that comes along; a lawyer is not a public utility. He may refuse to act because he has doubts about the justice of the client's position. Or the pay may not be good enough. Or he may simply dislike the man. Or he may be concerned about the principle his victory would support. Once he accepts the case, however, he fights as hard as the lawyer who had no hesitation. In fact, a degree of doubt may strengthen him; the lawyer with a total emotional commitment is apt to choke.

My friends sometimes expressed surprise that this lawyer or

that was on the other side of a censorship case. They would point out that he was a cultured man, or an urbane man, or a man affirmatively interested in civil liberties; they would assure me that the opposition would therefore not be too strenuous. They were uniformly wrong. The most difficult opponent was precisely such a man. A liberal attitude might affect the administrative question of whether to proceed against a particular publication, but when the decision was made (by him or for him), the liberal prosecutor tried his case with as much intensity as the most indignant censor. In the athlete's paradoxical phrase, he came to play—meaning not to play but to win. And his broader view of the subject increased his capacity to understand, and hence to deal with, our side of the case. He was just as combative as the lawyer who regarded his cause as a crusade, and he was free of the carapace that limits the crusader's agility.

But there is a mercenary aspect in the adjectival sense as well. A lawyer usually lives on what his clients pay him, an arrangement that clashes with his social function. The inconsistency appears in the curious transformation of the word "client." It originally referred to one who was a dependent, in a status inferior to that of the person he depended upon. Part of the protection the Roman *patronus* gave his clients was legal advice and representation in court. Now, however, there is too often a mutual dependency between attorney and client, an unhealthy symbiosis, and the dominance may point the other way. Lawyers need the patronage of their clients, which in etymological terms is a contradiction.

The practice of law, like other occupations that seem interesting, attracts too many people, and a buyers' market is created. (Conversely, for example, undertakers are hardly ever poor, and in small towns the undertaker-bank-president—in that chronological order—is a familiar phenomenon.) Most lawyers struggle to reach a level of living it is assumed they occupy easily.

Even with the largest and most prestigious firms, business-getting is an important part of the daily (and nightly) work. A partner's share of the firm's income depends on what business he has brought in more than any other factor, including his skill and effectiveness as a lawyer. Things have changed somewhat, but thirty years ago young lawyers looking for work were often told, "There's nothing so cheap as talent." The need to get and hold clients encourages a wooing and sycophancy utterly inconsistent with the dignity of the law. (The dignity of the law, fortunately, relies only in part upon the dignity of lawyers.)*

The word "client" has spread to other commercial activities, and its most recent meaning is its most debased. Even in the law, it denotes, to an unhappy extent, nothing more than customer. And nothing less: lawyers who accept that meaning also accept the postulate that the important client, like customers generally, is always right.

This is a poor state of affairs. It is not merely training and experience that the lawyer offers his client; there is also his detachment. He has a cool and distant perspective, and can see things clearer—not because he is always a clear-headed man, but because the problem is not his own. (The proverb tells us that a lawyer who handles his own legal problems has a fool for a client.) Partisanship and detachment are in no way inconsistent when the partisanship is professional, but financial dependence and detachment are not congenial. His objectivity is even more important in the lawyer's broader obligations. "The rules observed," I said a few pages back, marking the limits of the lawyer's singular devotion to the interests of this client. The limits are critical. The lawyer must be devoted at least as much to the law, to the interests of society. He is part of the judicial system, an officer of the court.

And so, like the judge, the lawyer ought to get his pay from the government. Such a proposal would at first provoke fiercer opposition than did tax-supported medical care in the American Medical Association; Medicare, after all, affects only part of a doctor's practice. But lawyers might be reminded, gently, that being officers of the court, they are by tradition in the service of the government. And in modern government—federal, state and local—a great number of lawyers are already public employees. As a practical matter, once the shock had worn off, the opposition would probably be less solid than that of the doctors;

---

* One result of the harsh economics of law practice is that a large proportion of those admitted to the bar do not follow their profession, and of those who do, another large proportion have income from activities that are mainly administrative or entrepreneurial.

there are impecunious practitioners who would stand to gain.

The idea would be attacked as radical and socialistic, but it would in fact be reactionary. The *patronus* did not charge fees for his advice or his advocacy. And the legal profession has never been entirely at ease with the way it earns its living. England and the United States differ on whether a lawyer may sue for unpaid fees and on whether contingent fees are permissible. (England says no to both.) Barristers' tailcoats still have a discreet pocket reached from the back, a vestige of the time when payment was made in a way supposed to keep the lawyer unaware of it.

The proposal would solve one of the acute problems of our legal system: how to provide counsel to the poor. The obligation has been recognized in criminal cases, and to a degree in civil cases. But the accused's celebrated right to counsel is less than it may seem. The energy and talent that Abe Fortas, the future Justice, devoted to the defense of Clarence Gideon is not commonly available to paupers. And in civil matters, the legal aid societies and the federal funds recently provided by the antipoverty program cannot come close to giving adequate service to all who need it. Moreover, it is not only the very poor who suffer. Every lawyer has had the excruciating experience of telling a client he must relinquish a just claim or yield to an unjust one because the client cannot afford litigation against a rich opponent. Contingent fees, a device to make payment easy, sometimes have unwholesome side effects; in any event they cannot help the poor person who is a defendant. And it is not merely cases that require the presence of a lawyer; it is often required where there is no case at all.

The law provides the structure in which we work and live. Our property and our incomes, as well as our freedom, depend upon the law; they are, in essence, no more than legal concepts.* Rights have a strange meaning when they cannot be en-

---

* The failure to acknowledge that the law creates property and income underlies the empty pronouncements we hear about government interference with free private enterprise. If the government, acting through the law, did not intervene at every moment, there would be no property. The government activities initiated under such labels as New Deal and Great Society, in relation to the effect of the law generally, are neither so new nor so great

forced; hence counsel must be available to everyone. The ability to pay fees is irrelevant to justice. That some people should be advised of their rights and represented in their enforcement while others are not—that some should have rights in fact and others have them only in theory—is a flat denial of law. It is therefore a crime.

---

as we tend to think. The rugged individual who damns the welfare state and wants to run his business unhampered would have to be rugged indeed. If the government were to take him at his word, he would lose his business to anyone with better muscles who decided to take it away. He could not even hire strong men to protect him; it is only the constantly intervening force of law that makes dollars worth anything.

It Seems There Were
These Five District
Attorneys . . .

MEMOIRS OF A WOMAN OF PLEASURE—THE TITLE
used by the author, and by G. P. Putnam's Sons two centuries
later, and by almost nobody in between—is better known as
Fanny Hill. When Putnam asked whether I would defend it, I
had never read the book. For that matter, I had not read *Lady
Chatterley's Lover* or *Tropic of Cancer* either, before the question of their defense came up. I may have been the only male of
my generation who had never seen any of the three. It appears
quite certain I was the only one paid to read them.

Memoirs is, legally, a more vulnerable book than the other
two. Had it been the first to be tried, the prospect would have
been hopeless. By the time it came to court, in New York, it had
the huge benefit of the *Chatterley* decision. It also had the huge
detriment of the New York *Tropic* decision. (*Tropic* was still a
year away from the Supreme Court.)

Fanny was vulnerable for two reasons. The first involves the
dual tradition of literary censorship. The cases, quite apart from
who wins, fall into two lines that are fundamentally distinct,
and in a sense opposed. Both lines involve the same statutory

prohibition, and the arguments of the prosecution are superficially the same. But the underlying objections are different.

One tradition is represented most prominently by *Ulysses* and *Tropic of Cancer*, the other by *Lady Chatterley's Lover* and *Fanny Hill*. For most people *Ulysses* and *Tropic* are not enticing; *Lady Chatterley* and *Fanny* are. In the one line of cases, the real complaint is that the books are offensive; in the other, that they arouse lust. In the one, public decency, rather than private morality, is at stake; in the other, it is sin, rather than the proprieties. The one book is attacked because it repels, the other because it attracts; the one because it disgusts, the other because it allures.

It is true that not a single word in *Memoirs*, standing alone, could possibly offend anyone. (Cleland's combinations, of course, are something else.) Bad words may be offensive, but different readers will give different answers to the question whether they add to or detract from sexual excitement. Most readers would be inclined to say Cleland did very well without the words. Their presence would have made a point for offensiveness (though it would not have been much of a point after the *Chatterley* and *Tropic* decisions), but it would hardly have added to the sin.

The taboo against illicit sex is much stronger and more deeply rooted than the taboo against bad manners. Where the book makes sex unattractive, the court is able to say that it will hardly affect anyone's morals. Thus Judge Woolsey concluded his famous opinion by disapproving the aphrodisiac and approving the emetic.

I disapproved of this approach and gave it very little scope even where it could be most telling—in the *Tropic of Cancer* cases. But whether I urged the point or not, it undoubtedly had its effect, and *Tropic*, though much rougher than *Ulysses*, was easier to defend than either *Chatterley* or *Fanny Hill*. As to these two, I felt obliged to concede—indeed, I asserted it before our opponents did—that the books were sexually stimulating. And from the point of view of those who contrived the antiobscenity laws, and whose drives now fuel their enforcement, the concession was damning; the worst thing you can do is make sex look good. *Fanny Hill* did this more than anything else the courts had considered.*

The other reason the book was so vulnerable was the general impression people had of it. In literature, as in life, Fanny did not have much of a reputation. Nor did her creator. In the literary world—most of whose members had read the book as avid adolescents and not since—as well as in the public estimate, it was disreputable. A 1961 treatise, whose authors were both learned in the field and liberal in outlook, used it as an example of the "deliberately and flagrantly erotic." One of our own witnesses was later to testify that the work was known as pornography—a classic of pornography perhaps, if that helped.†

When I read it I was surprised. Cleland, I thought, was a very good writer, and *Memoirs* a pretty good book. It has style and grace and wit, and when I recalled the gross and clumsy and witless volumes that help to stock our bookstore shelves, I was quite ready, in fact eager, to go to court.

The publishers, however, were influenced by the general attitude. They were, in my judgment, too defensive. They planned to publish *Memoirs* as "A Literary Curiosity." I persuaded them to be less diffident. It struck me as much more than a curiosity, and in any event I could not see that being curious refuted the charge of being obscene. The caption on the dust jacket was changed from "A Literary Curiosity" to "The Classic Novel about Fanny Hill"—leaving it to the courts to decide the category in which the work had achieved the status.‡

---

* Lenny Bruce, if he had wanted to win his cases, would ultimately have prevailed against his tormentors. In reality, offensiveness was the entire charge against him. Even though there was the additional difficulty that a performance rather than a book was involved, the value of his social comment and the absence of eroticism would have won for him on appeal.

† A past president of one of our most important bar associations telephoned me when the *Fanny Hill* case began and asked if I could lend him the book. He explained there had been a contraband volume in the Porcellian Club when he was at Harvard, but that he was never able to capture it. After he read the copy I sent him, he conveyed his gracious thanks and his sympathetic assurance that I had no chance of winning the case.

‡ I had not previously been Putnam's lawyer, and after the trial I asked Walter Minton, its president, why they had retained me. Minton said there were two reasons: one was the *Chatterley* and *Tropic* cases; the other

Fanny Hill was tried three times—in New York, in Boston and in Hackensack, New Jersey. The number of trials was pretty much a matter of the publisher's choice. Putnam, having seen what happened to Grove on *Tropic of Cancer,* decided not to indemnify the booksellers. Anybody who sold the book had to take care of himself.

Withholding indemnities does not, of course, insure against all legal expense. The publisher may itself be involved in litigation. If there is criminal prosecution, the case must be fought; conviction brings stigma, a fine for the corporation, and the risk of jail for its officers. If the authorities proceed by civil action, there is a choice: the publisher can accept an injunction where the action is brought, and write off that state as a market.

In New York, however, even a civil action would have to be defended. It was conceivable that the sale of a book forbidden in one place might go on elsewhere. But an injunction at the point of publication would make things difficult. Moreover, New York is itself a major part of the book market; the loss of sales would be by far the largest that a single adverse judgment could occasion. Finally, New York was Putnam's home and the center of the publishing world; in terms of morale, a surrender in the heartland is devastating. So if there was trouble in New York, the publisher would have to litigate.

On the assumption that we lost in the New York courts, we would try to get to the United States Supreme Court, and there the matter would be settled, one way or the other, for the whole nation. But suppose we won in New York. By throwing away all arguments based on state law, we might, as with *Tropic* in Massachusetts, induce the state court to give us a victory, if it gave us any, on strictly federal grounds. The opposition would then be able to go to the Supreme Court.

But even when a litigant confines his position to a single ground, he does not avoid the possibility that a court will rule in his favor on another ground. We might have a decision of little

---

was that we had several times met head-on when I represented authors he published and, he said, "I came away licking my wounds." I believe it was meant to be not a tribute to skill but a description of unremitting trucu-lence. This is a note to young lawyers on how to endear themselves to future clients.

use outside the immediate situation, and being the winner, we could not appeal. Besides, there is always the chance that a losing opponent will decide not to go farther, as had happened with *Tropic* in Boston.

In either of these events—a success based on state law or an opponent who decided he had had enough—the publishers would have a magnificent legal victory and a big practical problem. A New York decision against suppression would not stop prosecutors in other states. Unless the publisher were willing to give the indemnities and risk reenacting the Grove experience, the sale of the book might have to be restricted to the one state where it was cleared.

There was an intermediate course: the issue could be litigated in a few important states—important both for the prestige of their courts and for their share of the market. If the outcome in each case was favorable, prosecutors elsewhere might lose interest in the issue; meanwhile there would be substantial sales in these states. If the outcome in any of them was unfavorable, there would be an appeal to take to the Supreme Court.

Among the states right behind New York in pursuit of the book were New Jersey and Massachusetts. It was decided to turn and fight in those two jurisdictions, and to be careful not to sell the book in Chicago and Detroit and other hotbeds of morality. Hence the three concurrent cases on *Fanny Hill.**

New York did not keep us waiting. There was a 1941 act of the New York legislature that set up a special noncriminal procedure for the suppression of obscene material. The statute authorizes an injunction against any publication "of an indecent character." For the definition of "indecent character," it refers to Section 1141 of the Penal Law, under which Barney Rosset

---

* A federal case would have been preferable. For one thing, the decision of a federal court of appeals on a federal question usually has greater influence on a state court than the decision of the highest court of a sister state (though neither is controlling). For another, the chances of getting to the Supreme Court would be better; there would necessarily be a federal question. The government, we learned, had pondered whether to proceed against *Memoirs* and unfortunately had decided not to. This was consistent with its position on *Tropic*, although the renewed consideration of the subject indicated some feeling in Washington that *Memoirs* was a less defensible book.

and Henry Miller were prosecuted in Brooklyn. (As mentioned earlier, all these statutory epithets come down to the concept of the legally obscene.) *

The idea was to afford an alternative to criminal prosecution —an enforcement device that would not send anybody to jail unless he went ahead and sold the book despite the injunction. With the nice whimsy to which codifiers of state legislation are addicted, this eminently civil action is found in Section 22-a of the New York Criminal Code.

It is a book-burning statute: if the book loses, all copies must be surrendered to the sheriff, who "shall be directed to seize and destroy the same." Moreover, the statute encounters the "doctrine of prior restraint"—that is, the doctrine that there should be no prior restraint. Prior to the trial, the court may issue a preliminary injunction, which stops distribution while the case is going on.†

For these reasons the validity of the statute was open to question. In an effort to shore it up, the New York legislature provided that the defendant might have a trial within one day after joinder of issue and that the court must render its decision within two days after the conclusion of the trial.‡

---

* The "acquisition" or "possession" of the publication might also be enjoined. Ordinarily, it is distribution and sale that are the objects of official action. The fact that the statute also goes after readers is characteristic of the broad, sweeping, out-damned-spot spirit of legislation in this field. By way of comparison, consider wartime price controls, which never punished consumers, even though runaway inflation may be thought more of a threat to national survival than books about sex.

† Section 22-a says nothing about it, but the preliminary injunction is part of the traditional chancery suit for a permanent injunction, and the New York courts have construed the statute as implicitly authorizing provisional orders.

‡ "Joinder of issue" is the completion of the pleadings. Pleadings are the litigants' formal written statements of position. In modern practice, there are usually no more than three: the plaintiff's complaint, the defendant's answer, and if the answer contains a counterclaim (a request for affirmative relief against the plaintiff), the plaintiff's reply. Pleadings are supposed to state the basic facts—not the evidence and not the law—on which each party will rely. (The word "pleading" is commonly and incorrectly used to mean legal argument; in the law, it means only these papers or the act of preparing them.)

This, of course, contemplates an extraordinarily fast litigation; the procedure was designed to meet the charge that a preliminary injunction could cut off the sale at the outset and thus effect a prior restraint. The answer would be that if a restraint was imposed erroneously, it would not be for very long. A majority of the United States Supreme Court, speaking through Justice Felix Frankfurter, was impressed with the design, and the statute survived an attack on its constitutionality. (The decision came down the same day as *Roth*.)

The doctrine of prior restraint has a prestige it does not deserve. It plays a prominent part in the briefs of lawyers and the opinions of judges in First Amendment cases, and it has a considerable currency among laymen. The theory is that criminal punishment of dangerous expression (with the supposed safeguard of the jury system) is permissible because the word is already out, while legal restraints that operate in advance are abhorrent to the First Amendment guaranties.

The phrase "books on trial" has a fine rhetorical ring, and it is easy to feel noble when we allow anti-obscenity laws to act upon bad people and insist that books themselves must be kept inviolate. But in its final effect, a jail sentence after publication strikes at least as hard at freedom of speech as an injunction under a statute like 22-a. By and large, publishers would rather lose money than go to jail. If we consider only a single book, it may be argued that society's interests are served when the book comes out, even if the author or publisher is later punished. But if we consider the totality of expression, the jail sentence is the more baneful. Images of police and prosecutor, and prison itself, make a deep impression on authors and publishers, in no way

---

Pleading was a very fancy art in the old days. The plaintiff served his Declaration, to which the defendant, if he did not Demur, responded with his Plea. This might be followed by the plaintiff's Replication. The defendant might thereupon make Rejoinder, which was sometimes met by plaintiff's Surrejoinder. Defendant could then serve a Rebutter, and plaintiff a Surrebutter. The forms were rigid, and a failure to follow the form prescribed for the particular category of grievance was often fatal.

Pleading is still an art, but it is now a freer one, and the courts will allow lawyers to correct their mistakes; ordinarily, the principal penalty for poor pleading is a waste of time and effort (which can also be fatal, but less often is).

matched by the sporting risks of the civil suit; anticipation does the censor's work. Moreover, prior restraint by injunction is not the same as the licensing John Milton fought, which meant a total suppression at the source, with no judicial review whatever. Except when used to describe an *ex parte* order,* or administrative as distinguished from judicial enforcement, "prior restraint" is an out-of-tune rallying cry.

But these were not the thoughts that formed the basis of Justice Frankfurter's opinion. Instead he emphasized the importance of allowing legislators wide choice of method ("It is not for this Court thus to limit the state in resorting to various weapons in the armory of the law") and pointed to the provisions for speed in the statute: the interference with freedom, he said, is nearly negligible. But the legislative scheme for instant litigation is illusory. It is ordinarily impossible for the defender of a book to bring the case to trial in a matter of days. Most trial judges have had little experience with constitutional problems; a thorough briefing has more than its usual significance. And the people who can make good witnesses are not available on short order.

As to the quick decision the statute calls for, suppose the judge politely asks the parties whether he may have longer than two days. Does the lawyer assume that an overworked judge's natural irritation at being pushed will have no bearing on the outcome? And even if that assumption is made, the fact is (up to now, anyway) that the less thought a judge gives to the matter, the greater the probability he will decide against the book.

Justice Frankfurter, writing at a time in his life when he was not at his brilliant best, loaded his statement of the case. Although the question presented to the Supreme Court was limited to the constitutionality of the procedure, and had nothing to do with whether the publications were obscene, his opinion described the materials that led to the suit and referred to appel-

---

* An order made only after one side is heard. In some circumstances a court may act on the application of one party without giving the other an opportunity to oppose. The justification is usually some serious and continuing injury—a situation that gets worse with every passing moment and cannot wait for a two-sided hearing. In an obscenity case it would presumably be the headlong deterioration of moral fiber.

lants as "merchants of obscenity." It was none of the Court's
business. The issue was the validity of an enforcement
device—one that might be used, for example, against the writings of Sigmund Freud. The procedure, and not the character of
the books or the booksellers, was up for decision.

The case also presented the Justice with an opportunity to
express, as he did on so many occasions, his confidence in the
wisdom of state legislatures. In a sentence that expresses nostal-
gia for a curiously archaic legal concept, he said:

> If New York chooses to subject persons who disseminate ob-
> scene "literature" to criminal prosecution and also to deal
> with such books as deodands of old, or both, with due regard,
> of course, to appropriate opportunities for the trial of the un-
> derlying issue, it is not for us to gainsay its selection of reme-
> dies.

"Deodand"—adjective and noun—was part of the old common law. An animal or an inanimate object that caused the
death of a human was deodand. Under the law, it was forfeited
to the King, to be distributed in alms by his High Almoner—
"for the appeasing," says Coke, "of God's wrath." The word is
from *deo dandum*, "a thing to be given to God." Historically,
God got cheated. Whether deodands went to the Crown or, as
they did later, to the lord of the manor, their use for charitable
purposes was subject to the corruption of the centuries.

Although the English common law was imported into the
colonies and is the core of our legal system, deodands failed to
make it across the sea. They have never been part of our law, an
item with which to balance, say, the War with Mexico. But
corrupt or not, un-American or not, they are a splendid example
of unreason.

When the niceties of logic are applied to atavistic premises,
the results are garish. The law of deodand made distinctions as
to how much was to be forfeited. "Thus," says *Bouvier's Law
Dictionary*, "if a man should fall from a cartwheel, the cart
being stationary, and be killed, the wheel only would be deodand; while if he was run over by the same wheel in motion, not
only the wheel but the cart and the load became deodand. And

this, even though it belonged to the dead man." The widow and children have lost husband and father; it therefore follows that their cart and its contents must be taken from them. Taken from them and devoted (by the lord of the manor) to charitable purposes.

Blackstone, a true son of the eighteenth century, was romantic about reason, and his agile legal imagination could find reason even where it seems not to exist. Why should there be a distinction between the stationary cart and the moving cart, and the harsher penalty imposed where there is motion? Blackstone had a plausible answer: if the cart is in motion, chances are someone set it in motion. So negligence is involved, and the harsher penalty attaches because of the fault. This is a good idea, but not a true one.* The difficulty is that neither ownership nor control over the object that did the damage had any bearing on the legal outcome. If somebody stole your well-guarded sword and murdered a man with it, your sword would be forfeited. And the cart would be deodand even though the man who was killed was its owner and driver.

Probably the distinction is a product of anthropomorphism. A century later, Oliver Wendell Holmes, Jr., more logical than Blackstone, found a less logical basis for the concept. It was vengeance: deodand was institutionalized retaliation. Feelings of vengeance are not limited to human objects. Chairs over which we stumble get kicked; golf clubs that dub shots get broken. But the more an object moves, the more it resembles a living thing, and the more fitting the fury.

Blackstone's idea of where it began is disclosed in the opening sentence of his chapter: "In the blind days of popery. . . ." His historical view is foreshortened. Exodus, Chapter Twenty-one, verse 28, proclaims: "If an ox gore a man or a woman that they shall die, then the ox shall be surely stoned. . . ." And in this the Greeks were even more primitive than the Hebrews; the Greeks applied the concept to inanimate things. In Athens, under Draco's Laws, a statue that fell and killed a man was

---

* A good idea is fresh, ingenious and appealing. If it also happens to be true, it is a great idea. A great idea that has been around awhile is a truism. A while later it is a cliché.

thrown into the sea.* The practical Normans were at least careful to get the benefit of the deodand; the Crown, not the sea, would have the prize.

Horses, oxen, carts, boats, millwheels and cauldrons were the commonest examples. But as late as 1840 a railway train that killed a man was declared deodand. (The company was allowed to keep the train by substituting money—two thousand pounds.) It was just twenty-eight years later that reason had a further triumph in *Queen* v. *Hicklin*.

It was this primitive notion that came to Justice Frankfurter's mind when he ruled that the New York censorship statute did not offend the Constitution. The Justice might as well have held state legislatures empowered to provide that First Amendment questions be decided in trial by ordeal. (And Barney Rosset, caught in the welter of *Tropic of Cancer* litigation, might have felt that in truth they were.)

The Supreme Court majority, relying on the appearance of expedition in the statute, was unrealistic. The statute permits the publisher to proceed at a pace the courts cannot accommodate. But the doctrine of prior restraint, on which those who attacked the statute were relying, is not realistic either. Proceedings like that provided by Section 22-a are, on the whole, an improvement on criminal prosecution.

This was the statute under which the authorities moved—suddenly and powerfully. An action under Section 22-a may be brought by a district attorney or by a corporation counsel.† But

---

* In the fourth century B.C., in one of the speeches of Aeschines:

> We banish beyond our borders stocks and stones and steel, voiceless and mindless things, if they chance to kill a man; and if a man commits suicide, bury the hand that struck the blow afar from its body.

Holmes says Aeschines mentions this "quite as an everyday matter, evidently without thinking it at all extraordinary, only to point an antithesis to the honors heaped upon Demosthenes."

† In New York City and certain other cities, the chief legal officer for noncriminal matters is called the corporation counsel. The title comes from the fact that in legal form a city is a corporation. The concept of the cor-

to meet and destroy *Fanny Hill,* the guardians of decency sent out the corporation counsel and five district attorneys. There are five counties within the city limits of New York, and the district attorney of each of them joined in the action. Such a display of unanimity in a field marked by difference of opinion could hardly fail to impress a court. It was all the more impressive in that only one of these six officials had proceeded against *Tropic of Cancer.* For good measure, the New York City police commissioner filed an affidavit expressing his agreement and asking for an injunction.

The massing of forces recalled an earlier litigation. The recollection brought with it both a small shudder and a warming ray of hope. I had returned from a World War II military career that involved an education in how to fly an airplane, maximum exposure to the bureaucratic weirdness of the wartime army, minimum exposure to danger, zero glory and a net negative contribution to the war effort. On my return to civilian life, however, I encountered some serious fighting. I had been in the Office of Price Administration when I entered the service, and went back there after my discharge. My first assignment was a group of cases against most of the major oil companies. They were charged with violating price controls, and the cases were going on in various federal courts around the country. These great companies had staffs of "house counsel," lawyers on salary who form internal law offices for large business corporations. In addition, in each city, each company had on retainer a law firm, invariably one of the most imposing. Having evidently concluded that this double layer of high-priced legal talent (multiplied by the number of companies involved) was not enough, the defendants combined to bring in a specialist in oil litigation, somebody they evidently regarded as the champ. At the first few hearings, the parade of lawmanpower that pounded into court suggested a display of Soviet tanks crossing Red Square.

It was not that I was facing this legal horde unassisted; I had with me a recent graduate of Harvard Law School, very bright but not very experienced. He was a good four years younger than

---

poration was applied to ecclesiastical and municipal organizations long before it began to be used for business enterprises.

I and still had a trace of adolescent acne to certify his freshness at the bar.

The contrast turned out to be helpful. In their arguments, the defendants sought to create the impression that a powerful government agency, descended from the totalitarian New Deal, was persecuting patriotic businessmen who (Standard of Indiana, Texaco, *et al.*) were just trying to make an honest buck. The impression they in fact created was that a combination of powerful corporations was attempting to tyrannize a government reduced to sending boys to do a man's job. After they lost a few, the defendants got the point, and at the end they were represented (in court) by no more than a half dozen lawyers at a time. If we could do as well now . . .

The corporation counsel and the district attorneys started the action by moving for a preliminary injunction, which they did through an order to show cause. An order to show cause sounds like something more than it is. It is simply a motion, differing from an ordinary motion in that it is cast in the negative and comes on for argument sooner. The order directs the other side to show cause why the court should not do what the moving party is asking. But the other side has no greater burden of showing cause than when a motion is made in the regular way; it is still up to the moving party to convince the court it should act.

Newspapers frequently report the signing of an order to show cause as though it were a substantial victory. Ordinarily the only gain for the party getting the order is that his motion is heard three days earlier than it would have been. Occasionally, however, until the motion can be heard, the court will also put a stop to the conduct complained about. This temporary restraining order is a victory—a temporary one as its name indicates. But the order to show cause in itself has no effect other than to expedite the hearing of the motion.

The motion for preliminary injunction, toward which the corporation counsel's order to show cause was aimed, asks for a longer restraint—granted only after submission of papers and argument—that usually lasts through the trial.

In earlier 22-a actions, which involved various kinds of subliterature, the corporation counsel had obtained orders to show cause that included temporary restraining orders. But a higher court had frowned on the practice because of its *ex parte* nature. Accordingly, in our case, the corporation counsel departed from the traditional show-cause procedure; he gave us notice that he was going to ask the court to sign the order. This was intended to erase the judicial frown and refute the charge that the authorities were suppressing books without listening to both sides. The refutation was a little tinny. We got the notice late in the morning; the order, it told us, would be presented to the judge at two o'clock that afternoon. There was no time to prepare opposing papers. More important, since an order to show cause is granted or denied on the spot, the judge would have neither an opportunity to read the book nor time to consider the intricacies of the constitutional issues. If the order was to embody a temporary restraint, as the corporation counsel was asking, the court would be throttling the publication without giving the publisher any sort of a real hearing. This is exactly what happened.

At two o'clock the judge said he was not going to read the book: he could take the word of the corporation counsel and the five district attorneys that it was obscene. So while the plaintiffs' motion for a preliminary injunction was coming on, and while the judge (another one) would ponder it, and until the time when the motion would be decided, the publisher was enjoined from distributing the book, and the booksellers who were made parties to the action were enjoined from selling it—all without any judicial determination that the book ought to be suppressed.

Later a hearing on the preliminary injunction was held. The judge was a different one, but the result was not. A preliminary injunction was issued. *Fanny Hill*, the newspapers announced, was banned.

The ban, of course, would be lifted if we won at the trial. And at a full trial our chances would be better. But, it seemed, not much. There were a number of depressing elements. The Court of Appeals decision against *Tropic of Cancer* had come down, and the timing could hardly have been worse for *Fanny Hill*. The corporation counsel and the district attorneys started their action on July 8, 1963. On July 10 the *Tropic* decision was announced. The motion for preliminary injunction was heard on July 16 and decided on July 26. On August 20 the trial started.

As a matter of law, as I have said, *Memoirs* was harder to defend than *Tropic*. And aside from strict legal analysis, lower courts tend to follow what appears to be a trend in the higher courts. The general feeling now was that the Court of Appeals was opposed to "books like that." It would take an independent trial judge to go against the winds prevailing in the highest New York court. And independence apart, most judges of the New York Supreme Court were, as a matter of personal inclination, likely to be opposed to us. The decisions of the judges who had issued the temporary restraining order and the preliminary injunction were typical of the initial response of most members of the court.

These decisions were themselves an obstacle. "I find," said the justice granting the preliminary injunction, "that throughout its 298 pages, there is depicted in glowing terms a series of acts dealing with sex in a manner designed to appeal to the prurient interest. . . . The Court has considered the book as a whole in its impact on the average person in a community and I find that the book is patently offensive and utterly without any social value." This justice and the one who would preside at the trial sat on the same bench. Judges ordinarily do not like to overrule their brethren.

The extralegal considerations were no more auspicious. Political pressures were stronger than they had been. Mayor Wagner, during that July, had pledged to do something about "pornography." The mayor did not say exactly what he meant by the term. The Reverend Morton A. Hill of St. Ignatius Loyola filled it in for him. Father Hill said that *Fanny Hill* was an example. (The seemingly inevitable typo never took place; typesetters aren't what they used to be.) Later Father Hill went on a hunger strike, which ended only after the mayor designated Deputy Mayor Cavanaugh to head an anti-pornography drive.

Father Hill was not alone. Rabbi Julius Neumann, of Congregation Zichron Moshe, joined his fast. The flame, however, did not burn quite so pure for the rabbi; he hoped also to draw attention to Soviet anti-Semitism, which, he said, was "even more tragic" than the sale of pornographic books. These two clergymen worked together with the Reverend Robert E. Wittenberg of the Immanuel Lutheran Church. (The roster of religions was complete, an occasion if not for a Hallelujah at least for a Bingo.) They were all involved in Operation Yorkville, a group active in the anti-pornography struggle; the Operation exhibited a motion picture which showed what they were against.

My opponent in the case was Seymour Quel, one of the assistants to the corporation counsel. He was experienced, knowledgeable, courteous and—of chief interest to me—formidable. The trial was assigned to Justice Arthur Klein. Quel and I went to see him to work out a schedule. At one point during the conference the judge said, "I suppose I'll have to read the book before the trial. Do I have to be seen carrying that thing around with me?" This was mostly a joke, but only mostly.

Apparently Klein knew *Fanny Hill* and regarded it as not only notorious but embarrassing. Another depressing factor had been added. This did not mean, of course, that he would prejudge the case. But even the best judge cannot come to a trial with his mind *tabula rasa*. If he knows a book, or knows its reputation, he necessarily starts with some preconception—in this case that there was something shameful about the book.

Then we ran into difficulty getting witnesses. We had expected some difficulty, but not so much. In general, nobody wants to be a witness. For one thing, it takes time. There is the time spent in preparation, and the time spent in court. Courts do not make appointments to hear witnesses. In ordinary litigation in New York the lawyers hope to begin a trial on a particular date, but they may have to wait several days (because the last case took longer than the court estimated) and the witnesses have to wait along with them. And even when a trial is set for a certain day, it is not possible to forecast the hour when the turn of a particular witness will come, and so he usually has to be in court all day. Nor can it be said in advance whether the trial will last one day or two or three. It is not a matter of borrowing an hour or so, and the kind of people we wanted to testify were busy people.

But there is something more elemental, and even more of a

problem, than the sacrifice of time. Courts are scary places. Being a witness is a scary business. I will return to this in a moment.

In this case, being a witness would take a real devotion to principle. D. H. Lawrence and Henry Miller are literary heroes. There is more of a consensus on Lawrence, but if Miller's laurel is not bestowed by acclamation, he wins it by virtue of the intensity of those who feel he should wear it. A critic could only enhance his reputation by taking the bold but socially approved (in the society of letters) step of going to court for *Lady Chatterley's Lover* or *Tropic of Cancer*. *Fanny Hill*, in any view, is another story.

That we should have impressive witnesses was particularly important here, and we needed a number of them. D. H. Lawrence was so great a name that two experts—Malcolm Cowley and Alfred Kazin—were enough. More would have created an imbalance of argument. For Henry Miller we had offered a wealth of literary endorsement, some of it elevating him to the highest place in the ranks of literature. Moreover, *Tropic of Cancer* was considered Miller's most representative writing. His best book, most people thought.

Poor John Cleland. That last could be said about *Memoirs*: it was his best book. But this was only because he had done nothing else worth mentioning. He had published very little, and his one other novel, *Memoirs of a Coxcomb*, was terrible— not terribly shocking, just terrible.*

As far as documentary evidence was concerned, there had been no critical writing about the book for the first 214 years of its existence. It was mentioned occasionally, but only under the heading of pornography. Nor were the current reviews much help. On the contrary, the two most prominent were so strongly

---

* The writing in *Memoirs* is so clearly superior to Cleland's other work that it has been suggested it was written not by Cleland, but by his father, who was a friend of Alexander Pope's. Both extrinsic and intrinsic evidence, however—particularly its relationship to other novels of the 1740's—are such that *Memoirs* appears almost certainly to have been written close to the time it was published. Cleland was then about forty, and the hypothesis that his father was the author would involve an extraordinary instance of doing-the-boy's-homework.

against the book—one with some qualification, the other a ring-ing denunciation—that they were used by the corporation coun-sel. Other reviewers had some good things to say, but they all included a sentence or two that the opposition could make much of on cross-examination or rebuttal. And some reviewing journals ignored it altogether, possibly on the theory that there was no longer any news value, the original publication date of *Memoirs* having slipped by.

So the flesh-and-blood witnesses would by themselves have to carry the burden that in the other trials had been divided be-tween them and the paper witnesses. We needed people with authoritative names and strong sentiments who could express those sentiments in court. It is one thing to state a brave opinion at a cocktail party, where brave statements are so splen-didly orchestrated, or even in print, where your cross-examiners can only write letters. It is another to take an oath and state it from a witness chair, under the cold eye of the judge and the hot breath of the cross-examiner. And we needed more than two witnesses; two might be ticked off as eccentrics.

On the preliminary injunction we had submitted the affida-vits of Louis Untermeyer, Maxwell Geismar, Dwight Macdon-ald, John Gassner and Norman Podhoretz—an all-star group that evidently made no impression on the judge who decided the motion. But the decision was not due to any weakness in the affidavits, and our affiants would have constituted a fine nucleus for the trial. Unfortunately, none of them was available. Unter-meyer had gone to Japan, Geismar to the Adirondacks, a place just about as remote in travel time. Macdonald had testified in the Ralph Ginzburg trial, and in my judgment that appearance (which in all probability would be known to the other side) laid him open to cross-examination. Podhoretz and Gassner had commitments that stood in the way.

Walter Minton and I tried to get replacements. The bravest of those we asked, and the fairest as well, was Barbara Epstein, one of the two editors of *The New York Review of Books*. The thought of going to court alarmed her, but she agreed to do it. She also got in touch with John Hollander, who said he would testify. So did Eliot Fremont-Smith, Gerald Willen and Harry Karl. Some of these people have earned considerable recognition since that time, but they were then young and not widely known. Their testimony would be good, I thought, but their names would not impress the court. A week before the trial we still did not have the witnesses we needed.

Then three unexpected things happened. J. Donald Adams, in his "Page 2" piece in the *Sunday Times Book Review*, wrote a perceptive and favorable little article about *Memoirs*, and then offered to repeat in court what he had said in print. He would come in from his vacation. Morris Ernst lent a hand, and met with Adams on Martha's Vineyard. Then Louis Untermeyer unexpectedly returned from the Far East. Finally—and really finally, when the trial had already begun—Eric Bentley said he would fly down from Cape Cod.

Now we had a fairly strong list of names. The only question was whether they would give us a fairly strong line of testimony. If they did, there would at least be a respectable record on appeal. (As it turned out, we had in addition a witness we did not expect.)

All of them had read my trial brief, so they had some understanding of the legal background and the issues. But in two instances there was no opportunity for the usual preparatory conference without which a lawyer is reluctant to chance what the witness may say. I did not see Untermeyer until just before his turn to testify, and I did not see Bentley at all. The others sounded good in advance, but courtrooms are special, and fine forthright statements in the lawyer's office often become diffident quavers on the witness stand.

This phenomenon, I think, has a great deal to do with the privilege against self-incrimination that the Fifth Amendment grants us.* The clause states that no person "shall be compelled

---

* The Fifth Amendment also protects us from double jeopardy, from major accusation except upon indictment, and—the broadest of the rights in the Bill—from deprivation of life, liberty or property without due process of law. But it is the assurance that we will not be forced to condemn ourselves that has lately been heard of most, the phrase "criminal case" having been construed to cover proceedings outside court that might lead to prosecution, such as congressional hearings. "Take the Fifth" became part of the American idiom in the fifties, the numerologists apparently having taken over history.

in any criminal case to be a witness against himself." Its roots are commonly thought to lie in the use of torture to extract confession; the Star Chamber was only a century and a half gone when the Bill of Rights was appended to the Constitution. If the defendant's testimony may not be used unless he wants it to be, then the Star Chamber method is defeated.

But this was not all, I would think, that the authors of the Constitution had in mind. The privilege is a thin shield against a government bent on Inquisition. (Consider the Stalinist trials, where the induced voluntary confession, in terms of the Fifth Amendment, would be simply a waiver of the privilege.) But the Amendment has a value outside the context of tyranny. It defends against something less extreme than the rack and the wheel. Externally applied torture repudiated, torture remains in the situation. It is milder, and self-inflicted, but it is there— often intense enough to affect the demeanor of a witness and the delivery of his testimony.

In our daily lives, we learn empirically that a direct, unhesitating, easy response usually marks the honest man, while hesitation, averted eyes, a tremulous voice and a groping for words identify the liar. Testifying in court is different from everyday conversation. The honest witness may hesitate, look away, speak with a tremor and mislay his vocabulary (while the well-coached perjurer reels off his tale). Jurymen, however, are not often in court and cannot make the appropriate discount. And the defendant, the man with most at stake, is most likely to be disturbed and unnatural. Hence it is simply unfair to make him testify unless he chooses to.

Everybody, almost everybody, is nervous in court—inexperienced lawyers especially, and witnesses who are parties most of all. But even experienced lawyers feel a tightening when the court is called to order, and all rise, and from a hidden chamber the man in the black robe goes to his high armored place.

The lawyer may have had lunch with the judge the day before, but he looks different up there on the bench. ("Bench" is an outrageous misnomer; it is an imposing seat of power. "Throne" would be closer.) Excluding the dishonest witness, who has good reason to feel anxiety, and the unprepared lawyer, who may be more anguished, the uneasiness remains.

Parties, witnesses and lawyers are all about to be put to the test, and whatever their interests in the outcome, the intensity of their feeling usually goes beyond anything appropriate. There is a residue of malaise, a stirring of submerged remorse. Fears come boiling up that have little to do with the matter at hand —forgotten crimes of childhood reach close to the surface— when we encounter the visible and majestic embodiment of authority in the courtroom. We are confronted at once with the twin and awful powers to inquire and to punish.

The eighteenth-century lawyers who drafted the Bill of Rights must have been aware of this. They understood in a general way, I believe, what has become explicit in this century. A defendant-witness may give every indication of guilt, and these indications can lead him to be judged guilty, although the guilt he betrays (and which betrays him) may have nothing to do with the accusation that brought him to court, or with transgression of any governmental law at all.

Judges themselves have confessed to an anticipatory apprehension. And a judge will sometimes refer to his presiding at a trial—without any conscious punning—as his being "on trial." After all, he knows very well—though we may be confused— who it is inside that robe.

The pressures that bear on witnesses are a problem for litigants generally. We had some special problems—the high court's still steaming decision against *Tropic*, the paucity of witnesses to the eve of the trial, the strong opinion against us on the motion for injunction, the judge's hint of embarrassment and the infirmities of the book itself. The hot and sultry midsummer held a bleak and wintry prospect. About a week before the date of trial, I told Minton that it must be viewed, realistically, as an opportunity to build a good record for the appeal we would be taking.

The litigant at trial has two objectives. One is to convince the trial court; the other is to build a record for appeal. Their relative importance varies from case to case. In the present situation, it seemed pretty clear that we had to concentrate on making a record. Chances of winning in the lower court seemed to be roughly zero, give or take a percentage point.

But I spent most of the week writing our brief, and a lawyer working on a brief is in a sense singing in a shower; as the ideas come and the argument takes on tone and rhythm, it begins to sound good. You polish the draft and read your own paragraphs with a pleasured appreciation.

I allowed a discount for the shower effect, and still the brief seemed to make arguments that would be hard to reject—not impossible to reject, but hard, for a judge who wanted to act and sound like a judge. I revised my estimate; the trial would not be solely an effort to make a record. I told Minton I thought we had a ten percent chance of winning.

It Seems

There Was This

Country Girl . . .

THE TRIAL BEGAN WITH MY WAIVING OUR STATU-
tory right to have a decision in two days. ("Although the statute
gives the defendant the privilege of having a decision within two
days after the trial, the defendant in this case is willing to waive
that requirement. . . . Since the Court is faced with the making of a constitutional judgment of the most delicate and sensitive kind, we do not want that judgment to be hurried.") Then
came the opening statements. Normally plaintiff's counsel
makes his statement first, and after defendant's counsel speaks,
he has a chance to reply. Quel and I had arranged, however, that
the normal sequence would be reversed. Each of us thought he
had something to gain from the switch. I was thinking of the
opportunity to speak twice. No countervailing benefit Quel
might be thinking of occurred to me. (If it had, I might have
turned down the proposal.)

My opening statement was not an exposition of the law. The
judge had my brief. Instead, I talked about the ends that anti-
obscenity legislation is thought to serve, and compared them
with the objects of the First Amendment. Quel's opening statement was a response not so much to my opening statement as to
my brief. He reduced my construction of the *Roth* case to this:

Now Mr. Rembar takes those two sentences [in the *Roth* opinion], and he says what they mean is this: no matter how obscene something is, if it is not utterly without redeeming social importance, anywhere in the book, you cannot proceed against it under Section 22-a.

The *Tropic of Cancer* decision, he said, made it plain that the highest court of New York did not agree with my argument that there were three independent tests:

> Now I submit, your Honor, that that is not the view of the Court of Appeals. Mr. Rembar, in his brief, admits that it is not the view of Judge Scileppi, who wrote one of the two prevailing opinions in *People* v. *Fritch*, which is the [New York] *Tropic of Cancer* case . . . and Mr. Rembar admits that he [Scileppi] didn't accept this business that it has to be utterly without redeeming social value.

He added an argument that the Court of Appeals had not made:

> Only one other thing, your Honor. The reason why Mr. Rembar's tests, it seems to me, must be inapplicable, is because in the *Roth* case itself, where they were dealing with the question of obscenity, one of the documents as to which the defendant had been convicted, and as to which the conviction was sustained, was a book, and that book had a section in it on literary history. Now it is very hard to say that a discussion of literary history is utterly without redeeming social importance. Certainly it has as much social importance as anything you can find in *Memoirs of a Woman of Pleasure*. But that fact did not prevent the majority of the United States Supreme Court from affirming the conviction in the case.

I used my reply mainly to shift the court's gaze from the concept of obscenity to the concept of constitutional rights:

> MR. REMBAR: With all due respect to my brother, his last statement involves a serious misreading of the *Roth* case. The *Roth* case arrived at the Supreme Court on certified questions, which the Court noted had nothing to do with the specific material involved. The counsel for the defendants in those two cases attacked the statutes as being altogether un-

constitutional on their face—void—without any consideration of the specific publications involved. . . .

Now what is obscene, of course, at this stage, is merely the
obverse side of the medal of "not constitutionally protected."
. . . It is not quite right to say that our position is that
although a book is obscene, it may nevertheless be under the
protection of the First Amendment. Our position is that if it
is under the protection of the First Amendment, it cannot be
deemed obscene.

The opening statements completed, the city and the district
attorneys presented their case. As in the *Chatterley* trial, it was
simply the book itself. But Quel would have the right, if we put
in testimony, to call witnesses in rebuttal.

I made the routine motion to dismiss, on the ground that
plaintiffs had failed to prove a case; the motion was routinely
denied. It was really no more than a stance in opposition: yield
nothing (in this instance) and assert a great deal. Quel contended that one had only to read the book to see that it was
obscene; the ground of my motion was that one had only to read
the book to see that it was entitled to protection. I would have
been even more surprised than Quel if my motion had been
granted. It was now up to me to go forward with evidence.

Our first witness was J. Donald Adams. After he had been
qualified as an expert on literature, I asked for his appraisal of
the book. Quel then made one of the plaintiff's fundamental
points:

> MR. QUEL: If your Honor pleases, I object to that at this
> time, because, as I read the decision in the *Tropic of Cancer*
> case, the literary merits of the book are irrelevant to the de-
> termination of the question of obscenity.
>
> THE COURT [addressing Rembar]: Do you want to say
> anything about that?

The principal opinion in the New York *Tropic* case, by Judge
Scileppi, explicitly rejected the value test. Consider first, the
opinion said in effect, whether the book is obscene, and if it is
obscene, its literary qualities only make it more pernicious.
My brief pointed out, however, that though three judges of the
Court of Appeals agreed with Judge Scileppi that *Tropic* was
obscene, only one agreed with his statement of the law. Hence

Judge Klein was not bound by the Scileppi opinion, as he would
have been by an opinion that spoke for a majority.

While Quel was talking, I thought of an additional point,
one I had not made before. The thought was prompted by my
fondness for looking out the window. Outside this particular
window was the federal courthouse. The echelons of judicial authority are strictly observed, and the lower state courts must ordinarily follow the rulings of higher courts of the state. But perhaps this case was different. We were relying on the doctrine
that a court may refuse to enforce an unconstitutional statute, a
doctrine based on the judge's obligation to support the Constitution. State judges as well as federal judges have this obligation,
and the United States Supreme Court is the final authority on
how the Constitution should be read. This being so, would a
state judge not be free to disregard the higher state court if he
believed its decision conflicted with the Constitution as interpreted by the Supreme Court? And if the judge felt the Scileppi
opinion was inconsistent with *Roth*, was not that conflict presented? I had no precedent to cite, but it seemed a good idea; it
could lose us nothing, and at the minimum it would emphasize,
for Judge Klein, the organic, national nature of the issue he had
before him.

> MR. REMBAR: Yes sir. If the court please, I thoroughly dis-
> agree with Mr. Quel about the meaning of the New York
> Court of Appeals *Tropic of Cancer* decision—that group of
> opinions which constitutes the court's decision. I would point
> out that this court, as well as the court across the street,
> which is called the federal court, has taken an oath to support
> the Constitution of the United States; that we have involved
> here a federal constitutional question; that on that question,
> with all due respect to the court in Albany, the Court in
> Washington is the final arbiter; that the decisions of the
> United States Supreme Court have made it very clear that
> expert testimony on the value of the book is admissible in
> cases of this type, and that—I submit finally—Mr. Adams has
> certainly qualified as a literary expert.
>
> THE COURT: The objection is overruled.
>
> MR. QUEL: I respectfully except.*

---

* The taking of an "exception" is a rite derived from ancient appeal

THE COURT: You may answer the question, sir. Do you remember it?

(The question with which the court concluded was a courteous one, seriously intended. It was also, necessarily, slightly comic— a reminder of what happens to a witness's concentration while the lawyers are arguing over a question put to him.) In permitting Adams to answer, Klein was rejecting the Scileppi view, at least for the time being. Whether he would accept mine was another matter. His ruling could have meant that he considered literary testimony relevant but not controlling—that he might balance literary worth against the degree of obsceneness he found in the book.

Allowed to testify, Adams, who had been the editor of the *Sunday Times Book Review*, made an excellent witness. His standing, his style and the cool and honest dignity of his answers all contributed. He described *Memoirs* as "to some degree, a work of art," and compared it to the drawings of Hogarth; like them the book "gives a social picture of the period which, I grant, is exaggerated at times, but is a realistic picture nevertheless." He mentioned "ancient Greek vases" on display at the Metropolitan Museum; these, he said, depicted "men, often with their sexual organs in a state of erection, the same sort of thing that is described in a book like *Fanny Hill*."

Adams said Cleland was a gifted writer, though not a great one. We then went into contemporary community standards:

Q. Mr. Adams, as an editor of perhaps our foremost literary periodical, I assume that you see and read a great many of the books that are currently published and have seen and read a great many of the books that have been published during the past decade; is that right?

---

procedures. The treatises tell us that at the present time it has two purposes: to make it clear "that the party unfavorably affected by the ruling is not satisfied" and to "preserve the precise terms of the ruling" for the appeal. The first purpose involves the assumption that lawyers are made happy by adverse rulings. The second assumes that what the judge has said somehow gains clarification if the lawyer says "Exception." Some states, including New York, no longer require exceptions, though the habit lingers. Others permit them to be taken wholesale. A few, like Massachusetts, still clutter their records with repeated orisons of the magic word.

A. Right.

Q. Would you say that the limits of candor that have been established by books of reputable and respected authors that are sold through the normal channels of book distribution—would you say that those limits of candor are exceeded by the book which is the subject of this action?

A. By no means. I think there are books being freely distributed in which there is a greater degree of what you referred to as candor.

He mentioned, as an example, James Baldwin's *Another Country*—a good choice because of the respect accorded the book and its author.

THE COURT: Let me interrupt you. I don't see the need, frankly, for mentioning other books and giving them, perhaps, undeserved publicity. There are newspaper reporters here who will probably quote this witness, as well as mention names. . . .

MR. REMBAR: I might say, your Honor, that if, in an attempt to arrive at a just solution of this very grave question before the Court, it is necessary to give certain books publicity, I am afraid that that will have to be done. However, I would like to allay your Honor's fears with respect to the book that has just been mentioned.

THE COURT: I have no fears. I don't know anything about it.

MR. REMBAR: It is already a best seller. Its trade book distribution has been completed. It is now available in paperback. I am sure that nothing that Mr. Adams will say will increase its sales, which are already considerable, and my purpose in directing these questions to the witness is twofold. One is to establish the literary merit, which I think, under the social-value test, entitles this book to free publication. The other goes to another test, a test which the Supreme Court has announced, that involves contemporary community standards, and I think it is important for this court to know—this court, after all, like these lawyers [there was a gesture taking in all the lawyers present, including me] cannot keep up with everything that is published; we have people here whose business it is to keep up with what is published and who can tell us what the community generally tolerates with respect to works of literature.

I am not, at this moment, speaking about the trash we see on newsstands. I am speaking only about respected books of reputable authors, and I would like to introduce a few of those books, because I think it is important that they form part of the record.

THE COURT: All right, I will overrule the objection and permit the testimony, but frankly I don't know the purpose of introducing these books in evidence, because I hope you don't expect me to read all these books. I have a problem, just reading this one, with all the work that I have to do, as you know.

Adams made some further comparison of *Another Country* and *Memoirs*, and I offered the Baldwin book as evidence. There was a long argument, which ended with Klein's refusing to accept any books (other than *Memoirs*) but permitting our witnesses to describe them. This, of course, was a satisfactory outcome, but the contest itself had only a collateral significance. No matter what were used as measures, there was small chance that a court would say *Fanny Hill* went no farther than currently accepted literature. The primary purpose of my arguments and the testimony on contemporary standards was to make *Fanny Hill* seem just a little less shocking, and to make the courts a little more receptive to the only theory that was apt to save the book—the value theory. For this purpose, the testimony of distinguished witnesses was more effective than a judge's direct comparison of our book with the others.

Adams now concluded his direct testimony:

Q. Mr. Adams, in the book which is the subject of this case, do you find any philosophical or moral values?

A. Yes sir. It interested me very much that in contrast to much that is published today in the field of fiction—I won't name any specific titles—Cleland makes a distinction, through his chief character, Fanny Hill, between sexual relations on a purely animal level and sexual relations which are reinforced by the feeling of affection, or love. He places one distinctly on a higher level than the other.

Now if that is not moral tone, I don't know what moral tone is.

MR. REMBAR: Thank you, Mr. Adams.

THE WITNESS: Enough?

Quel began the cross-examination by reading a description of *Memoirs* from the corporation counsel's affidavit on the motion for preliminary injunction. He asked whether Adams agreed with it. The affidavit was cast in language gleaned from opinions in earlier obscenity cases:

> Described in lurid detail are repeated, meticulous recitals of sex acts, including acts of sexual perversion, set forth in a style which is a blow to the sense of the reader, and for the evident purpose of teaching the reader about sin of impurity and arousing him to libidinousness. In its two hundred ninety-eight pages, the book describes in detail instances of lesbianism, female masturbation, the deflowering of a virgin, the seduction of a male virgin, the flagellation of male by female and female by male, and other aberrant acts, as well as more than twenty acts of sexual intercourse between male and female, some of which are committed in the open presence of numerous other persons, and some of which are instances of voyeurism.

The affiant himself yielded to no man in point of luridity. Quel then asked Adams:

> Do you agree or disagree, and if so to what extent, with that definition? . . .
> A. I do, up to a point, because—
> Q. What point?
> A. Because, let me say this, that the heroine, if you wish to call her that, or the chief character, views these sexual aberrations with disfavor. She looks upon them with distaste. They are repugnant to her. The normal sexual relation is not, and I see nothing impure in the sexual act itself, and that statement used the word "impurity." There is nothing impure about sexual love between men and women.

Quel went into the specific incidents described in the book and was at pains to show the pleasure in them. He made the point that Fanny did not disapprove of everything she experienced. There was then a dispute about a piece of paper:

> MR. QUEL: Your Honor, I have prepared here a list of the pages in this book which I deem objectionable and within the purview of this case. I realize that this particular paper has no evidentiary value—it is simply my summary of the book—but

rather than cross-examine the witness in detail as to the incidents which I have set forth here, I would like to give him—I
would like to mark this for identification, give him a copy of
it or give him the original—and ask him whether he agrees
with the accuracy of this summary of the book. Otherwise it
is a matter of my going through it incident by incident, and I
want to save some time. I will be glad to show it to Mr.
Rembar.

THE COURT: Let me understand your point. What are
these, pages which you consider erotic or—

MR. QUEL: No, not—

THE COURT: —obscene or objectionable?

MR. QUEL: No, no, pages that describe certain incidents. It
will be easier, perhaps, if your Honor looked at it.

THE COURT: I have read the book, as you know.

MR. QUEL: Surely, I know that.

THE COURT: What is your purpose in asking him—you
want to ask him whether—

MR. QUEL: Whether that is accurate, rather than go
through it page by page.

THE COURT: Mr. Rembar will concede probably that it is
accurate.

MR. QUEL: Fine, if he will—

MR. REMBAR: I will concede without checking it; I rely on
my brother to have made up an accurate list. My question is
relevancy.

I referred to the Scileppi opinion, which though it had not undertaken to abrogate the whole-book rule, had painstakingly collected individual passages:

MR. REMBAR: Despite the opinion of Judge Scileppi, a majority of the Court of Appeals holds that—this includes the
concurring judges—that you may not consider isolated pages
in a book.

MR. QUEL: I agree with that.

MR. REMBAR: Therefore I object to this list as meaningless. Your Honor, in reading the book, can make up his own
list. The book speaks for itself, and this adds nothing to the
case except to point in the direction that the Court of Appeals and the Supreme Court have disapproved.

MR. QUEL: There is no question you have to consider the

book as a whole; this is simply a summary of the various incidents.

THE COURT: I will accept it. You don't even have to offer it in evidence. Perhaps you might submit another memorandum, and you can include that in your memorandum.

MR. QUEL: All right, I will. I will give your Honor a copy now.

THE COURT: If this will obviate the necessity of a brief, I will take it.

The judge was agreeing with me that the paper was not evidence. It could be submitted in a memorandum (in this context, a synonym for "brief"), but that could not have been what Quel was after; his present brief already contained much the same list, and a brief is only argument, not proof. Apparently he had wanted the enumeration of passages to gain the status of evidence. The judge continued:

Do you want to ask this witness any more questions?
MR. QUEL: Yes. Yes, I do.

What Quel was so eager to get to was the John Ciardi piece on the book that had appeared in the *Saturday Review*. He read large portions:

"I am not well disposed, let me say, to banning any book. I believe that parents who have reared their children in sympathy, and yet within a sense of this world as it goes, have nothing to fear from what the children read. And it is always likely—it seems, in fact, certain—that any statute framed to suppress pornography will be used to suppress the work of serious writers. It is, I believe, socially irresponsible to let moral indignation bring about statutes that cannot, by their nature, be responsibly phrased to cover all cases. The only consequence of such statutes is that the good will be damned with the bad—a clear affront to the legal principle that it is better for a hundred guilty persons to go free than to punish one innocent person. These, I submit, are ponderable reasons for opposing legal censorship of any sort, and I must take them to be sufficient. But to the specific question 'Is the *Memoirs* a pornographic book?' I can give only one answer. It certainly is: It was written as such, it has had a clandestine history in which all scholars have held it to be such, and such it is today and will be to the dark end of time's last bookshelf."

Q. Do you agree with that, Mr. Adams?

A. That would—

MR. REMBAR: With what part, may I ask?

MR. QUEL: Then let the witness say.

A. That would depend upon what definition you gave to pornography or what it means to one. There is a whole business of what is obscene, and so subjective, what makes the obscene to me may not to you; to some people some passages in the Bible are obscene. We all differ in our reactions. I am quite well aware that statutory definitions of what is obscenity may differ from personal definitions, but I am not a lawyer; I am concerned with my attitude toward what is obscene, your attitude, again the reader's attitude.

Q. Excuse me, Mr. Adams, but the word which was used in this review was "pornographic." Do you agree?

A. They are closely allied.

Q. Do you agree that the book is pornographic?

A. What do you mean when you say it is pornographic?

MR. REMBAR: If the Court please, counsel is now asking the witness for a legal conclusion.

MR. QUEL: All right, I will withdraw that question.

I had discussed the many meanings of the words "obscene" and "pornographic" with our witnesses, and told them that a witness may insist on having an ambiguous question clarified. The meaning counsel for the prosecution usually have in mind, when they use these words, is "illegal"—obscene within the language of the statute. But that, naturally, is a conclusion of law, and witnesses may not be asked for their legal opinions. Quel went on:

Q. I would like to read to you another page from Mr. Ciardi's review and ask you whether you agree with this: "With all scholarly details in place, however, and with all incidental stylistic merits recognized, the book still remains an overt piece of pornography. It was conceived and written with no intent but to titillate the reader by ringing the sexual changes in minute (and yet evasive) detail, the author's catalog of sexual variations being limited only (and considerably) by his own lack of imagination. (He might at least have read

the classics and given Roman substance to English manner-
isms.) With Cleland's theories of sexual encounters there is
no effort to depict the lives of men and women seriously. The
details of sexuality are, in fact, suggestively exaggerated. The
seeming naïveté of Fanny's memoirs is not the result of simplicity but is an artful coloration of the tone, clearly designed
to heighten the suggestiveness of the sexual narration. And
the author himself could not have begun to believe that life
in a London brothel was remotely as he described it."

A. I can't fully agree with that because there is very
marked characterization in Mr. Cleland's work and I did not
notice that the first time I saw the book, but when I read it
more carefully in this edition I became aware of that, that he
several times characterizes people in a very interesting way,
and that is why I say he is a writer of some merit, not only for
that, but for the picture he gives of the morals and manners
of the period. They are sometimes exaggerated, I admit,
and—

THE COURT: Mr. Quel, whose review is that?

MR. QUEL: John Ciardi in the *Saturday Review* of July 13.

THE COURT: July 13.

Q. Do you recall offhand, Mr. Adams, any of these
characterizations of Cleland that you were referring to?

A. I would have to see the book. I have been struck several times by what I thought was clever characterization.

Q. You don't remember any particular one?

A. Not at the moment.

MR. QUEL: That concludes my cross-examination.

Having begun with an older, eminent witness who might not
remember all the specific passages, but spoke with authority, I
decided I could now take a chance on a younger and flashier
one. John Hollander, poet and assistant professor of English at
Yale, had said some very good things in my office, but even there
he seemed nervous. The effectiveness of his statements, naturally,
would be diminished if the manner of their delivery indicated
uncertainty or diffidence.

So I felt some tension when I called him. He, apparently, was
feeling more. I had been watching him solicitously (solicitous,
of course, for the case, not the witness). Waiting his turn, he

suffered visibly. The day was hot, and the courthouse was not air-conditioned. The courtrooms had majestic windows, but construction was going on outside, and for the sake of audibility they had to be kept nearly closed. Hollander was sitting in the first row of the benches beyond the bar, most of the time with his elbows on his knees and his head in his hands. On the floor between his feet, directly under his chin, was a tiny pool of sweat.

But once he took the stand and began to talk, his tension disappeared. So did mine. Hollander reacted like the anxious athlete after the first pitch is thrown or the first tackle is made. His testimony was splendid. (It was also garbled in the transcript. Hollander talked fast and used a number of words that are not too commonly heard in courtrooms. Afterward, hours were spent in translating his part of the record.)*

During the time that I was asking the qualifying questions, I decided to give Hollander his head:

Q. In order to save the time of the court, instead of asking you these various questions specifically, I will ask you to give your opinion about the literary merit, the historical significance, the psychological values that may be found in this book.

MR. QUEL: I object, your Honor, for the reasons stated in my objection to a similar question to Mr. Adams.

THE COURT: Objection overruled.

MR. QUEL: Exception please.

A. Am I to proceed? *Fanny Hill* is a very remarkable book indeed, I think. It is, after all, one of the few novels that are really novels written in English before the middle of the eighteenth century. . . . It is very much in the tradition of

---

* There is a tendency to attribute finality to documents that can be called official. Many people have the impression that what the official court stenographer puts down is necessarily the record. It is, only if no one makes a successful objection. After the trial either side may suggest to the other that there are mistakes in the transcript. Usually the mistakes are corrected by agreement. The lawyers recall what was actually said, and their recollections generally jibe. If they differ, a motion may be made for the correction of the transcript, and the judge will decide whether the stenographer was accurate or, if he was not, what in fact was said.

the eighteenth-century novel, and what he has done is to set out and from the very beginning—may I quote, your Honor? Thank you. From the very beginning I think it is apparent that this book is going to be a record not merely of the life of the senses but to a very considerable degree of the life of the mind.

Fanny says in her very opening remarks, on page 29 in this edition, that she had learned—she had "exerted more observation on the characters and manners of the world than what is common to those of my unhappy profession, who looking on all thought or reflection as their capital enemy, keep it at as great a distance as they can, or destroy it without mercy."

Fanny, the narrator of this book, certainly does not look upon thought or reflection as her capital enemy, as I think it is incredibly obvious throughout the book. She is constantly applying her intelligence and insight to the narration of her exquisitely sexual adventure, and she is capable of observations not only about life and manners, for example, about the relationships between peoples, specific sexual impulses and their characters, and other ways; even physiognomy comes into this . . . she makes it very clear, I think, that the two most admirable characters in this book are entrepreneurial people. This is a book that refers to the world of middle-eighteenth-century London; it is a time in which the very roots—well, more than the basic roots, the trunk and the branch, the bottom branches of modern industrial capitalism —are beginning to be seen for the first time, and what she does is to present a view of the world which is that of the entrepreneurial man, the self-made man.

Her older protector at the end of the book, the man who virtually is responsible in a sense for making her the kind of character she is rather than a completely mindless sort of sensualist, the man she refers to—although he isn't named in the book, but he is her benefactor; indeed he leaves her with a considerable amount of money—he is said to be a rationalist of pleasure. This is a term we might expect from a French eighteenth-century philosopher. This man and also I believe the rather more favorable of the two bawds for whom she has been employed at various points in the book, these are really the two very admirable figures for her because they are both self-made. They are both not of the aristocracy, but rather of the bourgeoisie, and she reinforces this view at several points in the book when she claims that the whole notion of sensual gallantry is not merely an aristocratic province. . . .

Now she is saying that of course a possibility for a range of feeling and a possibility for the heightening of one's feelings because one is intelligent is possible for all sorts of people. In a sense it is a very democratic possibility as well as being a very sentimental and sweet one, and her constant sense, I think, that feeling and knowledge, that feeling and intelligence, are not enemies of each other but rather go to enhance each other is a doctrine of the Enlightenment—of that part of the development of Western minds in the eighteenth century which is called the Enlightenment—and I think it is an extremely healthy attitude. . . .

After commenting on Cleland's style, Hollander concluded with what he called a Jamesian passage in the book, "obviously written by somebody that thought with a great kind of humanistic skepticism about the whole domain of human sexuality and human experience in general."

I will read it out loud now: "But, as the main affair was now at the point the industrious dame had laboured to bring it to, she was not in the humour to put off the payment of her pains, but laying herself down, drew him gently upon her, and thus they finish'd, in the same manner as before, the old last act." Now this is what I call a remarkable passage—

THE COURT: I didn't hear you, what did you call it?

A. This is what I call a remarkable passage, this is certainly not the kind of thing that somebody would want to put in a book if he were only interested in grossly stimulating the sexual desire of the reader, because it is a reminder, I think, in that phrase "The old last act," of the whole idea of what the ancient Romans called the notion of *post coitum triste*, the notion there is a kind of inevitable sadness that does follow all human sexual experience, and certainly if there were only a desire on the part of the author of this book to excite the readers and do nothing else, he would stay a million miles away from such notions as that. . . .

One might say she lies, in English literature, halfway between Defoe's Moll Flanders, who is a very self-seeking sort of person without any kind of sense of sensual refinement, and James Joyce's Molly Bloom, who is in a sense at the other extreme. I think Fanny is a character, is a great female char-

acter in English literature, and she does in a sense lie somewhere along the literary genealogy of these two people.

MR. REMBAR: Your witness, Mr. Quel.

I disagreed with parts of what Hollander said; as evidence,
though, it was magnificent. The rush of thoughts snarled some
of the sentences, but it gave the testimony the tone of a heart-to-
heart talk. Now confident of his ability to maintain his position,
I delivered the witness to his cross-examiner.

Quel began by challenging the comparison with Henry
James; the association seemed to jar him. Then, having brought
in Ciardi on the cross-examination of Adams, he brought in
John K. Hutchens on the cross-examination of Hollander. Quel
read a portion of the Hutchens review:

"The presence on these premises of Mr. Quennell, an
eminent English student of the eighteenth century, attests to
the present publisher's design to cloak Fanny in an unfamiliar respectability. Mr. Quennell makes a game try as he goes
about attributing to Cleland's erotic classic a degree of 'elegance and energy,' 'undoubted historic value' and even 'a
definite literary appeal.' The publisher too offers a prefatory
note, pointing out how far in advance of his time was Cleland's insights into the psychology of sex.

"There is a little something in this although if you could
get a subsidy from one of those rich foundations you might
enjoy a long, profitable career before you found anyone who
ever read Fanny Hill's memoirs for any of the above noted
reasons."

"Do you agree with that?" he asked. Hollander, alert to the cue
in the objection I had made on the cross-examination of Adams,
pointed out that several different things were said in the passage
quoted, and suggested they be taken up one at a time. Quel took
them up one at a time. Hollander found that he could not agree
with any of them.

Quel then got to the jacket copy of the book, and brandished
the word "priapic." Hollander engaged in an erudite tour de
force:

Q. And what does priapic mean, Mr. Hollander?
A. Phallic.
THE COURT: What does it mean?

THE WITNESS: Phallic.

Q. I will read from *Webster's New International Dictionary*, second edition unabridged; I couldn't find priapic, but I found priapism.

A. Well, no, don't. Priapism doesn't mean the same thing; priapism is a physical nervous disease.

Hollander was now a thoroughly relaxed witness. Indeed, he was no longer in the witness box; he was back at Yale.

Q. Wait a moment. One of the definitions of it is: a lewd act, image, et cetera, also indecency, debauchery.

A. This is a definition of priapic or priapism?

Q. Of priapism.

A. That wasn't the first definition of it.

Q. The first definition was a medical definition.

A. Yes, that is what I thought.

Relegated to the runner-up definition, Quel continued:

Q. . . . I am taking the second definition.

A. Yes.

Q. Doesn't priapic mean the same thing?

A. No, not—no. Priapic refers to phallic worship, the god Priapus, also the Roman god, the phallic god, and these representations of him are just that.

Q. You are talking about Priapus, the god?

A. Yes, about Priapus, and priapic, which is the adjective form from Priapus, would mean phallic. I think what Mr. Quennell means by calling this a priapic novel is his reference to—and I think he is very explicit about it in his own point to the Introduction—to the hyperbole, the overexaggeration, in the description of the male sexual organs in this book. This is—I call it hyperbole, which is the literary term used for exaggeration—there is hyperbole of sentiment, and there is hyperbole of physical sensation, just as when Fanny, almost quoting a well-known epigram of Plato, said, at one point, "I wish I had a hundred eyes to see you with instead of merely two."

Q. That is what I meant to indicate, that the book is one which deals predominantly with sexual intercourse in its various forms?

The pedagogue reborn was patient with new students:

A. No, that is not what I would take priapic to mean. Mr. Quennell is a man of vast vocabulary, and he singled a word out because, I think, he meant a particular thing by it.

Quel moved to Ciardi:

Q. For example, do you agree with his statement that the book is unquestionably pornographic?

A. I don't know how Mr. Ciardi used the term "pornographic." Many people use it in many different ways. Pornographic means literally, from the Greek, *pornos* plus *graphein*, writing about whores; that is all the word means. . . . Certainly in the broadest sense of the word this book is pornographic, but so indeed are vast sections of the Old Testament, et cetera. I obviously don't need to go into that. I don't know what he means by a pornographic book in this sense. We all use the word; a lot of us use it in very different ways. In one sense I can clearly agree with him; in another sense I cannot. . . .

Hollander had left all his nervousness in that little pool of sweat.

The court announced the noon recess.

In this half-day of trial one thing had been made plain: whatever the judge's personal feelings about the book might be, he was resolved to treat the issue as one of law, and to decide it according to what he believed was required by the Constitution.

I went to lunch with Untermeyer; we had not had an opportunity to talk about the case before.

When the trial resumed, we offered such book reviews as we had; they weren't much. (Useful reviews came out after the trial.) I chose this particular time for the offer in order to make a point of what Quel was doing with the pieces by Ciardi and Hutchens.

The theoretical purpose of the "Do you agree?" cross-examination is to explore and challenge the testimony that the witness gave on direct. Actually, however, it is often used to bring to the trial court's attention, and to make part of the record for the appellate court, material that would not otherwise be admissible. The tactic in reality violates a fundamental concept about evidence, but it has been accepted for a long time and Quel's use of it was entirely legitimate. Nevertheless, the effect was to put adverse reviews into the record at the same time that Quel was opposing the direct introduction of favorable reviews. To emphasize the anomaly, I made an argument I knew would be rejected.

> MR. REMBAR: In his cross-examination of defendants' witnesses, Mr. Quel has referred to and read portions of two book reviews, one by Mr. Hutchens, one by Mr. Ciardi. Since these passages have now become part of the record, I would like to offer as evidence a group of other book reviews that have been published since the publication of this book, and which have to do with this book.
>
> MR. QUEL: I object to that, your Honor. It is well recognized that when you are cross-examining an expert witness, you can quote from other works or books and ask him his opinion, but that does not mean that on direct testimony you can put other reviews in.
>
> THE COURT: You are absolutely correct. . . .

I then moved to the better reason for the admission of our reviews:

> MR. QUEL: If he is withdrawing that—
>
> MR. REMBAR: I am not withdrawing it.
>
> THE COURT: He is not withdrawing it now. He is not offering it now either, but I understand what he is going to do, if he does offer them, will be simply to offer them, rather than call those people as witnesses.
>
> MR. REMBAR: I offer them on the authority of *Grove Press* v. *Christenberry*, the *Ulysses* case, *Smith* v. *California* and other decisions, which have held that published reviews are competent evidence on the subject of literary value.
>
> THE COURT: The same as these witnesses that you are calling, of course. On that theory, I will permit them.
>
> MR. QUEL: I object to that. It gives me no opportunity to cross-examine. If he can go out and get book reviews and just put them in, by the same token, I can go out and get statements of people, never bringing them to court, and just put them in. The whole purpose of a trial is to both examine and cross-examine.
>
> MR. REMBAR: There is a little difference between private

statements and published reviews. We have letters sent to us by distinguished people. I am not offering them, because I realize that the objection that Mr. Quel has now made is well taken as to that. But it has been established that what has appeared in publications with respect to a book, what has appeared in newspapers and magazines as book reviews, is admissible.

MR. QUEL: I don't think so, your Honor. I am not objecting, in fact I do not object, to your Honor's taking into account a general community standard, which is one of the things that your Honor must determine. But to put in a favorable book review without producing the author of that book review deprives the defense of an opportunity to cross-examine, and I object to that.

THE COURT: I am going to overrule your objection. . . .

As things turned out, I never used the hard-won opportunity. The testimony had begun well; I decided to wait before offering our meager documentary evidence on literary merit. The testimony finished stronger than it began; I concluded that offering the reviews could only dilute its strength.

Quel's objection to our book reviews—there was no need for him to expound his reasons—went to both relevance and competence. He was saying that literary evaluations had no bearing on whether a book was obscene, and he was also saying the reviews were hearsay. The latter can use some explanation. Hearsay is the repetition of what someone else has said, and it is ordinarily not considered evidence; the law wants no second-hand information. For one thing, stories change in the telling, and to find out what happened we ought to hear it from somebody who was there. For another, if the words we are asked to believe are those of a person not in court, there is no way of testing his honesty or his capacity to observe.

The hearsay rule is simple enough in its affirmative statement, but it is laced with exceptions. An utterance, for example, that could only have hurt the man from whose lips it fell—a "declaration against interest"—is likely to be true, and hence may be repeated in court by one who heard it. Again, a witness may testify about a "dying declaration"—a statement made when death seems sure and near. The accepted rationale is that a man about to meet his Maker will be careful to speak the truth; a better one, if we are to include atheists, is that he may as well tell the truth because he will not live to have the profit of lying.

The hearsay rule applies also to written evidence (again with a number of recognized exceptions): the document is not its writer, and a piece of paper will not answer to cross-examination. The judge was not meeting Quel's objection when he said the book reviews I never offered would be admissible because they were the "same as these witnesses that you are calling, of course." They were the same so far as relevance was concerned; they were not the same in point of competence. In other cases, where I was pressed harder, I argued that since the purpose of the hearsay rule was to avoid untested statement and distorted translation, reviews constituted another exception: there could be no distortion on the printed page; and as to the untested statement, it was safe to assume that professional critics and scholars were not going to offer the public something other than their best judgment. (Occasionally I made another argument—that the reviews might be admitted not as proof of what they said but merely as proof that they existed, so that hearsay could not be involved at all, and the very fact that the book received reviews in reputable journals demonstrated that it was taken seriously as literature.)

Untermeyer was the next witness. He was described by Susan Drysdale in her report of the trial for *The New Statesman* as "the brisk, dapper little poet." Judge Klein evidently regarded him as something more. Courteous to all the witnesses, Klein treated Untermeyer with a special respect; possibly he had attended a high school that used his anthologies.

Untermeyer began by explaining that his first name was pronounced Looie, not Lewis. He then summarized, smoothly, what he called the virtues of the book: the skill and elegance of the writing ("I speak now as a writer, as a craftsman. It's an enviable piece of work"), its value as a historical document ("a picture of a fringe, and a rather wide fringe if history is to be relied upon, of the eighteenth century"), and its success as a novel ("at a time when novels were fairly few. . . . They are living people, and of course Fanny, to me, is a very definite living person. I may not approve of all of her acts, but I don't approve of the acts of all of my friends, either").

When Untermeyer had finished his summary, I decided to try to draw testimony on something we had not covered during lunch. I wanted to have a critic say that treatment, not subject matter, distinguishes a work of art; this would support my argument that there is no subject matter forbidden to the artist.

You may not lead your own witness on direct examination, and asking him questions in an area not previously discussed can be hazardous—particularly where your thesis depends on a distinction that a flat, nonleading question may fail to suggest. There is risk enough when you know the witness is familiar with the point; if, as here, the idea is one that for all you know may never have been part of his thinking, it is even riskier. The witness may not understand what you are after and give you no response; he may try to guess, and this can make things worse. I might have stopped to discuss the point with a witness still to come, but since the trial seemed to be going well I did not want to break its rhythm and lose momentum by asking for a recess. And Untermeyer's testimony up to now indicated that he was likely to say what needed to be said. Whether he would have, unaided, became unimportant. Outside assistance arrived in the form of an objection from Quel:

Q. [by Rembar]: Would you say that in this book the act of sex forms the subject matter of a piece of literature, as distinguished from a situation in which the act of sex, the depiction of the act of sex, is the sole object of the person writing the material?

MR. QUEL: Your Honor, do I have a continuous objection to this line?

THE COURT: No, I am going to surprise you, and I am going to sustain your objection, because here again, sir, this is something that I am going to determine myself, whether in fact this book depicts the act which you are discussing in a fashion different from what you say other books do. . . . But I don't think I am going to permit you, sir [now addressing Rembar], to compare it with acts, let us say, of sex, or other acts, and the manner in which it is depicted in this book, because this is something I will determine and can determine very easily, simply from reading the book.

MR. REMBAR: Would you not agree, your Honor, that whether the particular subject matter, say war, forms the material for a work of art, as distinguished from a situation of pure reporting—would you not say that that is a question on which a qualified literary critic can speak? Let us not think of sex for the moment. Let us think of the act of war as treated in, say James Jones's *From Here to Eternity*. Is there not a difference between that and a newspaper account of a particular battle, and is not this witness qualified to say whether that difference exists, and in what it consists?

THE COURT: Do you think, sir, that this witness is better qualified to make that determination than the court? This is not something that comes within his purview as a literary critic. If it does, I will permit it.

MR. REMBAR: I think that that is a literary judgment.

THE COURT: You mean, the manner in which this is written? I will go so far as to say that you are probably right there too. . . . I am going to overrule counsel's objection. . . .

After first sustaining the objection, a ruling reasonable enough when the necessarily naked question was considered, the court, having heard arguments, now ruled that the question should be permitted. And the argument had served the purpose of a pretrial conference with the witness. A lawyer may not tell his own witness what he is trying to get at, but this is exactly what he must tell the judge when the other side claims that his question is not relevant. We proceeded:

Q. You heard the question, I believe, as I phrased it for the court?

A. Yes, I did.

Q. And I would simply like your response to it.

A. All right. I will use your same image, or metaphor, or symbol, if you will. *The Naked and the Dead*, of Mailer, and *The Thin Red Line*, of James Jones, are both about war as a central subject, but what they treat of is human beings in the act of war, human beings in their response to war.

In other words, what is interesting in those books is not the taking of a hill, a victory or a defeat by a group of men, but it is the men themselves, how they react to it, and I feel very much the same way about the *Fanny Hill* book—that what is interesting to me in the book is not merely the description of the sexual act, which I have read before, but the reaction of the people toward it, and the variations which are played upon this central theme, which to me sum up, come to, a work of art, of literature.

On cross-examination Quel again invoked Ciardi and Hutchens; Untermeyer, like the earlier witnesses, was unable to agree. Quel asked Untermeyer, as he had asked Adams and Hollander, whether "particular instances" in the book were pornographic. Adams had said he did not know what the word meant. Hollander had said the book was pornographic only in the literal sense of the word. Untermeyer was willing to give the word a somewhat broader meaning:

A. Mr. Quel, it would be very hard for me to define pornographic, even in my own mind. I think I would say that pornography is what is written in the men's room in the subway. I don't think that pornography can be that generally applied to descriptions of the sexual act, if it is done with any kind of, I say, decency.

I mean, I may approve of the sexual act, but I also may approve of an artistic portrayal of it, the way we do in paintings or sculpture.*

Q. Mr. Untermeyer, you don't mean to imply that unless something is written in the men's room in the subway, it couldn't possibly be pornography?

A. Would you say that again?

Quel reached for the Ciardi review. Untermeyer said he had read it.

Q. Just to refresh your recollection, would you just glance at the last one, two, three, four paragraphs from where I have got the check mark (handing paper to witness)?

A. Yes, I remember reading them. I remember at the time disagreeing with him.

Q. You disagree entirely with this review?

A. I often disagree with Mr. Ciardi on other matters.

Q. I don't doubt that, but I am just talking about this one.

A. I particularly disagreed with him on this one.

---

* An interesting converse of Ring Lardner's "He was a weak hitter but he couldn't field."

Quel persisted; he wanted to know the specific parts that Untermeyer disagreed with.

> Q. Now what about the part "And the author himself could not have begun to believe that life in a London brothel was remotely as he described it"? How about that?
>
> A. I would answer I don't know the author. I don't know what he had in mind. I couldn't speak for Mr. Cleland. He may have done it as an active exaggeration. He may have done it as a kind of heightened reportorial—I wouldn't know how to answer that.
>
> Q. But haven't you an opinion as to whether he really believed that or believed that he was accurately portraying the details of it?
>
> MR. REMBAR: I don't think there is any question about what went on in the mind of an author over two hundred years ago that is at all appropriate.
>
> THE COURT: He can answer if he knows.
>
> A. I will be very glad to answer. . . .

His answer was that he didn't know.

On redirect examination I tried to meet Quel's point about the exaggerations in *Memoirs*:

> Q. Mr. Untermeyer, is the device of exaggeration employed by writers?
>
> A. It is a very well-known device. In poetry, it has a fancy name, called hyperbole, which nobody can really spell nor even understand. Of course, it is a well-known device. It is a device which is used not only in literature, but in practically every other form of art, the elimination of certain details, and the exaggeration of others. This is perfectly well known.
>
> Q. You will say, then, that a writer can tell you something about a situation, a time and age, a society, even though he exaggerates?
>
> A. Certainly.
>
> Q. You were also asked some questions about what the author of this book may have had in mind. As a literary critic, which do you think is more significant, the writer's intent or the writer's product?
>
> MR. QUEL: Well, if your Honor please, I object to that. I think this is irrelevant. I asked that question in my cross-examination because I was directing it to a particular state-

ment in another review, which said, in effect, that it was not an accurate portrayal.

MR. REMBAR: We didn't introduce that statement, your Honor. It was introduced on cross-examination.

THE COURT: For whatever it may be worth, I will overrule the objection and let him answer.

MR. QUEL: Exception.

A. The very simple answer—what is important, of course, is what the writer does, what he leaves behind him, what he says, what is on a piece of paper, a manuscript or a piece of print, not his intention.

Next came Gerald Willen, assistant professor of English at Hunter College. He spoke about the structure of the book, advancing the proposition that it is a novel of development, continuous rather than episodic. On cross-examination, back to Ciardi:

Q. . . . Do you agree with Ciardi's statement that the book is pornographic?

A. Well, I don't know what the term "pornography" or "pornographic" means. If the term should be defined, I would be able to give you an answer.

THE COURT: Well, you define it in your own mind, whether you think the book is.

MR. REMBAR: Your Honor, if I may say so, if he defines it in his own mind, he doesn't know whether he agrees or disagrees with Ciardi. Ciardi may have something else in his mind.

THE COURT: I will sustain the objection.

Quel then went to Hutchens's comments on Putnam's motives ("the present publisher's design to cloak Fanny in an unfamiliar respectability"):

Q. . . . My question on that is, Do you agree or disagree with that?

A. I disagree with it.

Q. What part of it do you disagree with?

A. I don't think the publisher has done anything for the book except to publish it.

Apart from a bit about the structure of the novel—"any novel consists of scenes; it is just a question of how the scenes are put together"—the rest of Willen's examination (cross, redirect and recross) was devoted to the book's descriptions of sexual aberrations. (Quel had chosen the word "aberrant," and I stayed with it; it seemed to me the least loaded of the several terms prosecutors had used for variations from the sexual norm.) It was important to the case—psychologically, rather than legally—that Fanny's disapproval should be shown. The questions and answers began to fly in various directions.

> Q. [by Mr. Quel]: Well, Mr. Willen, will you agree with me that except in the instance of flagellation, there is no express disapproval of any of those acts which I have mentioned?
>
> MR. REMBAR: Two [instances of disapproval] were mentioned on direct examination, Mr. Quel, of flagellation and homosexuality, both explicit.
>
> MR. QUEL: Where do you find a rejection of homosexuality?
>
> THE COURT: Whom are you asking now, the witness or Mr. Rembar?

The general subject of law enforcement became part of the literary analysis:

> Q. [by Mr. Quel, of Mr. Willen]: Where in that paragraph is there an explicit rejection of homosexuality?
>
> A. She calls it an infamous passion, for example.
>
> Q. Where is that?
>
> A. On page 257, third line, and then the fifth line, that "There was a plague spot visibly imprinted on all that are tainted with it, in this nation at least, for that among members of that stamp whom she had known or at least were universally under the scandalous suspicion of it, she would not name an exception," et cetera, et cetera.
>
> Q. Now Fanny is stating what Mrs. Cole told her?
>
> A. Yes.
>
> Q. Do you find any acceptance of Fanny of that statement, or the accuracy of it?
>
> A. She accepts the statement but rejects the practice.
>
> MR. REMBAR: May I direct the witness's attention to the paragraph immediately preceding that, in which Fanny Hill

is giving her own reaction, rather than that of Mrs. Cole?

MR. QUEL: As I read that paragraph, Mr. Rembar, she is just describing the scene that she witnessed.

MR. REMBAR: She wants to have them arrested; that is how she feels about it.

Quel had apparently missed this in the book. Or perhaps he found it difficult to accept—or at least to remember—a passage in which Fanny Hill and the police seemed to be on the same side of an issue. He continued:

Q. Do you see in that immediately preceding paragraph any desire upon Fanny's part to get anybody arrested?

A. Well yes, indeed. "The criminal scene they acted, I had the patience to seek to an end, purely that I might gather more facts and certainty against them in my design to do their deserts instant justice."

Q. What did she do about it? Did she have them arrested?

A. She was heartily—

Q. Did she have them arrested?

A. No, she didn't. But since we are dealing with thoughts; she wanted to have them arrested.

I wondered whether Quel felt relieved that the miscreants were not in fact arrested.

The next witness was Eliot Fremont-Smith, called to testify about the part sex plays in contemporary literature. Fremont-Smith, not then known as a critic, was a member of the editorial staff of the *New York Times Book Review*. From that post he necessarily saw what was current in literature, and could speak generally about books that are respectably published and seriously received. His testimony went not to value, but to community standards. As a witness, Fremont-Smith combined youthful earnestness with a tone of authority. His testimony was that the degree of candor in *Memoirs* did not exceed that in many current novels—the degree, that is; quantity was something else.

Fremont-Smith's testimony ended the first day of trial. It had been, I felt, a good day. I told Walter Minton the odds had changed; I was now quoting them at only three-to-two against.

That night Eric Bentley, phoning from Cape Cod, said he would come down the next day but that he could not arrive first thing (and if a Cape fog closed in, he would not arrive at all). From our telephone conversation I expected Bentley would be a strong witness.

I planned to make him our last witness. The record, I felt, was about right on literary value. Further testimony would probably not add much, and there is always the possibility that another witness may diminish the force of earlier testimony, or blunt a point already made. (So far, none had.) Moreover, there is the critical matter of locating the line that separates the judge impressed from the judge fed up.*

We started the second day of trial with Minton, hoping that his tenancy of the witness chair would last until Bentley showed up. It was important to have the publisher as a witness not so much for his testimony as for his presence. The publisher's failure to appear might be taken, logically or not, as a reluctance to stand by his book.

We used Minton's turn to record Putnam's high reputation. Quel was willing to concede the fact. I was unwilling to accept the concession, unless it was made very much a concession indeed:

> MR. QUEL: If your Honor pleases, I object to that [a question about what authors Putnam had published]. I concede that Putnam has been in the publishing business for a long time, and they have published many authors, but I think that is sufficient, and I object to anything else.
>
> THE COURT: Would you make a concession to go further? Evidently this is to show they have published books by well-known and prominent writers.

---

* Stopping with Bentley would have the collateral benefit of relieving Barbara Epstein of a task she expected would be disagreeable. (She was there all along though, and ready, and I would not have been considerate of her feelings if we needed another witness.) Harry Karl was also in court and would be more disappointed than relieved at not having to testify, but I had decided that one more literary witness, and only one more, would make the right number.

MR. QUEL: Yes certainly.

MR. REMBAR: I want to go a little further, your Honor. In the opinion of Chief Justice Warren of the United States Supreme Court, the conduct and character of the particular publisher is more important than the particular book. Now whether it is more important or not can be argued, but the character of the publisher is certainly relevant. And Putnam is not merely an old firm; it is one of the most respected publishing firms in the United States. I would like to establish that through testimony.

MR. QUEL: I object to that, your Honor.

THE COURT: Are you going to call anybody else to testify to that effect?

MR. REMBAR: No sir.

THE COURT: At this point?

MR. REMBAR: No one else.

THE COURT: Then Mr. Quel is willing to concede, not only that this is an old firm and that it has been in existence for one hundred and twenty-five years; it is reputable, it has published books by the best authors, and I would assume, Mr. Minton, you would not deny, that perhaps some of them were not so good?

THE WITNESS: A few.

THE COURT: Why do you want to go into the names of these people? If you insist, I am going to let you do it, but it would seem to me what you are up against here, Mr. Rembar, is that then you will have to have me determine that these authors, whose names you are going to mention, are the best authors. Since he is willing to make that concession, why put the court to the test of determining whether whomever he may mention as an author is one of the best? Although I must say that I think I might be in a position to judge that.

MR. REMBAR: Do we have a concession that Putnam is one of the best and most reputable publishing firms in the country?

THE COURT: Well, I think he will concede that Mr. Minton would so testify, if you asked him that.

MR. QUEL: Yes, I will agree that Mr. Minton would so testify.

MR. REMBAR: I want a concession as to the fact.

THE COURT: What he is conceding here, I think, is what you are trying to prove.

MR. REMBAR: He is not. He is conceding only that Mr. Minton would so testify. Either I want a concession as to the fact, or I want an opportunity to prove the fact.

MR. QUEL: I am not too clear about this. It seems to me that, assuming that this book is obscene as we contend, it does not make any difference whether it is put out by the most reputable publishing firm in the world or by some fly-by-night organization.

THE COURT: I would not agree with you on that, Mr. Quel, but let us go a step further, and taking Mr. Rembar's statement at its face value, that Judge Warren has indicated that in a case of this kind, reputation and type of a publisher is important, I would think that is so. What he wants you to concede now is that G. P. Putnam's Sons, which is the publisher of this book and the defendant in this case, is a reputable publisher.

MR. REMBAR: Is among the most—

THE COURT: Has published some of the finest writers in existence today.

MR. REMBAR: And over the past century.

MR. QUEL: Yes, I concede that.

MR. REMBAR: All right, thank you.

We went into editorial procedures and book distribution to show that publication of *Fanny Hill* was part of Putnam's regular course of business. It was handled as a book, not as an exploitation item; the only thing that set apart its distribution was the unusual number of orders (unexplained) from colleges and libraries. The reasonably chaste advertisements went into evidence.

The cross-examination of Minton was long and bad-tempered, on both sides. Quel was a large and solid man, sober and steady. He had been courteous to all the witnesses. His voice occasionally achieved some volume, but his temper was even. Minton put a few curls in it:

Q. . . . . Now in what sense was the word "priapic" used in the jacket cover on this book?

A. I would suggest the best way would be to summon Mr. Peter Quennell from England and ask him. I can't tell you in this instance in what sense he used it, exactly. I would suspect, if I might look at your definition, I might puzzle one out.

Q. On your suggestion that we summon Mr. Quennell (handing papers to witness), you published this jacket, didn't you? When I say you, I mean Putnam's?

A. Putnam's published it. We had considerable interchange of letters with Mr. Quennell about the writing of the introduction and attempting to make everything perfectly clear. I must confess that one word, that one word, that did not enter my mind, or that we did not bring up specifically with Mr. Quennell, was the word "priapic." I assume he did not mean that this was a book such as a book about a lost weekend.

Q. Well, Mr. Minton, don't you understand words when you publish them?

A. Not every word we publish, no sir.

Q. You publish a lot of words you don't understand?

A. Not a great many, but a few. . . .

Q. In your opinion, is it a pornographic book?

A. Pornographic is a word that has acquired meanings that are not in the original. If you mean it in the classic sense, let us go back to our dictionaries. . . . This is literally writing of or about harlots, harlotry, whoredom or prostitution. In that sense certainly this is a book which is pornographic. It also has acquired secondary meanings of obscene. Do I think it is an obscene book? Obviously I wouldn't—

MR. QUEL: No, no. Now, your Honor, I move that that be stricken out.

THE COURT: I think that he is going on. You have asked him now whether he thought this book was pornographic—

MR. QUEL: That's right.

THE COURT: —so he said according to the strict definition of the word it is, but he says that there is a secondary meaning of the word, and as to that he doesn't—

MR. QUEL: He started off on something else. As to obscene, I haven't asked him about that.

THE COURT: No.

MR. QUEL: It is not within his province to decide that question.

THE COURT: The objection [motion to strike] is overruled.

MR. QUEL: Exception.

* * *

Q. What about Mr. Ciardi's statement in the fourth paragraph from the end to the effect that—well, suppose I read to you parts of it.

"The details of sexuality are in fact suggestively exaggerated."

Do you agree with that?

A. I would agree with Mr. Untermeyer's statement yesterday, if you remember—

Q. Please, please, Mr. Minton—

A. Yes.

Q. Do you agree with Mr. Ciardi's statement?

A. I think that they are exaggerated.

Q. I am again reading from Mr. Ciardi's review.

A. I would like to add, if I might, to this—

Q. Now, please—

A. It is the function—

MR. QUEL: Your Honor, I move that that be stricken out.

THE COURT: All right.

MR. QUEL: This witness is trying to take over the examination.

The cross-examination at times ranged far afield:

Q. . . . Do you know many people who have read it prior to its recent publication?

A. Yes sir.

Q. So far as you are aware was it prescribed reading in any English course in any college?

THE COURT: How do you spell prescribed, with an *o* or an *e*?

MR. QUEL: That is a good question. I spell it—

THE COURT: I suppose you don't know of any? I don't know myself where it was prescribed reading in a college. Do you know of any case?

THE WITNESS: I know that it is not prescribed but it is mentioned in courses. . . .

One of the myths propagated by television and the movies is that a witness may be forced to answer "yes" or "no." It entails, of course, the foolish presumption that all questions are capable of yes or no answers. Here again the law is less mysterious than people suppose. The cross-examiner's thundering demand for the monosyllabic response may or may not be justified, and may or may not receive the support of the court. Indeed, there are situations where the appropriate answer is "Yes and no." Minton is a man less subject than most to the influence of myth:

Q. Didn't Doubleday-Doran refuse to handle this book?
A. That is a very interesting case.
Q. Yes, but would you please answer my question yes or no?
A. Yes and no. Now, can I explain?
MR. QUEL: Your Honor, I move that the answer be stricken out and the witness be directed to answer.
THE COURT: If it can be answered, answer it. If it can't be answered, you don't have to answer it.
THE WITNESS: It can be answered, and the answer is yes and no, because at first Doubleday, when we first asked them, said they did not think they wanted to give us an order at the present time. They then examined the book, my understanding is that George Hecht, who is the vice-president of Doubleday—
MR. QUEL: Can we have that stricken?
THE WITNESS: (continuing) —read the book, and they gave us an order.
THE COURT: They gave you an order. I see that they are one of the defendants in this case, or they were.
MR. QUEL: Yes, but we discontinued.
MR. REMBAR: Mr. Minton says at first they wouldn't, and then they said they would.
THE COURT: Of course. Let's move along.

Quel recalled Minton later for some further cross-examination. The mood carried over:

Q. Were you aware of the fact that in a review published, I believe in 1953, Ralph Thompson had characterized the book as "tediously and bewilderingly pornographic"?
A. It was not 1953. I believe it was in the 1930's, and I believe that you are reading, as you have done several times before, and then gotten mad at me when I pointed it out to you, you have read part [Minton came down hard on the word "part"] of what Mr. Thompson said.
MR. QUEL: Your Honor, I don't know how to handle these admonitions from the witness.

Despite the irritations, or perhaps because of them, Minton's testimony was good. On direct examination he supplied the data about the publisher and the publication that we wanted. On cross-examination he scored some points, and he didn't get hurt. Neither did the record.

Bentley came into the courtroom while Minton was testifying and took the stand immediately after Minton finished. He did not disappoint my expectations: his testimony was concise, and worth setting out in full:

A. I have just read the book for the first time, and—just once—it is still fresh in my mind. It struck me as an interesting and mostly enjoyable book. The interest that it had for me was, it seemed to me the author had a very challenging and far-reaching idea, and it was this—

MR. QUEL: Would you talk a little louder, please?

A. I am sorry. The idea I got from the book which I have just read was this, that there are two situations in ethics and morals in Western civilization as we know it. The one—I am simply trying to be quick—one is called pagan and consists of the enjoyment of the animal part of our nature, and the other is ascetic, having much to do with Christian tradition generally.

That the author's notion was through the example of sexual activity to arrive at some middle ground between these two extremes, one of which simply accepted the animal and the other is ascetic, having much to do with Christian ideas. One said that's good, and the other of which said no, that's bad and we are against it. And the compromise he arrived at was arrived at, as I say, in this way: he wrote a little parable of a girl, it is a traditional parable actually—

MR. QUEL: I am sorry; well, I will come closer, maybe I can hear him better.

A. He wrote this parable which I call the parable of the prodigal daughter. This is of the country girl who goes through the whole pagan experience of what the Bible calls riotous living—it is a phrase in the New Testament. The conclusion, however, is not the pagan conclusion, or else Fanny would just remain the same at the end and say these physical experiences were wonderful and completely satisfying, and that is it.

But this is quite different from the book which Cleland wrote, which is essentially a romantic love story, the love story between Fanny Hill and the man called Charles. Her conclusion is that there should be a synthesis of these two traditions, that while passion is good, it is even better to have a pure love with it, and her conclusion is—this you could either call the synthesis of the two traditions or a middle ground between them; either way, it is not one and it is not the other.

The idea is stated, I think, very boldly and resumed on the last page of the book. That is what I got out of it. I found it a very interesting, stimulating book.

Although what Bentley meant was pretty clear, no ambiguities should be left in the record—that is, no ambiguities that might work against you. "Stimulating" is a word that had appeared frequently in opinions in obscenity cases, and not in the sense in which Bentley used it. It was time for me to interrupt:

Q. I take it that in this particular sentence you are using the word "stimulating" in the sense of intellectually stimulating?

A. Yes. [Short pause.] Well, all good books are emotionally stimulating too.

The phrase "emotionally stimulating" could cover the emotion of lust. To a court, however, the connotations of "emotionally stimulating" and "sexually stimulating" were not the same.

He had covered content; how about style?

A. That took me aback at first; that is, I was very surprised from all the gossip to find the extreme elegance and artificial character of the book. As something of a technician in these fields it had a special interest for me, and that was this, that verbalizing this kind of material, even any verbalizing, sets it at a certain distance because we don't normally confront this material in words, but in action. But to verbalize it in words of considerable artifice and elegance in a tradition of prose which I am familiar with, English literature of the seventeenth and eighteenth century, this was essentially Cleland's idea, to set it at a further distance, so you have this very peculiar experience when reading it, that you try to think of the experience direct, that is one thing, but he actually doesn't invite you to do that, or he even stops you from doing that, by putting this double veil between you and the material, first the veil of the extremely elegant and indirect style, what he calls the indirect style in the passage, I notice, where he speaks of his own way of writing.

MR. REMBAR: That is all.

Quel began his cross-examination:

Q. Mr. Bentley, I believe you said you had just read the book recently?

A. Yes.

Q. Had you ever heard of it before?

A. Yes.

Q. Was it a prescribed reading when you went to college, as far as you know?

Bentley had evidently been a conscientious undergraduate:

A. No, or else I would have read it.

Then came the do-you-agree phase. Bentley's responses had a nice economy:

Q. Do you agree that the book is erotic?

A. Yes.

Q. Do you agree that it is pornographic?

A. No.

Q. Have you read John Ciardi's review of the book?

A. I have been listening to your reading it; that's all.

Q. Would you glance, particularly, at the last four paragraphs?

A. Yes. I get the idea.

Q. Do you agree or disagree?

A. I disagree with most of that.

Q. Well, let me take a sentence or two. "The details of sexuality are, in fact, suggestively exaggerated." Do you agree or disagree with that?

A. I don't understand the force of "suggestively." I agree with "exaggerated."

*   *   *

Q. You have heard me ask various witnesses about Mr. Hutchens's review?

A. Yes.

Q. May I direct your attention particularly to the two paragraphs starting from where I have the check point there, which I have read to the other witnesses.

A. Yes. I have read it.

Q. Do you agree or disagree?

A. I disagree.

Q. Let's take a specific part of it. Do you recall the first of those two paragraphs refers to "elegance and energy," "undoubted historical value" and so forth? "There is a little something in this though if you could get a subsidy from one of those rich foundations you might enjoy a long, profitable career before you found anyone who ever read Fanny Hill's memoirs for any of the above noted reasons." Do you agree or disagree?

A. I disagree, because I read it for those reasons.

Q. You mean, you think they could find you without engaging in a long profitable career?

A. That is right.

Q. Do you know other people who have read it for that reason?

A. Yes.

Q. Do you know other people who have read it for other reasons?

A. Yes.

Q. Would you agree that the vast majority of people who would read this book would read it because of its eroticism?

A. I couldn't give an opinion on that.

Bentley was our last live witness. There was still some documentary evidence I wanted to put in. Not the book reviews; I had decided not to use them. The evidence I now offered went not to the value test, but to the prurient-interest/community-standards test:

MR. REMBAR: As the court knows, there is reference in our trial memorandum to the fact that in newspapers of recent weeks there have been reported, not as fiction but as fact, stories in which the incidents of this book are curiously paralleled, and indeed heightened; that is, we have submitted that in these newspaper stories the acts of aberration, to which counsel for the plaintiffs has drawn attention on this trial, are more extreme than in the book which is the subject of the trial. The purpose of our calling attention to this is that if what is objected to in the literary work is put before six million readers every day in the form of factual reporting, it can hardly be said that this book can do any harm to the public.

I now offer a number of newspapers and *Life* magazine

containing articles reporting the so-called Profumo-Ward affair.

MR. QUEL: I object, your Honor. We can't go into a trial of a Profumo or Ward or anyone else. We are concerned with this particular book. I object to it.

THE COURT: I am going to sustain the objection. The Court will, however, take judicial notice of the fact that this trial was widely reported in the newspapers—of course, depending upon the newspaper. I might say, parenthetically, that the *New York Times* exercises a form of censorship on its readers. It doesn't always go too much into detail. I am sure some of the other papers did.

I see no point in cluttering the record with these newspaper clippings and articles, although, as I have indicated, the court will take judicial notice of how widely the newspapers have printed and reported the trial and the statements of the witnesses at that trial.

MR. REMBAR: May I have this marked for identification and noted as formally offered.

THE COURT: Yes. What does the box contain?

MR. REMBAR: Newspaper clippings and a copy of *Life* magazine.

The court would not accept the newspapers as evidence, but the court would take judicial notice of their existence and their contents.

It would have been better to have the newspapers formally received in evidence. Where the proof is hard to get, judicial notice is a great help. But where you have the proof ready, the point it supports is made with greater force if it is made through evidence. A judge ruling that he will take judicial notice is in effect saying, sometimes rather absently, "Yes, I know." It is not enough, for forensic purposes, that in a general way he is aware of the condition. What is wanted is the full appreciation that comes from a renewed examination of the specific facts, in the context of the trial. Yes, the court knew there was considerable reporting of the details of the Profumo affair, but the newspaper stories had a startling amount of sex in them, and a startling resemblance to *Memoirs*, and I wanted the judge to read them again, and closely, with the comparison in mind.

But to a degree, as a result of the argument on whether the

evidence should be admitted, these facts had been recalled to Judge Klein and given some emphasis. And having been offered and marked for identification, the newspapers and the magazine were part of the record. The appellate courts would have to decide whether this evidence should have been admitted; to make that decision, the judges would have to read it.

It was now Quel's turn to come forward with his rebuttal witnesses. They were three clergymen and a social worker. These were not the three clergymen who were involved in Operation Yorkville. Quel apparently felt that the Operation group would not make as good an impression as those he called. He was right, I thought. The witnesses were intelligent, reasonable men; he ran no risk that their statements would be dismissed as zealotry. But there was still the question of what they could testify to.

The first was Dr. William F. Rosenblum, rabbi of Temple Israel. It was established that in addition to his strictly clerical functions, Dr. Rosenblum engaged in various community activities. Quel then continued:

Q. Have you read *Memoirs of a Woman of Pleasure?*
A. I have.
Q. Can you give us your opinion as to the book, particularly with reference to the question of whether or not it falls within or passes the bounds of general community standards?
MR. REMBAR: I object to this question, your Honor. It is a matter that Mr. Quel and I have discussed before. There is a question of law involved. The defendant has used testimony of two kinds; one is the testimony of qualified literary critics who spoke about the literary qualities of the book, attempted to analyze and interpret it. The other kind of testimony related to what is objectively available—both in terms of serious works of literature and the limits of candor which we find in such works, which are reputably produced and sold, and with respect to the trash available on our newsstands. All of this testimony related to objective things. None of it related to anyone's subjective idea of what community standards may be. I submit that that, the latter, is a question for the court, and therefore, I object to this question.
MR. QUEL: It is undoubtedly a question for the Court.

But, on the other hand, there is no reason why the expert testimony on that score should be confined to literary critics. In effect, what Mr. Rembar is saying is that it is all right to put literary critics on to prove what contemporary community standards are, but nobody else can testify to it.

It seems to me that by putting that kind of testimony, he has opened the door to my rebuttal testimony.

MR. REMBAR: If I may say so—

THE COURT: I don't think it is necessary. As I understood the purpose of the testimony of the so-called experts, the literary critics or literary people, they were not testifying as to what the current standards were, but as to what their critical opinion was of this book. Rabbi Rosenblum is an old friend of mine. I would say I am very fond of him. I listen, usually with great attention, to anything that he may have to say. But, I am afraid I am going to have to sustain this objection. If you can set him up as a literary expert, I will permit you to have him testify what his personal opinion is as to the literary merits of this book.

Quel reasserted his contention, then directed his questioning along a different line:

Q. Dr. Rosenblum, in the course of your work, do you read many books?

A. I have to.

Q. Have you read many novels?

A. Not as many recently as I did in the past. I read quite a number of novels.

Q. Over how long a period of time have you been doing that?

A. Ever since I went to high school. Quite a long time.

Q. I won't ask you how long.

A. No.

Q. In the course of your lectures, do you on occasion talk about books?

A. I do. Many times.

Q. Have you an opinion as to the literary merit of *Memoirs of a Woman of Pleasure?*

I started to object.

MR. QUEL: My question is, whether he has an opinion.

MR. REMBAR: I don't think that the question of whether

Dr. Rosenblum has an opinion is relevant, because the opinion could be offered only if he were qualified as a literary expert. I don't think that Dr. Rosenblum has been so qualified.

MR. QUEL: Your Honor, I submit—

THE COURT: I am going to overrule the objection. I think the objection here goes more to the weight of the testimony that the rabbi is about to give than it does to its admissibility. I will overrule the objection.

MR. REMBAR: Exception.

Judge Klein was in effect ruling that since Dr. Rosenblum had some acquaintance with literature he could state his opinion of the book, but his opinion would have to be weighted (or unweighted) according to the extent of his literary knowledge. Presumably, since he was a doctor of divinity and not of letters, his testimony on literary merit would have less consequence than that of our witnesses.

Dr. Rosenblum then gave his opinion:

THE WITNESS: I think it has some literary merit. It is a novel.

After I had worked so hard to keep the witness from expressing an opinion, he produced one that was helpful to us. Quel decided he had better press his own witness:

Q. Will you describe, in some detail, your opinion as to the literary merit?

A. Well, I think, first of all, in accordance with the root definition and the acquired definition, it is a pornographic book, but written in a style that is somewhat different than would usually be accorded subjects of that kind. In that respect, it is a literary work on a certain subject.

MR. QUEL: I am sorry—

His sorrow was understandable.

Can I have the answer to the last question?

The stenographer read the answer, and Quel returned to community standards:

Q. In your opinion, Dr. Rosenblum, does the book transcend or fall within contemporary community standards?

MR. REMBAR: I object, your Honor.

THE COURT: Objection sustained. This is the same question that was asked before in another form.

MR. QUEL: That is true. May I call your attention to the concurring opinion in *Smith* v. *California,* which, it seems to me, forms the basis of the admission of such testimony, whether it is by a literary expert or by anybody else—always bearing in mind that the ultimate determination as to that question must be made by the court.

MR. REMBAR: I would like to say, with respect to that statement by Mr. Justice Frankfurter, that it is in a concurring opinion, and that he speaks on behalf of a defendant in a criminal case, to whom he feels the widest latitude should be permitted. I don't think the same considerations apply here.

THE COURT: The objection is sustained.

MR. QUEL: Exception, your Honor.

Q. Dr. Rosenblum, I believe you said that in your opinion the book was pornographic.

A. Yes.

Q. Do you draw a distinction between pornography and "erotic realism"?

A. To a certain extent, I do.

Q. This book definitely falls within the pornographic area, in your opinion?

A. It certainly does.

MR. QUEL: That is all, your Honor.

The phrase "erotic realism" came from *Obscenity and the Law,* by Eberhard and Phyllis Kronhausen. The authors suggested that pornography is typically filled with fantasy, and that "erotic realism" forms a different category. Quel was trying to show that *Memoirs* was essentially fantasy, and therefore pornographic. He had quoted the Kronhausens when he questioned Minton (in a passage that has been omitted), and he now repeated the phrase. I picked it up when I started to cross-examine Dr. Rosenblum:

Q. Mr. Quel, in examining you, referred to a passage from the Kronhausen book.

MR. QUEL: No, I did not. You are mistaken.

MR. REMBAR: You had it in your hand; and you used the words "erotic realism."

MR. QUEL: I used those words, yes.

MR. REMBAR: Which are in this paragraph.

MR. QUEL: Yes.

MR. REMBAR: The paragraph was read into the record by Mr. Quel.

MR. QUEL: In connection with the other witness; yes.

Q. The paragraph begins, "In pornography"—

MR. QUEL: What page are you reading from?

MR. REMBAR: Eighteen. The same passage you read into the record.

Q. (Continuing) —"(hard-core obscenity) the main purpose is to stimulate erotic response in the reader. And that is all."

I take it that you agree with that definition of pornography; or do you not?

A. Part of that definition, yes. I agree that is one of the aims of pornographic literature, and pornography would be that; yes.

Q. You do not agree with the sentence that says, "And that is all"?

MR. QUEL: The witness didn't say that.

THE WITNESS: I didn't say that.

MR. REMBAR: I didn't interrupt you.

THE WITNESS: I didn't say that.

Q. I wanted to get your position clear.

A. That definition is an almost exact definition of what I would give.

Q. You mean, the two sentences I read?

A. Yes, what you read.

The essential part of the Kronhausen definition, for present purposes, was the second sentence: "And that is all." If a book had qualities other than the ability to stimulate erotic response, it would not, in this analysis, be pornographic. Although Dr. Rosenblum started by saying he agreed with only part of the definition, he ended by agreeing with all of it. And he had already testified that *Memoirs* had something other than the "purpose to stimulate"; it had "some literary merit." So his testimony showed that according to an authority Quel himself had invoked, our book was not pornography.

There was a pause in the proceedings after Dr. Rosenblum finished. Quel had obviously been acquainted with the rabbi before this litigation, and Judge Klein had spoken of him, for the record, with both fondness and respect. Witness and cross-examiner are, in the nature of things, adversaries, and if you do not actively dislike the man, there is an impulse afterward to make it clear that the animosity is professional only. During the pause I went over to Dr. Rosenblum, shook hands and offered a pleasantry. Judge Klein noticed this and asked, "Oh, are you a friend of Rabbi Rosenblum too, Mr. Rembar?" "No, your Honor," I said, "but it seems that everybody else is; so I thought I'd better introduce myself."

Quel's second witness was Father Edward Soares, a Roman Catholic priest assigned to the educational offices of the archdiocese of New York. He was director of the Archdiocesan Committee for Decency in Literature, and like Rabbi Rosenblum he was active in community groups. Quel asked for his opinion "as to whether the book falls within or crosses over the line of community standards." I objected. The ground of my objection had been explained earlier—that the expression of such an opinion was the judge's job, not the witness's.

MR. REMBAR: Now I press the objection.

THE COURT: I might indicate, there is no doubt in my mind what the father's opinion is. I know the Catholic Church has a list of books which they don't consider proper for their people or their children to read. Isn't that so, Father?

THE WITNESS: For the young.

THE COURT: I am certain that this book is not one of those books that they would want anybody to read. I have indicated here earlier, sir, that I wouldn't want my daughter to read this book. Unfortunately for all of us, this is not the test. I have to decide legally whether this book is obscene; and if it is, it should be suppressed; if it isn't, it shouldn't be, of course, according to the standards set up by the Supreme Court in the *Roth* case.

MR. QUEL: Of course, what I am trying to do is to establish community standards. I am well aware of the fact, as I said before, that your Honor must decide the question; but I am trying to make a record on that.

THE COURT: I have indicated what my ruling will be. Objection sustained.

As with Dr. Rosenblum, Quel's principal purpose in bringing this witness to the stand—to get a statement that *Memoirs* went beyond community standards—was thwarted. So Quel turned to literary merit. Father Soares was unwilling to concede the degree of merit Rabbi Rosenblum allowed the book. But the father's literary opinion could not, under the law, count for much; on my objection the judge had said:

I am afraid that this witness, with all due deference to him, has not been qualified as an expert in the field of literature. He is no more, in my opinion, than the average reader. However, I will overrule the objection. With due deference to the cloth, I will let the father answer the question.

Next came Julius Nierow, a social worker and deputy executive director of the New York City Youth Board. Quel went through the process which had now become routine. Had he read the book? Did he have an opinion as to whether it went beyond community standards? What was that opinion? Apart from the point that the statement of such an opinion was not evidence, Nierow's special experience was with children, and the decision in *Butler* v. *Michigan* (that what is safe for children cannot govern publication) stood squarely in the way. By this time my entire argument could be made in three words:

MR. REMBAR: Objection, your Honor.

Judge Klein pointed out that the witness worked with children. Quel then said:

As a matter of fact, if it will help any, I will specifically exclude children. All I am asking him is whether, in his opinion, the book conforms to general community standards, forgetting about children.

MR. REMBAR: I take it that this is the same as the question—

THE COURT: Yes, I will sustain the objection, for the reasons given in sustaining the same objection to the same question.

MR. QUEL: Exception. That is all, your Honor.
MR. REMBAR: No cross-examination.

Then Quel called his last witness, the Reverend Canon William S. Van Meter, Director of Christian Social Relations of the Protestant Council of the City of New York, and before that Director of Christian Social Relations for the Episcopal Diocese of Chicago. Van Meter was tall, slender and long-necked. In his face there were merged an appropriate dedication and an amused country look. He suggested Walter Brennan with a massive injection of intellect.

Quel elicited the background information and then embarked upon the community-standards questions:

Q. Canon, have you read *Memoirs of a Woman of Pleasure?*
A. Yes sir. I read it last night in some detail and have somewhat changed my views as a result of this; that is, I didn't find in it what I expect to find, but I read it last night until four o'clock this morning.

He had somewhat changed his views.

For some reason, the answer did not seem to make much of an impression on Quel. It was, after all, the end of two days of intense trial in a courtroom that had noise outside and heat inside. People were getting tired. Perhaps Quel was getting tired too. Or perhaps, convinced of the rightness of the position he was advocating, he was not attuned to the idea that a clergyman might take a different one. Possibly it was a combination of these factors. In any event, he simply went ahead as he had with the three preceding witnesses, following the course that Klein's rulings had made routine:

Q. Have you an opinion as to whether the book conforms generally with community standards? Just answer that yes or no.
A. Yes.
Q. What is your opinion?
MR. REMBAR: Objection, your Honor.
THE COURT: Objection sustained.
MR. QUEL: I respectfully except. That is all, your Honor.

I could not avoid making the objection. I had urged, and it had been ruled, that the city's witnesses, qualified only as participants in community affairs, could not give opinion testimony. When Quel asked for Van Meter's opinion, consistency required that I object. Yet it seemed likely that if Van Meter had answered, it would have done us more good than harm.

It was time for me to cross-examine. What I needed was a question that did not ask for the canon's opinion, but would nevertheless elicit it. Perhaps if the word "opinion" was not used there would be no objection:

Q. Dr. Van Meter, you said just now that after reading the book your views of it had changed somewhat. Would you please expand on that statement?

There was no objection.

A. Well, I had looked at this book very hurriedly. It came into my possession at ten-fifteen yesterday morning. I had looked at it hurriedly and had looked at passages. I was expecting to find a quite different kind of work. I was expecting to find something which was titillating, or some such thing, and looked at passages which looked, at first examination, as quite lurid, and then I read the book as a whole, and I came out with a quite different view.

Q. What view did you come out with?

A. I came out with a view that this was a serious book, that there was some serious consideration of plot and character development, that it had some sociological importance, if a person were concerned with that period.

I am primarily concerned with contemporary problems. I am not concerned with this period, but if a person were, I think this is something a person would want to look at.

This was better than I could have hoped. Rosenblum had grudgingly conceded some literary merit but had made clear his disapproval of the book. Van Meter was taking an affirmative position on the book's value, and he was the city's witness.

Testimony favoring one side that comes from the other side comes with unusual force. It is expected that plaintiff's witnesses will favor plaintiff and defendant's witnesses will favor defendant; there is a large discount for partisanship. The statement of an impartial outsider would have much more weight. (Though there are of course no impartial outsiders in court; every witness is called, for a purpose, by the litigants.) But a statement in your support by someone presumably partial to your opponent (else why would your opponent make him a witness?) has a sharp and memorable impact, even stronger than that of the hypothetical neutral observer. Instead of a discount, his testimony carries a premium. The courtroom reacted accordingly; there was a stir and a murmur.

But the next thing that happened made my heart sink. As one faced the bench, the windows were in the wall to the left, and the witness stand was to the right, toward the blank wall. Against the blank wall was the jury box—in this trial occupied by journalists. There were tables and chairs for the lawyers directly below the bench. We had the table to the left, the one nearer the windows. Questioning Van Meter, I was standing over on the other side of the room, to the right of the witness stand, near the jury box. The judge had turned his chair to the windows, his gaze in the general direction of Foley Square, an attentive back toward me and the witness.

When this beautiful testimony (I thought it was beautiful) had been completed, the judge swiveled around. His face was set and, it seemed to me, grim. He spoke in clipped syllables:

I couldn't quite hear you, sir. Will the reporter please read that answer?

The reporter did. The judge's being irritated could mean only one thing: he had by now made up his mind, against us, and this testimony was awkward. The record would show that a witness called by the city had testified that the book was not at all what the city charged—that indeed the book had merit. It would be a nuisance to have to deal with something like that in an opinion holding the book so worthless that it should be suppressed. Hence, I thought, the judge's annoyance. He had reached his conclusion, and it was the wrong one for us.

I had misread his face. What I could not see from where I stood could be seen from the end chairs at our counsel table. My associates, who were sitting there, later told me that when Van Meter made his answer, Judge Klein, looking out the window, began to smile. That the city's witness should give such testimony was, after all, not only significant; it was pretty funny. But courtroom etiquette requires that judges be impassive; at least they are expected to try. Klein wanted to make sure he had heard correctly, and so he turned to the stenographer to have the answer read. But when he turned, and was facing the courtroom, he had erased the smile. What I thought was an expression of annoyance was actually the facial set that resulted from an effort to compose his features.

Quel came back in an attempt to repair the damage. There was not much he could do:

Redirect Examination by Mr. Quel

Q. Well, so far as the contemporary times are concerned, what is your opinion of the book?

A. I think that qualitatively it doesn't vary from a great deal of the literature which is currently available.

Q. How about quantitatively?

A. I think that there is a quantitative difference.

Q. By that, you mean that the sexual incidents occupy an undue proportion of the book. Is that what you mean?

A. Within my experience. I am speaking only in terms of my own personal knowledge. I wouldn't want to make a value judgment. I would say that it occupies a greater part than other books that I have read and examined.

MR. QUEL: That is all, your Honor.

Recross-examination by Mr. Rembar

Q. When you said just now that you did not want to make a value judgment, you were referring to the use of the word "undue" by Mr. Quel?

A. Right.

The last to testify was Minton, recalled for further cross-examination—a notable display of devotion to duty on the part of Quel, considering how abrasive their first encounter had been. The additional testimony did not change anything.

Both sides now rested. The judge asked whether counsel wanted to make closing statements. Quel said he did. He argued again that I was misinterpreting the law. He said the Scileppi opinion confirmed the rule of *Roth*—that material is obscene if according to the average man and in the light of community standards its dominant appeal is to prurient interest—and that social value is no part of this rule. Quel was, of course, stating what had been the generally accepted reading of the Brennan opinion.

Judge Klein knew my basic argument, and it was not necessary to repeat it:

> MR. REMBAR: I will leave the appraisal and assessment of the various cases to the consideration of your Honor upon the brief which we have filed. I don't think it is necessary to take the court's time in discussing these precedents now.
>
> In closing, I want to make only two very brief points. One is that while Mr. Quel may have been justified in referring over and over again to the opinions of Mr. Hutchens and Mr. Ciardi as a vehicle for cross-examination, I think it is significant that neither Mr. Ciardi nor Mr. Hutchens appeared to testify as to the literary merit, or lack of it, of this book.
>
> The second point that I wish to emphasize is this—I am sure your Honor is aware of it but it cannot be emphasized too strongly—the question we have is not whether from a personal, or a family, or a religious point of view this is or is not a good book to read. The question is the extent to which the law may be permitted to interfere with its publication. . . .

The trial was over. I told Minton our chances were now at least even.

The decision came two days later. *Fanny Hill* won.

Judge Klein had indicated quite strongly that he would need more than the statutory two days, and we had waived the requirement. He then managed to comply. Some people—a few—work better without deadlines. In any event, the opinion came down within two days, and it was a good one.

A note *obiter*. Just after court adjourned, I was standing out in the corridor, talking about the trial (more precisely, listening), and waiting for Irving Klein and Ellis Levine, associate counsel, who had been a great help. They were gathering up our papers and the exhibits. When they came out, they told me that a curious thing had happened after most of us left the courtroom. There was a sudden alarming clatter. They looked up from their paper-gathering. High on the wall behind the bench was the legend "In God We Trust," spelled out in metal letters. Two of the letters had fallen from the wall to the floor.

There is more than one explanation. There are three. God was reminding Judge Klein of the importance of making the right decision. Or the jackhammers used in the construction work outside, which had played us an obbligato throughout the trial, had finally shaken the letters loose. Or the First Amendment having been in issue for two days, God was drawing our attention to another great concept involved in the Amendment. He was pronouncing the judgment that references to Him should not be part of government buildings. He was giving a more than gentle hint that Church and State should be separate. As a matter of fact, God was separating them.

The Enlightenment
in New York

THE ELECTIONS OF 1966 INDUCED SOME INTEREST-
ing lapses of memory. Frank O'Connor, one of the five district
attorneys who, with the corporation counsel, had brought the
action against *Fanny Hill*, and who later became New York City
Council president, was running for governor. Judge Klein was
running for surrogate, a New York judicial office concerned with
wills and estates.*

Judge Klein's decision in the *Fanny Hill* case had been cou-

---

* The surrogate has frequent opportunity to appoint fiduciaries, who
receive compensation, sometimes substantial amounts, out of the estates
involved. The office has accordingly been a focus of political power. In a
fierce primary struggle waged on "organization"–"reform" lines, Klein lost
out to Judge Samuel Silverman, one of his brethren on the Supreme Court
bench. (The personal honesty of the two candidates was never in issue.)
O'Connor won his party's nomination, but was defeated by Nelson Rockefeller in the general election.

It may be noted that the famous Peter Zenger case, a pre-Revolutionary
landmark in the history of freedom of the press, had its source in the association of political position with profit—more precisely, in a squabble over
who was entitled to the profit. The royal governor of the colony of New
York had customarily received certain fees as perquisites of the office. The
incumbent died, and while his replacement was sailing from England, the
senior member of the New York provincial council—Mr. Rip Van Dam—

rageous. If he had further ambitions, he must have been conscious of the political detriment in what he did: vacating another judge's order and letting *Fanny* loose to mingle with the citizens of New York. The anti-pornographic stance was the politically advantageous one. Judge Klein, I felt, could not have been unaware of the fact that if he ever ran for another office, his ruling might cost him votes. Being a real judge, he was not deterred.

But three years later, in his campaign for surrogate, he gave an interview to the New York *Post*. The newspaper quoted him on *Fanny Hill:*

> I thought it was junk, but not obscene junk.

The second part of the statement was the expression of a logical and consistent position; a judge may think very little of a book that he feels constrained by the Constitution to protect. But this had not been Judge Klein's position when he decided the case. His opinion was based "upon a careful reading of the book." It said that "there is present herein an additional factor, not normally encountered in cases where books are sought to be suppressed, and that is the high literary quality of the book."

In the same season, District Attorney O'Connor was the subject of a profile in the same paper. His particular position on the political scene made liberal support a problem. The *Post* quoted him on various matters, and reported that:

---

acted as chief executive and took the fees for himself. When the Englishman arrived, he claimed the money, and, turned down, he sued (but apparently being a moderate man, sued only for half). The suit touched off a battle for power that went far beyond the original controversy. The faction opposing the governor hired Zenger to publish their propaganda in a new weekly journal, and a prosecution for criminal libel followed. At a time when anti-government speech was not at all free, Zenger was acquitted. A Philadelphia lawyer came up to New York to defend him—Andrew Hamilton, considered the best lawyer in the colonies. Hamilton's defense was based not on the law as it had been understood up to that time—"the greater the truth, the greater the libel"—but on what, he argued, the law ought to be: that truth should be a defense where criticism of public officials is concerned (as it now is, no matter who has been libeled). It will be of interest to Henry Miller that the grand jury did not indict Zenger; he was prosecuted on an information.

He is against "censorship of any work that has a claim to literary merit." He was the only DA here to oppose the banning of *Fanny Hill.*

If O'Connor had opposed the banning, his opposition was a very private thing, and his official action showed a self-effacing deference to the wisdom of his colleagues. The corporation counsel had filed an affidavit urging suppression, and the five district attorneys had filed their amens. The counsel denounced *Memoirs* in strong terms, saying it was " 'hard-core' obscene material. . . ." O'Connor's affidavit stated that he had read the counsel's affidavit and "for the reasons set forth" in it, he joined in the prayer for a restraining order.

Neither, I believe, was offering a conscious misstatement. The prosecutor of the book was presenting himself as a defender of literature. The savior of the book was demeaning what he had done. Each was in the grip of the tug to the middle that American politics traditionally exert.

Judge Klein's decision ended the temporary restraint, and sales took off like a shot from a sling drawn taut. The city and the district attorneys filed notice of appeal. An appeal takes time to get under way, and since the appellant has to file his brief first, it would be a while before the heavy work on our side began. So far as the Putnam balance sheet was concerned, victory or defeat at the trial level—the trial being in New York— was more significant than anything else. It gave the publisher a period of unhampered distribution long enough to insure a profit. With that accomplished, I suggested to Putnam it might make business sense to stop litigating and submit to an injunction before legal costs resumed. If the fight were carried all the way, the case in New York alone would go through at least two appeals (to the intermediate and highest New York appellate courts) and possibly a third (to the United States Supreme Court). Even if there were an ultimate victory, the expenses— legal fees and the printing of records and briefs—could conceivably outrun the additional income, and if there were an ultimate defeat, the money would have been badly spent.

As counsel to my clients, it was my duty to make the point.

As a citizen—and for myself—I hoped they would reject it. They did. Walter Minton and Victor Thaller (the treasurer of the company) said that Putnam had made a considered decision to publish the book. They wanted the company to be vindicated in that decision, or told it was wrong by the highest court they could get to. I argued the utility of stopping now. They were not persuaded. I was greatly relieved.

The appeal by the city in the *Fanny Hill* case brought into focus one of the central weaknesses of our case—the author's intent. In the older cases, it was irrelevant; the courts had said that obscene material was not made pure by the fact that the author had what he considered a righteous aim. Under the *Hicklin* rule, obscenity was what tended to corrupt, and a work was no less corruptive for being innocently conceived.

But if value was to become the test, then the author's goal would indeed be relevant. The roads to hell and to the remainder shelves are paved with good intentions, but serious resolve at least points a writer toward a work of art. Moreover, an exploration of novelistic purpose is part of critical analysis, and thus part of expert testimony on literary merit. We had testimony of that kind in the *Chatterley* trial (where I also argued that it had some bearing on appeal to prurient interest). Judge Bryan gave weight to it, and Judge Clark concluded his opinion with a reference to "the author's central purpose." It was important again for *Tropic of Cancer*.

In the course of these cases I was often asked how the law stood. At this time, 1963—*Chatterley* decided and *Tropic* a good bet to win when it got to the Supreme Court—I usually answered that it would soon be settled law that no serious writing could be suppressed. ("Serious" meant both seriously intended and seriously received.) Whether the Supreme Court would accept social value as an independent test was still very much an open question, but I felt that it would accept it at least to this extent: a writer who had evidently set out to create literature and produced something that was given attention as literature would see his book protected by the First Amendment. We had just moved from a situation in which, in most courts, the purpose of the author counted for nothing, to a situation where an honest purpose would get him halfway home.

But this was no help to *Fanny Hill*. On the contrary, it hurt. The other side could urge the converse of the proposition: if serious purpose was relevant, surely the anti-obscenity laws must be allowed to operate against a deeply objectionable book whose author's purpose was not at all serious. Our opponents, I thought, might have made more of this at the trial; they might have put less emphasis on what they called the "aberrations," and more on how nicely the writing was gauged to meet the common quest for sexual excitement. They could have argued that *Fanny Hill*, and Fanny Hill, were excellently designed to stir a sexual response and that the design was confirmed by the circumstances that prompted Cleland to write. He was broke and debtors' prison was more than an abstract possibility; he had been there. When prosecution threatened, he said not a word about having written a good book, or even that he had tried and failed. Instead, he promised he would never do it again. Whatever freedom might be allowed the serious artist, the courts were not ready to allow any to the conscious pornographer. If her creator's object were the key, Fanny Hill would surely get herself locked up.

At the argument in the Appellate Division (New York's intermediate appellate court) some of the judges hit hard at the aspect of the case that had been worrying me. Didn't Cleland write this book in order to make money? Wasn't it, really, a book consciously directed to the libidinous instincts of the reader? Didn't the author expect to sell lots of copies? (Cleland gave up the manuscript for a flat sum—twenty guineas—but cash in hand would be more attractive than future royalties to somebody as down and out as he.) Wasn't this, if not dirt-for-dirt's-sake, then dirt-for-money's-sake?

Cleland's motives, I answered, presented a question of literary history, not a question of law. The courts simply could not decide, two and a quarter centuries later, what had gone on inside Cleland's head. And in any event, only the writer's final product was important. Literary testimony might deal with artistic ends, as disclosed by the work itself—the ideas the writer was trying to convey, the view of life he sought to share with his

readers—but that was not the same as the personal reasons that
led him to sit down and write. (In a particular case, the two
might coincide, but only the first belonged in court.) I mentioned William Faulkner's Introduction to *Sanctuary*. It begins:
"This book was written three years ago. To me it is a cheap
idea, because it was deliberately conceived to make money."

It would be both futile and unbecoming, I suggested, for
courts to inquire into the diverse springs of artistic endeavor.
The miserable record made by artists as critics of their own work
—the ludicrous verbalizations that we sometimes hear from
talented people in the nonverbal arts—shows that their stated
plans are of little consequence; what they create is of the greatest consequence. *Memoirs*, not Cleland, should be the subject
of inquiry.*

The court was evidently satisfied with the answers on this
point, but not—a majority of them—with my arguments generally. Three of the five judges held that *Memoirs* should be suppressed. They did not, however, say anything about Cleland's
intent. Judge Breitel, since then elevated to the highest court in
the state, and Judge Botein, the presiding justice of the court,
dissented, Breitel writing for them. He had been my most persistent and difficult questioner, but in his opinion he said:

> Thus, it is inconsequential whether an individual or an offi-
> cial finds only obscenity in a book or that even a primary
> motivation two centuries ago was a purveying of obscenity.
> The test must be objective if constitutional standards are to
> be applied.

It is a mistake to forecast decisions on the basis of an appellate
judge's questions; a judge who gives a lawyer trouble during argument may be expressing an adverse attitude, but he may also be
testing a favoring attitude, or neutrally exploring a problem.

---

* A fourteen-year-old shortstop and quarterback of my acquaintance, to
whom the subject of art was a bore, produced interesting and graceful
ceramics, by far the best in his high school class. When I asked how come,
he explained by drawing on his athletic experience. "Good hands," he said.
I have seldom heard a better explanation of artistic accomplishment from
an artist.

Without bothering about intent, the three-judge majority labeled the book "hard-core pornography," and made no concession whatever to the value theory. They referred to *Roth* only in
connection with the prurient-interest test and accorded literary
merit only the significance given it thirty years before in the
Ulysses case. Quoting Judge Augustus Hand, they pointed out
that the erotic passages in *Memoirs* were not " 'submerged in
the book as a whole.' " "To the contrary," said the majority, "it
is the inconsequential and almost nonexistent nonerotic passages that are so submerged."

The Appellate Division's reversal would reinstate the injunction, but the court accepted our suggestion that its order be delayed for ten days, during which we might ask the Court of
Appeals, the highest court of the state, for a stay. A stay would
keep Judge Klein's decision alive, and there would be no injunction for the time being. We did not have in mind further sales
in New York; whether or not there was an injunction, booksellers could be prosecuted, and the fact that a majority of the Appellate Division had said the book was obscene was ample
warrant for any district attorney who chose to proceed.

The reason we sought the stay was to enable Putnam to continue national distribution. Did a ruling that the book violated
New York law affect shipments going to other states? Quel's
contention was that the statute governed all conduct that took
place in New York, and therefore covered the act of the New
York publisher in selling an obscene book even though the particular copies were to go elsewhere. Mine was that the only
basis for the statute was the protection of the citizens of New
York, that nothing except putative good was done to the character of New Yorkers when copies of the *Memoirs* left the state,
and that the legislature in Albany could not be permitted to dictate the reading habits of other states. There was no direct
precedent on this question, and the only way Putnam could be
certain of avoiding trouble was to get the upper courts to keep
Judge Klein's decision in force, despite the reversal, pending a
further appeal.

When the Court of Appeals is not in session, an application
for a stay may be made to any one of its seven members. Normally it is made to a judge who lives in or near the place where

the litigation is going on—in this instance Stanley Fuld. Fuld was one of the very best of American judges. He was also a man of considerable humor and had the detachment that goes with it. At the same time, he was acutely conscious of the obligations of his office. Quel and I went to Fuld's New York City chambers and put the matter to him.

On a motion for a stay, the merits of the case (that is, the ultimate questions) are of course not decided, but they are usually examined, because unless there is a real possibility of reversal, the decision appealed from ought not to be disturbed. Judge Fuld first indicated that there was grave doubt as to the validity of my position on obscenity. He then indicated that there was also grave doubt as to the validity of the opposing position. "Have you read the book?" he asked Quel.

"I've read it twice," said Quel.

"Do you think it's pornographic?"

"I do," said Quel unequivocally: "it deals with practically nothing but sex."

"But it tells the story of a prostitute," I argued, "what else should it deal with?"

"Yes," said Judge Fuld. Then, after a pause, "It's autobiographical, isn't it?"

The question was directed to Quel. It was not possible to tell whether the judge was serious. A momentary uncertainty spread over Quel's face—the birth of panic every lawyer occasionally feels when something suggests that there is a large and relevant fact of which he has been unaware. "It's written by a man," he said very firmly to the judge, and then to me, somewhat less firmly, "isn't it?"

Judge Fuld gave us the smallest of smiles. "Probably a ghost writer," he said.

He then became obviously serious. His concern was whether a single judge should act alone to negate, even temporarily, the decision of the last court that had spoken. He reminded me that what I was asking involved a delicate exercise in intercourt relationships. I agreed, but suggested that in this instance a stay would continue, not disrupt, the status quo. (The theory of a stay is that while the appeal is being decided, the status quo ought to be preserved. Ordinarily, this means the condition that

existed before the lower court issued its order; the full phrase is
status quo ante.) The book had been permitted to circulate by
the trial court, and the appellate division's three-to-two reversal
was what would change things, and rather late in the day. Moreover, I said, this case was different from most, because it involved the First Amendment; if there was doubt, judicial discretion should be employed on the side of freedom.

Judge Fuld suggested that he might order an exceptionally
fast hearing of the appeal so that what happened meanwhile
would have less importance. Quel and I thought we could do
the briefs quickly. Fuld set the case down for argument in fifteen days. At that time the full court would consider whether to
continue the stay while they were deciding the case. The issue
we were arguing was now reduced to a matter of two weeks. But
how about those two weeks? Fuld returned to his doubt about
overriding, for however short a period, the judgment of the Appellate Division. "I have to think of my place in the court system of the state," he said. "Think rather of your place in history," I said. He grinned. "Oh, that's secure," he said, "for
about two weeks, anyhow; I'll grant the stay."

When the appeal was heard, the full court kept the stay in
force. Three years later, Fuld moved to his proper place in the
court system of New York—in a sense quite different from that
in which he had used the phrase. He succeeded Charles Desmond as Chief Judge of the Court of Appeals, and took the seat
that once belonged to Benjamin Cardozo.

The Court of Appeals had heard my main arguments a year
earlier, in the *Tropic of Cancer* appeal. But we could not simply
submit a second edition of the *Tropic* brief. For one thing, the
testimony was different. For another, my opponents were different, and their arguments were different. For a third, we were
dealing with a book whose vice was allure, not repulsion. And
finally, in this case, though my interpretation of *Roth* remained
essentially the same, I had been presenting a fullblown "three
test" theory of the law of obscenity (Harlan's *Manual Enterprises* opinion adding support to the idea that the prurient-
interest test was not the only test). Before a book might be suppressed, it had to be demonstrated (1) that it predominantly
appealed to prurient interest, (2) that it was patently offensive,

and—*and*, not *or*—(3) that it was utterly without social importance. (In the *Tropic* appeal, I saw nothing to gain from drawing attention to the matter of patent offensiveness and had used
Manual Enterprises only to attack the asserted exclusiveness of
the prurient-interest test.)

The taste and elegance of *Memoirs*, my brief asserted, pre-
cluded its being condemned under the *Manual Enterprises*
standard; in its patent characteristics the book could not fairly
be called offensive, no matter how objectionable the underlying
subject matter might be. It was not prurient, because though it
might be sexually stimulating, it did not have the morbidity and
thoroughgoing nastiness that were indispensable elements in the
Supreme Court's concept of prurience. And it was not utterly
without social importance, because literary merit was socially
important, and there was overwhelming evidence that the book
had literary merit.

At the oral argument I took a few minutes to return to the
question of the ends the anti-obscenity statutes were supposed
to serve. Sin, evidently, was central—at least where the fastidi-
ous *Fanny* and not the boorish *Tropic* was on trial. The censors'
concern was for the reader, and the crime of the publisher was
in providing him with an opportunity to sin. But opportunities
to sin were all around us. Yet the law stayed clear, except where
lust was the sin and a book the occasion. The law ought to be
more consistent.

I reviewed the Seven Deadly Sins. The legislature did not
penalize a restaurant for setting a fine table and thus leading its
customers into Gluttony. Television provided constant seduction to Sloth—especially among the young—but it was not for
that reason criminal. And certainly the legislature did not seek
to prevent men from becoming rich, though their riches often
provoked other men to Envy. We did not banish biographies
that spread success stories before our envious eyes, nor children's
programs, nor cookbooks. Why, then, I asked the judges, should
the fact that a book spoke about sex in such a way as to awaken
Lust bring down the law's intervention?

The material of the argument was archaic, but not simply for
the purpose of putting a novel cast on what, to the judges,
might have become a too familiar subject. I used it to emphasize

the point—phrased in less archaic terms—that so far as books were concerned, the only kind of morality the legislature seemed to be interested in was sexual morality. If the comparisons seemed ridiculous, it was because the law's exertions—aimed at one sin alone—were ridiculous.

Six of the seven judges were the same as those who decided the *Tropic* appeal. One who had been against *Tropic*, Sydney Foster, had retired during the year, and been replaced by Francis Bergan. Judge Bergan had made a liberal record in the lower courts, but this was a thin basis for predicting how he might regard *Fanny Hill*. Indeed, it was conceivable that this court would vote seven-to-nothing against the book. And it was inconceivable that more than five would hold in its favor.

Four did. They were the three who had dissented in the *Tropic* case, plus the new judge. Bergan wrote the principal opinion, which seemed just barely able to arrive at the conclusion that the book should not be suppressed. The dissents, in contrast, were vigorous, but in a curious way they gave support to our legal position. They did not really dispute my theory of how the United States Supreme Court viewed anti-obscenity statutes and the First Amendment; rather, they deplored it. They were not so much dissents as protests.

On the day before our case was argued, there was another case in Albany involving *Fanny Hill*. It was a prosecution under a different statute, one that dealt only with minors, and Putnam had nothing to do with it.

It is settled law, as I have said, that a book may not be suppressed on the ground that it is bad for children. But how about a statute that merely forbids sales to children? Such legislation, it is urged, does not deny freedom of the press, because the books remain available to adults.

The suggestion is appealing. The world of the child is not the world of the adult, and the reasons that impel us to respect the First Amendment do not require that every book be made available to every child. But there are questions. Such a statute necessarily works some impairment of free circulation among adults. The bookseller earns a small profit on each item he sells and ordinarily has no interest in becoming a martyr to liberty. Must he, at his peril, determine both the nature of the book and his customer's age? Will he not simply refuse to carry books that seem to him doubtful (not the most profitable ones, of course) rather than run the risk of prosecution? Moreover, the arguments that make such legislation attractive—that children are impressionable and may not be able to understand or handle everything they read—themselves suggest a rebuttal. Is there not danger in giving government power to curb the free range of young minds? Should we allow our legislatures to issue reading lists (or, rather, no-reading lists) for our children?

During the time when the *Fanny Hill* case was on appeal, a woman in New York City sent her daughter to buy a copy. It was a deliberate, knowing act. Evidently convinced that the book would corrupt morals, and that something must be done, she was gathering evidence for a prosecution. There is no reason to suppose that the girl, without having read the book, was in the eyes of her mother already corrupted, so that the lady felt there was nothing to lose. We must therefore assume that she was willing, *pro bono publico*, to lay the moral fiber of her daughter on the altar of clean literature. Such resolute exclusion of ordinary parental feeling in the face of a higher imperative had probably not been seen since Abraham led Isaac into the land of Moriah. In the case of Isaac, the Lord stayed Abraham's sword. Nothing stayed the bookseller, however; he sold the girl the book. The mother then complained to the district attorney, who proceeded under a statute specifically prohibiting sales to minors.

I recommended to Putnam that it make no effort to participate in the case. I did not feel that the general problem of child-protection versus untrammeled circulation had an obvious answer, and the publisher was already, and directly, engaged in a legal struggle over a much more fundamental question of freedom. If the particular statute had defects, that was a matter for the defense of the particular bookseller, who was well represented.

The prosecution ended in a decision that the statute was too poorly drawn to be constitutional. (There is no reason why such a statute cannot be put in a constitutionally acceptable form. It is historical fact, however, that the best legal minds are not often on the side of censorship.) Later, another statute of the same nature but, according to a majority of the highest New York court, drawn a bit better, was sustained (in a case not involving *Fanny Hill*).

Overall, my feeling is that the matter is less important than at first it may appear. On the one hand, it is hard to see how anti-obscenity legislation, with its limited scope, could be used to raise a stultified generation. On the other, books constitute so small a part of the total sexual environment in which our children grow that the benefit of such a statute is just as hard to see. And assuming that there would be some benefit if the statute could be made effective, it is doubtful that it would keep the proscribed books out of the hands of our determined and affluent youngsters. The very fact of prescription would be a challenge and a goad, and would likely put the burden of policing back where it belongs—in the home. Let me say only that the legislation on the point that I have so far read strikes me as worse than none, and that I reserve judgment on the case of some future marvel of an antibook, child-protecting statute.

At this writing the Supreme Court has yet to deal with legislation directed solely to the protection of children; I expect it will approve such legislation in principle, even if it holds a particular statute invalid.

Legislative

Wisdom

A COUPLE OF CHAPTERS AGO—DESCRIBING Justice Frankfurter's opinion upholding Section 22-a, the New York procedure later used against *Fanny Hill*—I mentioned his recommending a deep judicial deference to the wisdom of legislatures. Other judges are less indulgent, and in appraising the split among the judges, we might consider an example of what our legislatures produce—an example which, if not typical, is neither the best nor the worst that comes out of our state capitols.

Article 27, Section 41, of the Public General Laws of Maryland, enacted in 1950, reads as follows:

CONTRACEPTIVES—*Sale by Vending Machines Prohibited; exception.*

It shall be unlawful for any person, firm or corporation to sell or offer for sale any contraceptive or contraceptive device by means of a vending machine or other automatic device whether or not such contraceptive or contraceptive device is advertised as such or as a prophylactic, except in places where alcoholic beverages are sold for consumption on the premises. This exception is not to include railroad stations, air and bus terminals. Nor shall it include places where alcoholic beverages are sold for consumption on the premises in Howard County.

Apart from specific constitutional restrictions (such as those of the First Amendment), a statute—whether state or federal— must be directed toward an end that the legislature has power to pursue (ours is a government of limited powers bestowed by the people), and must employ means reasonably related to the accomplishment of that end ("substantive due process"). Both the affirmative provisions of a statute and such exceptions as it may allow are subject to this requirement of reasonableness.

In this instance, the satisfaction of the constitutional demands is plain to see. First there is a purpose long held to be legitimate—the prevention of sin. Then there is the reasonably related mode of attaining it: banish contraception (by vending machine, that is) and you banish sin. Finally, there is the reasonable exception of "places where alcoholic beverages are sold for consumption on the premises"—bars, cocktail lounges, restaurants that sell liquor. The logic of the statute is apparent to anyone willing to give the matter a little thought: if the citizen is sinning anyway, what the hell. Lechery may as well be added to revelry. Damnation being eternal, there is nothing to lose. The Maryland legislature could hardly have been more reasonable.

This assumes, of course, that there is no mistake in punctuation. If, as sometimes happens in drafting statutes, a comma was inadvertently omitted, we should have to revise the reading. Perhaps it was intended that a comma should follow "sold" and precede "for consumption on the premises." That is, the lawmakers, frustrated by a careless draftsman, meant to make it illegal:

> to sell any contraceptive by means of a vending machine, except in places where alcoholic beverages are sold, for consumption on the premises.

On this hypothesis, the legislative worry was not about the mechanistic vending of contraceptives generally, but only about the possibility that the consumer might use the goods at the point of purchase. At the same time (if this were the intended punctuation), it appears that the legislature was willing to make a more liberal exception than the statute, absent the additional comma, would permit. The prohibition would be narrower (only vending for consumption on the premises), and the exception would be broader (everywhere liquor is sold, not merely where it is also drunk). It would be lawful to have the machines in package stores as well as in cocktail lounges, and—by clear negative implication—to consume both lines of merchandise on the spot.

A moment's consideration reveals that this construction must be rejected. Evasion would be too easy. We might envisage establishments (apart from those utterly unaffected because they sell liquor) that could bootleg the product—a bookshop, for example, wishing to supplement the meager receipts that come from its usual trade. It would have two machines. One, legitimate, would bear the legend "To Take Out." The second, typically kept in a curtained corner, would be labeled "For Consumption on the Premises."

We cannot suppose that the State of Maryland would allow itself to be so simply trifled with. The phrase "consumption on the premises" must be read as applying to the alcohol, and thus as limiting only the exception, not the main provision. The legislators knew what they were doing when they left the comma out.

The last two sentences of the Act have their own interest. Not only did the assemblymen show they could temper stern prohibition with tolerant exception; they also showed they could contain the urge toward toleration, and avoid the extremes of moderation. Drunk with reasonableness, as it were, they made exceptions to their exception. First they excluded railroad stations, bus terminals and airports. Purchase on the fly, so to speak, will not do. Then they made the mysterious second exception to the exception. On this, the face of the statute tells us little; we must wait to hear from the residents of Howard County.

To move to a more serious subject, or rather to a more serious treatment of what is essentially the same subject, the question of the deference due the legislature is, of course, the converse of the question of how far courts should carry the doctrine of judicial review. All judges agree that they should have no interest in whether a given statute is desirable or undesirable, so long as it is an exercise of granted powers and violates no constitutional prohibition. The requirement of reasonableness is only that the statute be not "arbitrary and capricious"—that it lie somewhere within the range of the arguably rational. The judges do not have to like the statute, and often sustain what they oppose. But these are matters of degree, and judges differ on how broad the range is, how rigorous the review must be, how much leeway the legislature ought to have.

Essentially, it is a matter of the extent to which the restrictions of the Constitution should be enforced against the current mood of the electorate, as that mood is expressed by its elected representatives. In the event of a conflict, where is the principal judicial virtue—in the circumspect use of the power to review, or in an active devotion to constitutional freedoms? Do our democratic principles call more strongly for giving the legislatures room to experiment, or for a strict allegiance to our organic law?

Curiously, on this basic issue of government, the concepts "liberal" and "conservative" have gotten up and exchanged seats during the last three decades. In the time of the New Deal, when a Roosevelt-led Congress was trying to legislate its way out of the Depression, the conservatives were all for a busy application of judicial review to Acts of Congress. As the Court struck down some of the new legislation, the liberals cried out in pain; the hurt was so bad that most of them gave support to the partially successful Court-packing plan. The conservatives cited the Bill of Rights, while the liberals invoked the Will of the People. The prayer for the holy freedoms of the individual was heard not on the left but on the right.

After World War II, economic problems became less critical, and the assertion of personal rights (as distinguished, roughly, from property rights) created the principal legal issues. Security —that is, anticommunism—grew to be the chief preoccupation of the lawmakers. Liberals began to worry about what Congress and state legislatures, thus bemused, were doing, while conservatives began to think the courts were interfering too much with legislative pursuits. It was now the Americans for Democratic Action, rather than the National Association of Manufacturers, who demanded that the Court arise and fight for liberty.

The positions were maintained through the sixties. The Court's interference with attempts to legislate loyalty, assist religion, maintain segregation and stamp out obscenity were, in general, deplored by conservatives and applauded by liberals. In 1967 Ronald Reagan, clasping hands with the radicals of our early history, complained of the "tyranny by the courts" and judges who usurped the power of the people.

And so at present the Justices who are labeled liberal are those who have less hesitation in striking down statutes, and those who are labeled conservative feel that the others should exercise more restraint.* Theoretically, it would seem that principles of democracy would require a diminished judicial role. The members of the Supreme Court are appointed, not elected, and they are appointed for life. The legislatures are more closely connected to the people, who periodically put them in office. But the theory does not square with history; so much depends on the particular legislature and the particular court. The best legislative body the world has seen was the one that produced the Constitution. What it enacted should be carefully preserved. On the other hand, to anyone who has watched the happenings under our statehouse domes . . .

Not that I would trade it for another form of government. The great recommendation for democracy lies in its alternatives. But we ought not to get sentimental about our elected representatives. And we ought to know what a rock and a fortress and a deliverer is our Constitution.

---

* The doctrine of judicial review applies also to actions of the executive branch, and a similar shift in attitude occurred there. Conservatives had asked the courts to intervene against the work of the New Deal agencies, such as the National Labor Relations Board and the Securities and Exchange Commission. After World War II, liberals began to seek the same intervention, but against different bureaucracies—notably, the Department of Justice in its deportation proceedings, and various agencies in their loyalty investigations. We sought it against the Postmaster General in the *Lady Chatterley* case. Later the conflict between executive and judiciary was waged mainly in the field of anticrime procedures.

ℱanny Hill

in Scollay Square

THE SECOND OF THE THREE *FANNY HILL* TRIALS was in Boston. It was a homecoming for *Fanny*. The book had been in the Massachusetts courts before, in 1821, in the first American obscenity case.

Reports of decisions in the early nineteenth century are sketchy. Volume seventeen of the Massachusetts Reports tells us there was a conviction followed by an appeal. It quotes parts of the indictment, and the argument, and some of what the appellate court said. The indictment started by charging the defendant with "publishing a lewd and obscene print, contained in a certain book entitled *Memoirs of a Woman of Pleasure*." It then added, almost as an afterthought, "and also for publishing the same book." *

The defense contended that the indictment was defective: since it failed to quote the passages alleged to be obscene, it did

---

* The indictment went on to say that the defendant published *Memoirs* "with force and arms." This might appear to be a rather interesting comment on the book business, suggesting that the 1820's anticipated the newspaper circulation battles of the 1920's. Actually, it is one of those phrases vestigial in the law, that hangs on, deprived of content by legal history, in formal documents. The origin of our criminal law lay in breaches of the King's peace. Eventually the law recognized crimes that involved no violence,

not fairly apprise the defendant of the charge. The court rejected the contention, not on any primeval whole-book rule, but because it would be wrong "to require that the public itself should give permanency and notoriety to indecency." There was awareness, even at this early date, that using the law to restrict obscenity might spread the poison farther. The court's antidote, however, had that common characteristic of literary censorship —futility. (Futility is not the same as ineffectiveness. Censorship is effective. It is just that its effects are not always what the. censors intend.) Since the prosecution could not escape naming the book, there was plenty of advertising. Omitting quotations would merely make customers of people who might otherwise have been satisfied with the court records, which, they might reasonably assume, had all the best parts.

The upper court affirmed the conviction. The defendant, whose name was Holmes, was sent to jail.

In between the two *Fanny Hill* cases, a good deal happened in Massachusetts. The commonwealth grew famous for its prosecution of books. "Banned in Boston" became part of the language. Then, in the last few years, things changed. The most important victory for *Tropic of Cancer*, until it reached the United States Supreme Court, was won in the Supreme Judicial Court of Massachusetts.

As with *Tropic*, the *Memoirs* case was "in rem"—"against the thing," as distinguished from the usual legal action, which is brought against a person. The attorney general of the state, the "petitioner," starts the action, and it may be defended by anyone interested in the distribution of the book, the "intervenor." * The procedure was established by a 1945 statute, the result of Zechariah Chafee's efforts to mitigate the harshness of obscenity prosecutions. Professor Chafee (of Harvard Law School), an important figure in the struggle for freedom of speech, devised it to permit the question to be resolved without

but the pleadings were slow to change; indictments (and declarations in the private action of trespass) continued to speak of *vi et armis*.

* There was a similar litigation in Rhode Island. For reasons described earlier, Putnam elected not to defend. The Rhode Island case is notable chiefly for the fact that the attorney general alleged in his petition that the author was one John Cleland, "believed by the Petitioner to be deceased."

subjecting the publisher or bookseller to criminal trial. The book is held obscene or not obscene, and no one is punished unless after an adverse judgment (whether or not he was party to the litigation) he goes ahead and sells it. Many who oppose censorship disapprove particularly of this kind of procedure on the ground that a book itself ought never to be put on trial. The expression of this splendid devotion to the repository of man's thought comes easiest from those who run no risk of a long-term sentence in jail.

The action is similar to that under Section 22-a in New York. The principal difference is that in Massachusetts there can be an *ex parte* determination (of doubtful constitutionality) that will prevent sales while the action is going on; in New York there is at least a two-sided hearing (although not a full trial) before a preliminary injunction may be issued. But the Massachusetts statute was passed in 1945, and at the time it was a gain: it took some of the terror out of the anti-obscenity law.

The trial, presided over by Judge Donald M. Macaulay, was held in the spring of 1964—after the Appellate Division in New York reversed Judge Klein and after the argument in the New York Court of Appeals, but before there was a decision from that court and before the Supreme Court decided in favor of *Tropic of Cancer*. Whether the value test, by itself, could save a book—whether indeed there was a value test—was still very much in doubt. There should have been less doubt in Massachusetts than anywhere else: the one court that had thoroughly accepted my theory (though by the narrowest margin) was the Supreme Judicial Court of Massachusetts. (We could not give full measure to the California opinion on the constitutional issue because the new California statute made explicit reference to social value.) But the reluctance of most lower-court judges to recognize the value test, plus the close vote and the ever-present question of whether a decision on one book furnishes a precedent for another, compelled me to make the argument all over again in my trial brief.

The opposition met the argument with a counterattack that was novel in the history of these cases. They agreed with me that the various tests of obscenity were to be applied separately and if a book had social value it had the protection of the First

Amendment. They then argued that *Fanny Hill* lacked that value—that it was no more than a collection of sexual episodes, written to sell to those seeking titillation, without any real merit and, because of its continuous emphasis on sex, prurient and patently offensive. (Carrying this one step farther, they might have said that it was a sort of literary stag film; fortunately, they didn't.)

The lawyers for the commonwealth were John E. Sullivan and William I. Cowin. In my judgment, their refusal to do battle over whether there was a value test was not merely sophisticated; it was tactically sound—not only civilized, but (for reasons I will describe later) the best way of winning their case.

The evidence on our side was to a great extent similar to the evidence in the New York case that preceded it and the New Jersey case that followed, and so I omit the direct testimony of our witnesses. But the trial had one prominent feature that the others did not—a witness called by the prosecution to speak on literary merit. He was Dr. John E. Collins, and his direct examination began:

Q. How are you presently engaged, Dr. Collins?
A. I am headmaster of the Newman Preparatory School.
Q. How long have you served in that capacity?
A. Four months.
Q. Would you give the court your educational background, starting from the secondary school?
A. I graduated from Boston College in 1925 with a B.A. degree. I have a Master of Arts degree from Boston University, 1926. I have a Doctor of Philosophy degree from Boston College, 1936. I did graduate work at Harvard and at Oxford.
Q. How have you been employed since the completion of your education or during your education?
A. I was a classroom teacher at the Boston Latin School for twenty-two years. I was head of the English Department at the State College at Boston for sixteen years, as well as dean, academic dean and dean of the graduate school, until February 1 of this year, when I came to Newman Preparatory School. My area is English literature.
Q. In connection with your profession, have you lectured?
A. That has been my life.
Q. Prepared articles?

A. Yes.
Q. Contributed articles?
A. Yes.
Q. Have you read the book commonly called *Fanny Hill?*
A. Yes sir.
Q. In your opinion, is this book obscene, Doctor?
MR. REMBAR: If I may, your Honor, I object to that question. It calls for a conclusion of law. It deals with the ultimate determination that this court must make, and it is not the subject of testimony. . . . The word "obscene," as your Honor knows, is a legal concept, a constitutional concept. The opinions of the United States Supreme Court and the opinion of the Supreme Judicial Court of this state in the *Tropic of Cancer* case have made that very clear.
THE COURT: I can recognize that the legal concept of what obscene means is one thing; however, a concept of what obscene means in literature has some bearing on determining what the legal concept of obscene means. I will allow him to answer.
MR. REMBAR: May I have an exception, your Honor?
THE COURT: Exception noted.
Q. I will repeat the question, Doctor. In your opinion, is the book commonly known as *Fanny Hill* obscene?
A. Yes.
Q. In your opinion, is the book indecent?
A. Yes.

I made another objection; the judge rejected it and noted my exception without my asking him to. But for the most part he insisted on our little antiphony unabridged. And he permitted Dr. Collins to testify that the book was "impure," "prurient" and "pornographic." Then:

Q. Are you familiar with the phrase "hard-core pornography"?
A. To a degree.
Q. To the degree that you are familiar with the phrase, would you classify this publication within hard-core pornography?
MR. REMBAR: Same objection, your Honor.
A. In my opinion—
THE COURT: Just a moment.
Of course, that term "hard-core pornography" you [Mr.

Sullivan] took out of the decision of the Supreme Judicial Court.

MR. REMBAR: By the same token, your Honor, the term "a prurient interest" is taken out of the Supreme Court decision.

THE COURT: "Prurient" is a word of many years'—hundreds of years'—usage.

It was not clear how that distinguished the one word from the other. Each was ancient; each had been given a special legal meaning by the courts. But Judge Macaulay was in no mood for analytical argument.

I will allow him to answer. Exception noted.

THE WITNESS: May I have the question again?

Q. The question is, in view of your familiarity within certain bounds of the term "hard-core pornography," is this book in your opinion within the bounds of your understanding of that phrase?

A. Yes.

Q. Did you find the book offensive, Doctor?

A. Yes.

Q. Would you go so far as to say you found the book patently offensive?

MR. REMBAR: I object to that question, your Honor. There again, there is a precise legal formula developed by the United States Supreme Court to express a legal conclusion, in the case of Manual Enterprises.

THE COURT: I know, but aside from the legal definition of "patently offensive," it might be a literary definition of it, or understanding. In that sense, I think the question is admissible.

I will allow it.

MR. REMBAR: Exception.

THE COURT: Exception noted.

Q. You may answer the question.

A. Yes.

MR. SULLIVAN: Your witness, gentlemen.

My cross-examination began with a few warm-up questions, and then:

Q. Had you been a teacher before you became headmaster?

A. Where?

Q. Anywhere.

A. Yes.

Q. What course did you teach?

A. Well, the English novel, comparative study of the novel, contemporary novel, three courses in Shakespeare, a course in biography—do you want a list of them all? I could go on forever if you want. I have been around a long time.

Q. Are you familiar with the English novels of the eighteenth century?

A. Yes sir.

Q. Which of the eighteenth-century novelists do you rate highest?

A. I don't rate any of them highest. I could give you five or ten names. I refuse to put one as supreme above twenty others.

Q. Would you name two or three that you regard as outstanding?

A. Richardson, Fielding, Jane Austen, Defoe, if you want to call him a novelist—I presume that's where you are building, anyway; and Smollett and Sterne, Edgeworth, Fanny Burning.* Go ahead.

Q. You testified in answer to a question put over my objection that you regard the book which is in issue here as appealing to prurient interest?

A. That's correct, sir.

Q. What do you understand by the word "prurient"?

A. Do you want to try Webster?

Q. I want to know what you had in mind when you answered the question.

A. Well, I can start with the word "dirty." I can go on with the word "sexual"; I can go on with "esoteric."

Q. Esoteric?

A. Yes. I can add "erotic"—in other words, for the purpose of stimulating sexual reactions.

Q. So that if a book could be described as erotic, you would also describe it as prurient?

A. Those words are not synonyms in every case. They may

---

* The error was the stenographer's, not the witness's. The stenographer was making an unconscious but understandable merger—the name of the author of *Evelina* and the personality of our heroine.

be and they may not be; you have to have a particular incident and a particular case.

Q. Well, could you give me an example of a book that you would regard as predominantly erotic that you would not regard as predominantly prurient?

A. Why yes. Zola's *Nana*.

Q. That book is erotic in the sense that it stimulates a sexual response in the reader, is that what you mean?

A. To a degree, but it has other literary merit. It lifts it up above and beyond the word "prurient."

Q. I see.

A. It is a human document.

Q. Correct me if I am wrong. As I understand what you are saying now, it is that there are books that are erotic in the sense that—

A. Well now, yes. Certain parts of *The Arabian Nights*, for example, may be.

Q. Certain parts of the Bible?

A. Yes, there are many cases where the words—

Q. The answer was yes to that?

A. I don't know what the question was.

Q. I said certain parts of the Bible.

A. Yes. That's an oldie.

Q. But nevertheless true. Well, let me put my question to you again because I am just trying—

A. You are trying to distinguish between the two words, correct?

THE COURT: Just let him ask the question, and you answer it.

Q. I want to know if I am correct in summarizing what you have been saying just now as follows: that there are certain books which you would deem erotic because they stimulate a sexual response in the reader, but which you would not call prurient because they have certain literary merits or literary values?

A. Well, I wouldn't condemn the whole book as erotic. I say there may be passages and parts in it which may be that.

Q. You know you have to consider the book as a whole, so let's say that there is a book that has these passages and parts which stimulate this sexual response in the reader, but the book also has some literary merit. How do you designate that book?

A. Masterpiece.

Q. You also answered affirmatively to the question whether the book in issue is obscene. How do you define that word?

A. Disgusting.

Q. Obscene equals disgusting?

A. I will go along with that for a while. Go ahead.

Q. You say for a while you will go along with that?

A. Well, if you start refining it, I will have to start refining.

Q. Don't you think we ought to refine these terms? After all, the publication of a book is at stake here.

A. Yes, I understand.

*   *   *

Q. Do you know of any books that do not deal with sexual subject matter that you could call disgusting?

A. Offhand, I wouldn't say so, no. I don't think that point is at issue, but go ahead.

Q. The judge will decide what points are at issue, but as of now you say that the word "disgusting" is confined to books that deal with sexual subject matter?

A. For the time being, yes.

Q. And those books you would call obscene?

A. Yes.

Q. Another question to which you answered affirmatively was whether the book at issue is indecent, and I would ask you again what you mean by that word?

A. Well, I would say that it was contrary to public mores, to the customs of the people and the common standards of a given time and a given place.

Q. Tom Paine's *Common Sense*, would that fit your definition?

A. I don't think so.

Q. Another term that was used on direct examination was the term "patently offensive," and you said that this book is patently offensive. Does that have any different meaning from these other words we have been discussing?

A. Well, I believe patently means open, doesn't it?

Q. It means "on the face of it," I think, yes.

A. Offensive—it is merely another way of picturing the same thing. You said that is in a Supreme Court phrase.

Q. In your opinion, is Henry Miller's *Tropic of Cancer* patently offensive?

A. Yes.

Q. Is it indecent?

A. Yes.

Q. Does it appeal to prurient interest?

A. Yes.

Q. Is it obscene?

A. Yes.

Q. When did you read the book in issue last, Dr. Collins?

A. Last night, first and last.

Q. Could you give me a brief recapitulation of the story in the book?

A. Well, I don't see how I could without being patently offensive.

Q. You are in a court of law, Dr. Collins. I am sure you will be excused.

A. Well, autobiography of a girl that comes from the country up to London and gets herself into a brothel and goes through the various adventures of, first of all, lesbianism, and with detailed descriptions of sexual actions. That's about all I could find in the book.

Q. Does she ever get out of the brothel?

A. Well, I should say no, she doesn't get out of the problem, no.

Q. Out of the brothel, I said.

A. Oh yes.

Q. She does. How?

A. Well, originally, she is taken out by one of her customers.

Q. And what happens then?

A. Well, it goes on the same—

Q. It is not the same. She is out of the brothel now. What does she do?

A. Well, she rides in a coach and so forth, and she has various adventures.

But for Dr. Collins it evidently was "the same," so much so that characters and incidents dissolved in the cross-examination—"I took no notes," "I haven't got it annotated," "I remember something like that."

Q. How about her first sexual experience with a man?
With whom does that take place?

A. Well, some old rake. I don't know whether his name is
even in there.

Q. An old rake, you say?

A. An old rake who had—it was not completed, as I remember, on her part.

Q. With whom does she first actually have sexual intercourse?

A. Now, let's see. It was with this young man who rescued
her, as it were, from the brothel.

Q. Do you remember his name?

A. No, I don't.

Q. You read the book last night, though?

A. Yes.

Q. Does the book end with Fanny Hill married or unmarried?

A. She was married.

Q. To whom?

A. I don't remember now.

Q. You don't remember?

A. No, not now. I didn't take notes on it.

Q. It didn't impress you, did it, that the man who is her
husband at the end of this book is the same young man with
whom she had her first sexual experience?

A. Wait a minute. You lost me on that. I think you are
right, and that that was supposed to be the moral in it.

When we reached the matter of definitions, Dr. Collins relaxed. He was a teacher of English, a Ph.D. who had studied at
Harvard and Oxford, and I was asking him about the meaning
of words. Lecturing, he had testified, had been his life. He lectured me.

But teacher had neglected his own homework. His answers,
as I mentioned in summation, showed that he had not done the
assigned reading very carefully, or else, for whatever reason, he
was unable to absorb it, or to retain it overnight. Moreover, his
opinions about the book had no real relevance. Assuming testimony in terms of legal conclusions were proper at all—a point
on which I disagreed with Judge Macaulay—the language Dr.
Collins spoke was not the language of the courts. If *Tropic of
Cancer* was, in his lexicon, patently offensive, prurient and ob-

scene, then his use of these terms to describe *Memoirs* was legally meaningless—in Massachusetts, at any rate. I referred to
this also when I summed up:

> In addition, while he testified that the book before the
> court is obscene, prurient, offensive and indecent, his under-
> standing of those words is demonstrated by the fact that he
> would apply each one of them to a book which the Supreme
> Judicial Court has held to be not obscene. That book, of
> course—
>
> THE COURT: By a four-to-three vote.
>
> MR. REMBAR: Still binding on this court, your Honor.

In an earlier chapter I described two objectives of the lawyer
at trial: persuading the trial court and building a record for
appeal. There are other prizes—false ones—that lawyers sometimes strive for. One is persuading the spectators (however few
they may be). This is a trap of vanity, deepened by the movies
and television. (Contemplating the effect of television courtroom drama on legal style, I have sometimes felt a chill at what
must be happening to medical techniques.) The other false
prize is persuading the witness. Here the natural urge to win an
argument can do a lawyer in. The crestfallen witness is largely
a literary invention. Very often after an obliterating cross-
examination, a man will leave the stand looking fat and happy.
If the edge of his testimony has been dulled, or if he has been
led by his own words to subvert the proposition that he was
called to support, the job has been completed. It is not necessary
that he acknowledge his defeat; it is not even necessary that he
be aware of it.

Nor is it necessary that the judge or jury (let alone the spectators) recognize the significance of what has happened. At the
time it may not be fully understood by anybody but the examining lawyer. It may take some pointing out. But this pointing
out is better kept for later—for summation or appeal. If the
lawyer insists on proclaiming the ruin of the testimony in the
course of the examination, the principal effect is to give the witness a chance to explain or retract or in some other way repair
the damage.*

---

* Although the two often go together, many courtroom situations offer

In Boston some of the spectators reported that Dr. Collins appeared pleased when he stepped down from the stand and walked out of the courtroom. He had been a virtuoso on the definitions.

Later there was an opportunity to strike all of his testimony. The Boston action was based on the paperback edition of *Memoirs*, published jointly by Putnam and Dell. It differed from the hardcover only in that some material about the New York litigation had been added to the introductory note. By this time there had also been a competing paperback by a California publisher using the imprint "Brandon House." On the cross-examination of one of our witnesses, Sullivan asked if there was any homosexuality in the novel. Our witness answered that there was "a reference to a homosexual episode" but that it was "not described in detail." Sullivan seemed puzzled:

Q. It is not? Have you read the paperback or just the hardcover?

A. I understand they are the same. . . .

MR. REMBAR: They are the same in that regard.

MR. SULLIVAN: I have a specific page in mind.

A. I understand that there is a passage that the editors believed a later publisher inserted and therefore was not written by Cleland, but does occur in some eighteenth-century editions of this book.

THE COURT: We are only interested in this particular book that is in litigation here.

THE WITNESS: The particular episode I have in mind is the one in which Fanny is disgusted by what she sees.

MR. SULLIVAN: That is what I have in mind.

THE COURT: I didn't hear you.

THE WITNESS: I said, the passage I have in mind is the one

---

a choice between looking good and doing good. The lawyer should never concentrate on trying to look good. There is an old story about an attorney whose reputation for eloquence had grown irritating to some members of his community. One of them went around town saying that while the lawyer might be clever, he wasn't clever enough to fool *him;* if *he* was ever on the jury, he damned sure wasn't going to be taken in by legal tricks. He got his chance. The jury gave the bright lawyer's client a quick victory. Questioned about it afterward, the iconoclast said he had not been impressed at all; in this particular case, he explained, the man just happened to have the law and the facts on his side.

in which Fanny expressed disgust at what she had seen. The actual episode itself, I said, is not presented in the detail that the other episodes are presented.

MR. SULLIVAN: I had for reference, your Honor, a book that Dr. Collins read and it was somewhat different from this.

If the book that Dr. Collins read was not the book on trial, a motion to strike his testimony would in all probability have been successful. Evidently he had been given the Brandon paperback, which included a passage that the Putnam editors had rejected as spurious. Reuben Goodman, the Massachusetts attorney associated with me in this case (he had defended Hubert Selby's *Tra La La* in the Provincetown trial that was the banner event of the 1962 Cape Cod summer season), spotted the discrepancy instantly.* He asked, in a co-counsel's courtroom whisper, whether I did not want to move to strike. I shook my head. It would have been a small victory, one that would sacrifice what seemed to me an important advantage. Dr. Collins' testimony had, I thought, been more than neutralized; taken as a whole, it suggested that *Memoirs* was proof against attack from literary sources. It would give the appellate court a sign of what might be expected when the prosecution sought to make an issue, through testimony, of whether the book had literary merit. Possibly other literary witnesses might have done a better job for the attorney general; John Ciardi, for example, would have made things interesting. But I had to make a decision on the spot, and my decision was that on this record Dr. Collins had done us more good than harm.

Sullivan used the cross-examination of our witnesses to establish the proposition that there is a large amount of sex in *Fanny Hill.* "Percentagewise," he asked Professor Fred Holley Stocking of Williams College, "what proportion of this book is devoted to depicting sexual relations of one kind or another?" I objected that the problem before the court was one of freedom, not

---

* *Tra La La* became a chapter in Selby's later-published *Last Exit to Brooklyn.* The court decided the story was obscene, but when it was appealed, the attorney general, with bigger fish to fry, dropped it.

arithmetic. If sex may be the subject of art and literature—and the Supreme Court has said that it surely may—then it should make no difference how much of a book is devoted to sex. The whole-book rule had been in effect in Massachusetts for almost twenty years (and longer elsewhere), but the judge denied my objection. The process was repeated with four of our witnesses. They answered the questions, but their answers must have seemed to Sullivan hardly worth the trouble. The cross-examination of Professor Bullitt, for example, included this:*

Q. Of the characters in the book, how many of the characters are depicted in relation to nonsexual happenings? A rough estimate.
A. May I ask a question?
Q. Certainly.
A. To clarify your question, do you mean in their total life span given to us, because some of the characters who are involved in sexual exploits have a good deal of other things—
Q. Any time they appear in the book.
A. Any time. Very few, if any.
Q. Very few, if any.
MR. REMBAR: I'm sorry—would you repeat the question, please?
THE COURT: How many characters in the book were concerned with nonsexual activities.
MR. REMBAR: At any time, was that it, or wholly?
THE WITNESS: At some time.
Q. At some time in the book concerned with nonsexual activities. What was your answer?
A. My answer to that would be no.

While one of our witnesses—Professor Norman Holland of M.I.T.—was being asked to reckon the percentages (something that proved difficult even for one from so scientific a station), it occurred to me that I might make my point through testimony.

---

* John Bullitt was a professor of English at Harvard, specializing in eighteenth-century literature. He was also the master of Quincy House. He was also an ex-boxer, and he had the boxer's habit of keeping his chin in and looking up at his antagonist from under his eyebrows. He did a lot of bobbing and weaving in the witness chair, but not in what he said: his testimony was straight and forceful, the caper that follows a bizarre exception.

If Judge Macaulay could not accept the idea, put in the form of an objection, that preoccupation with a single subject matter did not condemn a book, the idea might still be demonstrated, for the record at least, by analogy.

Redirect Examination by Mr. Rembar

Q. Mr. Holland, are you familiar with the Horatio Hornblower novels of Mr. Forester?

A. Dimly. I used to read them when I was a kid.

THE COURT: You say dimly?

THE WITNESS: Dimly.

THE COURT: It reminds me of the use of the words "dim beacon" in the *Tropic of Cancer* case.

MR. REMBAR: In the minority opinion, your Honor.

Q. Would you say that those novels dealt in large part with the activity of sailing?

A. Yes.

Q. Would you also say that there is almost no character in that book who is not involved in some way or another in sailing ships?

A. Right; I think that's correct.

Q. As a student of the novel, can you tell me whether it has ever been thought to be a literary requirement that a novel deal with all aspects of life?

A. No, not particularly. A novel necessarily has to limit itself to the scene somewhat and that sort of thing.

Q. Does it deprive a novel of its quality as a work of art if it deals almost entirely with one aspect of life—as, for example, sailing ships?

A. No, not at all.

MR. REMBAR: That's all; thank you.

Bullitt testified about the portrayal of character in *Memoirs*, and by way of comparison, spoke about other eighteenth-century novels. At this point, the record had been loaded with names—names of writers, names of the people in their books, and names of critics and scholars. It led to a droll application of a rule of evidence:

Q. (by Mr. Rembar): You just mentioned, Mr. Bullitt, two characters who are quite distinct in the book. Is there in general the treatment of character and the development of character in this book that is typical of the novel as a literary form?

A. Very much so. Perhaps the proper way to start answering your question is to refer to a critical remark made by Henry Fielding in *Tom Jones*—

THE COURT: No. You can't bring hearsay in there.

THE WITNESS: Sorry.

Evidently Macaulay thought the witness was about to repeat "a critical remark made by Henry Fielding to Tom Jones." Since neither Fielding nor Jones was in court, the judge must have felt his quick intervention saved the record from a double dose of hearsay.

Some of the witnesses were asked a pair of questions that rather mystified me. They had to do with the language used in *Memoirs*. Counsel addressed them first to Bullitt. They also mystified Bullitt, but he recovered:

Q. (by Mr. Sullivan): I would like to ask one question. Are you married?

A. I am indeed.

Q. The language used in this book—is this the type of language you would use over the breakfast table with your wife?

A. There isn't a single dirty word in this book.

Q. Would you answer my question?

A. Yes indeed. Indeed.

MR. SULLIVAN: No further questions.

Sullivan put the same questions to Holland, who made a graceful response:

Q. Are you married, Dr. Holland?

A. Yes, I am, Mr. Sullivan.

Q. Would you use the type of language that is used in this book over the breakfast table with your wife?

A. I would, were I so skilled to speak it.

We had an asset at the time of the Boston trial that had been lacking in New York: some good reviews. After the New York trial, V. S. Pritchett and Bridget Brophy had written about *Memoirs*, the former in *The New York Review of Books* and the latter in *The New Statesman*—both fine pieces of critical writing. There were things in Brophy's article that worked against us; my opponents could have picked damaging sentences out of it. But she treated the book as literature and as something worthy of attention, and this, so far as we were concerned, was what counted. Pritchett was even more helpful. Apart from its general excellence, his article made some of the very points I was making. This was not entirely coincidence. The editors of *The New York Review* had told me Pritchett was going to write about *Fanny Hill* and had asked for copies of my briefs in the New York case. So we find Pritchett saying, among other things:

> the real test is not what the average man thinks; it is the test of artistic merit, and if he is called upon to judge, it is the average man's duty to find out what artistic merit is. . . . I believe one can see it also [the transmuting process of art] in that minor amatory exercise *Memoirs of a Woman of Pleasure*. No one is asked to say *how* meritorious an artist is in these matters, but it is essential for the transmuting element to be recognized.

And corroborating the argument that the 1821 case was not a pertinent precedent, because the indictment referred primarily to the illustration rather than the writing:

> After [the original] publication, the real pornographers got to work on *Fanny Hill*. The book was pirated. The pirates supplied obscene illustrations. (One set of these by Cruikshank must have been good, but it has been lost.) They dirtied the text, added episodes. The illustrations led to prosecutions.

Here we had impressive documentation for points that had previously been advanced rather nakedly in the briefs—a prime example of bootstrap jurisprudence.

Sometimes an objection can be made too soon. Normally this is an error that the lawyer commits; in this case it was the judge. At the New York trial, when I was seeking to establish the quality of the publisher, I had asked Walter Minton whether Putnam had ever been in trouble with the law of obscenity. The ideal answer, of course, would have been no, never. But the actuality was not too bad either: just once, with Dr. Marie C. Stopes's *Married Love*. The fact that this modest and gentle manual could at one time have been the subject of attack was itself a helpful bit of history.* In Boston, I tried to get the same testimony. But this time there was an objection, not from my opponent but from the court:

> Q. Prior to the publication of *Memoirs of a Woman of Pleasure*, had Putnam ever been involved in an obscenity case?
>
> THE COURT: What is the purpose, please?
>
> MR. REMBAR: I want to show the standing and reputation of the firm that published this book, your Honor.
>
> THE COURT: This action is against the book itself, not against the publisher.
>
> MR. REMBAR: Very well.

It was very well indeed. It appeared that I was asking Minton the question counting on a negative answer—that Putnam had never been involved with obscenity. Judge Macaulay did not want that to go into the record. But his silencing the witness left the clear, if inaccurate, impression that the answer would have been no. The appellate court could assume that in all one hundred and twenty-five years of its existence Putnam had never once been charged with publishing a dirty book. It was not incumbent upon me, on the appeal, to negate the implication Judge Macaulay had created. As a matter of fact, there would be

---

* The case, which Putnam won, involved a Customs ban, and as in all such cases, the parties were the government and the book. Such actions are brought by the government to effect a forfeiture of the object being imported, which is itself nominally the defendant. Accordingly, the official title of the case was *United States* v. *One Obscene Book Entitled* Married Love, but it is usually referred to as *United States* v. *Married Love*.

no way to do that without going outside the record, and appellate courts frown on such excursions. If I had been asked, I would have said; nobody asked.

The Massachusetts trial had a feature that the New York and New Jersey trials lacked—a hostile judge. I do not mean Macaulay was discourteous.* I mean he came to the trial with a preconception and was loath to let it go. For example, with our witness Ira Konigsberg, a young and acute assistant professor at Brandeis, the judge himself became the cross-examiner. Konigsberg said that compared to certain contemporary novels, *Memoirs* was "obviously more healthy."

> THE COURT: More healthy?
> THE WITNESS: Yes sir, more healthy. . . .
> THE COURT: What about the three other girls whose history is given in the book besides Fanny? Remember about three other associates of hers in whatever you might call her calling?
> THE WITNESS: Yes. . . . One ends up married and the other two do end up happy, but various aspects of their professional life are attacked by Fanny at various times in the novel as being perverse or in bad taste or without love, and when they do undergo these experiences—for example when one of the girls dresses as a man and ends up with another man, Fanny is quite willing to expose this as in poor taste. . . .
> THE COURT: Would you say these three other girls told about their experiences with a sense of pride?
> THE WITNESS: No.
> THE COURT: Sense of exaltation?
> THE WITNESS: I wouldn't use those particular words. I think they are too strong for that. . . .
> THE COURT: What about the whipping incident?
> THE WITNESS: That too is held up—
> THE COURT: The homosexual incident?

---

* Not to be confused with the Macaulay who said:

> We find it difficult to believe that in a world so full of temptations as this, any gentleman, whose life would have been virtuous if he had not read Aristophanes and Juvenal, will be made vicious by reading them.

THE WITNESS: Yes sir.

THE COURT: The lesbianism?

THE WITNESS: They fit into the pattern. The homosexual incident is held up with scorn. It is undercut throughout by a very strong comic element. The same can be said of the whipping. She reacts violently to both of them.

Konigsberg *sir*'ed the judge throughout but finally showed his irritation:

THE COURT: Would you describe the description given by the author of these acts as pornographic?

THE WITNESS: Could you tell me what you mean by pornographic?

THE COURT: You don't know what I mean?

THE WITNESS: I don't know what *you* mean. I know what *I* would mean by pornographic.

THE COURT: If you don't know, you need not answer.

This is not a harsh criticism. Macaulay was nothing like the anti-law nonjudges who ran some of the *Tropic* trials (not, incidentally, those I have described in detail); I would have guessed that in general he was fair and able. It is just very difficult, in these cases, for the judge to keep his eye, fixed and unwavering, on the law. Fanny Hill is too beguiling, and *Fanny Hill* must suffer the consequences. Before the trial was over it was pretty clear that Macaulay would rule against us. He did.

A curious phenomenon in censorship is the censors' personal immunity to the infectious book. The moral fiber in jeopardy is always somebody else's. In not one of these trials did the prosecution produce a witness—or his doctor, or his clergyman—who, as a result of his reading, suffered physical, moral or spiritual deterioration. But the prosecutors are certain it can happen —to other people.

In his final words at the trial, Mr. Sullivan made a patently sincere peroration:

I necessarily read this book prior to trying this case. I am not a literary expert, although I did major in English in college. I am not one easily offended, but I was offended by this book, and I feel there is no literary merit in it. It did arouse prurient interest and impure thoughts in me. Fortunately I am well adjusted enough so it did not affect my daily life, but I wonder if that could be said for everyone who has access to a book of this nature.

This might seem, to those who were not present, to sound a note of smugness. Quite the contrary; the coda rang with humility. It even appeared for a moment that Mr. Sullivan might knock on wood.

Two Hundred and Eighteen Simply
Said Man

THE PRELIMINARY DECISION BANNING *FANNY HILL* in New York may or may not have been heard round the world, but it easily carried across the Hudson. One of the two New Jersey counties that face New York City from the west shore of the river is Bergen. The magnificent Hudson Palisades are Bergen's brow. Behind them, to the north and west, there are pleasant suburbs and good-looking farms. To the southwest, the land sinks into the Jersey Meadows, where chemical plants, abattoirs and dump heaps combine with the marshes to produce a celebrated odor. At the edge of the Meadows is Hackensack, the county seat. Tightly girdled by a net of superhighways built for people intent on getting somewhere else, cut off by the Palisades from whatever sea breeze the Manhattan masonry might let through, and deprived of the west wind by the overprivileged suburbs in the hills, Hackensack, loveliest village of the plain, is a hot place in June. The New Jersey *Fanny Hill* trial was held in Hackensack. It was held in June.

Putnam has its warehouse in Bergen County, and Putnam's president, Walter Minton, lives in Bergen County. One day in 1963, after the New York preliminary injunction was issued but before the New York trial, the warehouse manager reported that two men came by, asking questions. They said they were from the county prosecutor's office. Were there copies of *Memoirs* in the warehouse? Were shipments being made? And was the manager aware that in New York the book was banned? At about the same time, American Book-Stratford Press, a large printing company that did work for Putnam and had a plant in Bergen County, told us they had a visit from the same two investigators; there again they talked about the New York banning.

The official whose title in most states is district attorney is called county prosecutor in New Jersey. The prosecutor for Bergen County was Guy M. Calissi, one of the most ardent and vigorous of the officials who played a role in these cases. When *Tropic of Cancer* was published, he had made a large number of arrests, and largely as a result of his efforts there was no distribution of *Tropic* in New Jersey for three years.

Activity in the prosecutor's office is disquieting. The prosecutor is, of course, concerned with crime, and we did not want a criminal trial—for two reasons. One was that it is always unpleasant, and sometimes disastrous, to be a defendant in a criminal case, and since Walter Minton lived in New Jersey, the court would have no jurisdictional problems in making him a defendant. The other was that we were in general better off with judges than with juries, and in a criminal case we might have to take a jury.*

In an earlier chapter, I said that an exercise in imagination is necessary to the understanding of a law or a constitution; you must envision its effect in situations other than the immediate one. Most people find this difficult. "Most people" includes some judges, but the chances that a judge will make the effort are greater than that a member of a jury will. Jurymen are to some extent interested in the law, but their interest tends to be

---

* Not every criminal trial is by jury. Federal and state constitutions give defendants in major criminal cases the right to have a jury. The right can be waived. In some states, however, the prosecution can demand a jury even if the defendant would prefer not to have one. Although the law on the point is not too clear, this seems to be the way it is in New Jersey, and the indications were that the prosecutor would make the demand.

academic. Their search for a verdict is likely to be unanalytical and narrowly focused: which side ought to win this case? Where censorship is involved, the question becomes: are we in favor of or against the publication of the book? That question in turn, for the generation that provided the jury panels of the period, came down to this: is it the kind of book we have grown up thinking of as a dirty book? But for a judge—that is, the man on the bench who deserved to be called a judge—the question would be different: does this book, whether or not I approve of it, lie outside the broad guaranties of the First Amendment? When this was the question, our chances, of course, were much better.

In England the situation was just the opposite; publisher's lawyers preferred juries. Apparently most of the judges there felt that constitutional liberties, which British courts have maintained against flesh-and-blood tyrants, must crumble when they come up against the terrible majesty of public decency. Meanwhile, juries gave verdicts for the defense, sometimes to the annoyance of the judge. The strictness of the latter was perhaps a consequence of the fact that Britain has no written constitution. Probably the tolerance of juries was a social rather than a legal response—the British public, at this point in history, pleasurably tearing down the edifice constructed by their ex-betters.

By and large, the people who oppose censorship fit into the sloppy concept "liberal." Trial by jury is associated with rule by the common man, and considered a feature of democracy. Many of our sympathizers were puzzled that I should decline the boon of a jury. Authors who have suffered from the censorship laws go even farther in this direction. Some of them tend to be emotionally if not philosophically anarchistic, and they distrust profoundly that embodiment of authority, the judge. Henry Miller gave us a particularly ironic example. In 1959—a few months before *Lady Chatterley* was published in the United States—the Supreme Court of Norway was considering whether his book *Sexus* was obscene, and Miller wrote a letter to the court. The letter states, *inter alia* (everything Miller states is charmingly *inter alia*), that he has questions he would like to put to the court. He asks whether such a thing can be done. He then answers himself, incorrectly:

I am afraid not. The judicial body is a sacrosanct body.

Having endowed the judiciary with a protective sanctity that Chief Justice Warren, for example, would find interesting, Miller continues:

> This is unfortunate, as I see it, for when issues of grave import arise the last court of reference, in my opinion, should be the public. When justice is at stake, responsibility cannot be shifted to an elect few without injustices resulting.

When Miller had his large encounter with the law, on *Tropic of Cancer*, he did very poorly with his last court of reference, the public, and its operating arm, the jury. He was saved by that elect few, the judges.*

It is part of a deeper fallacy—that democracy is mere majoritarianism. Democracy is more than rule by numbers. It is a group of values, kept alive by a defined process. Freedom of expression is one of the values and, at the same time, one of the working elements in the process.

As soon as we heard the prosecutor was active, and before he could take any steps, we started a suit for declaratory judgment —a suit, as I have said, that asks the court to state the rights of the parties. This was partly an effort to shift the battle from the criminal courts to the civil, and partly an application of the doctrine of Don't Just Stand There, or Hit Him First. (It may be dignifying this too much to call it a doctrine; it may be more of a recurrent impulse.)†

---

* This, of course, was the issue argued in 1787 and for three-quarters of a century afterward—Miller taking the view of Samuel Adams, Jefferson and Patrick Henry, against that of John Adams, Hamilton and Washington. The triumph of the conservatives (the word is relative, of course; they had just participated in a leftist rebellion) insured the doctrine of judicial review, which today proves such an annoyance to conservatives. It is a fair guess, however, that Washington, Hamilton and John Adams, alive today, would not be conservative, and Jefferson, Henry and old Sam Adams would favor judicial review.

Miller, incidentally, lost the case in Norway; as much as we admire the Norwegians and their government, they do not have our First Amendment.

† There was the case against the Washington police in the very beginning of the *Lady Chatterley* troubles, before any government official moved

Not every difference of opinion is appropriate for declaratory judgment; there must be an existing controversy, not just the prospect of one. On the other hand, the controversy must not be the subject of litigation already under way. And whether the procedure can be used where a crime is being charged is a question that the courts find vexing. The law here is in a delicate and awkward position, involving as it does an intrusion by one court into the affairs of another, and the precedents are not consistent. But this at least can be said: where First Amendment rights are concerned, prosecutors must be scrupulous to confine themselves to prosecuting, and must not use the weight of their office to regulate the sale of books. (They often have, of course. "Must not," in the law, means that a court will do something about the situation provided one is willing to suffer the trouble and expense of asking it to.) The imminence of prosecution for obscenity would not, without more, provide a ground for declaratory judgment. But interfering with publication by official threat is something more. We were contending that Calissi's men had gone beyond investigation; their inquiry about the New York banning—a gratuitous inquiry, we said, unless it was meant as a threat—constituted our main evidence. It wasn't much.

Whether this was a proper case for declaratory judgment was never resolved. New Jersey has a statute like New York's Section 22-a, and the prosecutor filed a counterclaim to our complaint, seeking an injunction against the distribution of the book. The prosecutor had in effect agreed to have it out in the civil courts, which was all, procedurally, we were after.

The New York ban had triggered Calissi's moves. Before the New Jersey case came to trial, however, the situation in New York was turned around—twice. Judge Klein made his decision, more significant than the earlier one for the reason (among others) that it came after full trial. But then the Appellate Division reversed Klein, and this was still more significant because it came from a higher court. After the New Jersey trial, and before

---

against the book. A few years later, a Long Island district attorney seized copies of the *Evergreen Review* to use as evidence in an obscenity prosecution; on behalf of Grove, we brought an action which ended with the district attorney subject to a federal injunction.

the judge there had arrived at a decision, the Court of Appeals held *Memoirs* not obscene, making the third reversal in the New York case. Later, however, and also before the New Jersey decision, the Boston judge held the book obscene. The net effect of all this was pretty much an equilibrium; eight judges had ruled against the book, and seven had ruled in its favor. The conclusion that the New Jersey judge eventually reached was probably no different from what it would have been if none of the other cases had taken place.

The judge, Morris Pashman, was an excellent trial judge. He had a quick intelligence, and the fine blend of patience and firmness that constitutes the judicial temperament.

Ronald Picinich (a soft *c* and an accent on the second syllable) tried the case for the prosecutor. He was skilled, bright and humorous. He had an air of detachment that added force to his arguments and, incidentally, produced an unusual (and unreported) bit of courtroom humor.

Picinich was trying to elicit certain testimony from a witness. I was doing my best to make it tough for him. He put a question to which I objected. Judge Pashman sustained the objection. He put another, aimed at getting the same sort of testimony. Again I objected, this time on a somewhat different ground. We argued. The objection was again sustained. It was becoming apparent that with these rulings it was going to be very difficult, perhaps impossible, to frame a question that would produce the answer Picinich wanted. And so he returned to the argument that his questions were proper. The judge, having shown the patience I mentioned, now showed the firmness; he had heard enough from both of us. He cut Picinich off with a brisk "All right, what's the next question?" Picinich thought for a long moment. "The next question," he said, "is *e, r.*" He pronounced the letters separately, spelling out the distressed lawyer's—the distressed anybody's—favorite monosyllable and giving a complete description of the legal situation.*

---

* The stenographer told me afterward that he customarily left certain things out of the transcript, things he thought were not seriously intended; hence he had omitted this exchange. Censorship is everywhere.

But Picinich brought to court more than humor. His approach was sophisticated, and the case he sought to build was the most elaborate I encountered in all this litigation. Counsel for the attorney general in Massachusetts had been sophisticated in their legal analysis, but they had evidently decided on a low-key trial. Picinich made his attack through witnesses.

In the *Chatterley* case the government lawyers called no witnesses. Their theory was that the book condemned itself; this was the traditional approach of the prosecution in obscenity cases. With *Tropic of Cancer* the situation changed; in some of the *Tropic* trials, the prosecution used witnesses, but their testimony had little meaning. Usually they were called not because they had any facts or competent opinion to contribute, but because the prosecution thought their presence would make an impression on the judge or jury. The churches were a favorite source (not that the entire clergy, or even most of it, agreed the books should be suppressed), and district attorneys looked for the nice three-faith balance that Quel had attained in New York.

Picinich did something quite different. He offered to answer through testimony the big unanswered questions of the earlier obscenity cases: Does reading about sex—and in particular reading the book on trial—have a bad effect on the reader? Does it damage him? Does it prompt him to commit antisocial sexual acts?

Censors of the obscene had always maintained that reading the evil material was bad for people, but they had no proof. Defenders of books had pointed to the lack of proof and made an argument of it. When the *Roth* case was in the court of appeals, Judge Jerome Frank wrote a concurring opinion that attracted a good deal of attention. The opinion, quoting a respected sociologist, said there was no evidence that reading the disapproved material had detrimental consequences. On a less scholarly level, there was Mayor Jimmy Walker's celebrated remark that he had never heard of a girl who had been seduced by a book (a tribute to the impermeable virtue of New York womanhood perhaps, but an insult to literature).

But the libertarians' favorite reference was a survey made by the New York City Bureau of Social Hygiene in the 1920's. It was cited in law review articles and in judicial opinions—by Judge Frank, by Justice Douglas when the *Roth* case reached the Supreme Court, and by Judge Fuld in the *Gent* case. Part of its durability was that it was so cute. This was Judge Fuld's summary:

> And a survey made some years ago by the New York City Bureau of Social Hygiene showed that out of 409 college women who responded to the question inquiring what they found most sexually stimulating, 18 said "pictures," 40 said "drama," 95 said "books," and 218 simply said "man."

By this time the survey was nearly forty years old, and a tradition in the liberal attack on censorship. No prosecuting attorney challenged it. It had been repeated so many times that everybody assumed it meant something. In fact, it meant very little.

The object of the survey was to gather data on the sexual mores of female college graduates. Questionnaires were sent to ten thousand unmarried women. Fewer than one thousand came back, and most of them were incomplete. No personal interviews were conducted. There was no attempt, either extrinsically or by built-in tests such as the Kinsey researchers used, to check the honesty of the responses.

The fact that the largest number of those who returned the questionnaires seemed to find "man" more exciting than anything else was always good for an appreciative chuckle. But it does not answer the censor. A woman's sexual fantasy will normally involve a man, but, it may fairly be asked, what brings on the fantasy? Since "man" is in this context a constant, associated with all the other stimulants, it has no legitimate place as a separate factor in the inquiry. When it is eliminated, books are the winner, by a wide margin. The questionnaires, if they proved anything, proved more for the suppressors of books than for their defenders.

As research, the survey had no scientific validity. As material for legal decision, it added nothing to the simple you-can't-prove-it argument. As a forensic device, it had a wiseguy air that would only irritate a judge not already convinced. The defenders of freedom should indeed have something of the Jimmy Walker in them; mockery and breeziness can be an appropriate part of the response to the censor. But they are not enough, and while glibness is an aid to advocacy, the advocate must know, even better than his audience, just how much of his discourse is no more than glib.

There is another danger: the approach depends on a negative —the absence of proof. Suppose some evidence of a causal connection should turn up. Once you make an argument, you are liable to get stuck with it. When you go too far and too confidently, you may not be able to retreat. If it is a clever argument, the effect is all the worse; the judge (or any listener) will be embarrassed and resentful at having gone along with (and perhaps enjoyed) the fine little demonstration. You will end somewhere back of where you started.

The most important objection to the argument, however, is that it demeans the First Amendment. Freedom of speech does not need such a defense. The Amendment assumes harm will come of some of the expression it fosters.

I had cited the survey in a few of the earlier cases, but by this time I felt it was a mistake and made no mention of it, nor of any other published comment on whether pornography is harmful. But Picinich was not content with a stand-off. He called witnesses to testify that reading books such as *Fanny Hill*—and, specifically, *Fanny Hill*—would have very bad consequences. The issue raised, I found a witness to testify in rebuttal. But I relied mainly on cross-examination of the prosecutor's witnesses, and on the proposition that the whole inquiry was beside the point.

Some of this testimony can be fully understood only if it is seen unexpurgated. For this reason, I will set forth almost all of the prosecution's case, uninterrupted by narration, with such comments as I may make relegated to the lower part of the page.*

---

* On the question of literary merit, or its absence, Picinich relied, as Quel had, on the offstage voices of Ciardi and Hutchens.

ℱanny Hill
in Hackensack

WILLIAM P. REILLY, sworn*
Direct Examination by Mr. Picinich†

Q. With respect to the book, John Cleland's *Memoirs of a Woman of Pleasure*, introduced in evidence, have you read that book?

A. Yes sir.

Q. Can you state for the court what the dominant subject matter of that book is?

A. Yes, the dominant—

MR. REMBAR: Excuse me.

THE COURT [to the witness]: Just a minute.

MR. REMBAR: The defendant objects to the question on the ground that it calls for a conclusion of law.

THE COURT [to Picinich]: You said dominant subject matter. The phrase is a bit difficult. You are talking about just the underlying theme?

MR. PICINICH: Just the general subject matter. How does that

---

* Dr. Reilly's face was highly mobile, rather fleshy and generally beneficent. Except under stress, he had a jolly look, a sort of secular Friar Tuck. The resemblance was only skin-deep.

† The testimony on the witness's qualification is omitted; its substance appears below.

call for a conclusion of law? I am not calling for something forbidden here; I am calling for what is the subject matter, what does the book deal with.

MR. REMBAR: On that I would say the question is improper because the book speaks for itself.

THE COURT: I will overrule the objection. The witness may answer just that question, nothing more than that. Go ahead.

A. The overall theme, the dominant theme of this book, is a portrayal of abnormality and perversion as being normal.

Q. What does the book deal with?

A. The book deals with abnormal sex.

Q. Now are there instances of abnormal sex portrayed in this book?

A. Definitely.

Q. Can you point to some of those instances which you consider to be abnormal?

A. Sure. I don't know if you want the exact page or not, but there are certain articles in here in which voyeurism is indicated, which is abnormal; homosexuality, which is abnormal; flagellation, which is abnormal; fetishism, which is abnormal. If you want the specific mentioning of these I will be glad to do that.

THE COURT: You are mentioning them.

THE WITNESS: But if you want the specific part of the book, all right.

THE COURT: No, just that phase.

Q. Just the topics.

A. Yes, there is no question about it—yes, that is the dominant theme of this book.

THE COURT: You have answered that. What is the next question?

Q. My next question is, What effect would reading this book have upon the average person?

MR. REMBAR: My objection to that question again is that it calls for a conclusion of law. It is an attempt to get from a witness an answer to one of the tests set up in the *Roth* opinion, in the words of that very test.

MR. PICINICH: I am not asking for legal opinion but for medical opinion—how does this reading experience or how does this portrayal of abnormal sexual experiences affect the average person? It is medical.

THE COURT: Which average person, according to the courts, does not exist.

Q. [MR. PICINICH]: All right, the normal: how does it affect the normal person?

MR. REMBAR: I don't think the witness is qualified as an expert to answer that question. He is qualified as a pediatrician and as an army psychiatrist, and with experience in psychiatry which took place over twenty years ago or about twenty years ago.* The effect of the book on the normal person is simply a question which this court from its knowledge of the law and of normal people generally will have to answer for himself.

THE COURT: For whatever benefit it has, I am going to overrule the objection and allow the answer to be given, with the understanding, as I indicated earlier, that I may reconsider on these questions which are being objected to and reconsider the competency of the evidence. Upon that reconsideration, if it is to be stricken, counsel will be so notified prior to any decision as to which evidence has been stricken and which has been permitted to stand. You may answer the question.†

A. The question about an average person, your Honor—you just mentioned no such thing exists. It is proven by law. I am speaking as a layman, as a pediatrician. A pediatrician does not simply hand out pills and watch for formulas. One of the biggest things we have to do is watch for the mental health, and health takes in that whole broad expanse of mental health and, of course, physical health.

THE COURT: The answer will be stricken as not being responsive.‡ Read the question.

---

* This was a fair summary of the qualifying testimony. Reilly had not mentioned any work in psychiatry apart from his military service, and since leaving the army (to which he had gone immediately after medical school) he had practiced as a pediatrician.

† In general a judge sitting without a jury tends to decide disputed questions of evidence on the side of admissibility. The theory is that while a jury may be improperly influenced by testimony that should not have been heard, the judge can himself determine (if not instantly, then upon reflection) what should be taken into consideration and what should not. In this case the questions of relevance and competence were particularly difficult, and at the pretrial meetings Judge Pashman announced he would allow the doubtful evidence to be given, and after the trial, having weighed the legal arguments, decide what might properly be considered and what might not.

‡ "Responsive" in the law means simply what it seems to mean: the witness is expected to respond to the question—no more, no less. The word

MR. PICINICH: Perhaps that is one of the reasons; there was a long objection after the last question, your Honor. Maybe that is why it wasn't responsive.*

THE COURT: As the case goes, objections will be made and very properly so.

(The reporter reads the pending question as follows: "QUESTION: My next question is, What effect would reading this book have upon the average person?")

THE COURT: Answer that question.

A. Your Honor, all right, I will answer the question. I will simply say this. In the field of medicine, like in the field of law, it makes it very difficult; you can't make a flat statement like that; you have to modify your answer to a certain extent based upon contingencies.

The effect on the average person of this kind of material is definitely detrimental to their mental health, and I say definitely. To the average person a constant perusal—a constant perusal of this kind of material—would definitely stimulate them to acts of sexual activity.

Q. When I use the word "average person," would your answer be the same if I removed that word and said "normal person"?

A. Yes, definitely.

BY THE COURT: †

Q. Is part of your answer stimulation, as you use it, is objectionable—just that emotion?

A. To abnormal sex, abnormal sex.

Q. I don't understand that.

A. This is what I mean. Perusal of this type of material—

Q. No. You said that this book would stimulate an individual.

A. I don't know.

MR. PICINICH: It was to acts of sexual activity.

---

came up with unusual frequency in this case, on both sides; some of the witnesses would ignore the question asked and answer an imaginary question they would have preferred.

* The implication is that the witness was so bemused by my objection that he forgot what the question was. A further implication, moderately impolite, was that I had planned it this way.

† This means that until the stenographer says "By Mr. Picinich," the questions—here the next half-dozen—are the judge's.

A. All right, to acts of sexual activity.

Q. You consider this objectionable from your standpoint, just stimulation in itself?

A. Stimulation as such?

Q. Yes.

A. Of course not. I am referring, of course, when this is being geared to the average person and it isn't under the proper circumstances. For example, if a husband and wife were to be reading this book, say, when they retire to their bedchamber at night, I don't see where it would be so bad, I grant you that, but we are speaking to the average person under ordinary circumstances.

Q. You condone the book under the setting you just described?

A. I wouldn't condone anything. Your Honor, I am simply saying taken in that broad context that it would not be too bad.

THE COURT: Go ahead.

BY MR. PICINICH:

Q. This stimulation to sex, would you say that the normal person would react to this, the stimulation would be normal, or a healthy or a wholesome stimulation?

A. It would be an abnormal, an unhealthy stimulation.

Q. In what way, and how does that differ from the normal and healthy stimulation?

A. If you make sex as the end-all and be-all of existence, as the pleasures of sex and nothing else, without assuming the responsibilities that go along with sex. Sex as we know it is a God-given act. It is able to evoke the most intensive human pleasures with a definite reason behind it, as most average people will see it, as procreation of the races, to perform your functions of civic-minded citizens, to take your place as citizens. But when you make the sexual pleasure an end in itself you are going to end up with anarchy, you have nothing else left. Hedonism, which is what this is, is pure pleasure for pleasure's sake. It offers nothing. It offers nothing to a society.

Q. And would the manner in which the author treats the variety of sex weigh in that analysis that you have just made?

A. Of course it does; certainly.

Q. In what way?

A. For example, we would have many kinds of books in the field of medicine where we do have certain types of books that we use for young people getting married to explain sex in its entire effect. That is a beautiful thing. There are certain parts of the human body which were intended to be stimulated for pleasure as a direct result of the married act, with the end result in most cases the idea of procreation, quieting the passion, and things of that type. But in this particular situation it is made sex for sex's sake, just a pleasure in itself. This type of book, certainly we would not take it into our home, read it aloud. I would never be allowed to read this over the TV. I would never be allowed to read this over the radio.*

THE COURT: Is this in answer to your question or a lecture generally on life?

Q. Don't give legal conclusions. The last bit about the television I don't think is properly in the case. The other is.

THE COURT: Suppose we stay with the answers to the questions, Mr. Picinich, nothing else.

Q. Now do you find in this book any reference to people receiving pleasure out of pain or rather a painful experience?

A. No question about it.

Q. Where did you find that, in what instances?

A. There are a couple of instances here, in one of which this young idiot boy who was seduced by this—I can't think of the girl's name, I think Louisa—and his penis was described, with all due apologies to the ladies in the audience if there are any, described as practically as big as her arm, and she couldn't hold this boy back, but she enjoyed it tremendously even though she was practically, not exactly, screaming in pain, but she was willing to bear this pain because of the exquisite nature of this that accentuated her sexual pleasure. This belongs in the field of abnormality. This is not normal sex by any means. That is one item.

Q. Are there others?

A. Oh yes.

Q. Do you find in this book anything of a philosophy expressed?

A. Yes, there is a philosophy of pleasure for pleasure's sake, hedonism.

Q. Do you find anything redemptive in this book?

A. No.†

---

* This testimony is obviously objectionable, on the ground, among others, that it is not responsive to the question that was asked. I made no objection, for reasons that follow.

† It may be noted that during Dr. Reilly's direct examination there

* * *
Cross-examination by Mr. Rembar

Q. Dr. Reilly, have you had any psychiatric practice since the war or have you been associated with any psychiatric clinics?

A. No.

Q. Are you a member of any psychiatric medical societies?

A. No sir.

Q. A diplomate of—

A. —of psychiatry? No. I emphasized that initially. I said qualified army psychiatrist.

Q. Your principal experience, then, is in pediatrics?

A. Yes. The greater emphasis today, I might add, in pediatrics is on mental health.

Q. Your chief concern with mental health, then, is with the mental health of children. Is that right?

A. As a pediatrician, yes, as a pediatrician.*

Q. Apart from being a pediatrician, your concerns are those of a layman rather than of a physician?

A. I don't consider myself actually as an ordinary layman, I have to admit that, because of the duties I have. I feel I am a little bit better qualified than the average physician in the field of psychiatry, and I have done this on and off in my own practice with young people thirteen, fourteen or fifteen. I have advised considerably young people ready to get married.

Q. You mentioned that all the states of the union make obscene the publishing or selling of obscene literature a crime? †

A. Yes.

Q. Except, I believe you said, New Mexico.

---

were many more interruptions from the court than from counsel—an inversion of the usual situation. After the doctor had been on the stand for a while, it appeared to me that the revelation of his habits of thought and underlying attitudes was weakening the prosecutor's case and strengthening ours. I decided that giving his biases full display was worth whatever loss might come from allowing him to make all the points he wanted to, whether or not they constituted admissible testimony.

* My aim here was to show that if the witness was an expert at all, he was an expert on a subject the Supreme Court had held not pertinent to the inquiry: the interests of children cannot control publication (although they may justify statutes regulating sales to children).

† On direct, during his qualification.

A. That's right. It is part of the education law in New Mexico.

Q. Do you know whether—so far as behavior is concerned as distinguished from reading—whether the general moral level in New Mexico is any lower than that of the other states?

A. I don't know.

Q. Do you know whether there is any greater incidence of sexual offenses in New Mexico than in the other states?

A. I just mentioned it is part of the education law. I am not a lawyer, so you have me right over a barrel on that. Frankly, I cannot make any statements how they enforce it or what they do.

Q. I am not asking you for that. I am just asking you whether you know as a statistical matter. It doesn't require a lawyer to answer this.

A. New Mexico is only one state out of fifty. I don't know.

Q. You don't know whether there is a higher incidence of sexual offenses in New Mexico than there are in the other states?

A. No, I don't know.

Q. You mentioned, I believe, that the theme of the book before the court is the portrayal of abnormal sex.

A. Yes.

Q. Does it deal with the portrayal of normal sex?

A. No.

Q. How do you define normal sex?

A. Normal sex? Normal sex, I would say, would be the actual act of sexual intercourse between male and woman with the avowed purpose of—married people, I would say—it is an act between married people for the avowed purpose of fulfilling the marriage contract, primarily with most people to procreate the race and with quite a few people as a secondary motive the quieting of passion.

Q. If there is no motive whatever on the part of the two people to procreate the race, would you regard it as abnormal?

A. Not necessarily. I just mentioned to you, sir, that primarily the average person when they marry—primarily the average person when they marry they wish to bring children into the world. But there are others for reasons of their own

—I am not going into the moral issues involved—for reasons of their own they may hold off on children five, ten years. It is their business, and they are entitled to that course, but certainly living together and the reason of the sexual act is quieting of passion, yes.

Q. Now I want to give you a specific hypothetical situation so that you may give me a very precise answer. You have a married couple. They definitely do not want any children. They do not want to procreate the race, for whatever reason, and they engage in sexual intercourse, taking every care possible to see to it that there is no procreation of the race. Do you regard that as normal or abnormal sex?

A. In the context of the statement, that is normal sex. I mentioned that to you before.

Q. That is normal sex?

A. I would say that is normal sex, yes.

Q. Now let's change the hypothetical.

A. For certain people now, people whose moral values are such that they feel it is perfectly all right, it is perfectly okay?

THE COURT: He is asking you what you think.

THE WITNESS: Now wait a minute, he is asking me what I think?

MR. PICINICH: I think he is asking what the doctor thinks about other people.

THE COURT: Just make objections, Mr. Picinich.

Q. In the hypothetical question nothing is given to you as data as to what the moral views of these people may be. I am just giving you the facts, what they are doing and what their intent is, and I ask you whether that is normal or abnormal in your view.

A. In the broad context of the question as you have given it to me, it is normal.

Q. Now let me add one more fact to this situation. They are not married. In your view, is what they are doing normal or abnormal?

A. Abnormal.

Q. Abnormal?

A. Yes.

Q. You, in one of your answers on direct examination, postulated a situation in which a married couple in bed read this book.

A. Yes.

Q. I think you said under those circumstances the stimulation it gave was one that you did not disapprove of.

A. I would go along with that.

Q. Well now, I would like you to explain that to me. Are you saying that you feel that this book is obscene in some circumstances and not in others, depending on what the situation in which it is read may be?

A. In one situation, Mr. Rembar, one situation, which I felt it may not be abnormal.

Q. What may not be abnormal, the book?

A. To read the book itself. I will have to rephrase that. In the one situation a married couple in bed, where almost anything goes in marriage as long as the sex act ends up where it is supposed to go, stimulation of almost any type may well be accepted. Under those circumstances, I will say the stimulation engendered by the reading of this book would not be considered abnormal.

Q. Then you are not talking about the book, you are talking about the reaction of the people?

A. The reaction of the people to the reading of this book. What could I say about the book? The book is an abstraction here.

Q. You said, I believe, a book is to be condemned if—and here I copied down your exact words—"if it stimulates to acts of sexual activity." Do you want to modify that answer?

A. Repeat the question, please.

(The reporter reads the pending question.)

A. If I said condemned, I should not have used that word because in the first place we condemn nothing.

Q. "We" meaning who?

A. Myself, my associates, particularly on the Citizens for Decent Literature.* We condemn nothing. We say nothing is obscene. We simply ask the people to read these things and draw their own conclusions.

Q. So you are not saying the book is obscene?

A. No, I am not saying the book is obscene at all. I'm simply saying it is detrimental to mental health.

MR. PICINICH: I object to the question.

THE COURT: What question?

---

* On direct, Dr. Reilly had said he "happened to be" New York State president and national vice-president of the CDL.

MR. PICINICH: The one the witness answered that the book is not obscene.

THE COURT: He said the book is not obscene.

MR. PICINICH: Excuse me. On cross-examination the witness is being asked for legal conclusions, and I don't believe this witness is competent—nor is any other witness competent—to give a legal conclusion as to whether or not any book is obscene.

THE COURT: I agree with you, it is a legal conclusion, but, as I say, the witness answered.*

Q. On direct examination you stated that this book had a detrimental effect because it advocated hedonism, because it advocated sex as a pleasure in itself, right?

A. Yes.

Q. And because it advocated sex outside marriage?

A. Yes.

Q. Let me give you another hypothetical. You have a book, not fiction, in the form of a treatise, in which a writer of the highest argumentative skill—say, a man whose skill rivals that of Cardinal Newman—takes the view that hedonism is a good thing, that sex outside marriage is a good thing, and that sex as a pleasure in itself ought to be pursued, and in this book with all that skill he urges very strongly upon the reader that the reader should follow his ideas. What is your feeling about such a book?

A. I have to determine myself what is the dominant theme of that book. Is it an appeal to pruriency or isn't it?

Q. I'm telling you the dominant theme of this book very simply is that the reader go out and pursue sex as a pleasure in itself.

A. If it is a scientific book and it is so intended to be a book like in college work or postgraduate work, but it is not meant just for the average person—you are making a hypothetical case. I will give you a hypothetical answer.

Q. Give me an answer to my hypothetical question.

A. Your hypothetical question I cannot possibly give an answer that cannot be unhypothetical. A treatise—you are re-

---

* Meaning that the witness himself had brought the word "obscene" into the testimony. I had merely taken his word and asked whether his statement applied also to the book before the court. Accordingly, Picinich could not have a valid objection to my question.

ferring to of a man of equal stature to Cardinal Newman—is
not read by the average man in the street, not by any means.
It is meant for people who are highly educated, meant for
people taking postgraduate work—under those circumstances
it would be entirely different. Like me, as a physician, I have
to know everything about syphilis and gonorrhea and everything else.

Q. Let me change the hypothetical to make it easier for
you. The standard of comparison for this particular author
will not be Cardinal Newman; it will be Dale Carnegie, certainly a popular author read by the great mass of people.

A. I get your question now.

Q. Answer the question.

A. Oh yes, Dale Carnegie's works are intended for the average person. If a Dale Carnegie plays up beautifully hedonism
as such—I haven't read the book, and it is a hypothetical
question—I have to know is he actually trying to put something
across that is really good?

Q. That is the hypothetical question. He is really trying to
put across the idea that his readers should go out and pursue
sex as pleasure in itself.

A. If the dominant theme of that book was one of an
appeal to pruriency, it is up to the court to make the decision,
and not to me.

Q. I am asking you for *your* opinion about that book. You
gave your opinion about *this* book.

A. Yes.

MR. PICINICH: Your Honor, may I state for the record I
object to the question. I am certainly confused, and I think
the witness is confused as to what conclusion he is being
asked to draw.

THE COURT: The witness has not said he is confused. If he
is, I would like to know it from him.

MR. PICINICH: I would object on the ground it is ambiguous.

THE COURT: I will overrule your objection. I think it is a
proper question. If you understand the question, please answer.

A. I understand the question.

THE COURT: If you are confused, please tell us.

THE WITNESS: No, with all due respect to the prosecutor, I
am not confused. I know precisely what Mr. Rembar is get-

ting at, but again I say a book of this type, if the appeal of that book is to pruriency—

Q. I am not sure I understand that answer. What I am asking you is, If this book with all the popular skills that Dale Carnegie has, a book which a great mass of readers is likely to read, if that book, the dominant theme and the main purpose of that book is to convince the reader—

A. The average person, you are talking about?

Q. —the average person, that he, the average person, ought to pursue sex solely as a pleasure in itself—

A. If it portrays hedonism, the philosophy of hedonism as such, just as an abstract philosophy without going into all these gross details as this book does, I would have to say no— as a philosophy, an abstraction, without going into all the details of it, of course I couldn't. You have asked me a question. I said this book is hedonism as a philosophy, but I am not disputing hedonism as such.

Q. Even though the average reader may very well get the idea from this that it is a good idea to go out and pursue sex as a pleasure in itself?

A. If the average person in this country and the great majority of people, national standards and so forth—the great majority of people felt this was so, I have nothing to stand on, I grant you that. But I doubt very much they would feel that way.*

Q. I would like to ask you, Dr. Reilly, whether you agree or disagree with this statement: "The paths of Vice are sometimes strew'd with roses, but then they are for ever infamous for many a thorn, for many a cankerworm: those of Virtue are strew'd with roses purely, and those eternally unfading

---

* Although the syntax of this answer is a bit difficult, its purport and effect are clear. In the several preceding answers Reilly has agreed that there should be no suppression of a book which, perhaps even more than *Fanny Hill*, would induce people to commit acts Reilly regards as "detrimental." His reserving decision where the book is "prurient" is irrelevant. He was not called as an expert on prurience; he was called to testify on the harmful consequences of reading, and he and Picinich have been making the point that *Fanny Hill* should be suppressed because reading it will lead to sexual activity that Reilly regards as abnormal—for example, sex out of wedlock. But he is now saying that even though the hypothetical book would cause the same evil conduct, he would not have such a book suppressed.

ones." My question is whether you agree or disagree with that statement.

MR. PICINICH: I object, your Honor, unless it be understood by myself and the witness on what basis, as a literary expert or as a layman.

MR. REMBAR: On the basis on which you qualified him.

MR. PICINICH: What basis is that?

MR. REMBAR: Whatever that may be. I feel he is not qualified at all.

THE COURT: Are you finished with your objection?

MR. PICINICH: No, I am not. I think he is qualified on a medical basis essentially.

THE COURT: I do not follow you.

MR. PICINICH: The statement as read to this witness, and it is asked whether or not he agrees with that, I would like to know what part—this is an expert—on what basis should he be confronted with the statement and asked whether or not he agrees with it. Is this a medical fact? Is this a philosophical fact? Is this a psychiatric fact? Or is it within the domain of literary knowledge or value?

THE COURT: I do not believe that the objection made is a legal objection to the question. It will be overruled. Will you please answer the question?

Q. The question was whether you agree or disagree with the sentence I read to you.

A. Will you repeat the statement, please?

Q. "The paths of Vice are sometimes strew'd with roses, but then they are for ever infamous for many a thorn, for many a cankerworm: those of Virtue are strew'd with roses purely, and those eternally unfading ones."

A. I don't profess to be a literary expert. I would rather not answer the question.

Q. You would rather not answer the question?

A. I don't fully understand the question.

Q. You do not quite fully understand the statement?

A. I don't feel I should take the time out now to try to understand.

Q. Let me understand you.

THE WITNESS: I don't want to make an answer—

THE COURT: One at a time.

A. I don't want to make an answer on the basis of a quick try, a quick absorption of that particular statement.

THE COURT: Then your answer is that you feel you cannot answer that question at this time, Doctor.

THE WITNESS: Yes sir.

*   *   *

Q. You mentioned homosexuality, flagellation, fetishism, voyeurism. Is there any sex in this book that you regard as normal?

A. No, not in the context of this book.

MR. REMBAR: I am not sure I understand the last part of the answer.

THE COURT: Can't you answer yes or no to that, and we will get along much easier.

THE WITNESS: It is a very difficult thing.

THE COURT: You cannot answer that last question yes or no?

THE WITNESS: I can't answer it in that manner.

MR. REMBAR: I will accept that, that you cannot answer that yes or no.*

THE WITNESS: Okay— Wait a minute.† Let me get that expression again.

THE COURT: Do you want the question read back?

THE WITNESS: Yes, I would like the question read back.

(The reporter reads the last question.)

A. In the broad context of the book, no; individually, yes.

Q. What individual examples do you regard—

A. As it describes the plain ordinary intercourse where she was with this fellow Charles at one point after she realized how much she loved this man, that the ordinary description of the sexual act to me with the describing of the intensity of the pleasure, I would go along with that particular part as such, but in the context of this book I see nothing normal of any sexual activity whatsoever.

Q. Then the only normal sexual activity you find in this book is the intercourse between Fanny and Charles. Is that your answer?

A. After the first or second time they had relations I would say that particular part in describing normal activity,

---

* The question Dr. Reilly said he could not answer yes or no was whether there was any sex in the book that he regarded as normal.

† There was a pause between "Okay" and "Wait a minute." The pause was filled with a lovely double take.

describing normal activity with the pleasure that was induced in her and shown that there was a certain amount of actual love here, but only in that particular thing. . . .*

Q. You testified on direct examination, Dr. Reilly, that you are familiar with contemporary literature? †

A. Within reason as an educated man I would say, not a literary expert.

Q. I am not asking you now your opinion as a lawyer, but just your opinion as a doctor. Did you approve or disapprove of the decisions of the federal courts in the case involving *Lady Chatterley's Lover?*

MR. PICINICH: I object, your Honor.

THE COURT: I will sustain the objection.

Q. Are you familiar with the writings of James Baldwin, Doctor?

A. Within reason. He is considered to be a contemporary good writer, a well-known writer.

Q. Did you happen to read his novel called *Giovanni's Room?*

A. No.

Q. Did you read his novel called *Another Country?*

A. I perused it. I would not be considered an authority on the subject.

Q. The answer is, you did not read it well enough to tell us what is in it.

A. The answer is, I did not read it well enough to discuss it intelligently, yes.

Q. Are you familiar with the works of John Updike?

A. No.

Q. Are you familiar with the works of Mary McCarthy?

A. I haven't read her book. I have just read reviews of it. I don't know it intelligently enough to discuss it.

Q. Have you read *Lady Chatterley's Lover?*

A. I have.

---

* It would be pointed out in the post-trial brief that the instance of normal sex the witness cited did not fit the rule of normality he had proclaimed earlier. Fanny and Charles were not concentrating on the procreation of the race; "fulfilling the marriage contract" was hardly their "avowed purpose"; and they would have recoiled from the suggestion that they should "quiet their passion."

† During direct, in a portion omitted.

Q. Have you read *Ulysses* by James Joyce?

A. No.

Q. What contemporary novels have you read?

MR. PICINICH: Is this interrogation? *

MR. REMBAR: It *sounds* like a question.

MR. PICINICH: I object to the question.

MR. REMBAR: He testified he was familiar with contemporary literature.

THE WITNESS: Yes.

MR. REMBAR: I want to know what he has read.

THE COURT: Generally speaking, we do not want to go through every book he has read.

MR. REMBAR: But he has not mentioned one yet that he has read.

THE COURT: I understand what your observation is, Mr. Rembar. [Addressing Picinich]: What is the problem?

MR. PICINICH: The basis of my objection is that I think it's improper to make a comparison of contemporary books that are on the market as compared to this one here. I think that what we are getting into—

THE COURT: Maybe we are getting in, but there has not been any question offered by way of comparison.

MR. PICINICH: The question is—

THE COURT: Have you read them?

MR. PICINICH: Yes. What has he read?

THE COURT: Here is a man who is qualified in certain avenues, and counsel wants to explore his expertise in that sense by trying to find out what he has read. I think it is a proper source of inquiry, a legitimate avenue of questioning. What is the question?

THE WITNESS: Your Honor, may I just—

THE COURT: No. There is nothing pending. You just answer the question.

THE WITNESS: Yes. Thank you. I will.

THE COURT: What is the question?

MR. REMBAR: Will he name what contemporary novels he has read?

THE COURT: Generally, Doctor.

A. I keep myself in good contact by reading of course all

---

* Picinich was evidently using the word "interrogation" in the sense of the third degree. I chose to take it in its innocent literal sense.

the book-review sections. I grant you that does not give me
the right to discuss a book. I have read *The Carpetbaggers*. I
have read *The Chapman Report*. I have read about a million
of the paperbacks which we can't consider decent literature. I
will grant you that. I am acquainted with *Ulysses*.

Q. What does acquainted mean, Doctor?

A. Just know a general idea about it. But I don't know
enough of the book *Ulysses* to discuss it intelligently. But—
all right, your Honor just wants me—

THE COURT: You have answered the question.

THE WITNESS: I'm sorry. I lost my temper. I apologize.

THE COURT: No, there is nothing to apologize for.*

Q. Other than *The Carpetbaggers,* is there any novel that
has been published in the last ten years that you have read?

A. Of course. I can't recall all those things. I am not
prepared to discuss the articles.

Q. Can you name a few that you have read?

THE WITNESS: This is silly.

MR. PICININCH: I object.

THE WITNESS: *Andersonville.*

MR. PICININCH: Just a moment.

THE WITNESS:: I'm sorry.

MR. PICININCH: I think it is apparent that the doctor does
not profess to be a literary expert, and yet he is being questioned on areas which he is not an expert in.

MR. REMBAR: I wish to say only that on direct examination
the witness testified that he was familiar with current literature in answer to one of Mr. Picinich's questions.

THE COURT: I think he has answered your question in that
field, Mr. Rembar, as to generally what he has read.

MR. REMBAR: Thank you.†

Q. Dr. Reilly, I won't keep you much longer, but I want
to read something else to you and ask you whether you find
yourself in agreement or disagreement with it.

THE COURT: Mr. Rembar, these excerpts, of course, are not
being utilized, I take it, in the fashion in which the cases say

---

* There had been no display of anger or rudeness on the part of the
witness. His temper was not what he had lost.

† "Thank you" is frequently used as a form of punctuation; it can mark
the end of the witness's testimony, or the end of a particular line of questioning. Or it can mean "I see we understand each other, your Honor."

that they should not be utilized. I think we are all in accord that this book should be judged in its totality, not page 23 or 37 or a paragraph here and there.

MR. REMBAR: Yes.

THE COURT: That is part of the *Hicklin* test, which we also agree has somewhat been abandoned so far as the United States Supreme Court is concerned.

MR. REMBAR: I agree, your Honor. All I am trying to explore by these questions is precisely what the attitude of the witness is.

THE COURT: With reference to the contents of the particular—

MR. REMBAR: Of what I have just read—not as a comment on the book.

THE COURT: All right.

Q. This that I am reading you is from an opinion in a federal case: "Although the whole subject of obscenity censorship hinges upon the unproved assumption that obscene literature is a significant factor in causing sexual deviation from the community standard, no report can be found of a single effort of genuine research to test this assumption by singling out as a factor for study the effect of sex literature upon sexual behavior. What little competent research has been done points definitely in a direction precisely opposite to that assumption."

A. That is wrong.

MR. PICINICH: I object to the question.

A. I would love to answer.

THE COURT: There is an objection, Doctor, before you answer.

THE WITNESS: I'm sorry. I'm not used to this.

THE COURT: The prosecutor has an objection.

MR. PICINICH: On this basis, apparently the witness is being asked whether or not he agrees with an authority, and in this case it being a decided—

THE COURT: Not the authority so much; counsel says with reference to the ingredients, the content of that statement.

MR. REMBAR: The content of the statement.

THE COURT: Forget about who said it.

MR. PICINICH: I take it that the issue of it having been decided by a court is not in the case or not in the question.

THE COURT: I agree with you.

MR. REMBAR: I did not say that that was decided by a court. I said I am quoting a statement from a federal court opinion, to find out whether the witness agrees or disagrees with it.

THE COURT: You disregard the observation that it was something taken from a case. Counsel wants to know whether or not you agree with the content of that statement.

A. I disagree very strongly with the content of that statement, and I am prepared to elaborate on it.

Q. I will be happy to give you that opportunity, Doctor. What is the factual basis for your disagreement?

A. The basis of my disagreement is this: Frankly, I am not too sure when that particular statement was made. But we at the present time have a hard-core group of evidence proving within a certain reasonable degree that there is no question—there is no question in the minds of eminent psychiatrists, psychologists, social workers and so forth—there is a definite cause-and-effect relationship between the reading of this type of literature and the increase in vandalism, juvenile delinquency, promiscuity, et cetera, et cetera.

Q. You mentioned you have a—what was it, a hard core of evidence?

A. Yes.

Q. Do you have it with you?

A. I have it downstairs, yes. I can quote you if you wish the quotation. I spoke before the New York Academy of Medicine.

THE COURT: We are not getting into that, Mr. Rembar, so don't invite him to go downstairs and get it.

THE WITNESS: No, not for fisticuffs, sir. Shall I continue with this?

THE COURT: No.

MR. REMBAR: You have answered the question, I think.

THE WITNESS: I'm sorry, your Honor.

Q. I gathered from your testimony on direct examination, Dr. Reilly, that your chief concern about the class of books that you disapprove of is that they contribute to juvenile delinquency.

A. As a pediatrician, yes.

Q. You as a witness.

A. As a witness, no; it is not my primary purpose.

MR. REMBAR: I did not ask you that.

A. My primary concern is with the average person in the United States.

Q. What does it do to the average person, would you say?

THE COURT: What does what do?

MR. REMBAR: The literature which the witness—

THE COURT: Are you talking about the book?

MR. REMBAR: No. He testified generally that there is a class of literature which he feels has some bad effects.

THE COURT: Yes.

THE WITNESS: Yes.

THE COURT: Your question, Mr. Rembar, is what?

MR. REMBAR: My question is whether his chief concern was with juvenile delinquency, and I believe his answer was that he was also concerned—

A. As a witness, I am not concerned primarily with juvenile delinquency; as a pediatrician, of course. But as president of the Citizens for Decent Literature, I am concerned with the effect on the average person.*

Q. Did you tell me in answer to my previous question that you have evidence—

A. Yes.

Q. —that the literature you are referring to—

A. Yes.

Q. —has damaging effects—

A. Yes, definitely.

Q. —on the average person?

A. And I am prepared to name them.

Q. Name whom?

A. The different psychiatrists who have done the work so far.

Q. You are not talking about evidence then in the sense of empirical results? You are talking about evidence in the sense of statements of other individuals?

A. Empirical results at the present time are being worked upon by Dr. Frederick Wertham in New York.

Q. Do you have any of those results?

A. Not with me.

Q. Do they exist?

---

* As a physician, he might be an expert, but he has been shown to be an expert only on children's diseases. So far as "the average person" was concerned, his presidency of a censorship organization would qualify him not as a witness but as a protagonist.

A. They exist. They have not been published as yet.

MR. REMBAR: That is all.

THE COURT: Is there any redirect examination?

MR. PICINICH: Just one question.

Redirect Examination by Mr. Picinich:

Q. You said that you addressed the New York Academy of Medicine in this area.

A. Yes sir.

Q. Will you tell us about that occasion?

A. Yes. I addressed the New York Academy of Medicine last April. And these people, as anyone knows, are the cream of the crop as far as medical minds in the whole United States. We presented the facts and figures as we know and see them, and I will be glad to give it if Mr. Rembar wants it. We presented the facts and figures as we know them. They were aghast. They were just as aghast as Senator Kefauver was as chairman of the committee investigating this kind of material.

THE COURT: Is this all right with you?

MR. REMBAR: Fine.*

THE COURT: Go ahead.

Q. What were the facts which you presented?

A. They confined their remarks primarily to the effects on

---

* What the witness was now saying went so far beyond the boundaries of permissible testimony that the judge felt called upon to intervene even though there was no objection from me. Dr. Reilly was not only offering his opinions, he was offering what purported to be the opinions of other persons who were not present to be cross-examined. And they were not only absent; they were unnamed. Moreover, it was emotional reaction rather than opinion that Dr. Reilly was describing.

A judge need not call breaches of the rules of evidence to the attention of the opposing attorney, but sometimes a judge will. Here Judge Pashman was not merely calling them to my attention; his tone indicated some wonder at the fact that I had not been protesting. But it was "all right" with me—as a matter of fact, "fine"—because it helped show the rambling, subjective, unfocused nature of the witness's testimony. It would indicate— to an appellate court that would have only the printed stenographer's transcript before it—the witness's emotional involvement and the contrast between what he was saying and what is ordinarily regarded as proper testimony. The more he talked and the wider he ranged, the more likely it was that the higher court would get a clear impression of this singular witness.

the adolescent. I have to admit that. They studied this and I have this, not right in my hands—I presume—they put out a special bulletin on salacious literature which was prepared recently on homosexuality of sick people. They have said that it is their considered opinion that the perusal of erotic literature—

MR. REMBAR: You were talking about a speech that you gave to a certain group.

THE WITNESS: I gave to the New York Academy of Medicine.

MR. REMBAR: Are you still talking about that speech?

THE WITNESS: Yes, I gave a speech.

MR. REMBAR: Now you are saying that they—

THE WITNESS: This is what they have done as a direct result of my speech, Mr. Rembar. That is the gist of the question as I have gathered it from the prosecutor.

THE COURT: Are you finished?

MR. REMBAR:* I object to it from this point on.

THE COURT: I tried to ask that before because I did not understand why you thought a particular speech to an individual or group and what their reaction was would be evidential in this case. I am not clear.

MR. PICINICH: Your Honor, I think the doctor is using statistics and studies in the field of medicine just as any other doctor does.

THE COURT: The objection is not to statistics. What statistics is he using? †

MR. PICINICH: I thought that is what he is getting into.

THE COURT: He is telling us about the reaction of a group. Is that statistics?

MR. PICINICH: No, if that is what he was telling us about. I thought it was that he was telling us about his address to the medical society.

THE COURT: That is what we started off with, and now he is telling us the emotional reaction of the audience. At least that is the way it started.

THE WITNESS: No.

THE COURT: Go ahead.

---

* But enough was enough.

† It is of course preferable to have the judge make your argument for you.

MR. REMBAR: "Aghast" is an emotional word.

THE WITNESS: Pardon me.

MR. REMBAR: "Aghast" is an emotional word.

THE WITNESS: Yes, I agree.

MR. PICINICH: I object to that.

THE COURT: Yes, I sustain the objection. What is the next question?

Q. The next question is the facts and the statistics that you addressed the New York Academy of Medicine with.

A. The facts and the statistics as we gave them were based upon the works of Dr. Nicholas Frignito of Philadelphia, who was the chief psychiatrist for the court of Philadelphia, who deals with adults—children and adults—mostly adults. We dealt with the work of Dr. Frederick Wertham and Dr. Pitirim Sorokin.

MR. REMBAR: I object. I don't think he is answering the question.

THE WITNESS: Yes, I am.

MR. PICINICH: Doctor, don't answer Mr. Rembar. This is to await the court's ruling.

THE WITNESS: I'm sorry.

MR. PICINICH: You may not be familiar with this kind of proceeding.

THE COURT: Go ahead.

A. I mention these people because these are the people who have said it is obvious to them—

MR. REMBAR: I object now, your Honor.

THE COURT: I sustain the objection as to what they have said.

Q. [by Mr. Picinich]: Do you, in arriving at your general opinion, accept this medical information?

A. Of course. What would I be talking it for?

Q. Why don't you listen to my question—and make this a part of your own medical opinion? *

A. This is the psychiatric opinion today.

MR. REMBAR: Your Honor, I submit—

THE COURT: This is your opinion?

THE WITNESS: This is three out of four psychiatrists in America.

---

* This kind of leading question is objectionable, and I would have objected to the form of the question except that its tone was so obviously plaintive.

THE COURT: Is it your opinion?

THE WITNESS: Positively, sir.

THE COURT: Then give it to us.

MR. REMBAR: He has already given his opinion on direct examination.

THE COURT: What is the question, now that we have cleared up that he is giving his opinion?

MR. PICINICH: That he is of the medical opinion—

THE COURT: Put the question to him. Then I will rule on it.

Q. What is this opinion which you have expressed to the Medical Society of New York?

A. The opinion I expressed to the Medical Society of New York is that this increase of this cesspool publication, this subliterature, has a definite correlation between the increase in vandalism, juvenile delinquency, promiscuity, illegitimacy, et cetera.

Q. In arriving at this opinion, you have taken the opinions of psychiatrists who have done clinical work in this field. Is that correct?

A. Yes.

MR. PICINICH: I have no further questions.

THE COURT: That is all. Thank you, Doctor.

JOSEPH F. ZIGARELLI, sworn*
Direct Examination by Mr. Picinich

Q. Dr. Zigarelli, are you a licensed physician?

MR. REMBAR: I will concede that Dr. Zigarelli is a medical expert.†

MR. PICINICH: Let's go into some of the background. I

---

* There was a marked difference between the prosecutor's first witness and his second. Dr. Zigarelli was urbane, highly articulate, calm and confident. He looked and sounded important. He had neat gray hair, and a set of neat features gave off an air of knowing tolerance. Quite evidently his testimony was the product of careful thought; he did not waste words. That is, he avoided gratuitous statements that would not be helpful to a position he was advancing; he spoke at length when he felt it accomplished something.

† Where you know, or can anticipate, that the items of experience by which your opponent's expert will be qualified are likely to be impressive, it is better to concede the qualification and avoid the recital.

think it's valuable for the court if we go into some of the background.*

Q. Are you a licensed physician, Doctor?

A. I am.

Q. Have you specialized in any particular field?

A. Yes, neurology and psychiatry.

Q. Do you belong to any organizations within the medical profession within these fields?

A. Yes, I do.

Q. What organizations or societies would they be?

A. I am a diplomate of the American Board of Neurology and Psychiatry. I am a fellow of the American Psychiatric Association, a member of the New Jersey Neuropsychiatric Association, a member of various organizations in New Jersey referable to neuropsychiatric electroencephalography. That's my qualifications.

Q. Are you in the course of your practice, Doctor, connected officially with any hospitals in the area?

A. Yes, I am.

Q. Would you name those, please?

A. I am formerly—I think it might be best to go back in the routine.† After graduating from Yale University School of Medicine, in the army I became a division neuropsychiatrist of the First Armored Division. Prior to that I was the psychiatrist for the Twenty-first General Hospital, which is the Washington University School of Medicine unit.

Subsequent to the army, I became resident psychiatrist at Greystone Park, then clinical psychiatrist there. And at the present time I am consultant at the New Jersey State Hospital at Greystone Park. I am an attending neuropsychiatrist at Paterson General Hospital, a consultant psychiatrist at various hospitals in Bergen, Passaic and Morris County.

Q. Doctor, have you read the book that is introduced into evidence, *John Cleland's Memoirs of a Woman of Pleasure?*

A. Yes, I have.

Q. And, Doctor, are you able to determine whether or not there was a dominant topic or subject matter dealt with in this book?

---

* Picinich was aware of this too.

† The word "routine" is something of a slip, but not an important one. It shows that Dr. Zigarelli had frequently been an expert witness (not, however, in censorship cases).

A. I did.

Q. What was that subject matter? *

* * *

A. Before answering that question, I would like to stipulate, if I may, that as a neuropsychiatrist I prefer to just give my opinion from a psychiatric standpoint. And for the court I would like to define psychiatry as I practice it. As a psychiatrist, I observe, study, diagnose and treat mentally and emotionally sick individuals. As a psychiatrist, I have to have some basic knowledge of psychology, and also some knowledge of sociology. I must have some knowledge of religion, the morals of our country, and I also have to have some idea of the society in which we live presently in 1964.† So if I can confine my remarks to psychiatry alone, my impression psychiatrically is that this particular book was the product of a psychopathic author.

MR. REMBAR: I object to that, your Honor.

THE COURT: Yes. The answer will be stricken as not being responsive.‡ Isn't the question about what the general topic

---

* I made my usual objection, and the judge made his usual ruling: he would provisionally accept the testimony.

† Dr. Zigarelli was obviously well prepared. Here he is relating his specialized experience to more general subjects. He knew that the Supreme Court had talked in terms of the average person, and that we would say the Court's use of the term was meant only to exclude particularly susceptible readers. So he was explaining that as a psychiatrist he must use society at large as a frame of reference. This is a tribute not merely to the doctor, but to the lawyer. Zigarelli's understanding of the law and of the respective contentions of the parties very likely came from the preparation Picinich had given him.

Lawyers prepare their witnesses for trials. This is sometimes confused with "coaching the witness"—making up a story for him to tell, or advising him to lie. There is nothing reprehensible in directing the attention of the witness to the critical issues, or in helping him articulate what might otherwise be poorly expressed. He may also be prepared by anticipating probable cross-examination, so as to avoid upset and confusion.

‡ The only trouble was that Dr. Zigarelli made his statement at a time when nobody asked for it. Accordingly, it was stricken as unresponsive. Nevertheless, it had been made, and the judge had heard it.

When a witness's answer is "stricken," it is of course not stricken from the hearer's consciousness, nor is it even stricken from the written record. As the transcript shows, everything is taken down, and the judge's order to strike the answer is carried out merely by reporting his order. (It is as was? Let's try and stay with that question. Wasn't that your question?

MR. PICINICH: My question was—

THE COURT: What was the general topic? Or something to that effect.

MR. PICINICH: Yes, what was the general subject matter? What was the general dominant topic of this book?

THE COURT: You are in accord that the answer is not responsive thus far.

Q. These sexual acts and these sexual experiences that are portrayed in this book by this author, can you tell me whether this in toto is healthy or a normal or wholesome treatment of sex?

A. In my psychiatric opinion, it is not.

Q. In what manner is it not healthy, normal and wholesome?

A. One, it portrays perverted acts of sex.

Q. Such as, Doctor?

A. Such as voyeurism, various phases of homosexuality, masochism, sadism. Two, the description by the author of these various acts, in my opinion, could stimulate abnormal sexual desires in the average individual as we see them, the average individual in all age levels. Three, it portrays in my opinion, again psychiatrically, sex in a debased way. It portrays the life and experience of a prostitute. Sex in itself need not be described that way in my opinion. These are just the major factors.

Q. Apart from this sex which you have described, Doctor, is there any expression of a philosophy, any other type of philosophy in the book?

A. Here again, if the author was attempting to portray a philosophical note I was unable to grasp it. If he were attempting to be another Voltaire, I don't know. I did not get any philosophical note from this book.

Q. Were you able to discover any redemptive values of the book? If there is such a thing from a psychiatric viewpoint.

---

though the King said "Get me my bowl," and the Chancellor said "The King wants his bowl," and that was the end of the matter.) There is, however, something to be gained from pointing out to the judge that the testimony is inadmissible, and more from getting the judge to take the affirmative action of ruling it so and directing that it be stricken.

A. I don't understand the word "redemptive."

Q. Was there anything redeeming trying to be portrayed by the author?

A. No, I think the author in himself did his best to portray what he was attempting to do. He himself was able to put down in words his ideas, his feelings, his emotions. He accomplished what he wanted to. But I don't feel that there is very much redeeming in this book whatsoever.*

Q. Now you have described masochism. This book deals with physical harm or pain, Doctor.

A. In certain areas the particular experience of the female in her experiencing of pain and discomfort is masochistic; that is in this book.†

Q. Is this a healthy or a normal view of a person? Is this a normal person who enjoys this pain?

A. Masochism is definitely an abnormal perverted act sexually.

Q. Now you spoke something about the author. This is the product of the author. Is that correct?

A. Yes, it is.

Q. And the expressions of the author. Were you able to conclude from his product his mental well-being?

A. I used the term "psychopathic individual." Based upon—

THE COURT: Did you hear the last question, Mr. Rembar?

MR. REMBAR: I am sorry. Dr. Decker had some appointment, and I wanted to tell him that he could leave at this point.

THE COURT: Read the question.‡

---

* Picnich was advancing one of two possible meanings of the word "redeeming" in Mr. Justice Brennan's "redeeming social importance." It was the meaning that reflected the old law: enough importance might redeem— that is, outweigh—a book's purience. I had assigned the word a different function. The test, I said, permitted no balancing: if the book had value, prurience would not matter. The weighing of the competing social interests all took place in the formulation of the rule, not in its application, and the word "redeeming" described the legal effect of social importance—any social importance.

† It may be observed that, with an example of outright, classic masochism in the book, both Reilly and Zigarelli instead chose descriptions of pain which, if masochistic at all, were hardly abnormal.

‡ I was caught between the need to hang onto a witness I wanted to use later and the need to follow the testimony. Dr. Decker, one of our witnesses, had some business to attend to and was getting restless. Rather than ask for

(The reporter reads the last question.)

MR. REMBAR: I don't think that the well-being of the author is relevant to the case, your Honor.

THE COURT: How is this material, Mr. Picinich?

MR. PICINICH: Your Honor, I think that the author's literary reputation is important. I think Mr. Rembar will bring that out. I think that his mental make-up in writing such a book is important.

THE COURT: But you are talking about a man now that concededly Dr. Zigarelli knows nothing about. We just were not around at that time.

MR. PICINICH: Only from his expressions.

THE COURT: Based upon the book, you are asking for a psychiatric diagnosis, something like that. That is quite a stunt.

MR. REMBAR: Two hundred years later.

THE COURT: Two hundred years later; that is quite a stunt.

MR. PICINICH: If the doctor can do it.

THE COURT: I know he will try. We do not doubt his qualifications.

MR. REMBAR: Your Honor, what is in issue is the literary product of John Cleland and not his mental state.

THE COURT: Yes. I am going to sustain the objection.

THE WITNESS: Your Honor, I was going to disappoint both of you.*

THE COURT: I have enough faith in you, Doctor.

MR. PICINICH: I have no further questions.

THE COURT: Cross-examine.

Cross-examination by Mr. Rembar†

Q. Dr. Zigarelli, you said that as a physician, as a psychiatrist, you dealt with mentally and emotionally sick individuals. Is that correct?

---

a recess, I decided to risk a moment to tell him he might go out now and come back later. It was a bad risk, but the judge was kind. He expected an objection from me because my pretrial brief had argued against any attempt to investigate Cleland's motives.

* The implication of this statement was that Dr. Zigarelli would not have engaged in a time-machine diagnosis of John Cleland. His earlier testimony, however, suggests that he might very well have done exactly that if the intervening argument and ruling had not taken place.

† Dr. Zigarelli's stricken statement about his special competence had not

A. That is correct.

Q. You also said that in your activities you felt that you had to be aware of, conscious of general standards of ethics and morality in the country. Is that correct?

A. That is correct.

Q. So far as those general standards are concerned as distinguished from psychiatric or neurological learning, would you say that you had to be more familiar with general ethical and moral standards than, say, a lawyer?

MR. PICINICH: Your Honor, I object to the question. I object to the comparison. I don't know what the lawyer is doing in the case at this point.

THE COURT: For whatever it is worth—perhaps it is not too valuable—but if the doctor can answer it I am going to allow him. If he cannot, certainly he will say so.

A. I can't answer it other than to break down what the psychiatrist must know of the moral issues, the sociological issues and the psychological issues. A psychiatrist, so far as I know, is trained differently from an attorney. And in his training I think he is exposed perhaps a bit more than an attorney to the sociological, psychological and moral issues in the United States.

Q. Would you make the same comparison with, say, a newspaper editor?

A. As far as training is concerned—

MR. PICINICH: Same objection, your Honor.

A. As far as training is concerned—mind you, many attorneys who reach the area of being learned judges must have a better sociological knowledge than a psychiatrist. There are many sociologists who perhaps can be more helpful in that area. But in answer to your question—a comparison with the psychiatrist and the attorney—generally speaking, in training, the psychiatrist is exposed to more than the attorney is.

Q. In training although not necessarily in experience, would you say?

A. According to how old you get to be.

Q. And newspaper editors, are they, would you say, generally familiar with—

A. Here again, I think the journalists—

---

been stricken from the memory of the judge. And since it would not be deleted from the record, it would be seen by, and might impress, an appellate court. So I tried to diminish its effect.

MR. PICINICH: I object.

THE COURT: I will allow it.

A. The individuals trained in journalism have a certain exposure to our social mores and so forth. Here again I am inclined to feel that the psychiatrist is more exposed to those factors.*

Q. Did I understand you to say on direct examination that the reading of this book would stimulate an abnormal sexual response in a normal individual?

A. I did not use that particular terminology. I said that it could, it could stimulate.

Q. It could?

A. It could. It is possible that this could, yes.†

Q. Could other types of books—say, *Mother Goose* or Andersen's fairy tales—stimulate an abnormal sexual response in a normal reader?

MR. PICINICH: I object to the question, your Honor, on the basis that the position of the State is that we should not be going into any other comparisons. What is on trial here is *Memoirs of a Woman of Pleasure.*

THE COURT: I don't think *Mother Goose* is being used here by way of comparison to *Fanny Hill.*

MR. PICINICH: Do you know where we are going?

THE COURT: I think I understand the avenue counsel is seeking to travel by way of cross-examination. I am going to allow it, if the doctor can answer it.

A. I will answer with a question by saying, your Honor, that the normal reader is a vast domain. What do you mean by normal reader?

Q. I am using your answer, Doctor; I did not suggest the term. You answered a question put to you by Mr. Picinich. You said as I copied it down—I may be wrong—that this

---

* At this point I felt that the answer stricken by ruling was finally stricken in fact. So far as his general frame of reference was concerned, the witness was reduced to claiming only a slight advantage for psychiatrists over members of other groups. This could not amount to the special and superior knowledge that would oblige a court to give particular heed to his opinions. Of even greater practical importance was his concession that "learned judges" would be more expert on these matters than psychiatrists, a concession that the bench would readily accept.

† In saying that it "could," the witness was safe but ineffective.

book could stimulate an abnormal sexual response in a normal individual. So it is your phrase.

A. A normal individual need not be a normal reader.

Q. All right, then: normal individual.

A. All right. Yes, I do feel that any literature in certain circumstances can stimulate sexual activity, but not abnormal sexual activity.

Q. Does the book have to deal with abnormal sexual activity in order to produce the effect we are talking about?

A. Not necessarily, no.

Q. So that a book that had no description of abnormal sexual activity could produce this abnormal response.

A. Not abnormal response—sexual response. Sexual response and abnormal sexual response are two different things.

Q. You are saying this book could produce the abnormal sexual response.

A. In my opinion, it can.

Q. In a normal individual?

A. In a normal individual.

Q. In a normal individual who is— Take the instance of homosexuality—an individual who is fully matured sexually, has no homosexual components in his make-up, he can be stirred by this book to commit an act of homosexuality? Is that what you are saying?

A. No. In my opinion he can. He can be stimulated. Now I disagree with your statement that an individual who is normal has no homosexual components.* We all do normally. All normal individuals have an unconscious homosexual component in their make-up. This book can stimulate homosexual activity in my opinion in a normal individual. It can excite the homosexual factors. For example, if this book were read by a sailor in a destroyer and there were no women around I think he could masturbate.

Q. He *could* masturbate?

A. Yes.

Q. Do you think he would be provoked to commit an act of overt homosexuality?

A. This is the field of probabilities.

Q. What is your opinion? You have been asked for your opinion.

---

* A statement I had not made.

A. My opinion would be that if the confinement in that ship were long enough, yes.

THE COURT: What is your next question? *

Q. My next question is, Taking what you consider to be the great mass of readers, not sailors confined in a ship for an extraordinary period, would you give the same answer to my question?

MR. PICININCH: I object to the question, your Honor.

MR. REMBAR: I think it is highly relevant.

THE COURT: I will overrule the objection. You may answer.

MR. PICININCH: May I say for the record that the mass of readers are not the test.

THE COURT: If the doctor is unable because of the factual presentation or otherwise to answer the question, he will tell us and we will respect his wishes on that score.

A. There again the answer would have to be in some way qualified, your Honor. I can't answer directly.

Q. You would say there would have to be some special circumstance such as confinement in a ship for an undue period?

A. The particular situation in each individual question would have to be specific, specific in the sense that there are so many variable factors, that each factor would have to be ascertained before giving an answer specifically to your question.

Q. Let me ask you whether you can answer this question, and if you cannot, simply say so. Taking a normal individual defined as you have, and I take it in your view the normal individual includes a latent homosexual component or some homosexual component—is that what you are saying?

A. Here again, don't misquote me. When I say homosexual factor, we individuals go through what we call a homosexual phase in life. We grow through homosexuality. This latent homosexuality exists in all of us. Taken in the proper concept of the individual then—latent homosexuality going back to the age of four, five, six, seven or eight years is what I am talking about; I am not talking about the latent homosexuality which borders on being abnormal—taking it that way then, I still feel that this could excite homosexual activity.

Q. Let me finish that question then. Taking such an indi-

---

* I had paused to make sure the judge had heard that answer.

vidual who lives here in Hackensack, who is an adult, who leads what we would all regard as a normal life—are you saying that the reading of this book is likely to stimulate him to an act of overt homosexuality?

A. Again in my opinion if you are speaking of the male, yes. If you are speaking of the female, yes. Both.*

Q. You are saying yes?

A. Yes.

Q. In your opinion—

A. Yes.

Q. In your opinion a normal individual not confined to a submarine living here in Hackensack and going through the normal activities of daily life, is he likely—

A. Well—

---

* This is a turning point. What has happened since the time he said "it could" has induced Zigarelli to take a more extreme position. Perhaps he sensed from the questioning that the "could" kind of statement was not going to get him very far. Any book may be said to hold the possibility of producing a given response in some one of its many readers. If *Memoirs* was to be suppressed on the basis of the behavior it caused, something more than that would have to be said. So Zigarelli went farther. But now his statements, while they were more meaningful, were much more vulnerable.

Cross-examination could not directly negate the testimony the prosecution was presenting. It was not like, say, the opinion of an orthopedic surgeon on a physical injury, or even that of a psychiatrist describing a psychosis; such testimony may be countered by questions relating to accepted medical knowledge, to the history of the particular patient, or other factual material. On the subject of reactions to erotic writing, however, there is almost no factual material; there is nothing with which the witness can be confronted that will compel him to contradict himself. It seemed to me, therefore, that the best way to deal with the prosecutor's witnesses was to lead them into excess.

It may occur to the reader that a strong point might have been made by demanding that Zigarelli back up his general proposition with specific facts —by asking him whether in his practice he had ever encountered a situation where a book had in fact caused abnormal sexual behavior. It also occurred to the writer; it would have been great to have had him admit that well, no, he had never actually seen such a case. But suppose he had said why, yes, of course, and ticked off a few. I would not have believed him, but there would have been no way of disproving what he said, and the lawyer's opinion of the testimony is not what decides cases. It was better, I thought, to let the cross-examination end with the witness making unsupported statements that were inherently improbable.

Q. That was my question. Is he likely to be stimulated to an act of overt homosexuality as a result of reading this book?

A. Again I will answer yes, with the qualification as I stated before. There are so many variable factors. But the answer is yes to both male and female.

Q. And my word was "likely."

A. Likely, again qualified by the fact—

THE COURT: You have answered the question, Doctor.

WILLIAM SCOTT MORTON, sworn[*]
Cross-examination by Mr. Rembar

Q. Dr. Morton, I guess the most convenient thing is to pick up where we left off. When you gave your answer to the question put to you by Mr. Picinich, what limits of candor were you referring to—in what area? Of conversation, among people in social groups, motion pictures, television—what?

A. I was referring, I believe, to the tenor of conversation among sophisticated people and among average people, taken overall, on topics of life and literature combined. . . .

Q. You are talking about two things: conversation, social intercourse?

A. Right.

Q. And literature?

A. Right.

---

[*] The Reverend Morton provided a further contrast. Dr. Zigarelli's amiable urbanity was replaced by the reverend's rather truculent earnestness. He had a high arching forehead, steel-rimmed glasses and a downturned mouth. There were now no smiles from the witness chair.

During direct examination he stated that he was a doctor of divinity and had lectured at universities; his subjects were "Mainly the Far East cultural civilization of China and Japan, comparative ethical matters and comparative religious field and in the cultural, of course, a good deal of literary comparisons too." He then said that the sexual experiences described in the book were "unhealthy," that the plot was "very weak," that there was a philosophy expressed in the book but one he disapproved of, that there were other historical sources for "the customs, manners and so on, ideas, of the eighteenth century," and finally, that the "content and subject matter of the book greatly exceed the average of candor in discussion of this matter." I had made an objection to his testifying on the last item, on the ground that it was a legal conclusion.

Q. I am now taking examples of current literature. Are you familiar with the novels of James Baldwin?

A. Yes.

Q. We referred previously specifically to *Giovanni's Room* and *Another Country*. Are you familiar with John Updike's *Rabbit, Run?*

A. I have dipped into all these works.

Q. You have not read them as a whole?

A. Not as a whole, no; not these ones that you have mentioned so far.

Q. How about James Joyce's *Ulysses?*

A. Yes, I read a good deal of that.

Q. Including the famous soliloquy?

A. I can't recall it.

*   *   *

Q. To refer to a work in which I am sure you have done more than dipped in, are there instances of abnormal sexual behavior in the Bible?

A. Certainly.

Q. In your opinion, does reading a description of abnormal sexual behavior make it likely that a normal reader will commit an overt act of the same type?

MR. PICINICH: I object to the question, your Honor.

THE COURT: I will overrule the objection. You may answer if you can, Doctor.

A. Yes. I think very often description of such behavior does incite people to it.

Q. Do you think it is likely?

A. I think it is likely. I think it is likely.* I think in the case of the Bible it has done so if the person has not read the rest of the Bible and tried to get the whole spirit of the book, the purpose of the author or authors of the book. Then I think this can happen.†

---

* Zigarelli's Syndrome was, I was pleased to see, contagious.

† A cross-examiner can begin to enjoy himself too much. Shortly after this, in the middle of a question, it struck me that Dr. Morton's testimony was at this point as good for our side, and as bad for the other side, as it could possibly get. Keeping him longer on the stand could only make it less good for us and less bad for them. I ended the cross-examination.

MAX LEVIN, sworn*
Direct Examination by Mr. Picinich

Q. Can you tell me some of your specialty experience? †

A. After I got my medical degree in 1924 I spent three years on the resident staff of the Henry Phipps Psychiatric Clinic, which is the psychiatric division of the Johns Hopkins Hospital. And ever since then I have devoted my entire time to neurology and psychiatry. I am the clinical professor of neurology at the New York Medical College in New York City. I am a diplomate in neuropsychiatry. I have written about ninety-five articles that have been published in journals of neurology and psychiatry. I am the psychiatric editor of *Current Medical Digest*, which is a monthly periodical for physicians. I contributed an article to the *Encyclopaedia Britannica* on their invitation. Well, I could go on and on, but I think that is sufficient.

MR. PICINICH: I think we have a good idea of your background.

Q. Dr. Levin, have you read the book *John Cleland's Memoirs of a Woman of Pleasure?*

A. I have.

Q. A copy of that is admitted in evidence by G. P. Putnam's Sons.

A. Yes, I read that book.

Q. In your opinion, Doctor, what is the dominant subject matter of this book?

A. Well, the dominant subject matter obviously is sex.

Q. How is sex treated in this book? Is it treated in a normal manner or healthy manner or wholesome manner?

A. Well, that is a matter that can't be put into a single word. But I will say that the impression that I get from the book is that it treats sex from the standpoint of a voyeur. The book is full, besides giving detailed account of many acts of

---

* Dr. Levin was older than the other doctors who testified. He was more controlled than Reilly, more didactic than Zigarelli. He used a hearing aid, and like many people whose hearing is poor, he was not always aware of the volume of his own voice. At times, usually without relation to emphasis, his words had a startling loudness.

† This followed testimony that Dr. Levin had been a practicing physician since 1924.

sexual intercourse, almost on every page, the book to a very great extent describes acts of sexual intercourse as they are seen by somebody. Now the voyeur is a person who does not get his greatest kick out of sex unless he sees two other people having sexual intercourse in his presence. And the theme of voyeurism to my mind is the dominant theme of the book. . . .*

Q. The motive of the author in writing the book—were you able to determine the motive of the author in writing the book?

MR. REMBAR: I object to that question.

THE COURT: I will sustain the objection.

THE WITNESS: Can I answer the question?

THE COURT: No. There is nothing pending.

Q. Can you tell us why the author wrote the book?

MR. REMBAR: The same objection.

THE COURT: I will sustain the objection.

Q. Do you think the author that wrote this book was a healthy individual?

MR. REMBAR: Same objection.

THE COURT: I will sustain the objection.

MR. PICINICH: I have no further questions.

THE COURT: Cross-examine.

Cross-examination by Mr. Rembar

Q. Dr. Levin, what is the subject of your article in the *Encyclopaedia Britannica?* †

A. Delirium.‡

It has nothing to do with sex.

---

* Levin then gave examples of what he regarded as voyeurism, including instances in which Fanny describes what she sees, and other abnormalities in the book, and challenged Cleland's sincerity in writing Fanny's final statement.

† I had no idea what the specific subject of the article was. From the doctor's description of his experience, however, it seemed likely that it would have to do with one of the more severe psychiatric disturbances, and indicate an expertise not so much in the problems of the "average man" as in fields that the court would regard as peripheral. I decided to gamble; it paid off. (If the subject had been, say, "Emotional Response to Erotic Literature," I would have been a sad gambler.)

‡ It happened that this was one of the times when the volume of the witness's voice suddenly expanded. The word "delirium" came out with a sonic boom. Levin paused, and then, in a softer voice, added the second sentence of his answer.

Q. I think you said you are a professor of clinical neurology.
A. Yes.
Q. You are not a psychoanalyst, are you, sir?
A. I am a psychoanalytically oriented psychiatrist.
Q. You define a voyeur as someone who does not get pleasure or satisfaction out of sex unless he has first witnessed it.
A. Yes. Witnessing the sex act stimulates his sex desire.
Q. The character Fanny Hill in this book, do you find that it is necessary for her to witness a sex act before she can enjoy her own sex act?
A. No. Fanny is not a voyeur.* But the book is written, it seems to me, by a man who was either a voyeur or who had voyeuristic tendencies.† But Fanny herself is not portrayed as a voyeur. In fact, you objected to the question why the author wrote the book. I was going to say—

MR. REMBAR: I still object.

THE WITNESS: What?

THE COURT: You can tell him privately when I am not around.

* * *

Q. Are you familiar with William Faulkner's novel *Sanctuary?*
A. No. I might say I don't have too much time to read literature, unfortunately, and I haven't read that book.

MR. REMBAR: That is all, Doctor. Thank you.

My main defenses against this psychiatric-clerical attack were, first, to argue (in my briefs, and by objection during trial) that whatever such witnesses might say was irrelevant, and then to try to show by cross-examination that what they did say was incredible. For safety, though, I thought we had better have a witness on our side; we brought to court Wardell B. Pomeroy, one of the three co-authors of the Kinsey Report.

Pomeroy had a pleasant, earnest, youthful, all-American look—a sort of cultured Ozzie Nelson. In contrast (perhaps) to the subject matter of his research, his manner was studious and

---

* This was not consistent with his testimony on direct.

† He is now saying that the author is the voyeur, leading to the obvious rejoinder (which I made in my post-trial brief) that every author recounts his experience, and that the writer of a first-person narrative is necessarily, and entirely, a voyeur.

reflective rather than worldly. He withstood cross-examination very well. At one point, Picinich was going over, one by one, the various aberrations in the book; he referred to the character Norbert:

> Q. Would you say that it is a practice which is accepted by the people of today, deflowering of virgins?
> MR. REMBAR: May I ask under what circumstances?

My interruption, which was a valid objection to the form of the question put by Picinich, was intended to direct Pomeroy's attention to the interesting problem of how the human race would survive if people were to reject the practice of deflowering virgins. Picinich finally got his answer:

> A. Yes. Every woman is deflowered at one time or another. This would be nearly one hundred percent.

Pomeroy's direct examination (which came on the second day of the trial) was devoted partly to showing the spread of sexual stimuli through the environment, in support of my argument that appeal to prurient interest could not mean appeal to sexual interest. In other trials I had simply asked the court to take judicial notice of the state of our culture; here I said that this testimony gave "the support of factual data to matters of which the court may take judicial notice." But the main reason for Pomeroy's presence was to contradict the prosecution's witnesses on what would happen to people who read *Fanny Hill*. He testified that sex books did not rank especially high among sexual stimuli. Where the prosecution's doctors based their statements on their individual practices, Pomeroy's were based on the interviewing of over eighteen thousand people, eight thousand of whom he interviewed personally. (Among the products of this research was the finding that criminals convicted of sex offenses were less often aroused by reading erotic literature than the rest of the male population.) If the term "average person" of the prurient-interest formula had anything beyond the limited significance I had been assigning it, then Pomeroy would be better able to tell us about "average" responses than would the prosecution's witnesses. Not only was his experience much wider, but, as I mentioned to the court, his field was "human sexual behavior"—not "delirium" (Levin) "electroencephalography" (Zigarelli) or propagandistic activities (Reilly).

Pomeroy had never testified before, and he approached his turn on the stand with an anxiety appropriate to this state of innocence. On the way to Hackensack, we had been held up by some road construction, and a good part of my preparation of the witness consisted of assuring him that he need not worry about whether we would be late. During his direct examination, however, his nervousness evaporated (we had made it to the courthouse on time), and he did a good job.

In addition to Pomeroy, we had our witnesses on literary value and on the treatment of sex in contemporary literature. They were particularly good in this case, partly because of the experience of the earlier trials and partly because of their own abilities, which Picinich's prodding cross-examination gave them ample opportunity to demonstrate. J. Donald Adams was present again—large, good-looking, white-haired and of an age to command respect. His manner was one of relaxed dignity, and as in the New York trial two years earlier, his failure to remember details seemed only to put the judge on his side and draw greater attention to his general statements. "Do you recall the character William, the young male messenger?" asked Picinich. "Not by name," answered Adams. Whereupon the judge told Picinich to refer to the incident rather than to "say Willie or John; that did not make much of an impression upon Mr. Adams." Later, when Picinich asked about "the introduction to the characters Harriet, Louise and Emily," the judge admonished: "The principle still applies. Tell him about the incident. Never mind Harriet."

Another veteran of the New York trial was Eliot Fremont-Smith, not yet a regular critic for the *New York Times*. He would have liked to talk about the book itself and about obscenity in general, but there were other people to talk about the book, and his comments on the general problem were the material of legal argument rather than the testimony of a witness. Most important, no one else could do as well on what was

happening in current writing—a much less interesting job that
Fremont-Smith graciously accepted.*

Walter Minton testified, as he had in the earlier trials, on the
character of Putnam as a publishing house and the nature of the
promotion and distribution of the book.

Another veteran—of the battle of Boston rather than New
York—was Fred Holley Stocking. His testimony in Boston had
been so good that I asked him to come down to New Jersey. He
was a strong witness, his delivery deliberate, his statements clear
and emphatic. Frequently in making his points, especially on
cross-examination, he smiled, perhaps out of courtesy, perhaps
in amusement at the thought that the answer was not going to
be what his cross-examiner wanted. He began by countering, almost mocking, Zigarelli:

> Like a previous witness I think I should explain the ground
> on which I base a professional opinion. . . . I am a profes-
> sional teacher of literature and my subject is an art, and my
> greatest expertise, if I have any, is in teaching young men
> how to interpret and understand literature as an art. And I
> firmly believe as a critic and teacher of literature that there is
> a difference between a sound or intelligent interpretation of a
> work of art and an unsound or stupid interpretation of a work
> of art.

He gave reasons why a reading of *Memoirs* that finds value in
the book is sound and intelligent. On cross-examination, Picin-

---

* His ideas on obscenity, which he expressed when we first spoke in 1963,
were, in rough paraphrase, that sexual excitement is just one of the emotions
that a reader may feel, that it is the object of writers (and other artists) to
evoke emotional responses, and that therefore pornography is a proper element in serious writing. I could not agree: the emotional responses the
writer seeks to elicit are empathic, not direct; the emotions ordinarily felt as
part of the literary or artistic experience have a different quality from responses to actual stimuli; and the pornographic response is a direct phys-
iological reaction to an immediate stimulus. It is as though, to create the
emotion of fear, a working model of a tiger were brought into the room.
Moreover, the pornographic response is differentiated from the artistic response by the fact that its catharsis cannot ordinarily come from the work
of art alone.

Though I might disagree, Fremont-Smith's idea was a good one, and it
appeared in articles by other writers later. But whatever its merits, it could
not, at this period in history, be used as legal argument.

ich brought up something that he might reasonably have thought would embarrass a professor, particularly the head of a department:

Q. Mr. Stocking, do you require your students to read this book?

A. I do not require my students to read this book.

Q. Is this the type of book you would want a young college student to read?

A. Definitely.

Q. Do you think that the sexual experiences described in this book would have any deleterious effect on the young college student?

A. Your Honor, I cannot answer this. Your Honor, may I make a little speech on it?

THE COURT: No speeches.

THE WITNESS: If I am to tell the whole truth I can't say yes or no.

THE COURT: We don't expect it if you can't, Professor Stocking; you certainly can answer as you find it necessary with some explanation, except we will try to minimize the speech portion of it. Just give us the answer.

THE WITNESS: One sentence. If he were to read this book in a course of mine and his chief response were the arousal of sexual passion and that dominated every other response, he would flunk my course.

Q. You mean that?

THE COURT: Publish that answer up at school so the boys can find out.

Q. You mean that if a college student were stimulated as a result of reading this book he would be reading with the wrong purpose in mind. Is that what you mean?

A. That's not what I said.

MR. REMBAR: I think the question has been answered.

A. I said if his chief response were the arousal of sexual passion, he would flunk my course.

Q. Well, if he were sexually stimulated, would he flunk your course?

A. Not unless that were his chief response. My students get sexually stimulated from reading *Anthony and Cleopatra,* but that isn't their chief response.

The next witness was John Owen McCormick, another department chairman—of comparative literature at Rutgers. Mc-
Cormick was the most elegant of the witnesses. He had his own
accent, and a musical voice, heavy on the woofer and light on
the tweeter. Some of his words were hard to catch, but what he
had to say was worth hearing, and the Judge was willing to lean
forward. Picinich taxed him with the "exaggeration" in *Memoirs*; the witness said he could think of very few novels that "do
not exaggerate aspects of human experience. That is part of
what novel-writing is." Picinich then asked:

> Q. How about this incident where all of the inmate prosti-
> tutes tell about their defloration? Is that an exaggeration?
> A. Again I couldn't say. One of the things about this
> novel, you see, that is fantastic is the attempt on the part of
> Cleland to place himself in a woman's mind. This is a very
> interesting attempt. And it is a very difficult thing to do in
> any literary work. As I said earlier, for a male writer to place
> himself in a female writer's mind, or vice versa, very rarely
> comes off. I think this comes off, that it succeeds. For the
> male reader this becomes more so of course; obviously this is
> a man's view, so how can one say?
> MR. PICINICH: Yes.

This was a smartly executed exchange of roles, followed by a
ruminative pause on the part of counsel.

> THE COURT: What did you say the next question was, Mr.
> Picinich?

In his questioning, Picinich suggested—as prosecuting attorneys
had, from the time of *Chatterley*—that there was no legitimate
reason for Cleland to write the way he did. I dealt with the
suggestion on my redirect examination of McCormick:

> Q. [by Mr. Rembar]: You were also asked whether a
> book designed to stimulate sexual response would necessarily
> contain certain scenes which my brother described on cross-
> examination. Is it possible that a book could create sexual
> response in the reader without having any of those items that
> he mentions?
> MR. PICINICH: I object, your Honor.
> THE COURT: I am going to allow him to answer.

A. Yes.

Q. In other words, you might have a book without defloration, without homosexuality, without flagellation, that might arouse a sexual response in a reader.

A. We have them.

Q. You might, would you not say, even have a book without any sexual intercourse at all that could arouse a sexual response in a reader?

A. Definitely, yes.

Another of our witnesses was Clarence Decker, vice-president of Fairleigh-Dickinson University and professor of literature there. The notion that "community standards" in the prurient-interest test referred to a local community—a city or a county or even a state—had already been rejected, for New Jersey at least, in a case that had gone to the New Jersey Supreme Court. But the fact that a witness is from your own neighborhood can have a psychological, if not a doctrinal, effect. Fairleigh-Dickinson is the seat of higher learning nearest Hackensack. On his cross-examination Picinich referred to an instance of "rape" in the book. I objected that there was no rape on the pages Picinich cites, and that Picinich as prosecutor would not have been optimistic about getting a conviction of the young man on the basis of what those pages related. The passage, incidentally, combines (conjoins, as Cleland would say) nice examples of the author's talent for the sentimental metaphor ("I now lay a bleeding witness of the necessity imposed on our sex, to gather the first honey off the thorns") and the comic punning metaphor ("All the struggles I could use . . . only served to further his point").

Five pages farther on, he could have found a better example, but even in the latter passage, there would be considerable doubt as to whether what is depicted is indeed rape, either in a legal or in a moral sense. The scene is one in which Harriet has been watching a young man swimming. She is keenly attracted to him. He disappears beneath the water. In a panic at the thought that he may be drowning, she rushes to the water's edge, where "fright and concern sunk me down in a deep swoon." The young man has actually only been engaging in an eighteenth-century form of skin diving. (Harriet has already lovingly described the skin; the diving is what confuses her.) He comes out of the water, finds her in a faint, carries her into the summerhouse and ministers to her, more or less tenderly—that is to say, first more, then less. At this point the prosecution would have a pretty good rape case. But the scene continues, and now Harriet is done with swooning. To her swimmer's further addresses, she gives her "tacit blushing consent." The consent, indeed, is so warm and affirmative that it must be considered a ratification of what preceded it. No man may be convicted by an ex post facto law, but does it follow that he should not be saved by ex post facto fond forgiveness? There cannot be rape where there is consent, and to the charge of rape there might be a defense of consent *nunc pro tunc*. Especially where the *nunc* so closely follows the *tunc*.

The trial closed with the testimony of two young professors of English—Paul Fussell, Jr., from Rutgers, and David Burrows, from Douglas (the Rutgers women's college). Each managed to make some literary comments that sounded fresh despite anything that had gone before. Picinich devoted a great deal of cross-examination to Fussell, who was cool and resourceful and, with the possible exception of Stocking, knew *Memoirs* better than any other witness in any of the trials. He should have; he had read the book twelve times. "Did it," I asked, "improve or diminish in your eyes as you reread it?" "It improved as a literary work," he answered, "it diminished as an erotic work."

The prosecution's witnesses, I thought, had failed to demonstrate that *Fanny Hill* would cause harm, or that any reading might cause harm. This does not mean that such a case could not be made.

I do not agree with those who say books can work no evil. The assertion is an affront to intellect. Books have great influence, much of it bad. But the risk that inheres in reading books is precisely the risk that the First Amendment contemplates. All the conflict is in the mind itself, and this is the conflict we cherish.

Some of the difficulty comes from the failure to recognize the distinction that lies at the heart of the Amendment. There is the moral or social or religious or intellectual question of what should or should not be published. Then there is the question of what, if anything, the law ought to do about it. The two questions are related but quite distinct.

We hear much controversy about whether it is a good thing or a bad thing that there are now available the books whose trials have been described, and the many other books that would not have been published were it not for these cases. The matter of quality enters into the argument. People say they started *Tropic of Cancer* and found it dull. Often enough, it is a genuine appraisal and not the cry of "Dull!" that masks the fact that one is made uneasy by a book. What good is it, these readers ask, to circulate something so unrewarding and at the same time so offensive? Others have pointed out that the wit and elegance of *Fanny Hill* is not apparent to most people, and why protect a book whose chief product is titillation? Is it wise to have the abominations of de Sade spread about? How about the tailored-to-measure paperbacks that are obviously designed for low-grade sexual excitement?

The questions are, of course, legitimate. Let us argue one, from the nonlegal point of view. I say that it is a good thing the Marquis de Sade is published. A number of people whose intelligence we must respect believe we have much to learn from him. But assume that they are wrong, that Sade, beyond being shocking, propagates false and ruinous doctrine. Is it better that his writings remain indirectly known but unexamined, a dread reservoir of vague fears? Or is it better that they be brought out and looked at in a strong light? Will the wide distribution of Sade's books bring him devotees? Or will it reveal them to be the product of a second-rate mind? (Second-rate, note, not evil; "evil" begs the question.) Isn't the devil we don't know harder to handle than the devil who has become familiar, and perhaps something of a bore? The defendants in the grisly "moors" murder trial of 1966 testified that they had read Sade and been influenced. Can we believe they would not have committed the crimes—or others as bad—if they had not seen the books? If they needed external inspiration, were there not sources else-where? *

You may consider that Sade has wisdom to give us, and approve the publication. Or you may consider his writing dan-gerous and disapprove it. Or you may think that if the one no-tion is doubtful, so is the other, and in any case let us uncover the horrid mystery and not let it fester. But this three-cornered argument should be carried on outside of court. If Sade's ideas are false, they are nevertheless ideas. The books undoubtedly have some importance, even if it is an importance with which they have been invested by others. They are therefore part of the press whose freedom the First Amendment guarantees.†

One can ask, with respect to each book that would have been censored but for the decisions of the last decade, whether it is for better or for worse that we have the book, and one will hear intelligent voices on both sides. Even as to the trashiest, there are those who argue the benefits of the pornographic experience.

The pornography-is-good-for-you school of thought includes proponents of two distinct, though overlapping groups. One ad-vances the proposition that reading pornography provides a re-lease for antisocial impulses that might otherwise be expressed in antisocial behavior. This, of course, is the hostile sibling of the proposition that obscenity must be suppressed because it induces such behavior. It has, in my opinion, precisely as much validity.

---

* ". . . Heinrich Pomerenke, who was a rapist, abuser, and mass slayer of women in Germany, was prompted to his series of ghastly deeds by Cecil B. DeMille's *The Ten Commandments*. During the scene of the Jewish women dancing about the Golden Calf, all the doubts of his life came clear: Women were the source of the world's trouble and it was his mission to both punish them for this and to execute them. Leaving the theater, he slew his first victim in a park nearby. John George Haigh, the British vampire who sucked his victims' blood through soda straws and dissolved their drained bodies in acid baths, first had his murder-inciting dreams and vampire-longings from watching the 'voluptuous' procedure of an Anglican High Church Service." Murphy, *The Value of Pornography*, 10 *Wayne Law Review* 668 (1964).

† In appraising the accomplishments of anti-obscenity statutes against the values of free speech, we may note that at the time the murderers read their Sade, the books were proscribed.

THE END OF OBSCENITY

The other members of the school declare that pornography provides a harmless pleasure of which we should not be deprived. But taking into account the various needs of all of us, I would say we would do well to be rid of the effluvia that choke our bookracks. The ground of my contention is not the same as that on which Lord Cockburn and Anthony Comstock stood, inherited now by the Citizens for Decent Literature. I would say, rather, that if pornographic trash provides a pleasure, it is a mean pleasure, and the net effect is anti-sex, a diminution of better pleasures. The question I address, however, is not a legal question. I would not argue that the law should interfere. I would argue the contrary.

One may consider any single publication—a fake weight-lifting magazine, for example—and come to the conclusion that we would profit from its removal. We can each of us play publisher, and decide whether, given the opportunity to put out a certain book, we would choose not to. But this is not the same as determining what others may publish. To do that, we must play another role: benevolent despot. Then, assuming we know what we are about, and that we are acting with true benevolence, we might consider the world improved by our decrees. The problems arise when we are asked whether we are willing to allow others—even a democratic majority—to have such power.

Half a year later Pashman rendered his decision—against us. The judge's opinion-writing, it seemed to me, did not equal his talented conduct of the trial; a fair example was his reference to Dr. Levin as a witness called by Putnam. I wondered for a while whether I was just being a sorehead. Then the *Stanford Law Review*, a neutral observer, commented:

> Perhaps the most striking example of the confused state of affairs in some lower courts is the opinion of a New Jersey Superior Court judge [in the *Fanny Hill* case].

By the time Pashman issued his opinion, however, the matter was largely academic. The Boston case was already on appeal to the Supreme Judicial Court, and it was the Massachusetts decision that would go to the United States Supreme Court.

The Majority

Below

A LAWYER CAN ALWAYS, IN A SENSE, HAVE THE last word. I do not mean getting an unfavorable judgment reversed; that, of course, is something more substantial than a last word. I am speaking of the small solace that comes from pointing out deficiencies in the opinion of a court that rules against him. On appeal, he can do this in his brief and argument.*

To affirm, an appellate court need not approve the opinion of the court below. It is error in the judgment, and not error in justifying the judgment, that appeal is designed to correct. But the lawyer should usually attack the opinion as well. If it is strong, the upper court may find it persuasive, and it becomes in effect an opposing brief. If it is weak, and its reasoning can be made to look bad enough, the conclusion itself becomes suspect; while sound results are sometimes reached at the end of a line of

---

* Even after the highest court has spoken, the lawyer may be able to put his case before another, larger, if less potent, audience. Assuming the matter is one of sufficient legal interest, and what he has to say about it is worth hearing, he can publish an article in a legal journal, and try to convince his readers the ruling was wrong. The article cannot affect the decision it complains about, but it may have some influence on future decisions. This is not, naturally, as satisfactory as winning in court, a sentiment that the client will no doubt echo. But it helps make the frustration bearable.

unsound reasoning, they are more often the product of, or at least accompanied by, good and articulate legal thought.

The Boston opinion was vulnerable, primarily because Judge Macaulay cited everybody. He treated Brennan's opinion in *Jacobellis* as "the opinion of the Court," and quoted, as though they were law, statements very good for us. At the same time he cited the dissents in the New York *Memoirs* case, which were denunciations of our position (but were, after all, dissents). He reached way down to retrieve the New York decision granting the preliminary injunction, a decision that did not survive the trial. In addition, he stood firmly on the New York condemnation of *Tropic*, although by now the New York court had itself said it was overruled, and—an item of some significance for a judge in Boston—the highest court of Massachusetts had earlier ruled in *Tropic*'s favor. Though he seemed to approve Brennan's statement that a book of literary value "may not be branded as obscene," he went on to say that the appraisals that counted were "those of average persons in the contemporary national community." My brief played upon the confusion.

It also, in a preliminary draft, contained the paragraph that follows:

> In more ways than one, Judge Macaulay demonstrated he could withstand the influence of the academic world. His opinion described the book as the "nadir of scatology." Calling the book pornography would have been, in our view, legal error, but it would have been arguable. Calling it scatological, however, indicates some confusion. *Memoirs* is scrupulously nonscatological. Indeed, the judge might have used this aspect of the book another way: on the question of literary merit, it could have been added to the points made by those who criticize Cleland for insufficient realism. The judge's word was appropriate to the memoirs of Chick Sale, not to those of Fanny Hill.

This is the lawyer working off his irritation at the adverse decision. The paragraph may soothe him when he writes it; it may even please him. But it will not please the judges. Appellate briefs are printed; our printer never saw the paragraph.

I not only had an opinion to attack; I also had a witness to attack. By the time Dr. Collins got through testifying, he was more of an ally to *Fanny*, I thought, than to her oppressors. (Apparently, on this one aspect of the case, Judge Macaulay agreed with me; his opinion made no reference to Collins' testimony.) There was a problem, however, in presenting this. It is difficult to be kind in depreciating the testimony of a witness, but appellate courts generally do not like overbearing lawyers. Here I wanted not merely to diminish the effect of what he said, but to reduce it to a cipher—to indicate that on the issue of literary merit it simply was not possible to give sensible testimony against the book. The task was to do this without losing penalty points for bad manners. I tried it this way:

> Although Dr. Collins testified to a long experience in teaching English, he used the word "esoteric" when asked what he understood by the word "prurient." This was not a slip; when asked whether that was the word he meant, he answered yes. The word "esoteric" is defined in *Webster's New Collegiate Dictionary* as follows: .
> (1) Designed for, and understood by, the specially initiated alone; abstruse; also, belonging to the circle initiated in such teachings. (2) Withheld from open avowal; private; as, an esoteric purpose.

The point is not minor; it indicates either that the witness, despite his experience, was not qualified, or that the matter before the court is one as to which he does not function with his usual competence or equilibrium. Another such indication is found in the witness's statement that the word "disgusting" could be applied to no books other than those that had a sexual subject matter.

Furthermore, Dr. Collins testified that *Tropic of Cancer* is "patently offensive," "prurient" and "obscene"—conclusions which, particularly in this commonwealth, are directly contrary to law. The witness is, of course, entitled to his private opinions, no matter what the courts may hold; but since his testimony was based on concepts so different from those embodied in the prevailing law, it cannot illuminate the issue before the court.

Finally, it appeared that the witness had not read the book very carefully, if indeed he had read it through. Although he said that he had read it on the night before the trial, he had difficulty remembering with whom Fanny Hill first had sexual intercourse, and he could not remember at all who it was that she married. Either this is an astounding memory lapse (further indication that the witness was presenting not testimony but an emotional response to the issue before the court), or else it demonstrated that the witness had not read the whole book.

So far as the analysis of *Roth* was concerned, the Brennan footnote to the prurient-interest formula—the one that began "I.e., material having a tendency to excite lustful thoughts"— had received special attention in Massachusetts. My brief offered various reasons why it ought not be given much weight, but it had to be admitted that the Supreme Court opinion on which I was putting so much reliance was, in these ten words, flatly against us. So I asked the Massachusetts court to ignore the foreign body. The footnote, my brief said, was "an example of the occasional inconsistency that creeps into even the most distinguished judicial writing." The best of us suffer lapses. Sigmund Freud undertakes a long-distance psychoanalysis of Woodrow Wilson, whom he has never seen. Sandy Koufax, one summer night in '66, gets knocked out of the box by the New York Mets.

The argument that Brooke and Sullivan and Cowin made in their trial-court brief, reasonable and liberal, foreshadowed the argument of their brief on appeal, but it was now developed and made more explicit. They did not dispute the main elements of my explication of the law: they agreed there were three tests, each of which might save the book. But this book, they said, failed them all.

The theory I had been struggling to get the courts to accept —that at this date had the imprimatur of only two Justices of the Supreme Court—was now being blandly conceded, indeed asserted, by our opponents. This may seem remarkable to the reader. It would, I am sure, have seemed remarkable to the opposing lawyers in the other *Fanny Hill* cases. It would have been incomprehensible to our opponents in *Chatterley* and *Tropic*. But it struck me as valid and, in the best sense, clever.

If the concept of "dominant appeal to prurient interest" took in all writing looked upon as pornographic, and if social value had no independent status as a test, then *Fanny Hill* was immediately defeated. This, our opponents in all the other cases had argued, was what everybody had understood *Roth* to say. One might have expected the attorney general to join the chorus. In *Tropic* the Massachusetts majority had favored our interpretation of *Roth*, but it was a narrow majority. Other high state courts had differed. A lawyer could quite properly ask the Massachusetts court, in the next case that came along, to reconsider, and shift to the view of the *Tropic* dissenters.

Yet the attorney general and his assistants were willing to abandon a legal position which, if it prevailed, would give them automatic victory. I am guessing at their reasoning, but it may have run something like this: the question to which contesting lawyers devote the most time and attention—the question that becomes the center of controversy—is the one that is likely to shape the decision. We were proceeding on a view of the law that a majority of the Massachusetts court had already accepted, and we had done well in other high courts where the meaning of *Roth* had been made the principal issue. On the other hand, *Memoirs* was the most vulnerable of the three books. Would it not be better, then, to concentrate not on the law, but on the book itself? By joining with us in our view of the law, the attorney general might sweep the legal issues out of the case, and the court would not be distracted in its contemplation of the notorious *Fanny*.

There is an old saying at the bar: when you are weak on the facts, argue the law; when you are weak on the law, argue the facts. The attorney general was not, in my opinion, so weak on the law. But he was stronger on the facts. The salient fact here, he could argue, despite all the testimony we had offered, was *Memoirs* itself. Let us not argue about the law, he was in effect saying; if the law condemns anything, it condemns this book.

I admired the strategy. But its application, I thought, led into a wilderness less hospitable to them than to *Fanny*. I explored it in my reply brief, parts of which follow:

Petitioner [the attorney general] points out that Cleland was not a major writer, and that the book must be saved "on its own merit alone." The latter is true of every book. The defender of a book cannot prevail on the ground that its author was a major figure, nor its prosecutor on the ground that he was not. . . .

Petitioner then argues that *Ulysses* is a masterpiece—a consideration certainly irrelevant to a test under which only material "utterly lacking" in value may be condemned—and says that its author "had much to comment on beside the subject of sex." And petitioner attempts to distinguish *Lady Chatterley's Lover* by stating that Lawrence's "reactions to the effects of industrialization in England certainly redeem the book. . . ." Arguments such as these depend on a distortion of the Supreme Court's use of the word "redeeming." . . .

There is no doctrine that sexual material has to be "redeemed" by a counterpoised weight of nonsexual material. The author of a book that has merit puts nothing in pawn by dealing with sexual subjects. For purposes of the social-value test, it may be assumed that the work is in one or more aspects objectionable. The word "redeeming" as used by the Supreme Court signifies only that what might otherwise be condemned is saved by the fact of its value. It does not mean that there must be a leaven of comment on the second industrial revolution.

In the concluding paragraph of his Point II [the section of his brief dealing with the prurient-interest test] petitioner says: "Had it been the Court's purpose to extend the First Amendment to cover all writing no matter what the quality or subject matter, the Court would have said so." Having brought elements of the prurient-interest test into his discussion of the social-value test, petitioner now brings elements of the social-value test into his discussion of the prurient-interest test. We agree that the Supreme Court has not extended the First Amendment to cover all writing no matter what the quality or subject matter. But quality has to do with social value, and not with prurient interest. . . . As to subject matter, we assert that if the necessary quality exists—if there is that literary merit or other value which calls the First Amendment into play—then there is no subject matter that is excluded from the range of literary endeavor. . . . There is nothing in creation that the artist may not deal with, provided that he is indeed an artist. . . . Petitioner proves nothing when he says "the dominant theme of this book is sex and its portrayal. . . ." We can agree with the statement; we must deny its relevance.

The final words of petitioner's Point II are that the book "clearly appeals to the interest or desire of the ordinary person to examine the unusual and ordinarily forbidden material that it offers." For one thing, this is a necessary consequence in each case where a previously suppressed book has been held entitled to publication; formerly forbidden material is made available, and this very fact will create interest. For another, the point that readers are interested in reading about sex is neither news nor a constitutional consideration. The courts that held *Lady Chatterley's Lover* and *Tropic of Cancer* to be within the protection of the First Amendment were as much aware as petitioner that many people would read these books for their sexual interest and the sexual excitement they offered. . . . Some seven million copies of *Lady Chatterley's Lover* were sold. Over two million copies of *Tropic of Cancer* have now been sold, and its sale in many states has only recently begun. The judges who decided those cases were not innocent of the possibilities upon which petitioner put so much stress. . . .

The brief then draws a distinction in quantitative terms. A book containing "an occasional description of a sexual encounter" will, according to petitioner, pass the test; one that contains many will not. Petitioner's distinction is not valid, either legally or psychologically. One radical décolletage in a roomful of conventionally dressed women is more shocking, and better calculated to arouse sexual response, than a beachful of bikinis. One vivid description of an act of sex in a book composed mainly of nonsexual incidents has an impact far stronger than that of a book whose subject matter is sex and which, by its nature, contains a number of sexual descriptions.

* * *

After starting his brief by emphasizing that only "material utterly lacking" value is "beyond the purview of the Amendment," he ends by arguing that *Memoirs* should be suppressed because, in his opinion, it is not as valuable a book as *Ulysses, Lady Chatterley's Lover* or *Tropic of Cancer*. He begins by quoting the language of the Supreme Court "that material dealing with sex . . . that has literary or scientific or artistic value or any other form of social importance may not be branded as obscenity" and that "the constitutional status of the material [may not] be made to turn on a 'weighing' of its social importance against its prurient appeal." He concludes by asking this court to engage in that very weighing process. When the petitioner applies the Supreme Court's tests as the Supreme Court has held they must be applied, the facts embarrass his contentions.

The argument took place in January 1965. As in the *Tropic* case, all seven justices sat. Six of the seven were the same; one judge had retired and been replaced. Representing the appellant, I spoke first, and spent some time reviewing what had gone on in this field of law since I was last before the court. In the *Tropic* appeals, California and Wisconsin had agreed with Massachusetts; New York and Illinois had not. This combination of decisions, I mentioned, permitted Boston booksellers, for the first time in history, to advertise a book as "Banned in New York." I described the Supreme Court cases of the previous June, and the subsequent reactions of the Illinois and New York courts. I said that Mr. Justice Brennan had evidently responded to Chief Justice Wilkins's complaint that the *Roth* opinion was "too dim a beacon" and brightened it considerably.

This won a smile of acknowledgment from the chief justice— a dim smile of acknowledgment. But he was still not satisfied with the social-value test. If the presence of any value, he asked, can save a book—if only books "utterly without" value may be suppressed—then wouldn't a favorable reaction on the part of one judge automatically decide the case, no matter what the other six might think? If one judge thought it had value, then how could it be said to be "utterly without" value? I answered, respectfully, that the question involved a fallacy, and I cited analogous situations in the law.

Often the issue on appeal (in any kind of case) is whether there is credible evidence in the record to support a trial court's finding of fact. The function of the appellate judge is not to decide whether the evidence demonstrates the fact—not to decide whether he would make the same finding as the judge or jury below—but only to decide whether there is some credible evidence on which one might conceivably base such a finding. If a majority concludes that the record contains no such evidence, there will be a reversal. If some judges think they see supporting evidence, this does not mean the others must assume it is really there.

The appellate process on social value is, in this respect, similar. If a majority concludes that the book is utterly without value, the book will lose. If some judges see value not discernible to others, I said, this does not mean the value exists. The minority can be wrong, and the majority is entitled to say so.

At the trial, Sullivan had handled the case, with Cowin assisting him. On the appeal, Cowin made the oral argument. It was similar to his brief, which I have described: perhaps literary critics might note some recondite value in *Memoirs*, but their reactions should not be controlling; to the average man *Memoirs* was nothing beyond pornography. There were no ideas in it. Almost all the book was taken up with sexual description. Cowin gave this repeated emphasis: the book failed to present "ideas as such."

Most of what had to be said in response was in my reply brief, but the point about lack of ideas, I thought, needed special attention. I asked leave to refer to a recent personal experience. I had arrived in Boston the day before and spent the evening visiting friends. They had entertained me (Boston being Boston, I did not add) by taking me to a discussion group on poetry. The evening's subject was Yeats's "Leda and the Swan." It seemed to me a beautiful poem. But it did not have a single idea in it, in the expository sense in which my brother used the term.

He was concentrating, I said, on but one of the values that the First Amendment guarded. In its *Tropic* opinion, this court had used the word "attributes"—"literary or artistic attributes" —not "ideas." The Amendment had a broader scope than my brother would allow. Perceptions, attitudes, fantasies, visions— all these were part of speech and press, and beyond these, aesthetic elements that need not be termed ideas at all. If Yeats's sonnet were otherwise obscene, it would survive not by reason of a fresh philosophy; it would be saved by its art. One might think the literary merit of "Leda and the Swan" much greater than that of *Memoirs*, but the Amendment protected minor works of art as well.

The poem, I added, had another bearing on the matter. The attorney general argued that *Memoirs* should be suppressed because so many of its events and descriptions had to do with sex. But if sex was ninety percent of *Memoirs*, it was a hundred percent of "Leda and the Swan." The poem dealt exclusively with a scene of rape. Among its fourteen lines, the court might observe, there was not a single one that was not concerned with sex.*

The Supreme Judicial Court took a long time to decide the case, from the beginning of January to the end of March. When it came, it was another four-to-three decision, this time against us. Five of the judges divided as they had on *Tropic of Cancer*—

---

* The poetry meeting—in addition to being, as it turned out, useful—had been very interesting; I had never, lamentably, experienced such a thing. One of its aspects I found interesting was the close connection between the poetry analysis and television sportscasting. Sports announcers almost never say anything bad is happening; it is apparently impious to use descriptions outside the range of good-to-great. This applies particularly to a quarterback's choice of plays. If, say, it is third down and one yard to go, a conservative running play stands a good chance of giving the team a first down, while a more dangerous play, such as a pass, may bring larger rewards. If the quarterback chooses the running play, the announcers will compliment him on the soundness of his judgment. If he chooses the pass, they will admire his imagination and daring. The one call is great because it conforms to the logic of the situation; the other is great because it goes counter to the logic.

This poetry group was made up of intelligent, sophisticated people. But Yeats was their darling quarterback. Where the rhythm was smooth and the rhymes matched easily, the poem was commended for its loveliness. Where the rhythm broke, or the words did not quite rhyme, the poem was commended for the variation and the dissonance. If the expectation of the beat or the repeated sound was neatly met, there was a satisfying music. If they were not met, a tension was created and the writing had power. The poet even had an advantage over the quarterback. The running play may be defeated by a massed defense, or the pass may be intercepted by defenders who have watched television themselves. Yeats, though, could not lose. Once in a while someone challenged the general approbation, and then the leader had only to say very sweetly, "If you don't feel it, you don't feel it."

three for the book and two opposed. The new judge voted the same way as the man he replaced, against the book. One judge who had been with the majority that sustained *Tropic* went the other way on *Memoirs*. It was Judge Spalding, and he wrote the opinion for the majority.

On the concept of social value, the dissenters were very clear. Judge Whittemore, with whom Judge Spiegel joined, opened his opinion: "This book cannot be ruled to be 'utterly without redeeming social importance.'" Judge Cutter, who had delivered the majority opinion on *Tropic*, called attention to the problems that inhered in my reading of *Roth* but agreed with their solution; the Supreme Court decisions, he wrote, "declare in effect (if not in words) that to justify literary censorship there must be absent any form of worth." Cutter had an interesting variation to offer: while he believed the book could not constitutionally be kept from the general public, he suggested issuing a decree that would forbid its sale to minors.

But these were dissenters. As for the majority, since their exact language became important in the Supreme Court, I will not paraphrase. After stating some of the facts and reviewing the Supreme Court decisions and the opinion of the trial judge, Judge Spalding wrote:

> Whether the Supreme Court of the United States has laid down three independent standards, all of which (as the judge ruled) must be satisfied, need not be decided, for in our opinion *Memoirs* meets all the tests. As indicated above, we have little doubt that *Memoirs'* dominant theme appeals to prurient interests and that it is patently offensive.
>
> It remains to consider whether the book can be said to be "utterly without social importance." We are mindful that there was expert testimony, much of which was strained, to the effect that *Memoirs* is a structural novel with literary merit; that the book displays a skill in characterization and a gift for comedy; that it plays a part in the history of the development of the English novel; and that it contains a moral, namely, that sex with love is superior to sex in a brothel. But the fact that the testimony may indicate this book has some minimal literary value does not mean it is of any social importance. We do not interpret the "social importance" test as requiring that a book which appeals to pru-

rient interest and is patently offensive must be unqualifiedly worthless before it can be deemed obscene. . . .

The Massachusetts majority was unwilling to concede as much as the attorney general had conceded. It withheld approval of the three-test theory; Judge Spalding pointed out that it was not necessary to decide whether the tests were independent if the book failed them all. He applied the value test, essentially, in the way Cowin urged it should be applied, but unlike Cowin, refused to recognize it as a separate standard. In the Supreme Court, then, I would have two opponents to contend with—the attorney general and the majority below. As it turned out, I also had a third, who attacked from a third position, different and distant.

The Race

to Washington

MEMOIRS V. MASSACHUSETTS WAS READY FOR
the Supreme Court, but the Supreme Court was not necessarily
ready for it. The process of persuading the Court that a case is
one it ought to hear takes time, and for *Fanny Hill* the passage
of time might be fatal. Two other obscenity cases were already
on the docket, and would normally be argued long before ours.
In each, I feared, there was a substantial chance of an adverse
decision, which might bring with it a set of opinions that would
halt the course of the law, and a rule under which *Fanny Hill*
could find no salvation.

The defendant in one of the pending cases was Ralph Ginzburg. A federal court had convicted him of violating the Comstock Act. The defendant in the other was a man named Edward Mishkin, convicted under the New York anti-obscenity
statute.

In my view, the material Ginzburg had mailed was not, in
itself, sufficient for conviction. Or if the Court were going to
hold that it was, our own chances would not be good. The three
Ginzburg publications were not terribly lustful as compared,
say, to *Fanny Hill*. And two of the three appeared to have
enough literary merit or informational content to earn the protection of the social-value test—if the Supreme Court would ac-

cept that test. But the way Ginzburg had sold his publications created a problem. When a lawyer with whom I discussed the prospect said I was needlessly alarmed, I pointed to the opinion of the federal court of appeals that had affirmed the judgment. Its first paragraph contained the following:

> The record shows that in September 1962, appellant Eros Magazine, Inc., of which appellant Ginzburg was editor and publisher, after a great deal of deliberation endeavored to obtain what was considered advantageous mailing privileges from Blue Ball, Pennsylvania. Meeting with no success there, a similar try was made with the Post Office at Intercourse, Pennsylvania. Again rejected, a final successful effort was made at the Middlesex, New Jersey, Post Office, from which over five million advertisements of *Eros* were mailed.

The opinion went on to describe other aspects of the operation and spoke of "experts in the shoddy business of pandering."

The court of appeals held the publications obscene in themselves. Disapproval of the methods Ginzburg used was not a necessary link in the reasoning. But, it seemed to me, these things had counted heavily in determining the court's attitude, and they might count heavily in the Supreme Court as well.

Mishkin's chances were even more doubtful, I thought. His books were trash, and it was not the first time he had been in trouble with the law. His record gave the impression of the inveterate commercial pornographer that the Chief Justice pictured in *Roth*; if, as Warren had urged, the issue should be a pattern of conduct rather than a book, Mishkin was vulnerable.

The Justices are conscious of their role as interpreters, and sometimes creators, of basic principle. They try to keep their gaze fixed on the general effect of their decision. But it is difficult to wash all the color out of a case. To attain the degree of detachment that would permit one to consider every question in abstract terms—to stay loose, and free from things, unique to the case and irrelevant to the principle, that excite sympathy on one hand or indignation on the other—would require judges more than, or less than, human.

Where the conflict between the demands of generalized law and the impulses drawn from the immediate situation is clear enough, the Court will submerge its feelings and concentrate on the principle that its decision will promote. But the detachment can never be perfect, and now and then the special features of a case will lead to a statement of principle different from what it would have been had the case borne a different countenance.

An example of these counterposed forces at work is *Terminiello* v. *Chicago*, a 1949 case decided by a five-to-four vote. There was a conviction under a breach-of-the-peace law in an Illinois state court, which interpreted the law to include speech that rouses the public to anger. Terminiello, addressing the Christian Veterans of America at the invitation of Gerald L. K. Smith, attacked, among others, Eleanor Roosevelt and former Chief Justice Stone. But his main target was the Jews, and the attack was vituperative enough to rouse a good part of the public to anger. (There were more angry citizens gathered outside the meeting hall than applauding citizens within it.)

The Supreme Court upset the conviction. The majority included the most liberal of its members, and it is a fair assumption they disapproved of Terminiello and his speech as strongly as the dissenters did. But, they reasoned, a conviction would constitute a precedent for an unduly restrictive interpretation of the First Amendment.

The minority, of course, also had more than Terminiello in mind. The statute's invasion of First Amendment guaranties was a small price, they felt, for a degree of protection against the horror he represented.

Breach of the peace, however, did not justify the Illinois action. Any utterance may provoke opposition, and the stronger the utterance the stronger the opposition. The expression may be strong enough, and unpopular enough, to create a riot, but if it is those who wish to silence the speaker that riot, they are the lawbreakers, not he. It is precisely where the opposition is most violent that the First Amendment is most needed. One wonders whether the dissenters would not have agreed with the majority if the speech involved had not been so repellent; Jackson, who wrote the dissent, had recently returned from his duties at Nuremberg.

There are several ways in which the needs and pulls of particular cases affect the development of principle. For one thing, the decision itself is important, quite apart from what the court may say in its opinion. An accumulation of decisions on one side or the other of a general question will have a heavy bearing on future cases. A corporate lawyer, for example, will be very cautious about recommending mergers after a series of adverse antitrust rulings, though mergers are in themselves generally lawful and despite the fact that each ruling was based on special circumstances that do not affect his clients.

For another, no matter how firmly the court focuses on larger issues, the immediate facts will determine the perspective in which they are seen, and hence give form to the large answers. The courts simply cannot anticipate all the possibilities, and what is before their eyes will influence even their broadest statements. No imagination is capacious enough to envision the many combinations of facts that a principle may encompass. If the publications in an obscenity prosecution appear to be valueless and perhaps harmful, the court will tend, in formulating its rules, to concentrate on prohibition rather than freedom. The law on the subject was in its infancy, and the infant would retain the mark of the wrappings in which it was brought to the Court.

Finally, opinions are usually written to provide the strongest possible basis for the decision. Although the judge may have been entirely judicial in reaching his conclusion, he is ordinarily inclined, in writing his opinion, to be an advocate for the conclusion he has reached. If the decisions in the pending cases were for suppression, the statements in the opinions would probably give general support to the idea of suppression.

And so, as I say, I was uneasy at the thought that *Ginzburg* and *Mishkin* might furnish the Justices their next opportunity to speak on the interaction of the First Amendment and anti-obscenity laws. The next pronouncements were likely to be crucial. The theory that value provides an independent test had never been explicitly propounded to the Court. (It will be recalled that *Tropic* was decided without argument.)

The Supreme Court's review of decisions may be either by certiorari or by appeal. Conceptually, certiorari is discretionary, while appeal, where it fits, is a matter of right. But the Court could not endure all the appeals that are filed, any more than it could endure all the cases in which certiorari is sought. To avoid suffocation, it entertains some appeals only summarily. An appeal will be dismissed unless it presents a "substantial question." On a basis of preliminary papers—without briefs or oral argument—the Court may think the point so well settled, or the objection so frivolous, that the decision below should be allowed to stand.*

The effort to demonstrate that the case warrants attention (that is, presents a substantial question) is made in a document called a Jurisdictional Statement. It is something very like a brief, but briefer, and it is directed primarily to the question whether there should be a full hearing of the case rather than how the Court should decide it. After the Statement has been filed, the other side has a certain time in which to move to dismiss (paralleling the opportunity, on certiorari, to oppose the petition).

The Statement here, I thought, had perhaps more than ordinary significance. If *Ginzburg* and *Mishkin* had already been decided by the time the Court got around to us, the Justices might regard the law as clarified by their decisions in those cases. Or, regardless of what happened in those cases, they might feel they had had enough of the subject, that if the law was not yet clear, it was about as clear as it was going to get, for a while at least—unless our Statement move them to think otherwise.

I had never had a Supreme Court case, and never written a Jurisdictional Statement. I asked a friend, who had a fine understanding of the Court and its procedures, and of the law in general, to go over my draft. My friend, Yastrzemski,† offered some helpful suggestions and one major objection—the Statement

---

* The precedential effect of dismissing an appeal is much different from a denial of certiorari. Certiorari may be denied for various reasons; it is not an expression of Supreme Court sentiment on the merits. Dismissal, unless it is for procedural defects, means that the Court regards the appeal as insubstantial, from which it follows that the decision below was correct. (The Court may also end a case without full hearing for the opposite reason: that is, on the preliminary papers the Court may decide that the decision was wrong, and so clearly wrong that a full hearing is unnecessary.)

† I also asked him to go over the draft of this chapter, to confirm the accuracy of the part that involves him. He found it thoroughly accurate, but was embarrassed by the laudatory description, and gave me the option of

was too long, he said, and too argumentative. A Jurisdictional Statement is, properly, a rather chaste document. Mine was elaborate and, in this company, garish. It devoted considerable space to a discussion of the book and the testimony about the book, and argued my theory of the law almost as much as the final brief would.

I was aware of the gaucherie. But there was *Fanny Hill*'s reputation to consider, and the fact that the other cases were pending. The Supreme Court might have no urge to stir itself unduly —to invoke the majesty of the First Amendment—for the sake of a book that was merely the best-known example of pornography, especially when its docket held other cases in the same general field. The Statement would be our first communication with the Court, and I felt it important that if the Justices shared the usual preconceptions about *Fanny Hill*, they be shaken at the outset.

Moreover, the value test had been put in issue. It was being relied on by Ginzburg's lawyers, and, at this time, opposed by the government lawyers. Even if the Court refused to hear our appeal, I wanted the Justices to have read my version of what the law was, and why it was what it was, when they came to decide the other cases. The Jurisdictional Statement thus had the triple purpose of getting the Justices to take our appeal, conditioning their view of the case if they did take it, and conditioning their view of the law if they did not.

But this did not make for the usual, proper kind of Statement. A first-class Supreme Court lawyer like Yastrzemski, sensitive to the nuances of the Court's procedures, would be troubled by my draft. He urged me to shorten it, and leave more to implication. I told him what I thought there was to gain. He pointed out that since my Statement was not what the Rules contemplated, and not what the Court ordinarily received, it might induce a negative reaction among the Justices.

As the discussion went on, Yastrzemski sighed the sigh of an

---

toning it down or removing his name. Since a less laudatory description would itself be an inaccuracy, and since I regard his standing among lawyers as equivalent to that of Carl Yastrzemski among ball players, I give him this alias.

artist who sees a beloved art form abused, and said, graciously, that despite his criticism, he really enjoyed reading the draft, and learned some things about the book that he had not known before. As a matter of fact, it now seemed to him that *Fanny Hill*, despite its celebrity, might actually be a pretty good book.

Suppose, I said, the Justices get the impression that Rembar is an ignorant lawyer, but that Cleland was a very good writer; will that be bad? All right, all right, said Yastrzemski.

Supreme Court terms run from October to May. The Massachusetts decision was rendered at the end of April, too late for any kind of action that term. Earlier in April, the Court had granted certiorari in *Ginzburg*, and "noted probable jurisdiction"—that is, accepted the appeal—in *Mishkin*. The Court would not consider whether to take our appeal until after it reconvened the following fall.

Ginzburg and *Mishkin* were scheduled for argument in November. Under the rules, the appellant has forty-five days to file his brief, and the opposing party has thirty days after that to file the answering brief; extensions of time may be granted, and a case is normally not called for argument until at least two weeks after all the briefs are in. The average interval between the acceptance of an appeal and its argument runs about four and a half months. In *Memoirs* v. *Massachusetts* the Court had not yet noted probable jurisdiction, and no matter how soon it did, this timetable would carry us well past the date set for the *Ginzburg* and *Mishkin* arguments.

The Supreme Court will on occasion, however, cut the time drastically. Although the occasion is typically a matter of public urgency, such as a lawsuit affecting an election, I saw a slim chance that it might happen here. The Court likes to have cases involving a single general subject argued together. If the attorney general and I would each forego the normal time for writing briefs, and if the Court would consent, we might be able to have our hearing on the day that *Ginzburg* and *Mishkin* had theirs. I spoke to John Davis, the clerk of the Supreme Court. (The position of clerk is an unclerkly one, highly important in the administration of the Supreme Court's business.) Davis said it was possible, but the Court had to be convinced there was good reason. And the collapsing of the periods would have to be agreeable to my opponent.

The Massachusetts attorney general, Edward Brooke (who later became United States senator), had indicated he would not move to dismiss our appeal. He would contest the case vigorously, but he wanted it heard; some elucidation from the Court would help law enforcement in Massachusetts. Right after I left Davis, I telephoned Cowin in Boston, and told him I was going to move to advance the case. Cowin said he would do everything possible to cooperate: what did I have in mind?

I had in mind, I said, that he would start work immediately, on the assumption that the Court was going to accept jurisdiction. He did not have to see my brief to be able to write his; the points I was going to make would not vary from those in the Jurisdictional Statement. Fine, said Cowin. I went on: if he could get his brief in fast enough, and the Court would dispense with the usual period between answering brief and argument, the case might be heard together with *Ginzburg* and *Mishkin*. So, I suggested, he ought to get it done in the next two weeks.

"Oh," he said, "I can't do that."

"Why not?"

"Because I'm getting married Sunday."

That stopped me, momentarily. Then: "How long will you be away—a week? That'll leave a whole week to do the brief. It shouldn't take you longer: we've been through this before."

"But I have other assignments from the attorney general; they have to be done."

"Ask him to relieve you of your other assignments. This is more important."

"I don't know if he will."

There was another moment's pause. "Who's going to argue this case in the Supreme Court," I asked, "you or the attorney general?"

"He hasn't said."

"Well, if we don't meet this schedule, there's a good chance neither one of you will argue it."

"What do you mean?"

"If we get to the Court after *Ginzburg* and *Mishkin*, there's a good chance they'll have said everything they plan to say for a while. Our case may be decided summarily."

"I'll get back to you," said Cowin.

He called me the next day in New York. Brooke had relieved him of his other assignments. He could meet the schedule. He was going to argue the case. I offered him felicitations on his marriage, and wished him a happy honeymoon.

The next step was to try to persuade the Court to take our case out of order. The procedure was by typewritten motion, filed a couple of days later. If the court was going to embark on a general review of the law of obscenity, the motion papers urged, it ought not to do it on the basis of *Ginzburg* and *Mishkin* alone; and the characteristics of *Memoirs* v. *Massachusetts* made it a good one for the Court to hear. Both sides in our case were submitting arguments different from those in the other two: "in the scheduled cases, the Court is being urged to overrule *Roth*, while the publisher's position [in *Memoirs*] is that the *Roth* standards provide ample protection for the book in question." The Court, however, might wish to give those standards additional "scope and definition," and *Memoirs* was a case well suited to such an undertaking. It presented the question of how the *Roth* tests should be applied "in a singularly precise and unmixed form": there were no procedural errors, no questions of search and seizure, no complications arising out of the general conduct of the defendants. Most important, while there was considerable evidence of literary merit, the book was "concededly erotic." I concluded with an offer to give them a brief in two days.

When the motion was filed, the Court had not yet noted probable jurisdiction. We were asking the Justices to speed along a case they had not yet said they would hear at all. Six days later the Court granted the motion. Meanwhile, something had happened that changed the schedule from hysterical to merely frantic: the Solicitor General asked for more time on his brief in the *Ginzburg* case, and the Court postponed the arguments in both *Ginzburg* and *Mishkin* to the first week in December. *Memoirs* v. *Massachusetts* was to be argued at the same session, immediately afterward.

The Court's
Friends and Mine

AT THE TIME THE *FANNY HILL* CASE WAS ON ITS way to the Supreme Court, there was great optimism among libertarians. People friendly to the cause I represented were more than encouraging; they were full of good cheer and confidence. A year earlier, after the Supreme Court decisions in *Tropic* and *Jacobellis*, a lawyer prominent in the field was quoted by *Time* as saying that it was now "impossible" for a book to be declared obscene. At the very least, it was generally assumed (in these circles) that the social-value theory was firmly established.

I did not share the optimism. I felt we would win our case, but I thought the law had not reached the stage my friends assumed it had, and that the Court was certainly not prepared to go beyond that stage.

To begin with, one could not easily ignore the fact that the Massachusetts court had decided against us. High state courts dealing with constitutional issues usually try to conform to the Supreme Court view of the law; in a sense, they are in the business of predicting what the Court will do. (I say usually, not always. But it is typical of a sophisticated set of judges like those in Massachusetts.)

And though periodicals reporting the cases that were approaching the Supreme Court spoke in terms of how they would fare under the application of "the three tests"—it is beguiling to have one's argument travel a circuit and return disguised as fact—the battle for the value test was still to be won. So far only two Justices (Brennan and Goldberg) had allowed there was such a thing, and one of them was gone from the Court. Indeed, *Jacobellis* and *Tropic* as precedents could be used both ways: the fact that seven Justices had not so much as mentioned social value was there to balance, perhaps to outweigh, the fact that two of them used it as an independent test.

Goldberg's replacement was Abe Fortas, who had a well-earned reputation as a liberal, on the basis of which a number of people assured me he could be counted on to take a libertarian approach to censorship—perhaps joining Black and Douglas to make a team of three. I took no comfort from this. Liberalism in other fields does not necessarily carry over into the First Amendment. (Nor does conservativism: two of the three judges of the New York Court of Appeals who voted in favor of both *Memoirs* and *Tropic* were Republicans.) The exchange of Goldberg for Fortas was the exchange of a judge whose attitude we knew for one whose attitude had not been expressed (or perhaps even formed).*

Stewart's reaction could not be predicted with any assurance. His voting in obscenity cases had been liberal, but he had declared that his judgment would be governed by a concept he had not defined.

Harlan had consistently adhered to the analysis he set forth in *Roth*. In effect, it was pro-censorship for state governments, anti-censorship for the federal government. A state government was moving against *Memoirs*.

White's views had not been spelled out, but his opinions on

---

* In *Roth*, Fortas had filed an amicus brief (a term explained below) on behalf of certain people opposed to anti-obscenity laws. This was hardly a basis for predicting how he would view things from the bench. He was acting as attorney for his clients, and there is no difficulty—legal or moral—in a lawyer's presenting an argument in one case that is inconsistent with an argument he has made in another. And there is certainly no difficulty in his taking a position, in the neutral stance of judge, contrary to a position once taken in the highly partisan stance of advocate.

other Bill of Rights questions strongly suggested that he would be conservative on questions of obscenity.

Clark had not written much in the field, but we could pretty well count on a vote against *Memoirs.* He had joined Brennan in *Roth,* but he had joined Warren in *Jacobellis.*

The Warren opinion in *Jacobellis* was perhaps the most troubling factor. Apparently concerned that too much of the Court's time was being taken up by obscenity cases, Warren had proposed that an adverse decision should not be disturbed if there was "sufficient evidence" to support a finding of obscenity. Since the book itself is always some evidence of its own obscenity, this in effect meant that the Court would never reverse a judgment of suppression except on procedural points. The Chief Justice defined "sufficient evidence" as lying between "no evidence" and "substantial evidence"—two standards familiar in appellate review. But a requirement of something less than "substantial evidence" is a requirement easily met.

This left Black and Douglas, whose votes my friends counted as sure because of their "absolute" reading of the Amendment. Even here, it seemed to me, there was something less than certainty. These Justices, like Warren, wanted to get the Court out of the censorship business, though by a different exit. They had commented that acting as a Supreme Board of Censors was an unbecoming role for the Court. If they became convinced that the other Justices would not come round to their position, they might feel obliged to qualify it in such a way as to relieve the Court of the unwelcome burden. Better to yield on one aspect of the Bill of Rights than to see the Court, the chief guardian of those Rights, impeded by the need to study hundreds, perhaps thousands, of publications challenged as obscene. If the end could not be accomplished their way, perhaps Warren's approach should be adopted. The yielding would involve no abdication of principle. It is hard to say just when a judge should stop dissenting, but at some point it may be an act of judicial statesmanship to announce that having several times presented his view—a view that he still believes to be correct—he now deems it necessary to join in a position less acceptable in order to secure the best possible administration of the law.

So I was dubious about my friends' optimism, and the doubt

was compounded when one thought of the Court not as a number of individual judges but as an institution. The Court is quite aware that it has a political function as well as a judicial one. There has been lively controversy over whether its decisions should come from strict legal analysis (an application of principle and precedent to the particular case) or from its understanding of social and political needs (decision-making according to what the Court feels is right and good for the country). The controversy has gone on for some years, but the Justices themselves seem less interested in it than the journalists. In fact, they are motivated by both ideas.

They are free with precedents, but not free of them. They look upon themselves as judges, expounding and applying the law and sometimes shaping it, but always dealing with a subsisting institution. They do not look upon themselves as unrestrained, paternalistic managers of the commonweal, who can write a new constitution for each case and leave the Constitution of 1787 to the historians.

They recognize, however, that they have too large an influence on matters of national policy to stay snug and comfortable within the ordinary confines of *stare decisis*. They will expand or contract the principle and accommodate the precedent more readily than if they were sitting in lower courts. Among the factors they must take into account is the mood of the people. The recent rulings against censorship, though they fell short of the demands of some citizens, were in the eyes of most of them too permissive. During this period, dealing with other aspects of the Bill of Rights, the Court had handed down decisions that gathered great clouds of opposition and abuse. The Justices are obviously not timid men, but opposition creates, if not anxiety, at least a problem—how long to persist in an unpopular course. Their fund of public support cannot be squandered. They might feel, it seemed to me, that enough of it had been spent in combating censorship, and more should not be lavished on the likes of *Fanny Hill*. Other difficult decisions had to be made—on civil rights, on police methods, on legislative apportionment ("one man, one vote"), on the church-state barrier, and on freedom of expression in political affairs (which was, after all, the kind of expression that the founding fathers had mainly in mind). It might be wisest for the Court—especially since there was so much overlap among the groups hostile to its various decisions—to begin to take a less uncompromising approach to this one aspect of liberty.

Finally, the euphoric haze obscured the fact that things do not go on indefinitely in a single direction. When the progress of the law is plotted on a graph, straight unbroken lines are rare. The law had moved very swiftly on the heading of freedom, and it might just be time for a change of direction.

An amicus curiae—a "friend of the court"—is one who is permitted to present his views in a case to which he is not a party. He may have a private interest in the outcome because his own situation is similar and can be affected by the court's ruling, or he may represent the public or part of the public. The government itself is frequently an amicus, in suits that bear upon the work of a federal agency. Or a nongovernmental organization, seeking to promote either the individual interests of its members or their version of the public good, may ask to be heard. Sometimes participation includes oral argument; usually it is limited to the submission of a brief.

Ginzburg and *Mishkin* brought the Supreme Court a whole host of friends. Briefs urging affirmance of the convictions were filed in both cases by the Citizens for Decent Literature, and in *Mishkin* by a group of enforcement officials. Briefs urging reversal were filed in *Ginzburg* by the American Civil Liberties Union, the Authors League of America and the American Book Publishers Council, and in both cases by a group of writers and publishers gathered for the purpose.

The amici aiding *Ginzburg* and *Mishkin* reflected the prevailing liberal-optimistic attitude. On the premise that the social-value theory was already part of the law, all but one demanded further diminution of restraints. The writers of the briefs were not merely hoping; they felt there was a good chance the Court would accept what they proposed.

Ordinarily a lawyer is pleased to have a friend at his side. Especially where the amicus is a respected organization, such as the Authors League or the Book Publishers Council—even more where the organization has no financial stake in the result, not even an indirect one, but only a devotion to principle, such as the Civil Liberties Union—its presence lends prestige to the litigant's position and gives it a sponsorship not provided by the necessarily narrow interest of the litigant. Apart from presence, the brief itself may be a help; it may offer additional arguments or put existing arguments in a more congenial form.*

In our case, however, I felt amici would not be helpful. The Publishers Council was now accepting the theory of an independent value test—contrary to the view of *Roth* it had taken earlier—but its policy was to speak only in abstract terms and to disclaim any opinion "as to the obscenity or nonobscenity" of the publication under attack. The disclaimer might carry a negative implication. If we were to have outside support, I wanted support for *Fanny Hill*; on statements of principle, I preferred my own version.

While the Council did not go far enough, the other amici seemed, for present purposes, to go too far. The Civil Liberties Union argued that there should be suppression for obscenity only where the prosecution could demonstrate a "clear and present danger" of harmful consequences. This was a concept brought over from the field of political freedom. It made, I thought, an awkward fit where the object of suppression was not subversive speech but obscene writing. The argument that they could not prove a chain of causation leading to antisocial behavior failed to meet the censors' fundamental objection—that reading the book was itself sinful and constituted all the harm that had to be noted. In any event, acceptance of the Union's argument would effectively erase the anti-obscenity statutes, since the required proof was unavailable. Whatever might be said for or against such a result was, to my mind, irrelevant: the Court was not nearly ready for it.†

The brief filed by the *ad hoc* group urged an explicit renunci-

---

* I pause to pay tribute—although I have from time to time disagreed with its actions or its arguments—to the magnificent work done by the Civil Liberties Union.

† I was not alone in my misgivings; among those who shared them were two lawyers for whom I had the greatest respect—Morton Yohalem and Louis Lusky (professor of constitutional law at Columbia).

ation of *Roth*; here again I felt the Court was being asked to do something that none but Black and Douglas had any intention of doing.

The Authors League, in a brief by Irwin Karp, submitted what I thought was the most effective of the amicus arguments —half exhortation, half practicality—and if this had been the only one, my attitude toward amicus participation might have been different.

Apart from the ideas presented, there is the matter of tone. When the writer is devoted primarily to a vision of what the law ought to be, the art of the advocate may suffer. His eye is on something larger and more distant, and sometimes the product may sound less like a brief than a dissent from a decision not yet rendered and denounced in advance. An amicus is exceptionally vulnerable to such seduction. One of the briefs that had been submitted, otherwise an excellent piece of legal writing, seemed in places like a lecture to the Court.

Everything considered, I came to the conclusion that we would be better off going it alone. I was asking the Supreme Court to mark a point in the progress of the law. I was saying it was a point at which the Court had by implication already arrived. The Court, however, had not yet agreed that this was so, and might never. Certainly, for some of the Justices the acceptance of my arguments would involve an abandonment of existing views.

The legal theory I offered, if judicially endorsed, was enough to protect *Memoirs*, and enough to work a radical change in the law as it had been understood less than a decade earlier. I thought it more of an advantage that the Justices have their attention confined to this theory, and not dispersed over a range of proposals, some of which, I felt, most of them would regard as unreasonable.

The views of the amici were already before the Court, of course, in the briefs filed in *Ginzburg* and *Mishkin*. But I preferred not to have the indigestible contentions stated with specific reference to our book. I talked it over with the client, recommending that we forego the benefit of extra voices to blend with ours—that, in these particular circumstances, it would be better to present a single note and not a chord. Minton agreed:

Putnam would not consent to the filing of any outside brief. Amici might still participate by making a motion to do so, but withholding consent would provide a measure of dissociation. And most of them were not likely to press the matter. Requests were made; we refused on the basis of a fixed policy, and the result was that no amici briefs came in on our side of the case.

But some came in on the other side. The Citizens for Decent Literature, no friends of ours, became friends of the Court. Even-handed, we declined to consent, but they made a motion, and it was granted. The Citizens' arguments were quite different from those of the attorney general, and we had to write a separate set of briefs to meet them. But where our friends, I thought, might have done us harm, our enemies were helpful.

The Companion

Cases

ONE MIGHT SAY THAT IN OUR HASTE TO PUT OUR arguments before the Supreme Court, we had fallen among evil companions. Not so. At least, not so from the point of view of the true censor. *Fanny Hill* was more of a provocation—not merely to lust, but also to litigation—than the materials marketed by Ginzburg or Mishkin.

The Ginzburg conviction was based on three publications, and circulars advertising them. (The mails shall exclude, says the postal law, both obscenity and information on where to get it.) One was *The Housewife's Handbook on Selective Promiscuity*, described in the Supreme Court's majority opinion as a book that "purports to be a sexual autobiography detailing with complete candor the author's sexual experiences from age 3 to age 36."

Another was the first issue of *Liaison*, which promised to be a biweekly newsletter. It was a rather silly affair whose ration of prurience was not much larger than its ration of wit; both were fixed in a statement on the first page. *Liaison* was not going to use dirty words "merely to titillate gross palates à la Henry Miller." The words that it was not going to use were listed.

The third, *Eros*, was a fancy hardcover quarterly that cost ten dollars a copy. It combined elements of *Playboy, Captain Billy's*

Whiz Bang, and *American Heritage,* and suggested the coffee table at least as much as the bed table. The particular volume had a series of color photographs of a man and a woman who were not, so far as one could judge, having sexual intercourse. They were nude but not completely revealed, and the general effect was arty rather than salacious. The most sensational feature of the photographs was that the woman was white and the man was black, a circumstance that the Supreme Court majority, dutifully following its own integration decisions, never mentioned.

The materials themselves, as I say, put less of a strain on the law than did *Fanny Hill.* The *Handbook* appeared to be serious in intent, and a number of doctors and psychologists thought it had value. The miscellany of articles and fiction in *Eros* was obviously meritorious, and could not match *Fanny's* unswerving fidelity to the arousal of sex. Its pictures did not go beyond those of other current and unchallenged publications—except perhaps in their interracial aspect, an aspect which might make them more offensive in some sections of the country but would be socially redeeming in others. *Liaison* had the least claim to the protection of the value theory, and probably no chance at all on patent offensiveness. Dwight Macdonald, testifying for the defense, described it as "extremely tasteless, vulgar and repulsive." Its triviality, however, should have gotten it by the prurient-interest test.

In March the government had filed a brief opposing Ginzburg's petition for certiorari. It proceeded from the still widely accepted premise (outside literary-liberal circles) that *Roth* had established the prurient-interest formula as the sole definition of obscenity, modified only by the gloss of patent offensiveness. The brief allowed social value nothing more than the office it had traditionally held. If it were present in sufficient quantity, it might outweigh the prurience, which then would not predominate:

> We note only that even if works have, to some comparatively slight extent, a literary or scientific interest, this does not, in our view, immunize them from attack as obscene. . . . It is

only if the presence of other themes casts doubt upon the dominance of prurience as the intended appeal and overriding interest of the work that the publication is constitutionally protected.

A brief for the United States in the Supreme Court is a prestigious document. This is partly because the government's Supreme Court briefs have an established, and justified, reputation for legal excellence, and partly because the United States as litigant is known to take a somewhat more objective view of the law than does the private suitor. Government lawyers represent all the people, and they should be concerned, and often are, with the enforcement of the Constitution as well as the enforcement of the Act of Congress they are administering. The lawyer's normal urge to win is tempered by the precept that a degree of detachment is fitting. (The extent to which the precept is honored varies from case to case and from lawyer to lawyer.)

The Solicitor General is the government's chief advocate in the Supreme Court. He is the nation's second-ranking legal officer, subordinate only to the Attorney General. The office has usually been filled by a distinguished lawyer, supported by a stout staff of legal scholars. Attorneys from other divisions of the Department of Justice or other government agencies may collaborate, but the Solicitor General or one of his assistants will customarily make the argument in the Supreme Court and have final responsibility for the brief. If there is an intramural conflict, the Solicitor General has the last word (except in the rare instance in which he may be overruled by the Attorney General, or by his client the President).

The Solicitor General is very much aware of his status as an officer of the Court and of his obligation to the law as an institution, and the Court is aware of his awareness. This, combined with the acknowledged ability of his staff, earns a special reception for his briefs and arguments. Hence the fact that the Solicitor General was before the Court and refusing to recognize an independent value test created an additional difficulty.

It was a difficulty that disappeared in a surprising governmental pirouette. Ginzburg was granted certiorari in April, and before the next November, when the government filed its main brief, its view of the law changed. This might have been second thought, or a matter of new personnel; I did not know. Over the summer Archibald Cox had resigned as Solicitor General, and Thurgood Marshall had taken his place. The March brief, opposing the granting of certiorari, had been signed by Cox and three attorneys. The November brief, on the merits, was signed by Marshall and two different attorneys. I mentioned a while back that the government asked for an extension of time to file; perhaps this reflected reconsideration of the problem, or even internal disagreement. In any event, in November the government accepted the value theory.

The indictment against Ginzburg and his corporations had been framed in three separate counts, one for each publication, and there had been a conviction on each. The Solicitor General did not treat them with an equal vigor. Indeed, his brief could be read as extending a delicate invitation to the Supreme Court to reverse on *Eros* and the *Handbook* and to affirm only with respect to *Liaison*. Some value might be found in *Eros* and the *Handbook* the brief allowed, but, ". . . substantial portions of *Liaison* are composed of offensive matter concededly of no redeeming importance; the judgment of the district court that it was 'dirt for dirt's sake' was clearly a reasonable characterization."

This distinction represented a permissible, and perhaps persuasive, application of the law. But the government lawyers may have had something in mind besides pure legal analysis. Varying sentences had been imposed. So far as the corporations were concerned, there could only be fines; there is no point in incarcerating a corporate charter. Ginzburg himself, however, had been sentenced to both a fine and five years' imprisonment. Considering the nature of his offense—especially against the background of the general commercial use that is made of sexual material—five years was a harsh penalty. The jail sentence was on the counts involving *Eros* and the *Handbook*; the sentence as to *Liaison* was a fine.

Now suppose the Supreme Court were to hold that *Eros* and the *Handbook* were entitled to First Amendment protection but *Liaison* was not. The defendant would stay out of jail, and at the same time the prosecution would have a victory. The Comstock Law would be shown to be very much alive, and a warning would go out to those who use the mails for material more objectionable and less justifiable than Ginzburg's. The fines to be paid on *Liaison* may have been paltry in the light of the economics of the whole enterprise, but it is not the Supreme Court's function to enlarge inadequate penalties.

Assuming this was the government's strategy, it need not have been motivated by soft-heartedness. It could appear to a competent advocate the best way to win the case. The strict course of the law's logic, as I have said, is sometimes diverted by the equities of the particular case, and the government lawyers —aware of the possibility that the prison sentence might strike the Justices as excessive—may have been offering the Court a way in which to hold the statute violated without sending a man to jail for five years.

As it turned out, a majority of the Justices felt quite able, thank you, to resist the diversion, and silently declined the government's silent invitation to render a double decision. The fact of the five-year prison sentence, however, was not without its effect. Two of the dissenting Justices began their opinions with a reference to it. It could hardly have failed to enter the deliberations of the majority.

Whatever may have been the government's thinking on the special problems of the *Ginzburg* case, its thinking on the general principles of law involved was now clear. Its new brief meant that in one of the companion cases, as well as in our own, both sides were arguing from the premise that social value was an independent test.

But in *Mishkin*, paradoxically, the prosecution (the State of New York) accepted the idea of an independent value test, while the defense did not. The paradox, of course, is only superficial. The attorney for Mishkin evidently, and quite sensibly, decided that drawing attention to the question of value would not help his client.

Mishkin's books had four signal themes: fetishism, homosexuality, sadism (formerly known as cruelty) and masochism. (It seems unfair that the Marquis de Sade has become so famous, while Leopold von Sacher-Masoch—who gave his name to a propensity but for whose existence the sadists would be, in lawful communities, a frustrated lot—is hardly known. Possibly the injustice could be remedied if somebody wrote a blood-and-nudity play called *McKinley/Masoch*.)

On the point of contemporary community standards, Mishkin's attorney omitted to mention a pertinent current event. At the precise moment that these cases were argued, the Number One song in the popularity polls was "These Boots Are Made for Walkin'." Its chorus, addressed to the object of the singer's affections—or at least attentions—was concerned entirely with the promise that the singer's boots, made for walking, would one day walk all over him (or her). Three of Mishkin's themes were apparently not only acceptable to the average person, or at least to the average teen-ager, but eagerly accepted.

A hesitant prospective witness in one of our cases had been troubled by the thought that if *Fanny Hill* could not be banned nothing could, and he was not at all sure publishing should be entirely uncontrolled. I told him that while there might be no books more lustful than *Memoirs* (depending on one's tastes), there were books that might be said to have considerably less social value. He wondered. I gave him some examples. He testified. Mishkin's books, which I did not have at hand, could have been used.

Mishkin's trial had taken place in 1960, before a New York three-judge criminal court. One of the witnesses that the prosecution called was Mishkin's printer:

Q. You stated that on some occasions Mr. Mishkin gave you a book that had already been printed?
A. That's right.
Q. What would you do in that case?
A. In that case I didn't have to bother with the typesetter. All I would do is pull the book apart and photograph it and go through the same procedure.
Q. When Mr. Mishkin gave you a manuscript, would anything else be done?
A. Well, if he gave me a manuscript, he would have to give me a little information to go along with it.

Q. What would he do, sir?

A. Well, he would tell me what price to put on the cover. He would give me a picture for the cover.

Q. Would he do anything else?

A. And he would tell me what—usually, if it was a thin manuscript, if there wasn't too much to it, he told me to try to make it a little thicker.

* * *

Q. Did Mr. Mishkin ever give you any other instructions concerning the printing of these books that you remember?

A. Well, he—yes. Here it says, "Rainbow Publishing Company, Brooklyn, New York." He would tell me to put down a publisher's name on the back.

* * *

Q. And would he always tell you the name to put on?

A. Couple of times he gave me the publisher's name and address to put down, but after a while he just told me, "Make up any name and address."

Q. "Make up any name and address"?

A. Right.

Q. When you say "address," what do you mean by that?

A. Like here, it says, "Brooklyn, New York." Sometimes we put down London or Paris. No definite address. Just a town—

Q. Did—

A. —or city.

Q. Did Mr. Mishkin ever tell you to put down his name and address on any of these books?

A. No.

The prosecution also called as witnesses a number of people who did books for Mishkin. One was a woman who had "met Mr. Mishkin through another writer."

JUSTICE BRESLIN: Yes. Go ahead.

A. He indicated what sort of writing—what sort of book he wanted. Then I went home and wrote it.

JUSTICE BRESLIN: What did he say to you?

Q. What did he tell you?

A. He told me he wanted a book written that was full of sex scenes and lesbian scenes, and that sort of thing.

Q. Did he use any other words that you recall?

A. Well, they were sort of naughty.

JUSTICE BRESLIN: What were they?

Q. Tell us what he said.

A. This is a little embarrassing. He wanted a book full of the things that are in the book. It is—

JUSTICE GASSMAN: Well now—

A. —sex.

JUSTICE GASSMAN: —what did he tell you? The book wasn't written at that time, and he told you that he wanted something in the book. Now what did he say to you?

THE WITNESS: Well, he wanted a book in which there were lesbian scenes, the sex had to be very strong, it had to be rough, it had to be clearly spelled out. In other words, I couldn't be subtle about it; I had to write sex very bluntly, make the sex scenes very strong. . . .

JUSTICE BRESLIN: What were the words used? You said there were some words that you described as "naughty" were used. What do you mean by that?

Madam, we have heard all the words; and you have heard them, too, according to your own testimony, from the defendant. I just want you to repeat them. What were they?

THE WITNESS: Well, the sex scenes had to be unusual sex scenes between men and women, and women and women, and men and men.

JUSTICE BRESLIN: In what way? Did he go into detail?

THE WITNESS: Yes. He described what he wanted and, too, showed me the other books that he had there.

JUSTICE BRESLIN: What did he say? What did he say?

THE WITNESS: Er, he wanted scenes in which women were making love with women, and that sort of thing.

JUSTICE GALLOWAY: Well, he used more graphic language, I assumed, did he, from what you said earlier? He used naughty words, is that what you said?

MR. STEIN: I believe the witness said he wanted naughty things.

JUSTICE GALLOWAY: I don't know.

JUSTICE BRESLIN: No, no.

MR. STEIN: I am sorry.

JUSTICE GALLOWAY: What did he say? That's all we want to know.

THE WITNESS: He brought out books and showed me—

JUSTICE GALLOWAY: Yes?

THE WITNESS: —that had been written; and he said he wanted sex scenes like these in which there were lesbian scenes. He didn't call it lesbian, but he described women making love to women and men were making love to men, and there was spankings and scenes—sex in an abnormal and irregular fashion.

The next writer who testified was male.

Q. Did you ever have any conversation with Mr. Mishkin prior to the writing of the book concerning the book?

A. Yes, I did.

Q. Will you tell us approximately when you had that conversation and the nature of the conversation?

A. I had this conversation with Mr. Mishkin in the early summer of 1958, in which he explained to me that this book —in the first place, he gave me an unbound book that he wanted me to extend. He wanted me to put a story line behind it and extend it. He wanted me to deal very graphically with the implementation of wheels on a female's body

—this was probably the stenographer's misspelling of "weals," though possibly Mishkin may have been trying to tap the sado-masochistic and hot-rod markets simultaneously—

of the darkening of the flesh under flagellation; and he said that the people who read these kind of books didn't care particularly about sex.

Here, coincidentally, was empiric observation supporting the idea that "prurient" did not mean "sexual."

He wanted me to concentrate mostly on the changing of the color of the flesh when people were being flagellated, and he didn't want any blood in it.

Q. Mr. Johnson, I show you People's Exhibit 21, and also People's Exhibit 57, two copies of the same book entitled *Screaming Flesh*. I ask you, sir, whether you can identify that book?

A. Yes sir, I can.

Q. What is it, sir?

A. This is a book that I wrote for Mr. Mishkin.

Q. Approximately when?

A. Late in 1958.

Q. And at whose request did you write it?

A. This is a book on—this is a book on bondage and fetishism.

Q. At whose request did you write it?

A. At Mr. Mishkin's.

Q. And what does the book concern, sir?

A. The book concerns bondage and—I mean, light touch of bondage. It contains a lot of fetishism about rubberwear and leatherware, and it has a strong lesbian theme.

Q. Were you paid for that book?

A. Yes sir.

Q. By whom?

A. By Mr. Mishkin.

Q. How much, and where?

A. About forty-five or forty-seven dollars.

Q. Where?

A. At the Main Stem Book Store.

JUSTICE GASSMAN: How much did you say?

THE WITNESS: About forty-five or forty-seven. It was either forty-five or forty-seven dollars. At the time Mr. Mishkin was at Main Stem I never received over a hundred dollars for any book except *Raw Dames*.

Mishkin's scale of pay was mysterious; another witness had been paid two hundred dollars. But his titles were plain enough —given the key.

Q. I show you People's Exhibit 23, a book entitled *So Firm and So Fully Packed*. Can you identify that book?

A. Yes sir, I can.

Q. What is it?

A. This is one of the smaller books that I wrote for Mr. Mishkin. I received a hundred dollars in cash for it. It is a book about tight lacing, and I learned about tight lacing due to the fact that Mr. Mishkin had asked me, first of all, to write the—to learn about the fetishes; and tight lacing is one of the fetishes that these people like to read about.

* * *

Q. Is there an author's name that appears on that book?

A. No sir. I don't think there is. No sir, there isn't.

Q. I show you People's Exhibit 27, a book entitled *Violated Wrestler*. . . .

Here again there may have been appeal to two disparate—reasonably disparate—audiences.

Q. Do you recall anything particular—did you have any conversation with the defendant concerning the writing of this book [*Columns of Agony*]?

A. Yes, I did. Mr. Mishkin gave me an original copy of this manuscript. It was in an unbound form, and he told me practically the same thing that he had told me about other books that he wanted on flagellation, not too much sex, that the people were more—the people who buy this book were more interested in the reddening of the flesh and in no blood being let because he wanted not too much violence and in—in wheels appearing on the bodies of the victims because this is what the people who bought these books wanted.

Again the wheels, and again the demonstration that there was something to which the concept of "prurient interest" might apply that could be distinguished from a normal sexual interest.

*   *   *

Q. Do you recall ever having a conversation with Mr. Mishkin concerning the writing of these books?—

A. Yes sir, I do.

Q. —this book? Tell us approximately when you had that conversation and what the conversation was about.

A. In either October or November of 1958 I went in to Mr. Mishkin with a manuscript, and Mr. Mishkin gave me eight pictures, and he told me he wanted—he wanted a story built around these eight pictures, and he wanted the captions in the—in the—under the pictures to conform with the text of the material that I would write, and he wanted it done in a hurry; and I did it in two days.

One of Mishkin's defenses was that there had been no proof of scienter—that it had not been shown he knew what he was doing.

The Brief for
the Supreme Court

THE BRIEF I PRESENTED TO THE SUPREME COURT
consisted mainly of arguments already described. Some problems it dealt with, though, bear special comment.

One was "well-written obscenity." The cry had plagued us all
through these cases. Good writing, every one of my opponents
had declared, is no excuse. If not all of them said—as many of
them did—the better the writing the more dangerous the book,
they all agreed that literary quality could not make an obscene
book nonobscene. Every judicial opinion against us, and almost
every dissent from majority opinions in our favor, nodded agreement. When they used the language of *Roth*, they said that
good writing did not have sufficient importance to redeem a
pornographic book.

This, to me, was question-begging. I had argued from the
start that the connotations of obscenity outside the law had no
significance; as a legal concept it could not invade the area shel-
tered by the First Amendment, and writing that had value
therefore could not be, in law, obscene. But for a century American judges and lawyers had treated obscenity as something that
had objective existence and definition, and no relation to the
First Amendment. The standard approach was to decide
whether the book was obscene, by whatever definition was cur-

rently in use, and then to consider whether there was something else present—it would take a good deal—that would justify the publication. On this approach, the talented use of words was hardly enough.

I never agreed that the values of *Memoirs* were confined to style and rhetoric. But neither did I agree that good writing, even in this narrow sense, was a matter of no social importance. My reply brief in the Massachusetts court had said:

> We do not, of course, concede that good writing—the gifted use of language—is not in itself a social value. Certainly our society could use more of it. The deteriorating ability to write is one of the principal laments of contemporary educators, in our law schools in particular. The attorney general's well-written brief, for example, is an exception to an unhappy rule. It is fair to say that the deterioration in ability is connected with a deprecatory attitude toward good writing.

"Well-written obscenity," I maintained, was a contradiction in terms.

The logic, I felt, was inescapable, but if a judge thought he had escaped it, there was nothing I could do, except point to other merits of the book or take an appeal, and from the Supreme Court there would be no appeal. In that Court my brief said:

> Respected critics have written about the book, and what they wrote is part of the record. In addition, there appeared in court, to face whatever rigors cross-examination might produce, distinguished faculty members from the colleges and universities of the commonwealth of Massachusetts. . . . All of the witnesses and all of the documentary evidence agree upon the fundamental point: *Memoirs* is a work of literature that has considerable value. Its value is not confined to the excellence of the writing—although good writing is rare enough to make its suppression an act of social improvidence.

A second problem was peculiar to this stage of the case. I was now, in effect, undertaking to explain the Supreme Court to the

Supreme Court, presuming to act as translator to the Court of the Court's own language.

The presentation of my theory of the *Roth* case could not be quite the same as it had been up to now. It is one thing to say to a lower court: this is what the Justices really meant, even if they didn't exactly say so. It is quite another thing to say to the Justices themselves: this is what *you* really meant, even if you didn't exactly say so. The implication hangs heavy that either their thinking was poor or they expressed it poorly.

The implication, however, can be dispelled. The process of making new law is often exploratory, even groping. As in any kind of empirical intellectual effort, a concept not fully realized may be at work. It will gain definition as new instances arise in experience, or (where legal thought is involved) as new cases arise in the courts. A developing rule of law will quite naturally lack full expression in the earliest cases, and at times may influence decision without being expressed at all—the "inarticulate hypothesis" that philosophers of the law have called attention to.

One consequence is that both lawyers and laymen may interpret these early cases in terms that are familiar to them, in terms of the old law left behind. Another consequence, which was also to manifest itself here, is that the judges who join in an opinion that comes at the beginning of such a process can end in disagreement. At first, the concept may be vague, and permit divergent understanding; there is sufficient agreement for the case at hand. But later, when the concept is tested against varying sets of facts, some of the judges will find the results unacceptable. The mind of the man who writes the pioneer opinion may hold inchoate ideas not shared by all who go along with him. The ideas are at the time not explicit enough to force recognition of the disparity; they are still such young ideas, so pliant.

The judges of an appellate court try to act as a unit, and to submerge small differences, or differences that seem to be small, in the effort to produce an "opinion of the court." An opinion that has the adherence of a majority—even more, one that is unanimous—has obvious advantages in our system of precedent. Dissents, and concurrences that concur in nothing except the conclusion, come from strong conviction. But the Justices are inclined to agree upon a single opinion when they can.*

The ideas latent in Brennan's *Roth* opinion may not have been clear to all the Justices who subscribed to it, and (this is hardly criticism) may not have been entirely clear—at the time—to him. Certainly their full implications would not be recognized: this was the first case in which the Court, set out to describe the effect of the Amendment on anti-obscenity legislation; moreover, it was a case that presented a totally abstract issue, and paid no attention to the books involved. The ideas were there, however, inherent in the line of reasoning by which the opinion arrived at its result. I had argued that under established principles of legal analysis they were therefore part of the precedent.

These things could not be said to the Court in just this way. But they had to be said—the full implications of the *Roth* opinion had to be expressed—if *Memoirs* was to be sustained. The brief became an exercise in delicacy:

> In *Roth* and *Alberts* the statutes were attacked as unconstitutional *in toto* and there was no other issue.† The majority accordingly undertook a comprehensive statement of the

---

* A contrary impression is given by the multiple opinions of the present-day Supreme Court, but the only cases that reach the Court today bring close questions with them. For one thing, the Court will rarely take a case whose resolution is close to predictable; if nine good lawyers agree, it may fairly be said the resolution is close to predictable. For another, the expense of appealing a case through several judicial lawyers insures that the opposing parties both believe their chances of winning are substantial; unless one or the other of the lawyers is giving his client foul advice, this means that there is much to be said on each side. Then there is the immense increase in litigation of recent years; the more cases there are in the various lower courts, the more likely it is that only the toughest will appear on the exclusive Supreme Court docket. That there are more split decisions than there used to be is no indication of flightiness.

† *Roth* v. *United States*, the reader will recall, was decided at the same time as *Alberts* v. *California*, and the Brennan opinion spoke for the majority in both cases. It is generally referred to as the *Roth* opinion, but the *Alberts* case, like *Memoirs*, involved a state anti-obscenity law, and I wanted to remind the Court (especially Mr. Justice Harlan) that the opinion imposed as severe a restriction on state efforts at suppression as on federal. Accordingly, I used the double designation throughout the brief.

reasons why the First Amendment does not protect obscene material, and this necessarily entailed a description of just what this unprotected material is.

The majority held that it has two characteristics. One is appeal to prurient interest, discussed above. The other is the complete absence of social importance. It is not every worthless publication, of course, that the statutes can affect; it must be a publication that appeals to prurient interest. Nor is it every publication considered prurient that the statutes can affect; it must be a publication "utterly without redeeming social importance." For unless the publication is worthless trash, it is not possible to justify its suppression in the face of a Constitution that forbids abridgment of freedom of the press.

Laws affecting speech or writing have, of course, been held to have a valid operation in spite of the First Amendment guaranties. The *Roth* and *Alberts* opinion mentioned cases that had so held. They are cases in which the speech or writing amounted to conduct rather than expression, or was so entwined with conduct that the behavioral rather than the expressive aspect dominated. Prohibitory laws might also operate where material is so utterly devoid of value that it need not be regarded as speech or writing at all. This last category provided both the constitutional justification for anti-obscenity legislation and, within the area bounded by the line of prurient interest, the constitutional definition of obscenity. Anti-obscenity statutes, the majority held, have a discernible, though severely limited, validity. Legislatures, in the pursuit of goals relating to prevailing concepts of immorality or offensiveness, may ordain suppression despite the strong language in which the First Amendment is cast. But they may do this only with respect to material that has no social value, and only because it has no social value.

The First Amendment, of course, has its principal function where the majority disapproves. Where a work of any value is in issue, the fact that most of the citizenry views it as immoral or offensive cannot justify a forcible silencing. On the other hand, it may be said of material utterly without value that it does not rise to the level of writing—that is, "the press"—within the meaning of the Constitution. Once obscenity is defined as that which has no value, then—and only then—room can be found in our constitutional structure for anti-obscenity legislation. The mark of suppressible obscenity inheres in the constitutional justification of the suppressive legislation.

The social-value test supplied not only doctrinal validity but practical workability. The prurient-interest test was itself a significant step toward clarity. The elimination of the spectacular weaknesses of *Hicklin* represented an important gain, and the word "prurient" provided some content and character where earlier formulas provided only amorphous deprecation. But the prurient-interest test, standing alone, left the law to deal with these grave yet delicate questions in terms of judicial responses that must remain largely subjective.

The determination of whether the predominant appeal of a book is to prurient interest is a matter of direct and personal reaction. Evidence of contemporary community standards and customary limits of candor can give the court a background against which to make its judgment, but there is no further aid to decision. No witness is an expert here, except with respect to that background, and any opinion he might offer as to the presence or absence of prurient interest would be a legal conclusion. There is the challenged book, and the key word, and the court must decide whether they match or do not match; there is nothing in between.

Social value, on the other hand, provides a criterion that can be objectively applied, and by a process familiar to the law. Judges and jurors are no longer committed to a total reliance on their individual responses. Traditional judicial techniques come into play. There is evidence to be considered.

We are now on familiar judicial ground. The courts have long dealt with questions of value, and there are time-tested methods at hand. One method by which value may be shown is in the testimony of those who may be qualified as expert in the field. Real estate experts, for example, give testimony in condemnation cases and in tax cases, and security analysts estimate earning power in corporate reorganization cases. Similarly, those who are qualified to speak about the particular values that a book is alleged to have can offer the court expert testimony on the point. There are among us individuals who, by training and experience, are better qualified than most to appraise the literary or artistic or other merit of a book. Their opinion testimony provides the material of decision.

Opinion as to value is quite different from opinion as to whether a book is prurient or not prurient, or obscene or not obscene; these words signal conclusions of law, which are the business of the court, not of the witness. Nor is the witness asked to state whether the book has that value which brings it within the protection of the First Amendment. The determination of that question is the province of the court, and the witness has only his usual function of supplying evidence upon which the court will act.

Another source of objective evidence as to value is documentary. Where there are book reviews, or critical essays, additional data can be presented to the court. The stiuation is analogous to those in which there are indications of value apart from the litigation, in the form of appraisals or otherwise, where economic value is in issue. There is this difference: where literary or scientific or artistic value is concerned, it is not alone the content, but the very existence of independent and respectable appraisals, that is meaningful. Writing which is "utterly without social importance" does not become the subject of sober critical consideration. There naturally will be differences of opinion about any given work, but the fact that there is serious discussion of the work, by recognized critics and scholars, published in established periodicals, is an objective fact of the utmost significance.

A third problem, present in every appeal but different in every appeal, was the treatment of the opinion below. The opinion supporting the decision appealed from has to be given special handling, no matter how similar the issues may be to those of other cases, or to those of the same case in its earlier stages. The brief made these comments:

The majority below gave the criterion of social importance only grudging acceptance, referring to it as "one other possible test"—this despite the explicit affirmation of the test by the same court in *Attorney General* v. *Tropic of Cancer*. It was perhaps a reluctance to concede the test's existence that led the majority below to falter in its application. There was plain error on the constitutional fact of the value to be found in *Memoirs*: the majority ascribed to the book only "some

minimal literary value." A publication might have consid‑
erably less value than the testimony and the documentary
evidence show *Memoirs* to have and still rise above the level
of "minimal literary value."

The majority below stated that the test does not require
that a book "must be unqualifiedly worthless before it can be
deemed obscene." There is a question whether this can be
reconciled with the principle that the obscene, in a constitu‑
tional sense, is only that which is "utterly without redeeming
social importance," but the question is one that need not be
reached. The considerable evidence of value in *Memoirs* ren‑
ders *obiter* any exploration of the outer reaches of what the
social value test protects. The present case does not involve
any iota or scintilla theory of social importance.

Nor does it involve a situation where evidence *pro* and
contra must be weighed. The testimony of the attorney gen‑
eral's one witness cannot reasonably be said to create a con‑
flict with the evidence going to show the value of the book.

The opinion below mentions, in slighting, advocates'
tones, that the book "contains a moral." But the critics
treated Fanny's thoughts about life and love as seriously
meant and entitled to serious reading. . . . The witnesses
gave more detailed testimony to the same general effect—
that the observations, ideas and moral conclusions of the book
are thoughtful, substantial and perceptive.

Referring to the expert testimony, the majority said, in
passing "much of [it] was strained." We respectfully but
emphatically disagree. The testimony was careful and specific.
. . . It is one thing to assert that a book is "not obscene" or
"not pornographic." These are conclusory statements that
can always be defended on semantic grounds. It is quite
another thing for a professional critic or teacher to analyze a
book, to give detailed testimony about what values he sees in
it and to appraise the book in relation to other works of liter‑
ature. Even if a single individual might conceivably be so irra‑
tional as to do what the majority below suggests, it is not
conceivable that the entire roster of these distinguished men
should be willing to give disingenuous, distorted or otherwise
"strained" testimony.

Moreover, there was corroboration for what the witnesses
said in the published essays of Pritchett, Adams and Brophy,
and in the introduction by Peter Quennell. Celebrated critics

thus submitted to the judgment of the literary world opinions very similar to those which the witnesses submitted to the judgment of the court.

There was an apparent contradiction between the Massachusetts formulation of the value test and Mr. Justice Brennan's.* "Unqualifiedly worthless" is hardly different from "utterly without redeeming social importance." Massachusetts was thus saying that what the Supreme Court demanded as a precondition to suppression (if my theory of *Roth* was correct) was not a precondition so far as Massachusetts was concerned.

But I gave this only glancing treatment, for several reasons. One was that the contradiction was apparent. If the Supreme Court accepted the value theory, the point that the Massachusetts Court misstated it was plain enough. Another had to do with a common tactic in advocacy; there is no urgency to test the extremes of a principle if your case, you claim, is well within its boundaries. The contrast between Brennan's statement and that of the Massachusetts majority needed no emphasis, while the proposition that *Fanny Hill* was better than her reputation always needed emphasis.

The final problem in writing the brief (save one that I will discuss in a later chapter because my decision was not to deal with it in the brief at all) was not raised either by the court below or by our opponents. It had to do with whether the value test could operate in all situations and for all forms of expression. Up to this point I had never spoken of possible exceptions, nor did the language of *Roth* on which we relied suggest any. Though the problem had been on my mind, it was not something that I had thought it necessary, or desirable, to discuss. But now, I felt, it had to be dealt with, to some extent at least; the Supreme Court might be undertaking a fundamental review

---

* And between what the Massachusetts majority said in this case and what the Massachusetts majority said in *Tropic of Cancer*. Spalding, who wrote the *Fanny Hill* opinion, had joined in Cutter's *Tropic* opinion, but the two Justices evidently did not understand the value test the same way—an example of what I mentioned a few pages back.

of the law, and nine agile intellects would be ranging over the field of obscenity.

The value test had a valid conceptual basis in the First Amendment and a valid precedential basis in *Roth*, and it worked well—made practical sense—in the cases where we had sought to apply it. Yet one could conceive of situations where, though the test by its terms might seem to invoke the guaranty, the Court would certainly approve suppression. Let us assume a play in which an act of sex is performed (performed, not suggested). Let us also assume the play has dramatic merit. To make the point plain, let us finally assume it is broadcast on network television. (The reader may make his own choice of the particular variety of sexual act, and of whether the broadcast would be in black-and-white or living color.)*

I did not want to undertake a specific discussion of hypotheticals such as this. My opponents in the various cases had not brought them up. They did not argue that the value theory should be rejected because in some areas it was unworkable. Rather, they urged that *Memoirs* itself failed the value test (as the attorney general contended), or that there was no such thing as a value test (as the Citizens for Decent Literature were to contend). It would hardly be wise to spell out an argument against our position that our opponents were not making. Nevertheless, either during the hearing or in the Justices' private thinking, horror examples might come into their deliberations. I wanted to suggest a solution without posing the problem.

There were two things in the brief that I hoped would serve the purpose. One was the distinction between expression and conduct. The imaginary television show I described involves performance and public audiences. It may be true that the performers have something to communicate, and that to this extent expression would be silenced, but the situation may fairly be regarded as in its essence action. The Court had sanctioned the impairment of communication where elements of action were

---

* Things change, of course, and I do not speak of what might be considered suppressible in the next century or even in the next several decades. (It might be less or more.) It was the effect on the 1965 Court that I was concerned with.

present; it had, for example, approved restrictions on parades, and on the use of "loud and raucous" sound trucks, and on salesmen calling without invitation. A defendant charged with indecent exposure—in the streets, not on the stage—might also argue that his effort is to communicate, and no doubt it is.

Having drawn on the distinction between expression and conduct, I then suggested that another kind of distinction might be appropriate—among different forms of expression. Again, I did not offer it as a reply to something said on the other side, but rather as an affirmative part of our own argument, an additional reason for giving new freedom to writers. The final paragraphs of the brief were these:

> It has, of course, been held that the guaranties of freedom of speech and of the press go beyond vocal utterance and the printed word. It does not follow, however, that the guaranties are to be applied in the same way, or to the same extent, with respect to all forms of expression. Books have a certain primacy because of their importance to society. Moreover, such conflicts as there may be with interests sought to be served by anti-obscenity legislation are less intense where books are concerned.
>
> The audience for a book is the individual reader, not an assembled group. In a theater audience, for example, there is a simultaneous collective experience, and the social interaction itself creates problems. (The familiar hypothetical from another area of restraint—shouting "Fire!" in a theater—would hardly present a problem if there were only one other person in the theater.) Again, the reader of a book has instant control over his exposure to it; he can terminate the experience by closing the book, and if its reputation puts him off, he need not open it. In contrast, other means of communication—the sound truck, for example, or the advertising poster in a train or bus—make us their captive. Television, the great new medium of our time, presents both aspects: its communications are usually received in a social situation, and contact is not always easily broken off. (Typically, television-viewing is a family affair, and it takes a family consensus to end it.) Finally, forms of expression differ in their impact. Scenes described in commonly accepted books would, if performed by actors on a stage, or displayed in photographs on a billboard, become quite different in their effect. Unlike forms

of expression that make direct appeal to the senses, a book's communications must pass through the screen of the intellect.

There is no important channel of communication that is more private and more a matter of individual control than a book. There is none that is less inflammatory (except in the unassailable realm of ideas) or less involved with public decorum. Hence the possibilities of antagonism between the publishing of books and other interests of society are relatively small.

At the same time, books have a singular importance for society. Tradition gives them a special place. It was to liberty of printing that John Milton's *Areopagitica* was addressed, and the great controversies about freedom of expression that were resolved in the adoption of the First Amendment had to do mainly with books (including that predecessor of contemporary paperbacks, the pamphlet).

Books provide a vehicle for the transmission of thought that is not matched by other forms of expression. They communicate ideas not only by way of exposition, but also through the shared experiences and perceptions of poetry and fiction. Other forms of expression may be as good or better for entertainment, excitement, or provoking emotional response, but the printed word remains the most important medium for the communication between mind and mind on which our civilization rests.

Any exercise of governmental power that hampers the free circulation of books therefore threatens our society. Even where printed matter upon trial is shown to be utter trash, and may properly be called a book only because there are pages and ink and a cover, the use of the law to suppress it raises grave questions. The decisions of the Court leave room for the suppression of such material. But they leave no room whatever for the suppression of a book which, upon trial, is shown to have value—"literary or scientific or artistic." The contrary proposition, we submit, toys in a frightening way with the fundamentals of our government. If the concept of freedom of the press is not to be qualified beyond recognition, it must mean that, in a case where value is proven, a book may not be destroyed. That is the case before the Court.

If the television example and other *casus horribiles* should occur to Justices, these paragraphs would serve as a reminder that they involved modes of communication other than books. If one of the insupportable hypotheticals should someday become real, the Court could distinguish its *Fanny Hill* decision (assuming it was a decision in our favor) on the ground that the uncompromising social-value test had gained acceptance in a case that involved a book.

There was no precedent for separating media of expression, but neither was there precedent that stood in the way. The Court had declared motion pictures protected by the First Amendment, but whatever statements had been made by individual Justices, the Court had not ruled—there had been no case presenting the question—that motion pictures are entitled to protection in the same way or to the same extent as books. Nor does it follow. It would not follow even from Black's absolute view of the First Amendment. Black's premise is that the Amendment is to be taken literally. The Amendment states, the reader will recall, that "Congress shall make no law . . . abridging the freedom of speech, or of the press. . . ." Black's appealing argument is that "no law abridging" means "no law abridging." The majority's answer to Black, that the First Amendment had never been construed to confer an unlimited freedom, had behind it massive authority and little logic; it represented a conclusion, not a reason.

But there is another answer where books are not involved, one that Black might accept. If the Amendment is to be given a literal reading, then it may be said that films, and other art forms that are not entirely verbal, are not literally speech or the press. On the other hand, once "speech" and "the press" are expanded beyond their plain meanings, we are not reading the Amendment literally; if that is the way the game of interpretation is to be played, then a converse liberty may justly be taken with the word "abridging." The Amendment's prohibition against lawmaking need not be imposed strictly where what the law affects is not strictly speech or the press.

The extreme situations could thus be accounted for, whether the First Amendment is to be given a literal construction or the traditional loose construction. Two members of the Court subscribed to the literal construction, and of the others, there were three or four who I hoped would accept the value test; the two groups taken together would make a majority. It was that majority for whom, if they should be troubled by cases not present but envisioned, it was necessary to provide solutions.

I was of course not interested in suggesting candidates for censorship. But I was speaking to a Court which, as I saw it, had not the slightest idea of granting complete freedom for everything that might be called expression. I was saying that situations for which it might think anti-obscenity laws altogether fitting were different from ours; the precedent the Justices would set, by ruling in our favor, need not in future cases haunt them. Remote regions of constitutional law did not have to be mapped in detail. It was enough to point out that distinctions among modes of communication were permissible, that the Court's opinion need not state a single rule for all of them, and that the printed word was entitled to the greatest freedom. What the attorney general had proceeded against was the printed word.

The Argument in
the Supreme Court

THE SUPREME COURT IS NIGGARDLY WITH TIME.
It has to be. There is so much to do outside the courtroom
—reading briefs, doing research, conferring, writing opinions—
that the Court cannot spend many hours listening to argument.
It sets strict limits, and the Chief Justice is a rigorous, though
gracious, timekeeper. Two small light bulbs, a white and a red,
face the lawyer as he addresses the Court. Five minutes before
his time runs out, the white bulb lights up. When his time is
gone, the red one lights up. He finishes immediately, or the
Chief Justice tells him, sweetly, to stop.

A day's session ordinarily lasts four hours, from ten until
noon and from twelve-thirty until two-thirty. Indeterminate periods are devoted to announcing judgments, reading opinions
and admitting attorneys to the Supreme Court bar; hence the
end of an argument may fail to coincide with the end of the
session. When this happens, the case is carried over to the following morning, and the lawyer picks up where he broke off. At
two-thirty, the Justices arise and leave. It is an exaggeration to
say that a lawyer caught in the middle of a "however" must stop
with the "how-" and begin the next day with an "-ever." But it
is not much of an exaggeration.

Fanny Hill was argued on a bad day. In one sense it was a

good day; it was the date set for the other obscenity cases, which was what I had asked. It was also good in another sense; the weather was fresh and sparkling. But it came after a most unrestful night spent in a hotel room that an ingenious management had contrived to heat to an unalterable ninety degrees. Opening the windows only confirmed the fact that the street alongside had become a motorcycle drag strip. And perhaps I was a bit anxious. I got out of bed that morning with a scrim somewhere between me and the outside world, and my mind full of glue.

Each of the obscenity cases were assigned one hour—a half-hour for each side. *Memoirs* would be last, and I wanted to hear what went on during the argument of the other two. The Court convened at ten o'clock, as usual, and we were informed that the *Mishkin* appeal, which came first, would not begin before eleven. I used the hour walking around the big block on which the Supreme Court building stands, trying to shape pieces of argument. The sun was as strong as it can be in December, and the wind about as cold. The building was lovely. Its bright and shadowed planes met in sharp clear lines—especially impressive to one about to enter the gray amorphous reaches of the law—and the blue above the building was exciting. At eleven I was feeling much better, if not much smarter, and I went in.

I was not at ease, though. Listening to the other cases and waiting my turn, I experienced somewhat more than the usual pre-argument tension. For one thing, the questions from the bench indicated that the optimism of the libertarians had indeed been misgauged (even allowing that judges often ask hard questions hoping they will be satisfactorily answered). For another, the lawyers all had sheaves of papers which they took to the lectern, and from the sound of it most of them had their arguments written out. This is a matter of individual style, and it was not my first appearance in an appellate court. It was my first in the Supreme Court, however, and I wondered whether, for the august occasion, my accustomed method was perhaps too casual.

My feeling was that it was better—for myself at least—not to have an argument composed in advance. Judges have to sit still for long periods, and their attention tends to flag when they must be the audience for a speech, and tends to quicken when what they hear is merely conversation. Again, the ready-made argument often resembles the lawyer's brief; delivering an oral statement of what the judges have already read or will soon read accomplishes something, but not much. And it is well to adjust to the Court's interests—indeed to the Court's moods—as they are revealed in the course of the hearing. This is not so easily done when one has an investment in a composed presentation; it hurts to break up those carefully carpentered sentences and paragraphs. Finally, the hearing's greatest value, in my opinion, is the opportunity to answer the judges' questions. Extemporaneous talk is more likely to provoke questions than a set speech.

But now I wondered whether all this was wrong. If it was right, why did the other lawyers have those typewritten pages? Suppose I got up there and the thoughts failed to come? I had a vivid image of a lawyer standing before the Court with nothing to say and no notes to turn to. A question crossed my mind: had there ever been a case, in the history of the Court, in which a lawyer had risen to address the bench, stood mute for a long moment, and then, without a word, collapsed? (I was told later that there had been.) But the lectern looked so sturdy. A reasonably fit lawyer could hang on.

The question and the answer amused me—not for their wit, of course, but for their low comedy—and the uneasiness began to fade. In addition, the exchanges between Court and counsel were interesting. I was replaying them as they went along, thinking about what I would have been saying instead, on both sides. Before our case was called, my principal emotion had changed from concern to let-me-in-there-Coach.

Mishkin and *Ginzburg* produced no surprises; what the attorneys on each side said was in substance in their briefs. The most persistent questioning came from the Chief Justice. He asked about the burden the Court would have to carry if obscenity cases were entitled to consideration on the merits. Was the Court expected to read all the material that would be pouring in upon it? More and more publishers and booksellers would be asserting First Amendment privileges, and sometimes a prosecution would involve a large number of books or magazines. (*Mishkin* involved fifty.) During both arguments, Warren pressed counsel to solve the Court's administrative problem.

Apart from Black, whose theory saved him the trouble, the Justices in the cases succeeding *Roth* had examined the publications, and those who had spoken on the point had said they were obliged to examine them as a trial court would. This conformed to the general rule that on constitutional issues the Court should itself look at the evidence, and not rely upon the findings below. State appellate courts, following the Supreme Court's lead, had assumed the same obligation—that of *de novo* review. And earlier, in the *Lady Chatterley* case, the federal district and circuit courts had done the same thing when we challenged the findings of the Postmaster General.

At the time *Tropic* and *Jacobellis* were decided, there was another obscenity appeal before the Court. The State of Kansas had convicted a wholesaler in a case involving thirty-six different paperbacks. The conviction was reversed, the prevailing opinion being that the measures taken by the police amounted to an unlawful seizure, a violation of the Fourth Amendment. (Some of the Justices appraised the books: Harlan and Clark thought they were obscene; Stewart thought they were not.) Although Warren agreed that the seizure required reversal, the number of books in the Kansas case perhaps influenced his dissent: the "sufficient evidence" type of review would take less of the Court's time on any given appeal, and probably cut down the number of appeals. The Chief Justice's questions and statements during the *Mishkin* and *Ginzburg* arguments suggested that he was now making an effort to bring more of the bench around to his point of view.

It must be remembered that the Chief Justice has an administrative as well as a judicial function: it is his Court to run. He might well have been appalled at the prospect of his Justices, who surely had other important things to do, mired down in hundreds of books and magazines. He was in effect agreeing with Black and Douglas that the Supreme Court ought not be a Supreme Board of Censors. But while their solution was to forbid all suppression, Warren's was to leave it to the lower courts. The lower court in our case had held against the book.

I wanted to dislodge Warren from his *Jacobellis* position, or at least to prevent other Justices from joining him in it. Thinking about this gave me an idea on how to open my argument. It was an opening that would make a quick bridge from the arguments of the earlier cases, and emphasize the differences between those cases and ours. It would come as a surprise—nothing like it had been suggested before—and, at some risk, provide a prop to the level of attention. After all, this was the end of the day, and the Justices had already heard a good deal on the subject. I wanted their interest, and I wanted their questions, and a radical opening might be the best way to elicit them.

"At 2:10 P.M.," the stenographer noted, "the matter came on for argument." *

The argument of an appeal ordinarily starts with a statement of what it is about and how it got to the court. I made this as short as possible:

> MR. CHIEF JUSTICE WARREN: Number 368, *A Book Named John Cleland's Memoirs of a Woman of Pleasure, Appellant* versus *Attorney General of the Commonwealth of Massachusetts.*
>
> THE CLERK: Counsel are present.
> MR. CHIEF JUSTICE WARREN: Mr. Rembar.
> *Oral Argument on Behalf of Appellant*
> MR. REMBAR: May it please the Court: This is an appeal from a decision of the Supreme Judicial Court of the State of Massachusetts, which held that this book was not entitled to constitutional protection, by a four-to-three vote.

Now I tried the opening I had been thinking about:

> I am happy to say, Mr. Chief Justice, that I bring you a case in which it is not necessary to read the book. It's not that we don't want you to read the book—we urge you to read the book—we think it's a good book. We do not think it will adversely affect your moral fiber. We do not think that you

---

* There is no official reporter in the Supreme Court. There are private firms, however, whose stenographers are regularly in attendance, and their transcripts are available.

will find it deeply offensive, although if the members of this busy Court have not had time to keep up with the best-seller list, you may find the subject matter a bit unusual.

A reporter told me later that at this point one of his veteran colleagues in the press box commented, "He'll never get away with it." (After the argument, my informant said, his colleague added, "He got away with it." If I lost in the Court, there would be the dubious consolation of having won in the press box.)

I meant the opening to be more than an attention-getter, though. The proposal was that the Court could ignore the book altogether—not on Black's absolute view, but on the claim that extrinsic evidence demanded that the book be protected. If this struck the Justices as too much of an innovation, too abrupt a departure from the way obscenity cases had always been handled, it would at least outline the value test in thick black strokes, and serve as a proud statement of what our record showed.

It was strange that the idea should have arrived so late. Six and a half years before, I had started to build our case, and now, at the end of the effort—minutes before I would have my main, and last, chance—something came to mind that might help.

One object was soon accomplished: this argument would be a colloquy, not a speech. The opening produced a reaction from the bench in something under sixty seconds:

MR. JUSTICE HARLAN: Maybe I wasted my time, because I read it in advance.

MR. REMBAR: I don't think your time was wasted, your Honor. I think, as I say, that it is a book which has many values to offer the reader.

MR. JUSTICE BRENNAN: Then help me, because I haven't read it.

MR. REMBAR: Very good, your Honor. I will say this, though, if I may help the Chief Justice first: we have here a record in which there is an overwhelming demonstration of the kind of value that all counsel here today agree invokes the protection of the First Amendment. I would suggest that a possible answer to the administrative difficulty that the Chief Justice has outlined is that where you have highly qualified witnesses who come to court and stake their professional reputations on their analysis of the book and its values—where you have published reviews and critical essays, by people who have no interest in the outcome of the litigation, which also establish that value—then, on the record, the book is entitled to the protection of the First Amendment.

MR. JUSTICE HARLAN: But you've got three judges of your court who say, in spite of the conflicting evidence, in their judgment the book was obscene, and under both the state and federal constitutions.

MR. REMBAR: The majority below, your Honor, did not accept the test of redeeming social importance. It obviously made very small impression on them, and they committed an error which I believe this Court will find to be an error, on the basis of the record. They said the book has only minimal literary value.

Now this Court, of course, while—

MR. JUSTICE BRENNAN: I thought that expert testimony, if I get what you are saying, that a number of distinguished literary critics say a book has social value, that ought to be enough for us, but I gather they are the experts on it and that the ultimate decision was for us. I thought expert testimony was only an aid, not to decide the ultimate fact or other determinant—such help as it may give. I didn't take it it to be substitution for—

MR. REMBAR: I didn't mean to suggest the contrary, your Honor. What I am saying is this: You do not accept the conclusions of the so-called expert. He doesn't merely get up and say, "This book has value," and leave the court. And there can be testimony on the other side as well. It is for this Court to read the record, to appraise the testimony and decide whether a case has been made out for social value.

The witnesses in this case didn't make conclusory statements. They analyzed the book. They spoke of the various canons of literary criticism that could be applied. They found the book good under those canons.

Now in opposition there was one witness, and we would leave to the Court the appraisal of his testimony as well. He was a witness who spoke in conclusory terms. He called the book obscene and prurient. He said that prurient meant esoteric. When asked if that was really the word he meant, he said yes. When he was asked who it was that the heroine had married at the end of the book, he couldn't remember. He referred to Jane Austen as an eighteenth-century novelist. Well, all of these things can be considered.

At the same time, the Court can consider the qualifications and the statements of Professor Fred Stocking, chairman of the department of literature at Williams College; Professor John Bullitt, professor of English and master of Quincy House, Harvard College; Robert Sproat, associate professor of English literature, Boston University; Norman Holland, associate professor of English, M.I.T.; and the rest of the witnesses—

MR. JUSTICE BRENNAN: I might understand if this were a problem in nuclear physics, but I wonder if that carries over into this area?

MR. REMBAR: I submit, your Honor—

MR. JUSTICE STEWART: I take it it is your point that it is a matter of law—it is not a matter of fact, it is a matter of law—if witnesses of this caliber and stature and good faith testify to this, then the matter of how many people disagree with them, if there are those people of this caliber willing to testify and who are able to testify under oath with regard to this, then no court could hold that this was utterly without redeeming social importance?

MR. REMBAR: When your Honor said how many people disagree with them—may I ask, in court or out of court?

MR. JUSTICE STEWART: Witnesses.

MR. REMBAR: If there is substantial testimony that the book is without value, then the Court will make up its mind on the basis of the record, just as in other cases where there is dispute—

MR. JUSTICE DOUGLAS: Our test has been "utterly."

MR. REMBAR: Yes, your Honor, and that is what our test will be. But you will have to consider evidence on both sides of the case.

MR. JUSTICE DOUGLAS: If you had one Baptist minister on one side and a thousand on the other, you won't say "utterly."

MR. REMBAR: The Baptist minister would not be qualified to give literary criticism; he would be able to give religious testimony. He might testify to the religious value of the work.

MR. JUSTICE STEWART: I see what you mean.

Mr. Justice Brennan took over:

> MR. JUSTICE BRENNAN: I would like to follow this up, what Justice Stewart was saying, that where there is testimony directed to the issue of redeeming social value, and there is critical testimony of acknowledged experts in the field, that that ends any obscenity case without our ever reading the material?
>
> MR. REMBAR: Yes, your Honor.
>
> MR. JUSTICE BRENNAN: Is that what you are saying?
>
> MR. REMBAR: I am saying that.

The Justice raised a point that is not new to the reader, but was new, apparently, to the courtroom audience.*

> MR. JUSTICE BRENNAN: And that is, well-written pornography is outside? (Laughter.)
>
> MR. REMBAR: Your Honor, the word "pornography"—
>
> MR. JUSTICE BRENNAN: Doesn't it mean that? We are dealing with, I guess, by hypothesis, with what is pornographic material as to which, however, a number of acknowledged literary critics are willing to say it has some literary and therefore social value, because it is well written.
>
> MR. REMBAR: If by pornographic your Honor means sexually arousing, or "lustful" in the terms of the decisions. . . . I think it has been clear for some time that material whose effect is to stimulate a sexual response in the normal person is not for that reason to be denounced. I think that such—
>
> MR. JUSTICE BRENNAN: *Roth* said that.
>
> MR. REMBAR: Yes, your Honor.

Mr. Justice Black made a broadside attack on the value test. Black, of course, was not in favor of any kind of test; if the First Amendment is to be applied absolutely, then no distinguishing criteria are necessary. He had said in earlier cases that he had not read the books; under his theory, there was no need to. I had the feeling that he had not read my brief either:†

---

* The handsome courtroom was filled, and there were lines in the lobby. People were asked to stay for a short while only, so that others could take their place.

† Not yet, that is. It is up to the individual Justice whether to read the briefs before or after the argument. The argument is more productive, I feel, if the briefs are read beforehand, but often there just isn't time. When

MR. JUSTICE BLACK: If we need an expert as to whether or not it has social value, experts in that field, why not go to a member of the legislature? They are the ones who pass on that kind of policy.

MR. REMBAR: Because he is not an expert in that field, your Honor.

MR. JUSTICE BLACK: He is an expert on a proposal of law as to what has redeeming social value.

MR. REMBAR: The issue is not whether the book has value as legislation, but whether it has value as a book.

MR. JUSTICE BLAKE: That's right. It is a question of policy, and I would think that no one would be better qualified to do that under our concept of government than the legislative body, assuming that it doesn't violate the First Amendment.

MR. REMBAR: Mr. Justice Black, suppose what was urged was not that it had literary value, but that it had scientific value. . . .

MR. JUSTICE BLACK: Get a scientist.

MR. REMBAR: Yes, and if what is urged is that it has literary value, get people who know good literature.

Mr. Justice Black asked if literary value was "the only great social value." "Not at all," I answered; Mr. Justice Douglas had, in another connection, mentioned psychiatric counseling, and I used it as an example. Mr. Justice Black left off at this point. The value theory, I thought, stood up pretty well to questions of the kind he had put. The kind of attack I was more concerned about had not come up, and would not during the rest of the argument.

But there was the question of the legal authority for the value test. That did come up. Three of the four lawyers who had argued that day said value would in itself save a publication. But only one of the nine Justices whom they addressed had said so. Mr. Justice Brennan asked whether I agreed with the other lawyers on this, and when I said I did, Mr. Justice Stewart, perhaps shocking a number of people present, brought the matter down to legal reality:

---

the opinions in the three cases came down, they showed the close and careful study that the briefs eventually received.

MR. JUSTICE STEWART: Where do you get that, from what cases?

I was, of course, delighted to tell him.

Mr. Justice Douglas asked about the historical value we were claiming: did it reside in the demonstration of "how bad our ancestors were"? This gave me an opportunity to mention our clippings on the Profumo affair and point to the "parallel between the events related in the book and the events related in the newspapers, at just about the time this book was published." The stenographer was moved to insert two (*Laughter*)'s in the transcript, one for the question and one for the answer.

Mr. Justice Harlan inquired about *Memoirs*' other trials, and when I had responded, it was twenty-six minutes after two. The white light had come on. There were still two things I hoped to do, and there was just enough time left to do them. One was to try to budge Harlan from his position that the states could suppress what the federal government could not, or at least to dissuade other Justices, who had not yet committed themselves, from accepting his view. The other was to set up the Citizens for Decent Literature as an opponent. Their amicus brief was quite different, both in substance and in spirit, from that of the Massachusetts attorney general. The case, I thought, had a better color when we met the fierce contentions of the Citizens rather than the temperate arguments of the attorney general. The Court's acceptance of either would, or course, defeat us, but our chances might be improved by showing that a decision against us would be an aid and a comfort to the Citizens and those who shared their basic attitude. It was an attitude that went beyond the matter of censorship-for-obscenity, and the Citizens' brief inadvertently—if not, indeed, compulsively—revealed this. The precedent they made the most of betrayed them:

MR. REMBAR: I would like, if I may, to mention the brief amicus that was filed without consent of the parties, but with the permission of the Court. That brief deserves special mention because I think it represents more truly than the brief of the attorney general the nature of the opposition to this book.

The brief proceeds from *Curll's Case*—it cites that case eight times. *Curll's Case* was decided in the first year of the reign of George II. Curll was a rather rambunctious publisher who was hauled into court for two things he published. One was a book which the government felt brought the government into disrepute; the other was a book which the government thought obscene.

It was only the obscenity case that the Citizens for Decent Literature had cited. Legal reporting of the time was unofficial and informal, and the fact that there was also a prosecution for seditious writing came from other sources.

The court in the obscenity case decided that obscenity was a common law crime, and they decided it on this basis: they accepted the argument of the attorney general there that a breach of the King's peace is a common law crime and that a breach of the King's peace can come from writing. And, he said, it comes from three kinds of writing: writing that tends to bring the government into disrepute, writing that tends to go against religion, and writing that tends to go against morality. The court agreed with him on all three. Now I think this is extremely important, because it shows exactly what the kind of opposition to publication is that is found in the anti-obscenity laws.

MR. JUSTICE DOUGLAS: Does that extend to books on mathematics and on religion?

MR. REMBAR: Books on religion would be banned under this test. What I wish to point out is that when the First Amendment was adopted, all three aspects of this opposition were rejected. They came as a package and were rejected as a package.

MR. JUSTICE DOUGLAS: Was this book [*Memoirs*] prosecuted in the eighteenth century?

MR. REMBAR: The author himself was not prosecuted. A bookseller later was prosecuted, but it appears the book was not an authentic copy. This book through its history has had a reverse bowdlerizing. People have added things rather than taken them out. They have added illustrations, for example, and the illustrations formed the basis for a case in Massachusetts in 1821, in which a defendant named Holmes was convicted. (Laughter.) *

I want to say one thing more on a question that was asked previously, and that has to do with the federal-and-state question. An author lives in one state, a publisher in another. The book is printed and bound in a third, and it's distributed by wholesalers everywhere. None of these people observe state lines. In New Jersey, there was a stipulation that the book would not be distributed during the pendency of the case. Some books got into Camden because the Philadelphia wholesaler covers South Jersey. It is just not consonant with the realities of modern publishing to attempt a state-by-state censorship. We cannot have some states in which a book is published and others in which it is not. A publisher cannot gauge his ability to publish, which comes down to a matter of money, in that way. I say that this nation cannot exist half censored and half free.

Thank you.

MR. CHIEF JUSTICE WARREN: We will recess now.

(Whereupon, at 2:30 P.M., the Court recessed.)

In the Supreme Court, as in most courts, the side that argues first can devote part of its allotted period to reply. Reply, to me, is especially valuable; other lawyers prefer to use nearly all their time, save a moment or two, for the presentation of their main arguments. I had decided that morning to hold back as much as a third of the half-hour. It happened that when our case was called, just twenty minutes remained to the end of the session. If I could crowd the points that needed emphasis—and the interruptions I hoped for and the answers I hoped to be able to

---

* When the Justices came to read the case, they would see that defendant went to jail not a moment too soon, if the allegations of the indictment are to be believed. It described him as "a scandalous and evil disposed person, contriving, devising and intending the morals as well of youth as of the other good citizens of said Commonwealth to debauch and corrupt, and to raise and to create in their minds inordinate and lustful desires." The population of Massachusetts in 1821 was small enough so that people with the same surname might well have been kin; the Justices could ponder the degree of consanguinity between the defendant pornographer and the great Justice born twenty years later.

give—into those twenty minutes, I could wait to see what my opponent would say, and have some freedom of movement in meeting it.

When I was a boy, there was a prizefighter who impressed me. His name was Tommy Loughran, and he was the light-heavyweight champion. He was a superb boxer, known particularly for his timing, not only in the sense of being able to connect with a moving target but also in the sense of knowing when the round was ending. This enabled him to do something that delighted his fans and infuriated his opponents: as each round came to a close, he usually managed to have the action in his own corner. At the bell, his seconds put out the stool, Loughran sat down, and his opponent had to take a walk across the ring. (Loughran was quoted as saying that he developed the ability to do this by shadowboxing to popular records, which usually ran three minutes.)

At two-thirty, the red light came on with a clang that I, at least, could hear. I had made the affirmative points I wanted to make, answered the questions the judges had put to me, and the ten minutes were left for reply. I felt I had done something worthy of the old pug.

That afternoon I moved to another hotel.

The next morning, Cowin argued that while there were three independent tests, *Memoirs* failed them all. His argument was first-rate, in essentials the same as in Boston, but the flow even better and some of the more vulnerable passages edited out. If the view of the law I was advocating were accepted, he said, no book could be held obscene.

For a good part of his half-hour there were no questions. Then they began. Mr. Justice Black returned to his attack on the value test. Mr. Justice Fortas explored historical value. When Cowin, adeptly taking his cue from the Chief Justice, referred to the "dreary and unpleasant job" of "a wholesale reading of this type of material," Mr. Justice Douglas asked, "If this is all dreary stuff, why is it obscene?"

It often happens that a controversy among the judges is carried on through the medium of the lawyer. Questions are directed to the lawyer that are meant primarily for colleagues on the bench, and sometimes they are not so much questions as declarations that end with a courtesy inflection. The Chief Justice once more put forward the view he had expressed in *Jacobellis*:

MR. CHIEF JUSTICE WARREN: Well, in other fields, don't we very often take the finding of fact of the lower court in situations that involve even the life of a man?

MR. COWIN: Yes sir.

MR. CHIEF JUSTICE WARREN: We have a murder case, for instance, and a man claims that the confession that they took was involuntary. He was coerced into it. It is true that we say that we are not bound by the finding of the court below and that we have the right and we sometimes do review it and make our own judgment, but is the Court obliged to do that? Can it not in this case, as we often do in the course of confession cases, take the view that the evidence was conflicting and that the court below found that it was a voluntary confession?

MR. COWIN: The Court can of course, has of course, taken this view in those areas and could conceivably take the view in the area of obscenity.

MR. CHIEF JUSTICE WARREN: Why shouldn't it? My point is, why shouldn't it if we can do it where a man's life is involved and where he may have been beaten and tortured, as they often claim in such cases? If we can do it there, let a man go to his death, why couldn't we do it here? I don't know that this constitutional right is any greater than the one we deal with in the forced confession.

MR. COWIN: Perhaps only greater by the deference that has been paid to it by the majority of this Court by insisting there be a full review.

At this point, Mr. Justice Brennan intervened to defend *de novo* review:

MR. JUSTICE BRENNAN: I suppose a murder case, forced confession case, doesn't have the First Amendment involved.

I would have made a different answer, and Mr. Justice Douglas made it for me. Going back to the opening of the argument the afternoon before, he said:

MR. JUSTICE DOUGLAS: Another alternative [to accepting the finding of the lower court, on the one hand or, on the other, to the Supreme Court's reading all the material itself] is for us to hold that a publication is not obscene if there is in the record a respectable minority opinion that it has social redeeming value?

Mr. Justice Black also opposed the Warren view, playing Socrates to Cowin's Glaucon (in manner only—Socrates being an advocate of censorship, by Plato's account):

MR. JUSTICE BLACK: I'd like to ask you a question now about findings of the court. How many judges do they have?

MR. COWIN: On Superior Court, your Honor, there are in excess of forty.

MR. JUSTICE BLACK: How many do you know?

MR. COWIN: I know perhaps half of them.

MR. JUSTICE BLACK: Do you think we could reasonably expect to get the same kind of finding from all forty judges?

MR. COWIN: Not a chance.

MR. JUSTICE BLACK: Why?

MR. COWIN: Because the reactions to the material would simply be too different.

MR. JUSTICE BLACK: Reactions of the person, individual person?

MR. COWIN: Yes, your Honor.

MR. JUSTICE BLACK: Then how can we rely, how can we adopt a test that makes us rely on the findings of judges when we know there are likely to be no two of them alike?

MR. COWIN: We cannot rely on the findings, your Honor. That I agree with. If it's a question, we'll rely on the United States Supreme Court to be the final determining factor of whether or not the tests have been met. I say we have to. This is the court of last resort.

MR. JUSTICE BLACK: Well, you're right. But the problem still arises how the Court is going to do all this censorship and do anything else.

MR. COWIN: I agree.

MR. JUSTICE BLACK: And whether it's the right one to do it—if anybody.

MR. CHIEF JUSTICE WARREN: Mr. Rembar.*

MR. REMBAR: May it please the Court, I believe that my brother has stated not the position we have taken but the position that he wishes we had taken. We do not say that *any* book can now be published under these tests. Under the test that Mr. Justice Black has in mind, that would be so; under the tests that this Court has thus far enunciated, it is not so. We do say that this book before the Court now is well within the protection of the Amendment under the tests as they now stand.

MR. JUSTICE BLACK: Under the *Roth* test?

MR. REMBAR: Yes, your Honor. The *Roth* case—and here I believe my brother and I are in complete agreement—actually set forth two tests: One was the heritage of those cases which had been decided under the anti-obscenity statutes before they were ever considered in the constitutional context, and that was the prurient-interest test, which was a narrower, more rigorous definition of the kind of material that those statutes could deal with. That is, it moved from the old idea of anything which arouses lust to the kind of thing which is morbid and unhealthy in its appeal. But in addition, since the First Amendment was now involved, there had to be some justification for giving these anti-obscenity statutes any scope. After all, a book is pure expression. There is no conduct involved, except perhaps on the part of the person who sells it, but when we are considering the book itself, there is simply expression. How then can it be said that it is not speech or press?

MR. JUSTICE BLACK: Well, that's what the Court held, isn't it?

MR. REMBAR: They held it was.

MR. JUSTICE BLACK: Instead of saying that the First

---

* Warren calls on counsel with a fine style and courtesy. He addressed every lawyer by name; where it was a name that might have several pronunciations, he had the right one. Time limits could not have been imposed more firmly; neither could they have been imposed more gently. This is not simply a boon to individuals; insofar as counsel are put at ease, the arguments are improved, which in turn must have some bearing on the nature and quality of the Court's decisions.

Amendment was not absolute. The Court did not say that. What the Court said was, as I remember, that certain types of language are not included in the word "speech" and "press"; that there are certain things that are not. That was said in a case where the only thing that happened was invective and bad language was used on the street to provoke a fight,* but the *Roth* test, as I understood it, was that if a book could arouse prurient interest, it was all right to censor it and stop it from publication. Do you say the book does not do that?

MR. REMBAR: We say it does not do that, but we say—

MR. JUSTICE BLACK: You say it does or does not?

MR. REMBAR: We say it does not arouse prurient interest as it is defined. We say that a book about which the worst that can be said of it is that it stimulates a normal sexual response in a healthy adult is not prurient within the meaning of the *Roth* test.

MR. JUSTICE BLACK: Well, that gets back to the definition of the word "prurient."

MR. REMBAR: Yes sir, but I wish to go beyond that, because apparently your Honor and I differ in what there is in the rest of the majority opinion in *Roth*. The majority undertook to justify these anti-obscenity statutes, and so it said, how is it that we can deal with obscenity, that we can allow the legislatures to deal with obscenity? And they said, because obscenity is material utterly without redeeming social importance. The Court therefore necessarily, in justifying the statutes, defined the kind of thing that the statutes could deal with. It is reasonable to say that it is not really speech or press if it is just worthless trash; that something that really has no value may perhaps be reached by these statutes.

Now my brother has said that if you hold with me, there is nothing that these statutes can reach. Well, I say that that is utterly unrealistic. This Court has had before it, on petitions for certiorari, publications as to which no claim of social value was made.† It is inconceivable that witnesses of the caliber of those who appeared to say that this book has value could

---

* The Justice was referring to *Chaplinsky* v. *New Hampshire*, 315 U.S. 568.

† This was a reference not to the companion cases (though *Mishkin* would have fit the description), but to certain other cases still, as I said, in the petition stage.

have testified that this other material, in these other cases, had value.

MR. JUSTICE FORTAS: Mr. Rembar, you did not introduce any evidence on any subject, did you, except the literary value?

MR. REMBAR: Yes sir, it is our position that no one is an expert on the question of prurient interest. That is a question for the Court.

MR. CHIEF JUSTICE WARREN: The Court?

MR. REMBAR: It is a legal question, your Honor, and therefore the Court is necessarily expert.

MR. JUSTICE FORTAS: The point came to mind because a few moments ago you referred to the phrase "prurient interest" in terms of prurient appeal to a person having normal healthy responses, whatever they may be, but you made no effort to adduce testimony addressed to that point, did you?

MR. REMBAR: No, your Honor.

MR. JUSTICE FORTAS: You relied, insofar as your testimony is concerned, as I understand it, solely on the proposition that because this, in your submission, is defined as a literary work, it has redeeming social value?

MR. REMBAR: Yes sir.

MR. JUSTICE FORTAS: Is that a fair characterization of your case?

MR. REMBAR: Exactly.

The well-written-obscenity point came up once more, this time put forward by the Chief Justice:

MR. CHIEF JUSTICE WARREN: Do you make a distinction between obscenity that is dressed only in crude writing from obscenity that is dressed in skillful writing and perhaps colorful writing that would in and of itself appeal to people?

MR. REMBAR: Mr. Chief Justice, the word "obscenity" has a number of meanings, as you know.

MR. CHIEF JUSTICE WARREN: I know. We're trying to find out.

MR. REMBAR: In its constitutional meaning, which is what I think we are concerned with, it means the kind of material that can be constitutionally suppressed. And we say that under the decisions of this Court, if it has value, literary value or some other type of value, then it cannot be obscenity. Obscenity is worthless trash. That is its definition constitutionally.

MR. CHIEF JUSTICE WARREN: Yes. It would make no difference to you, then, whether it were dressed up in crude language or in very skillful and learned language?

MR. REMBAR: If it were skillful and learned enough, your
Honor, if it were really a work of consequence, then it would
make a great difference, because then I would say in constitutional terms it is not obscene.

In the closing moments, Mr. Justice Brennan questioned me
on how the social-value test should be applied:

MR. JUSTICE BRENNAN: May I ask a last question. I gather
you are saying that the *Roth* test is a constitutional test?

MR. REMBAR: Yes sir.

MR. JUSTICE BRENNAN: And because it is a constitutional
test, its application necessarily is a constitutional judgment?

MR. REMBAR: Yes sir.

MR. JUSTICE BRENNAN: And that constitutional judgment
is the last of the line, in this court?

MR. REMBAR: That's right.

MR. JUSTICE BRENNAN: And that it is not a matter of experts in this field, but ours is the ultimate constitutional responsibility, whether you call us experts or anything else. We
have to make the ultimate judgment, is that it?

MR. REMBAR: You have the responsibility, your Honor.
You are experts on law. In making that judgment, what I
suggested yesterday—

MR. JUSTICE BRENNAN: In other words, we are not making
a judgment as experts of literature or prurient interest or anything else, but experts in the application of the constitutional
test.

MR. REMBAR: That's right, your Honor, and you have the
record to help you. I said in this case it was not necessary to
go beyond the record, because the record itself is so persuasive. But that does not mean that if the record were more
conflicting, you should not go to the book.

Thus, "at 11:12 o'clock A.M.," as the court stenographer noted, I
had come back to where I had started at 2:10 P.M. the day before, and "argument in the above-entitled matter was concluded."

The Penumbra

THE CITIZENS FOR DECENT LITERATURE, INC., HAS
a twentieth-century name, redolent with affirmation. Its members, and the members of its predecessor, the National Organization for Decent Literature, apparently want to tell us that
they are not against literature, but on the contrary, for it. Anthony Comstock and John Sumner were not troubled by such
nuances. It was the Society for the Suppression of Vice, and no
nonsense about it.

When the Citizens filed their brief, the case became more
difficult, or at least more complicated. We were involved in the
toils, confinements, hazards and perplexities of a two-front war.
There was the danger that the muted and judicious arguments
of the Massachusetts attorney general might appeal to some of
the Justices, while the Citizens' shrill din might appeal to others
—enough together to make a majority. But their brief was also
an opportunity. The Supreme Court, I have said, cannot be
insensitive to public opinion. That part of the public in whose
opinion these books should have been banned was represented
more accurately by the Citizens than by the attorney general. If
the Justices were interested in the sentiment of the voters, I
would like to show them what transpired when the sentiment
was reduced to legal principle.

The Citizens' brief, almost inadvertently, laid it all out. I had drawn attention to this in the oral argument: the philosophy that would support suppression of materials dealing with sex was the philosophy that would support suppression of political divergence and heterodox religion. And doing my lawyer's heart good, the Citizens proved my point in the precedent they cited.

At the argument, the Court had given me permission to submit another brief, answering the Citizens'. This rejoinder—got out fast, and carried, not mailed, to Washington so that it would be in the Justices' hands as soon as possible—was occupied mainly in countering the Citizens' skillful plausibilities. But it opened and closed with *Curll's Case*. Curll—his name is variously spelt with one *l* and with two—had a colorful career, which included a great feud with Alexander Pope. The ancient antagonists were united in death by the Citizens, who cited, along with *Curll's Case*, Pope's quatrain advising that vice should not be "seen too oft"—an observation with which a reader of *Memoirs* might agree, though not necessarily for the same reasons. And Pope, had he known, might have been distressed by the use to which his verse was put, since he was a friend of John Cleland's father.

My brief began:

The CDL brief has many inaccuracies and much that is irrelevant, but it presents, plainly and truly, the essential view of things that underlies efforts to suppress books such as *Lady Chatterley's Lover*, *Tropic of Cancer* and the book now before the Court. . . . The theory is that standards of conduct —specifically, standards of sexual morality—can be preserved by forbidding certain kinds of speech and writing, that the preferred sexual morality ought to be preserved by such means, and that it is the business of government to do so.

This, of course, is a plausible political philosophy; indeed, it is a philosophy that has been adopted by other governments in times past, and at the present by governments in other parts of the world. But it is no part of our concept of government. It is explicitly rejected by the First Amendment, and apart from the First Amendment itself, it is thoroughly inconsistent with the genius of our Constitution. . . .

The brief ended:

The case was decided in the first year of the reign of George II, the year 1727. We do not deprecate the CDL argument because it rests on an ancient case. The date is important not because it is long past, but because it places the case in a time that is significant in relation to the First Amendment. It was a time of political and philosophical struggle. The case itself was a victory for the theory of repression. The larger contest, however, had a different outcome. By the end of the century our Constitution had explicitly rejected the ideas that prevailed in *Curll's Case*.

There were two concurrent prosecutions of *Curll*. One was for the publications alleged to be obscene, and this is the case on which CDL relies. The other was a prosecution for publishing the memoirs of a government spy; here the basis of the prosecution was that the publication was seditious. Curll was convicted in both cases. In the case that CDL cites, the King's attorney general argued as follows:

What I insist upon is that this is an offence at common law, as it tends to corrupt the morals of the King's subjects, and is against the peace of the King. Peace includes good order and government, and that peace may be broken in many instances without an actual force. 1. If it be an act against the constitution or civil government; 2. If it be against religion; and 3. If against morality.

1. Under the first head fall all the cases of seditious words or writings. . . .

2. It is a libel if it reflects upon religion, that great basis of civil government and society; and it may be both a spiritual and temporal offence. . . .

3. As to morality. Destroying that is destroying the peace of the government, for government is no more than publick order, which is morality. My Lord Chief Justice Hale used to say, Christianity is part of the law and why not morality too? . . .

The argument was accepted by the court and the motion to set aside Curll's conviction was denied.

The fact that the King's attorney general combined the three points in a single argument is significant. The same spirit that would stamp out sedition and heresy would repress art and literature in the supposed interests of an approved sexual morality. The three points are part of a unified pattern of government, a pattern that the First Amendment excludes. It is now well settled that "seditious words or writings," distinct from conduct, may not be suppressed, nor may heretical words or writings be suppressed. We submit that *Roth-Alberts*, considering the third aspect of restraint on expression, limits suppression of writing dealing with sex to material that is utterly lacking in literary value or any other form of social importance.

The Citizens' brief also urged—the attorney general's brief had not—that the Harlan view should be adopted, that each state should be permitted to suppress obscenity as it saw fit, with little or no interference from the First Amendment. And so my responding brief extended the remarks I had made during the oral argument:

> Moreover, the economics of publishing are such that the prospect of the loss of part of the national market may well produce negative decisions on whether or not a particular book will be published. The problem is not so much with the big best seller. The problem is with the first work of a new writer, or the work of an established writer whose merit has been recognized but whose books are marginal so far as economic return is concerned. If publishers do not have constitutional principles of nationwide application to go by—if distribution in some states is foreclosed or unpredictable—there will inevitably be a self-imposed censorship.

Harlan saw the states as laboratories in which legislative experiments could be carried out. This is a concept useful in certain fields of government action (zoning, for example, or public ownership of utilities) but not, I felt, if the First Amendment is involved. It was a chilling prospect—fifty little labs with state legislators performing their vivisection on freedom of speech.*

After our response was filed, the Citizens petitioned the Court for leave to submit another brief. To pass on the petition, the Justices would have to read it. In reading it, they would see

---

* In a case in New Jersey where the opposition took the Harlan approach and the book had been held not obscene by the New York courts, I asked the Court to contemplate the administrative consequences. Would roadblocks be set up at the Hudson River and Kill van Kull tunnels and bridges? Would briefcases and shopping bags be laid open and searched for contraband books?

the additional arguments that the Citizens proposed to offer. The petition was in itself another brief. So I filed an objection to their petition; my objection was in itself another brief. The petition was denied.

Thus, for the reasons I have mentioned, the Citizens' brief probably helped our case. But at the same time a concern of mine was deepened—not because of any particular arguments they made, but because the brief might keep the Court's attention fastened on the traits and features of the value test. It might bring to the surface a problem that had been troubling me, and that I had decided, until then, to ignore. I continued to ignore it, but only after a hotly contested internal debate. The sentence in *Roth* we were relying on declared that obscenity might be excluded from constitutional protection because it is "utterly without redeeming social importance." In the *Lady Chatterley* case, arguing that a converse proposition was embedded in *Roth*, I referred to the suggested criterion as "the social-value test." That is, I was reading the word "importance" in the sense of "value." "Importance," however, has other meanings—not synonymous with value—that would impose a higher standard. "Some value" might not be too hard to show; "some importance" could be something else again.

The test as yet had no legal existence; it was in the process of being synthesized, out of a phrase, an inference and a constitutional theme. I was free to formulate it the way I thought best. ("Best" in such a situation involves a combination of the proposition's chances of acceptance and of its usefulness if it is accepted.) I aimed for the less exacting meaning of "importance" —that is, "value."

The semantics were never challenged, possibly because in the beginning the opposition regarded the whole idea as preposterous. And as the theory gradually gained currency, "importance" and "value" came to be used interchangeably. Thus the Massachusetts attorney general, the Solicitor General in *Ginzburg*, and the New York district attorney in *Mishkin* all referred to "the social-value test." *

---

* A significant example of how thorough the identification became appeared in an article by a noted British-American legal scholar, Arthur L.

But did the theory as formulated take in too much? If the proposed rule did not contemplate a certain level of importance to society, but merely value of any degree, then the phrase "utterly without" would fix a very low standard indeed. The theory might appear to extend constitutional protection to things a majority of the Supreme Court would not want to protect.

I am not now referring to something that is just too shocking, though it may have substantial artistic merit—the kind of thing imagined in the chapter on our brief. The present problem does not involve performances offensive beyond the possibility of judicial approval, but rather borderline books, or other expression painfully acceptable, whose value is minuscule. Take, for example, a motion picture which by current norms is patently offensive and appeals to prurient interest, and has no artistic merit except in one regard. A cameraman once highly thought of, but now done in by drugs or alcohol or lack of exercise, has worked on the film for a handout, and the photography, in some of its footage, shows flashes of his old talent. Or suppose we have, in the shape of a book, a hackneyed repetition of the familiar events, delivered with heavy-handed lubricity and a laboring effort to crowd in all the formerly objectionable words. There is, in this hypothetical volume, a paragraph of beautifully written description (probably plagiarized, but the record does not demonstrate this).

The question of the earlier chapter had to do with situations in which the artistic level might be high but the presentation so indecent that no contemporary court could be expected to approve. This one had to do with works that might fail the prurience and offensiveness tests, but not by nearly so wide a margin; would the test I was proposing protect such a work because it had some value, even though the value was tiny?

Our main brief had dealt with the first question, not explicitly, but by drawing attention to the differences between expression and conduct, and between books and other forms of expression. The brief had not dealt with the present question at

---

Goodhart, former master of University College, Oxford. Writing after the *Memoirs* decision, Professor Goodhart referred to the Supreme Court in *Roth* as stating that "a book would not be held pornographic unless 'the material is utterly without redeeming social value.'"

all, though like the other it had been on my mind for a long time. In the earlier cases—*Lady Chatterley* and *Tropic* and *Memoirs* in New York—the opposition treated the value theory as altogether unacceptable, and therefore felt no need to trace its hypothetical applications. In Massachusetts, the attorney general, though he accepted the theory, also found it unnecessary to look beyond the book on trial: if *Fanny Hill* could be published, he said, then no book could be banned. But his commingling the tests (while agreeing they should be kept apart) put a mask on the problem. The court itself came closer to the problem, but in a way that did not force its exploration. Denouncing *Memoirs* as prurient and patently offensive, the Massachusetts majority refused to concede that an independent value test existed, and said that in any case *Memoirs*' "minimal literary value does not mean it is of any social importance." But the court's phrase "unqualifiedly worthless" was unfortunate (for the court's purposes) and saved me the problem of dwelling on the discrepancy between this formulation and Brennan's. Instead, I could concentrate on the book itself.

Choosing to join issue with the Massachusetts majority on whether the book had appreciable merit, I argued that our case did not involve any "scintilla theory of value." There was risk in spending so little time on what I felt was the legal error in their statement of the value test. But there was also risk in promoting a discussion of how the test would work if a book had only a speck of merit. My guess was that the Supreme Court, following our law's empirical inclination to deal with one case at a time, would not pause to meditate on how to handle a suppositious work of admittedly meager quality.

The inclination is empirical, but a legal system must have principles—devices for decision that apply to a plurality of cases. That is to say, a legal system must have laws. How far beyond the immediate circumstances a court should carry its speculations is, once again, something that involves the art of the law and the good judgment of the judge. With the entry of the Citizens for Decent Literature, the problem became more acute. This was not because they made the problem explicit; their total rejection of the value theory would make such points superfluous. They argued, accurately, that there had never been a statement by a majority of the Supreme Court that would justify a departure from the law as it existed prior to *Roth*, when literary merit was only something that might be weighed against the lust-provoking elements in the book. But their frontal attack was so vigorous that the Justices might be moved to consider, more than they otherwise would, the theory's side effects.

If the question were raised, I had an answer. The answer would not save the trash-in-the-form-of-film that had three minutes of good photography or the trash-in-the-form-of-book that had a paragraph of good writing. "Any value at all," I would concede, was not equivalent to "any importance at all"; it would take more than an iota of merit to make up an iota of importance. But very little more.

I would agree, if I had to, that although "social value" and "social importance" had come to be used interchangeably, they were not precisely synonymous. They had been used interchangeably because the value of *Lady Chatterley* and of *Tropic*, and, yes, the value of *Fanny Hill*, was more than sufficient to establish importance. Nevertheless, some degree of detectable value might be required, in order to achieve the smidgen of importance that the test demands.

I would argue this if I had to, but I would rather not have to. My object was to establish the value theory as a rule of law. So far as the development of the law was concerned, it was freedom's best chance, and so far as my client's direct interests were concerned, our case without it was very likely lost. One way to try to get the theory accepted was to present it with all conceivable objections rebutted in advance. Another was to present it in as simple a form as possible—as a basic principle rather than as a complete, all-purpose system. The more complicated the theory appeared, the less receptive the Justices might be.

The private debate was a close one, the outcome in doubt until I had corrected galley on my final brief. Whether my decision was right I do not know, except for the unreliable sign given by the fact that *Memoirs* v. *Massachusetts*, like *Memoirs*, had a happy ending.

The Decisions
of March 21, 1966

ON MARCH 21, 1966, THREE AND A HALF MONTHS after the cases were argued, the Supreme Court handed down its decisions. The convictions of Mishkin and Ginzburg were affirmed; the judgment against *Memoirs* was reversed.

Clark and White voted for suppression in all three cases. Black, Douglas and Stewart voted against suppression in all three. Harlan voted for suppression in *Mishkin* and *Memoirs*, but against it in *Ginzburg*. Warren, Brennan and Fortas voted for suppression in *Mishkin* and *Ginzburg*, but against it in *Memoirs*. Thus the vote was six to three to affirm Mishkin's conviction, five to four to affirm Ginzburg's conviction, and six to three to lift the ban on *Memoirs*.

The Court was not only divided as to what the judgments should be; there was a dazzling variety of views on each side of the divide. Only two Justices were content to let another speak for them throughout. Fourteen opinions were filed, a number that was reached even though several were thriftily made to serve for more than one case. Nevertheless—and this may be puzzling to those who formed their impression from published comments of the time—there was sufficient agreement among the Justices, sufficient overlap where there was not congruency, that important features of the law emerged with considerable clarity.

In each case, Warren and Fortas, the only Justices who did not write, joined in opinions written by Brennan. In *Mishkin* and *Ginzburg*, Clark and White also joined Brennan. Thus in these two cases there was a cohesive, though narrow, majority against the defendants, a single opinion of the Court to which five Justices subscribed. (Harlan's separate concurrence added the sixth vote in *Mishkin*.) In *Memoirs*, there being no other opinion that spoke for any but its writer, the three-judge Brennan opinion headed the list, and Brennan announced the judgment of the Court. The order in which the opinions were handed down reversed that in which the cases were argued: *Memoirs* came first, then *Ginzburg*, then *Mishkin*.

Douglas wrote two witty essays. He referred to Clark's denunciation of the book and said that he "would pair my Brother Clark on *Fanny Hill* with the Universalist Minister I quote in the Appendix"; the Universalist Minister had been enthusiastic about *Memoirs*, and had himself paired John Cleland with Dr. Norman Vincent Peale. Black made a forceful statement in support of his "absolute" position, though it was a statement that may have laid the foundation for a future delimiting of the position—a containment, not a modification of it. He used the words "discussion" and "views" in saying what must be kept absolutely free. I wondered whether he was not getting ready, should an appropriate issue be presented, to give the definitions of "speech" and "press" some rather tight lacing. But though questions such as I discussed in earlier chapters may have been implicitly reserved, both Douglas and Black reaffirmed their thesis that the First Amendment forbids all limits on speech and press.*

Stewart arrived at the same result as Black and Douglas,

---

* The two Justices do not state the proposition in the same language, and it is quite possible that in some future case they may disagree. Douglas follows the ordinary course of reading the material involved in the case. Black, pursuing his logic to the end, does not. There may have been an exception here, however. In his *Mishkin* dissent, Black said: "Neither in this case nor in *Ginzburg* have I read the alleged obscene matter." He did not mention *Memoirs*. Fanny does indeed inspire gallantry.

against suppression in all three cases, but on the Stewart axiom that only hard-core pornography may be suppressed. He added something though—I will describe it in a moment—that made the axiom rather less of a Magic Automatic Self-Bailing Little Wonder. Nothing here, he found, was hard-core pornography.

Harlan held to his position that the First Amendment does not apply fully to state legislation. Hence he voted to reverse Ginzburg's conviction, which was under federal law, but to affirm Mishkin's, which was under state law, and to affirm the Massachusatts ban on *Memoirs.* He made it clear that if the statute used against *Memoirs* had been a federal statute, he would have voted differently. ("To me it is plain, for instance, that *Fanny Hill* . . . could not be barred from the federal mails.") His opinions were well written, well reasoned and, given the premise, persuasive. But I was glad to see it was still a private premise; I had been concerned that the Harlan approach might have begun to look tempting to Warren.

The two other dissents in *Memoirs* had a different basis and a different tone. Clark began:

> I have "stomached" past cases for almost ten years without much outcry. Though I am not known to be a purist—or a shrinking violet—this book is too much even for me. . . .

He then presented a detailed digest of the book, which demonstrated, he said:

> There can be no doubt that the whole purpose of the book is to arouse the prurient interest. Likewise the repetition of sexual episode after episode and the candor with which they are described renders the book "patently offensive." . . .

But apart from how he saw the particular book, his view of the law was profoundly different from that of the majority. Clark, and White as well, protested the adoption of the value test. "There are three Justices," he said, "who import a new test into that laid down in *Roth.* . . ." Clark had been a subscriber to the Brennan opinion in *Roth.* He would not have been, he said rather bitterly, if he had thought it embodied such a rule as the prevailing group was stating now. This is an example of the judicial phenomenon I described in a previous chapter—the divergence of views that sometimes occurs when an opinion that has started a change in the law comes to be applied as a precedent. Later cases may turn up sharper issues and cut between disparate attitudes that had managed to cohabit in the roomy declarations of the early opinion.

The Brennan opinion in *Memoirs* made law of the value theory. It stated the theory in emphatic terms, and relied on nothing else. The Massachusetts majority was wrong, said Brennan, when it held that a book did not have to be unqualifiedly worthless in order to be suppressed. It had to be just that. If a book had any worth, it could not be suppressed:

> a book cannot be proscribed unless it is found to be *utterly* without redeeming social value. This is so even though the book is found to possess the requisite prurient appeal and to be patently offensive. Each of the three federal constitutional criteria is to be applied independently; the social value of the book can neither be weighed against nor canceled by its prurient appeal or patent offensiveness. . . .

Warren and Fortas joined Brennan in this statement—Fortas, who for the first time was considering the matter from the bench, and Warren, whose view in *Jacobellis* had been quite different.

Stewart also accepted the independent value theory. My brief had suggested that his concept of hard-core pornography, which he had not yet attempted to analyze, was an amalgam of all three tests.* His opinion described hard-core pornography as a "class of material in which all of the elements coalesce"—the elements being prurient interest, patent offensiveness and utter absence of social importance. Since all three had to coalesce, the presence of value would assure First Amendment protection.

Harlan said he too—though only where the federal government was concerned—would limit anti-obscenity efforts to hard-

---

* "Analytically," said the brief, "the concept appears to involve all three standards discussed above. It would seem to be a combination of morbidity, extreme offensiveness and utter worthlessness that denotes hard-core pornography."

core pornography, and he would describe it the same way Stewart did. He stated, moreover, that evidence such as had been given at the *Memoirs* trial demonstrated the value the test required (although he dissented from the judgment on another ground). So did Douglas (although he concurred in the judgment on another ground). Each came very close to agreeing with my (then) outrageous opening statement—that on a record such as we had made, the Court could save itself the trouble of looking at the book. Harlan:

> To establish social value in the present case, a number of acknowledged experts in the field of literature testified that *Fanny Hill* held a respectable place in serious writing, and unless such largely uncontradicted testimony is accepted as decisive it is very hard to see that the "utterly without redeeming social value" test has any meaning at all.

Douglas:

> If there is to be censorship, the wisdom of experts on such matters as literary merit and historical significance must be evaluated. On this record, the Court has no choice but to reverse . . .

Whether there were three or four or five Justices who subscribed to the value theory, it was enough, so long as there were two others who would forbid all suppression. But in fact there were five who now agreed the First Amendment shielded any book that had merit, even minor merit, subject only to the caveat that Harlan would not apply the principle to the states— a caveat that had little bearing on the future of publishing, since the Harlan variation had no adherents.

In addition to establishing the value test, the decisions of March 21, 1966, made another advance—less radical and less significant, but significant nevertheless. It was in connection with the prurient-interest test, and it came not in our case but in Mishkin's. A gain for freedom was marked in an opinion that sent the defendant to jail. (This was not something new; the opinion affirming Samuel Roth's conviction laid the basis for the vast liberalization that followed.)

Mishkin's defense employed the traditional concept of obscenity that I had been trying to overturn: obscene books were lustful books, books that excited a sexual reaction. Mishkin's books were not sexually exciting, his lawyer urged, except perhaps to special groups. And here he invoked the *Roth* "average person," whose prurient interest was not engaged, he said, by the depiction of deviant practices: ". . . instead of stimulating the erotic, they disgust and sicken."

Our opponents in all the cases had founded their principal arguments on this reference to "the average person." Taken together with their reading of "prurient" as lustful, the phrase meant, they contended, that if a book produced a sexual response in most people, it was obscene. Moreover—and this continued right up through the arguments of the Massachusetts attorney general in the Supreme Court—the use of "average person," in what was regarded as *the* definition of obscenity, showed that if there was such a thing as a value test, the needs and desires of intellectuals did not count. The average man was the arbiter.

But the decision in *Memoirs* made it clear that the average man had nothing to do with the value test. As for the prurient-interest test, the *Mishkin* opinion indicated that at least part of my gloss was being accepted. In the *Memoirs* brief (as in my 1959 *Chatterley* brief) I proposed that "average person" had a negative, not a positive function—that the *Roth* opinion employed the phrase to express "the final rejection" of the *Hicklin* rule. Among the weaknesses of *Hicklin*, I said, was that the book was judged by its effect on "the most susceptible."

The Court had no need to use this section of the brief for *Memoirs*; the decision was based on the value test alone. But in *Mishkin*, dealing with the average-person point made by the defense (which had so much in common with the points prosecutors had been making), the Court said:

The reference to the "average" or "normal" person in *Roth* does not foreclose this holding [against the defendant]. In regard to the prurient-appeal requirement, the concept of the "average" or "normal" person was employed in *Roth* to serve the essentially negative purpose of expressing our rejection of that aspect of the *Hicklin* test that made the impact on the most susceptible person determinative. . . .

The word "average," which had been so dear to opposing counsel and to many lower-court judges, had been cut down to a proper size.

As to the other limitation I had urged—that sexual interest did not equal prurient interest—the opinions made no comment, one way or the other. There was only the negative support that came from their refusal to accept Mishkin's argument that his books were not prurient because they were sickening. But there was affirmative support, from one Justice at least—the writer of the *Roth* opinion—during the oral argument of *Memoirs.* At one point I had said, ". . . material whose effect is to stimulate a sexual response in a normal person is not for that reason to be denounced." Brennan interjected: "*Roth* said that."

In *Ginzburg*, the Supreme Court enunciated what was generally taken to be a new concept. The way the publications were sold, the Court held, was pertinent, and in doubtful cases could make the difference. The majority was willing to assume "that standing alone, the publications might not be obscene." Indeed, said Brennan, affirmance implied no agreement with the way the trial judge characterized the material. But "the context of the circumstances of promotion, sale and publicity" might be considered "as an aid to determining the question of obscenity. . . ." Thus aided, the Court found all three Ginzburg publications obscene.

Among the circumstances noted by the Court were the attempts to send the mail from Pennsylvania towns that so innocently provided double-entendre postmarks. In addition, said the Court, Ginzburg's circulars "stressed the sexual candor of the respective publications and openly boasted that the publishers would take full advantage of what they regarded as an unrestricted license allowed by the law in the expression of sex and sexual matters." Then there were the slips labeled "Guarantee," which assured the buyer full refund "if the book fails to reach you because of U. S. Post Office censorship interference."

These things, the majority concluded, were "pandering." Since the publishers of the material "proclaimed its obscenity," the court below had made no error when it accepted the defendants' "own evaluation at its face value. . . ."

Cries of anguish and astonishment greeted the decisions. So did cries of joy and grateful hosannas. The *National Decency Reporter* (published by the Citizens for Decent Literature) said, "The final results were a major defeat to the smut industry." The Citizens had to struggle a bit with the *Memoirs* decision, but they managed to fit it in. The *New York Times* reported:

> Thirteen clergymen of all faiths, including three Cardinals, applauded two recent Supreme Court decisions on obscenity in a joint statement yesterday.

The clergymen were a little more realistic than the Citizens— they applauded only two of the decisions, lamenting *Memoirs* and expressing the hope that the Supreme Court would reconsider the value theory.

But a greater clamor came from the other side: the Court in *Ginzburg*, we were told, had invented a new doctrine, made new law to justify a repressive decision. It was an interesting spectacle—liberals decrying Supreme Court action because of its novelty. *The Nation* called the decision "beyond comprehension." *The New Republic* called March 21 "a grim day in the temple of justice." An article in the *Village Voice* said, "In the *Ginzburg* case, the Court for the first time equated sex with obscenity."

Twenty prominent intellectuals took a full-page advertisement in the *New York Times* to protest. Russell Baker of the *Times* said, "It is obvious that the Supreme Court is in over its head on the smut issue." The *Herald Tribune* said that the decision had "shrunk the limits of free expression." Michael Harrington, in the same paper, said, "The Court has sacrificed very real First Amendment freedoms."

It was not simply a New York-liberal-Eastern-Establishment

reaction. According to the *Chicago Sun Times*, the Court had "added a new dimension to censorship. . . ." The *Wall Street Journal's* evaluation was: "a defeat for civic-liberties advocates." The *Oakland Tribune* said the "censors' authority has been broadened by the law of the land." The *Detroit News* said the *Ginzburg* decision "does not augur well for the principle of government by law." An attorney prominent in the field repeated the general appraisal of the decisions and predicted: "Organizations interested in suppressing books and magazines will seize upon the novel device of censoring them on the grounds of salacious promotion."

In fact, the Court had added very little that was new on the side of repression. It had added a great deal that was new (in terms of established law, as distinguished from what many thought to be the law) on the side of freedom.

The pandering concept, which seemed to pinch the most, was hardly an original creation. Essentially, it was a variation on the ancient theme of estoppel. Estoppel expresses the feeling that you ought to be held to what you say. In private dealings you may be bound, even where strictly there is no contract, if you make a statement and somebody acts in reliance on it. The courts will not allow you to explain you didn't mean it; they put your money where your mouth was. If a publisher in selling his books declares they are obscene, the Supreme Court held, we will take him at his word.

But the pandering concept had more specific precedents. In describing the rush to put the *Memoirs* case before the Court, I mentioned my concern about how *Ginzburg* might come out. This was not an inspired insight. The way a book was sold had for a long time been deemed relevant in obscenity cases: prosecutors had sought to prove that books were peddled for their lewdness, and publishers sought to prove they were presented as serious literature. The Massachusetts anti-obscenity law provided for the receipt of evidence on "the manner and form of [the book's] publication, advertisement and distribution." Courts outside Massachusetts had not needed specific statutory direction; in a number of instances they had taken pandering into account, or the absence of it. If anybody had missed the point, it was given prominent display in Warren's separate *Roth* opinion.

In *Lady Chatterley*, Judge Bryan, taking note of the evidence we had introduced, said:

> There is nothing of "the leer of the sensualist" in the promotion or methods of distribution of this book. There is no suggestion of any attempt to pander to the lewd- and lascivious-minded for profit. The facts are all to the contrary.
>
> *   *   *
>
> No one is naïve enough to think that Grove Press did not expect to profit from the book. Nevertheless, the format and composition of the volume, the advertising and promotional material, and the whole approach to publication, treat the book as a serious work of literature.

(Brennan, holding against Ginzburg, agreed that his making a profit was not itself significant.)*

Such evidence, on either side, had usually provided only a makeweight argument, but in close cases it is important to make weight. The *Ginzburg* majority did not create a new concept; it took an old one and gave it sharper definition and a more explicit role than it had played in most earlier cases.

Moreover, the opinion was widely and grossly misunderstood. One heard such comments, seriously offered, as "*The Mill on the Floss* can now be held obscene if a bookseller advertises it in the wrong way." It was simply not so. The Supreme Court's approach was this: consider the book outside the context of its promotion; if the question of obsceneness is found to be arguable, pandering may justify a holding that the statute applies and the Amendment does not. *Fanny Hill*, said Brennan, presented an arguable issue (though it was one he would resolve in favor of the book), and he held open the possibility that if a bookseller promoted *Fanny Hill* as the Ginzburg publications were promoted, the Massachusetts attorney general, moving against that bookseller, might have better success. But

---

* Richard Kuh, writing about my opening statement in the New York *Fanny Hill* trial, where I spoke about the way Putnam was advertising and distributing the book, says that I was "seemingly anticipating that pandering standard that the Supreme Court's majority was to promulgate almost three years later . . ." *Foolish Figleaves?* (Macmillan, 1967). Mr. Kuh gives me too much credit; it was not prescience, but simple accommodation to what was already part of the law.

the pandering concept would apply only where the material itself was on the edge of illegality. And even there, in my judgment, a publisher's telling the public that the book was about
sex would not amount to pandering.

When the decisions came down, some companies whose
books might have been vulnerable asked me what to do about
their advertising. It was open and honest advertising, I thought,
neither gross nor arch, and I advised them to go on doing what
they had been doing. Nothing happened.

The air was full of calamity. "This is the opening the district
attorneys have been looking for," a well-known attorney was
quoted as saying. The Citizens for Decent Literature agreed.
The *Wall Street Journal* said, "The decision may encourage a
nationwide crackdown of local officials on sexy publications and
movies." Another attorney prominent in the field wrote: "It is
clear that the financially insecure artist who describes sexual
matters cannot promote his work when *Fanny Hill*, well supported by substantial witnesses and a solvent publisher, cannot
succeed." (This was after the decision; the publisher of *Fanny
Hill*, of course, went right on publishing the book, as the Supreme Court had held he was free to do.) His article added:
"The immediate result of the three decisions will be an increase
in arrests and prosecutions, both in the country and the city." *

At the date of writing, approximately a year has gone by. The
Post Office Department, which keeps careful statistics, reports
that in the past year there has been a decline in prosecutions
under the federal anti-obscenity laws. For several years prior to
the decisions that would loose the hounds of censorship, Comstock Law arrests had averaged between sixty and seventy a
month. In the period July 1966 to January 1967, there was an
average of thirty-four a month. Moreover, Post Office action to
ban books from the mails, which had begun to decline after the
Lady Chatterley decision, has now virtually disappeared.†

---

* Presumably meaning the nation generally, as well as New York. But
compare the statement of Whitey Bimstein, celebrated prize-fight trainer,
when, returning from a mountain training camp, he was asked how he
liked it: "The country is a nice spot."

† The official who gave the statistics called attention to complaints
based on advertisements that constituted pandering-without-obscenity, and

The fearsome new weapon lay idle. In New York City, a spokesman for the police department said he could recall only one case during the year in which the prosecution had thought the pandering concept worth invoking. As to the general effect of the decisions of March 21, 1966, he said they "didn't help one bit."

In fact, of course, there was much more freedom after the decisions than before. The works of the Marquis de Sade, openly published in unexpurgated form for the first time, encountered no interference from the government. *Last Exit to Brooklyn* had only minor difficulty. The notorious *Story of O* had none. *Candy* was everywhere. Restraints were relaxed on the stage and on the screen. *The Deer Park* was produced off Broadway and *Marat/Sade* on Broadway. Customs let through a film version of *Ulysses*, despite the fact that Molly Bloom's famous soliloquy was spoken out loud; a high customs official, according to the *Times*, explained that "recent court decisions protected all films except those 'completely without socially redeeming value.'"

It is quite clear that the doom-sayers were wrong. It is also quite clear that the joy of the Citizens was just whistling in the light. The thirteen clergymen were the most perceptive; although they approved *Ginzburg* and *Mishkin*, they viewed with dismay the *Memoirs* opinions.

The common view of the decisions, from the liberal side, was distorted by two factors. One was the lack of realism about how the law stood before March 1966. If you were in favor of freedom and misinformed about the state of the law, you would naturally feel deprived by the decisions, and inclined to take the bleakest view of their meaning. The other was that many people (myself included) felt there were aspects of Ginzburg's trial that seemed unfair and the five-year jail sentence was grotesque. For the individuals concerned, the results were unhappy, and to a part of the public scandalous. But for freedom of expression,

---

which, while they might furnish grounds for a mail-fraud prosecution, would not furnish grounds for anything else. One of the cases that he mentioned involved an advertisement that promised "a film of a girl and a dog on a blanket." Those who subscribed received a picture of a little girl playing with a dog, on a blanket.

March 21, 1966, was a very good day. The pandering rule would send Ginzburg to jail, but its future as an inhibiting force on speech and the press would be negligible. The acceptance of the value test would give writers and publishers a freedom they had never before enjoyed.

I do not mean by this that nothing in print can ever be censored. There remain the questions I described. Can a speck of value immunize a work? I think the answer is no—for the present Court at least. Though Brennan did not find occasion to say so, there will still, I believe, have to be a discernible, demonstrable value. And it will have to be a value that pervades the work—not one story with a good plot line in a magazine of otherwise consistent trash, or a few passable paragraphs in an utter stinker of a novel.

But there is no high line of value that a book has to reach. The prevailing opinion in *Memoirs* v. *Massachusetts*, the opinion that finally gave the value test legitimacy, spent no time differentiating between "importance" and "value." It simply substituted the latter for the former. In *Roth*, Brennan had said "social importance," and the value theory was at best only implied. In *Jacobellis* the theory had become explicit, but it had the support of only two Justices, and again Brennan had said "importance." In *Memoirs* the theory became a rule of law, and now the word was not "importance" but "value." A book cannot be proscribed unless it is found to be "*utterly*"—the italics were Brennan's—"without redeeming social *value*"—the italics are mine. The possibly more demanding word "importance" was not to be taken in its more demanding sense.

As to extreme situations in other media of expression, it may be significant that the subject of Brennan's sentence was "a book." In *Roth* and in *Jacobellis* he had used the word "material." Possibly, in choosing the word "book," he was preparing a basis for distinction if the imagined cases should come to court. But at least where books are concerned, the value test is now an established rule of law, a rule that protects even that classic of pornography, *Memoirs of a Woman of Pleasure.*

Literary censorship has its most important impact not on the publisher or the bookseller, but on the writer. If he must keep an eye on the law, we are deprived of his best creative effort. And this has been the condition of things until very recently (unless, of course, a writer was willing to limit his audience to those who could be reached through a private printing or a foreign distribution). Things are different now.

Consider the author at his typewriter. Pandering is irrelevant; he cannot be inhibited by the thought that his publisher must refrain from advertising his book in the manner of *Ginzburg*. Assuming he can produce something not "utterly without" merit, which is equivalent to assuming that he is a writer at all, he and his book will be safe. If he has some talent, and if he is making any effort to use that talent—whatever springs and urges may have put him (or John Cleland) to work—the law will never bother him. That is the meaning of the *Fanny Hill* case. So far as writers are concerned, there is no longer a law of obscenity.

Conclusion

THE CURRENT USES OF THE NEW FREEDOM ARE
not all to the good. There is an acne on our culture. Books enter
the best-seller lists distinguished only by the fact that once they
would have put their publishers in jail. Advertising plays upon
concupiscence in ways that range from foolish to fraudulent.
Theater marquees promise surrogate thrills, and the movies
themselves, even some of the good ones, include "daring"
scenes—"dare" is a child's word—that have no meaning except
at the box office. Second-hand Freud gives the film director a
line on which to hang his heroine's clothes; psychoanalytic
clichés create his reputation as philosopher-poet, while shots of
skin insure his solvency. Television commercials peddle sex with
an idiot slyness. We approach a *seductio ad absurdum.* A visitor
from outer space who had time to study only our art and entertainment would take back an eccentric view of the reproductive
process on earth.

This is indeed a lip-licking, damp-palmed age. My objection
is perhaps different from that of the Citizens for Decent Literature. I consider all this anti-sex.

But it will pass. It will pass because it is not the freedom
itself, but the taboo it displaces, that sets the stage for prurience.
(The Supreme Court, after all, did not choose too bad a word;
"lust" would dignify the emotion that the composers of movie-

advertising seek to elicit.) The truest definition of pornography requires that the act of reading itself be sinful, or illegal, or authority-defying, or at least sneaky. (Forgive me, friends.) The response cannot be the same when no book is forbidden. The long refusal to permit honest treatment of sexual subjects has conditioned a nation of voyeurs. As the courts move on their present path, they hustle pornography off the scene, a billy in its back.

A change, I believe, is already observable. It is the grownups who provide most of the adolescent reaction. They grew up when it took a trip to Paris, or a pass to a locked library alcove, to read Henry Miller. It is they, and not their juniors, who are most likely to be aroused (to sexual response, or to moral indignation, or to both) by the sudden release of forbidden books. The younger generation is much less excited by the new freedom in literature—in both senses: it is less alarmed and it is less titillated.

If writing will remain free for a sufficient time, some balance will be restored. I do not mean, of course, that the evocation of sexual images and empathies will—or should—be eliminated from literature, nor do I mean that the perversion of sex to commercial purposes will disappear. But the present distorted, impoverished, masturbatory concentration on representations of sex will diminish as the restraints on expression recede. Pornography, which is in the groin of the beholder, will lose its force —not, as Comstock hoped, by reason of the scope and vigor of censorship laws, but by reason of the constitutional restrictions put upon them.*

I respectfully dissent from the prevalent view that freer expression is part of a moral decline.† I do not, as do many of my contemporaries, believe that modes of expression and modes of behavior are all one, or that there is a tight connection between

---

* I realize, of course, that this may pose a problem for a current critical thesis that finds a new literary frontier in pornography.

† The phrase "new morality" is currently in fashion. "New morality" said fast, as it so often is these days, sounds very like "numerology." The connection is more than aural. The shibboleth and the science each provide a rich supply of ready-made answers.

the alleged changes in sexual morality and the alleged changes in other kinds of morality. (And I am skeptical about the extent of these changes—both kinds. I question whether differences in conduct that flow from lessened fears of pregnancy and illness can be considered changes in morality, and I also question whether our grandfathers were more honest than we are.) I would assert the wisdom of the law's separation of expression and conduct, and suggest that the removal of artificial restraints on expression may help to establish a sounder morality.

"Not all to the good," I said, but quite clearly much that is good has come from the liberty to speak about sex, and more is likely to come—altogether apart from the greater scope allowed our writers and artists. We can now, for example, see serious television presentations (commercially sponsored) of the population riddle—presentations that can talk in direct plain language about the source of population. (Note that the last phrase, now merely a choice of words, would once have been a law-enforced euphemism.) Our black-magic view of sex suffers from illumination, and we must benefit from its discomfiture.

But these are dicta. The cases in this volume have to do with expression, not with conduct. And among modes of expression, they have to do only with books; the treatment of sex in other forms of communication is another story. It is in relation to books that obscenity has had its main meaning. With the lifting of legal restraint, the kind of response in the reader—shocked or aroused or guilty—that marks what we are accustomed to call obscene will begin to disappear.

The word will not leave the dictionary. There will always, so long as there is society, be indelicate violations of social convention (though future convention may seem strange to us). And there will always be things obscene in a deeper sense, things that have a special kind of ugly evil. But obscenity as the term has been commonly understood—the impermissible description of sex in literature—approaches its end. So far as writing is concerned, I have said there is no longer any law of obscenity. I would go farther and add, so far as writing is concerned, that not only in our law but in our culture, obscenity will soon be gone.

Appendix

This appendix contains some references to sources and some comments too discursive for text and too long for footnote.

AS LONG AS IT DOESN'T OFFEND
OUR OWN IDEAS

The case involving *An American Tragedy* is *Commonwealth* v. *Friede*, 271 Mass. 318. The district court's opinion in *Ulysses* is at 5 F. Supp. 182, the court of appeals opinion at 72 F. 2d 705. The *Strange Fruit* case is *Commonwealth* v. *Isenstadt*, 318 Mass. 543. The *Hecate County* case is *People* v. *Doubleday*, 297 N.Y. 687, affirmed 335 U.S. 848. The *Tropics* case is *Besig* v. *United States*, 208 F. 2d 142.

The Eisenhower address, "Remarks at the Dartmouth College Commencement Exercises, Hanover, New Hampshire, June 14, 1953," is in *Public Papers of the Presidents of the United States* (Office of the Federal Register, National Archives and Records Service). The *Wall Street Journal* report is from its issue of March 15, 1967. The statistics on the "national cross-section" are from Stouffer, *Communism, Conformity and Civil Liberties* (Doubleday 1955). The Picasso story is in the *New York Times* of April 13 and May 29, 1965. The silencing of Father Coughlin is described in a UPI dispatch of April 3, 1965.

THE LAW TO THE TIME OF CHATTERLEY

Warburg's description of his trial appears in *The New Yorker* of April 1957. The early *Fanny Hill* case is *Commonwealth* v. *Holmes*, 17 Mass. 336. The case of the impudent posture is *Commonwealth* v. *Sharpless*, 2 S. & R. (Pa.) 91. Lyndhurst's speech is described in Paul, *History of Modern England*, Vol. 2, pp. 83–84. The citation of *Queen* v. *Hicklin* is [1868] L.R. 3 Q.B. 360. The *Frankfurter* opinion on the Michigan statute is in *Butler* v. *Michigan*, 352 U.S. 380. Mencken's letter is in *A Mencken Chrestomathy* (Knopf 1953).

In the beginning, treason and heresy were the main concern of the censors. They are, of course, related to obscenity, which is moral heresy, treasonous to religious and social authority. In the early days, treason was defined primarily as "compassing or imagining the King's death." Only in "the higher moments of English justice" did the judges interpret this to mean an actual effort to kill the King. (Brant, *The Bill of Rights*, Bobbs-Merrill 1966.) In its lower moments, such as the reign of Richard II, a member of Parliament who moved the repeal of any of the numerous laws defining treason was by that very act guilty of treason.

Obscenity censorship did not become prominent until the time of the Puritan revolution, but while the association with puritanism is easily made, it should be kept in mind that before this time not many people read books. As I mention in a later chapter, censors are concerned with the mass of men rather than with intellectual minorities. In any event, publishing an obscene book was clearly a crime from the beginning of the eighteenth century.

The actual defendant in the *Hicklin* case was not Hicklin, but a man named Scott. Hicklin was one of the local justices who had ordered the destruction of the pamphlet, and the Crown was on his side; the titling of cases, more in earlier times than now, followed a hidden logic, and "versus"—for which the "v." stands—does not necessarily mean "versus."

Scott was "a person of respectable position and character," and he took his stand as a member of "The Protestant Electoral Union," a body formed "to protest against those teachings and practices which are . . . un-English. . . ." The pamphlet was entitled *The Confessional Unmasked; Shewing the Depravity of the Romish Priesthood, the Iniquity of the Confessional, and the Questions Put to Females in Confession.*

ASPECTS OF THE LAW

An example of the quoting of the half-sentence is in *The Struggle for Judicial Standards*, by Justice Robert Jackson (Knopf 1941). Judge Van Orsdel's opinion is in *Children's Hospital* v. *Adkins*, 284 Fed. 613, affirmed 261 U.S. 525. The description of White's affliction is from Barber, *The Honorable Eighty-Eight* (Vantage 1951).

The common law covered both civil and criminal matters. It bestowed and enforced private rights and liabilities, and it defined and punished crimes. Just as certain behavior made one liable to pay money for infringing the rights of a fellow-subject, so certain behavior made one liable to punishment for a breach of the King's peace—in each instance, at least theoretically, by immemorial tradition. Criminal law today, however, is in most states exclusively a matter of legislation, while private rights and liabilities are still to a great extent determined by the common law.

In another, narrower sense, the term "common law" designates one of two kinds of nonstatutory law. The other kind is called "equity." At an early date, the courts' statement of the customs they were enforcing took a fixed form, and the common law became brittle. The human tendency to oversimplify—to impose systems upon nature—was naturally at work.

The common law remedy in a civil action was ordinarily a judgment for a sum of money, and the judgment was given only in closely defined sets of circumstances. These were described in the common law "writs," and the finite number of writs could not cover the infinite varieties of man's misconduct. Those who had grievances that did not match any of the common law writs began to petition the King, and the King referred the petitions to his chancellor. The chancellor was ordinarily a high ecclesiastic, and thus inclined to feel that he had a more direct communication with ultimate justice than had the laity. He intervened to give relief in cases for which the common law provided no remedy, or where he felt the processes of the common law would lead to the wrong result. The usual form of intervention was an order directing the perpetrator of the wrong to refrain. This is the remedy of injunction.

Sometime in the fourteenth or fifteenth century the number of petitions grew so large that the chancellors could no longer handle them without an organization, and they established their own courts. These were the courts of chancery. The body of law that the chancery courts developed became known as "equity."

The two court systems operated side by side, competing for

power. Coke had his battle with Ellesmere in the time of Elizabeth, and lost. In case of conflict, equity's injunction could stop an action at law. Two centuries later, the courts began to merge. The European revolutionary turmoil of the 1840's had a mild analogue in this country: legal procedures were altered, and New York in 1848 put law and equity into one set of courts. Not all the other states were in a hurry to follow; across the Hudson River in New Jersey, for example, there were separate law courts and chancery courts until after World War II, and in Delaware there still are. Although in almost all the states, and in the federal courts, law and equity are now combined in a single judicial system, the principles that come from the separate systems retain their ancestral characteristics. Depending on the facts presented or the relief sought, there may be a common law remedy or an equitable remedy. Moreover, the right to a jury in a civil action depends on whether the claim sought to be enforced is one that was formerly cognizable at law or in equity; the common law courts employed juries for most matters, while the chancellors felt that they could get along quite well without them.

Equity is generally, and mistakenly, regarded as something fairer, more devoted to justice, more on the side of the little man, than the rigid common law. History, as usual, refuses to conform. Those who championed the common law as against equity—Coke is the prime example—had democratic inclinations, while the chancellors were on the side of the Crown. Though he lost the battle to Ellesmere—equitable remedies can alter what the common law would otherwise provide—Coke comes down to us the winner. The historical process that had taken place in the common law courts was repeated; there was an agglutination of particularistic, justice-in-this-case decisions, and there evolved from precedent a set of principles. And the principles are infused with the genius of the common law.

It is fitting that the proponents of the common law were historically on the side of democracy. Law itself is on the side of democracy. The ad hoc settlement of controversy is not law; law implies generalization. (The laws of the physical sciences were named for the kind of law that we are talking about; there was, of course, manmade governmental law before there was science.) The special favor is anti-law. The broader the rule, the narrower the possibilities for the operation of privilege. The greater the number of instances that must be treated the same way, the more equally treated are those who are governed. The perversion of the common law is the unheeding invocation of doctrine; the perversion of equity is ticket-fixing.

An honest flexibility is, of course, desirable. A broad and firm rule works injustice in some cases, and its effects can be harsh. A more particular application of the power of government allows a nicer adjustment to the demands of fairness. But it also allows a nicer adjustment to the demands of privilege. To the extent that the law has a life of its own, independent of the persons who rule, it reduces the strength of the well positioned and adds to the strength of the rest of us.

Thus it was appropriate that those who were on the side of the people should be adherents of the firmer common law, and those who were on the side of the King should be adherents of the more charitable (or more corrupt, as the case might be) equity jurisdiction. History sometimes gives effect to unintended puns, and the term "common law" eventually attained the egalitarian aspect that was not part of its etymology.

THE ROTH *CASE*

The Supreme Court opinions in the *Roth* and *Alberts* cases are at 354 U.S. 476. The articles by Lockhart and McClure are at 38 *Minnesota Law Review* 295 and 45 *Minnesota Law Review* 5. The book by Paul and Schwartz is *Federal Censorship* (Glencoe 1961). The article by Gerber is at 112 *University of Pennsylvania Law Review* 834. Father Gardiner's statement is in *Catholic Viewpoint on Censorship* (Doubleday-Image 1961). Professor Kalven's remark is in "The Metaphysics of the Law of Obscenity," *The Supreme Court Review* (University of Chicago Law School 1960).

There are three ways in which the Constitution may be made the basis of resistance to governmental action. One is a total attack on the statute that the officials are seeking to enforce. (Federal legislation is vulnerable only to the charge that it conflicts with the federal Constitution; state legislation may be challenged under either the state constitution or the federal.) The statute is viewed generally; its effects beyond the circumstances of the particular case are contemplated. The attack if successful will wipe the statute off the books. It is held to be invalid "on its face" or "as a whole." This was the kind of contention that was made, unsuccessfully, in *Roth*.

Another kind of constitutional issue is raised without reference to any statute. The defendant says simply that the actions of the government officials violate a right, privilege or immunity that the Constitution confers upon him. A statute may be involved in the case, but its general validity is not in issue. For example, a defendant in a criminal prosecution gets his conviction reversed because his constitutional right to counsel has been disregarded; nothing is said about the statute under which he is prosecuted—a statute, say, making murder a crime.

The third kind of constitutional attack lies between the two. The focus is on the statute under which the authorities are acting, but the statute as a whole is not called in question. Instead, the litigant claims it is unconstitutional as applied to his particular situation. If he wins, the legislation remains on the books; the decision is that the Constitution does not permit its operation in the circumstances before the court.

In was the second and third kinds of attack that we made on behalf of *Lady Chatterley, Tropic* and *Fanny Hill.*

A decision that a statute is constitutional does not necessarily mean the court likes the statute, nor does a contrary decision necessarily mean the opposite. The court—that is to say, a worthy court— is moved by considerations quite different from those that move legislators to vote for or against a bill. In constitutional terms, the words "valid" and "invalid" are not equivalent to "desirable" and "undesirable." The fact that a statute is constitutional means only that the legislative body had authority to enact it and, in doing so, did not violate any constitutional prohibitions. The Constitution sets the limits within which legislative power may be exercised. It does not require—indeed, by strong implication it forbids—a judicial appraisal of the wisdom of governmental action that lies within those limits.

LADY CHATTERLEY: *THE FEDERAL COURTS*

The *Besig* case is at 208 F. 2d 142. The Learned Hand opinion is in *United States* v. *Kennerley,* 209 Fed. 119. It was one of the two L. Hand opinions mentioned during the trial; the citation of the other—*United States* v. *Levine*—is Gellhorn's statement from *Individual Freedom and Governmental Restraints* (Louisiana State University Press 1956). The opinion on the *Lady Chatterley* movie case is at 360 U.S. 684. The citations of *Grove Press* v. *Christenberry* are 175 F. Supp. 488 (Bryan's opinion) and 275 F. 2d 433 (the Court of Appeals opinions).

LADY CHATTERLEY: *POSTSCRIPT*

Some confirmation of my comments came later (too late to be included in the chapter) when the British banned *Last Exit to*

Brooklyn—on a jury verdict. The banning "threw British publishing circles into confusion" and raised questions as to whether "a serious work [can] now survive the 1959 Act" (*Publishers' Weekly*, December 11, 1967). If earlier obscenity cases had been decided on principle rather than on the sentiments of particular juries—if the courts had been forced to say what the Obscene Publications Act really meant—the suppression of this obviously serious writing might not have taken place, or, if the matter of principle had been considered and decided the other way, the pain, expense and confusion of a banned publication might not have been suffered.

Roy Jenkins later became Chancellor of the Exchequer and one of the leading figures in the Labor Party. St. John-Stevas was the author of a very good study of obscenity censorship—in this country unfortunately cited mainly in judicial opinions favoring censorship.

TROPICAL STORM

Judge Murphy's opinion is in *Upham* v. *Dill*, 195 F. Supp. 5. The 1965 decision holding that film censors must promptly go to court is *Freedman* v. *Maryland*, 380 U.S. 51.

TROPICAL CLEARING

The Massachusetts *Tropic* case is *Attorney General* v. *Tropic of Cancer*, 345 Mass. 11. The New York case is *People* v. *Fritch*, 13 N.Y. 2d 119. The Wisconsin case is *McCauley* v. *Tropic of Cancer*, 20 Wisc. 2d 133. The California case is *Zeitlin* v. *Arnebergh*, 59 Cal. 2d 901. *Manual Enterprises* is at 370 U.S. 478. The Supreme Court *Tropic* case is *Grove Press* v. *Gerstein*, 378 U.S. 577. *Jacobellis* v. *Ohio* is at 378 U.S. 184. The Illinois Supreme Court case is *Haiman* v. *Morris*, which has no citation because the opinion was withdrawn.

The case before the three-judge federal court in New Jersey is *Grove Press* v. *Calissi*, 208 F. Supp. 589. Though these federal judges refused to interfere with the activities of the New Jersey prosecutor, two years later I asked another three-judge federal court, in New York, to interfere with the activities of a New York prosecutor. The district attorney of Nassau County had seized all the copies of the *Evergreen Review* that were then at the bindery, for use in an obscenity prosecution. (The obscenity complaint was based on two items: a chapter from *Eros Denied*, by Wayland

Young, the second Baron Kennet, which dealt with the origin, use and effect of dirty words, and a portfolio of photographs by Emil J. Cadoo. The photographs were semiabstract and in color, and their subject matter was sexual embrace. The last phrase is not a euphemism; it was hard to tell exactly what the people photographed were doing. It was clear, however, that in one way or another they were embracing, that they had no clothes on and—as a fair deduction from the foregoing—that the action was sexual.) The New York case concluded with an injunction against the district attorney. The two decisions involved different facts and issues, but the second one (*Evergreen* v. *Cahn*, 230 F. Supp. 498) represents at least a shift in emphasis.

Article III of the Constitution enumerates the classes of cases in which the federal courts may act, and refers specifically to the Supreme Court, which is given both original and appellate jurisdiction. Its original jurisdiction, rarely exercised, has to do with litigation between states and litigation affecting ambassadors, ministers and consuls. Its appellate jurisdiction extends to everything else that comes within the federal judicial power—principally suits between citizens of different states ("diversity cases") and those that turn on federal statutes or the Constitution ("federal question cases").

Congress has authority to restrict the Court's appellate jurisdiction, and Congress has marked out two routes to Washington: appeal and certiorari. Assuming the correct procedures have been followed, the Court will consider and decide every case that reaches it via appeal (although some it will handle only summarily). Certiorari is different: it is granted only where the Court deems the case important enough to add to its crowded calendar. A petition for certiorari attempts to demonstrate the case's importance—where it is a federal case, for example, by showing that it involves a question to which different circuits have given different answers, and where it is a state case by showing that the state court has ruled, probably erroneously, on an important point of federal law. But whichever route is taken, the case must fall into one of the classes to which federal jurisdiction is confined by Article III.

The class involved in the *Tropic* litigation was "cases . . . arising under this Constitution." To create such a case, one of the litigants must raise a constitutional claim or defense. This reflects a primary feature of our legal system—that courts will act only on what the parties put before them—a feature on which the Supreme Court has been especially insistent where its own jurisdiction is concerned. It is ordinarily not enough that the facts of the case appear to involve the Constitution; the Court has stated time and again, with certain infrequent and well-explained exceptions, that the constitutional contention must be raised early and carefully preserved. It must be nurtured like a smoggy city tree; it is especially susceptible to waiver.

IT SEEMS THERE WERE THESE
FIVE DISTRICT ATTORNEYS . . .

The 1961 treatise has already been mentioned—Paul and Schwartz, *Federal Censorship*. The case upholding the New York statute is *Kingsley Books* v. *Brown*, 354 U.S. 436. The comments by Holmes are in his collection of essays entitled *The Common Law* (Little, Brown 1881).

THE ENLIGHTENMENT IN NEW YORK

The *Zenger* case stands for the proposition (if it stands for any legal proposition at all; it was a confused trial) that the damaging statement is not unlawful if it is true and if it is made "of and concerning" a government official. Truth, which for some time now has been a complete defense to any charge of libel, once was no defense at all. "The greater the truth," said the courts, "the greater the libel." If the plaintiff would be hard put to deny the bad thing you are saying, your statement is all the more damaging.

It is interesting that the great changes in the law of libel of the last few years have also concerned government officials. The Supreme Court has held that the First Amendment overrides (though the Court will not accept Black's thesis that it abolishes) the traditional law of libel. Where public officials are concerned, the statement complained of must now be not merely untrue, but made with knowledge of its falsity, or with reckless disregard of whether it is true or false. The concept has been carried into the action for invasion of privacy, and extended to cover public figures (a prominent left-handed pitcher, for example) as well as public officials. Going one step further, a recent federal district court decision, concerning the film *Titicut Follies*, has held the Amendment applicable where subjects of public interest are involved, even though the plaintiffs are government employees of subordinate status and not at all known to the public. (The Supreme Court cases referred to are *New York Times* v. *Sullivan*, 376 U.S. 254, *Time* v. *Hill*, 385 U.S.

374, and *Spahn* v. *Messner*, 387 U.S. 239. The district court case is *Cullen* v. *Grove Press*, not yet reported.)

There are good accounts of the Zenger trial in Brant, *The Bill of Rights* (Bobbs-Merrill 1966) and in Deutsch, "From Zenger to Garrison," *New York State Bar Journal*, October 1966.

In discussing with my clients the question whether an appeal should be taken, and then, upon their decision, handling the appeal, I was performing two of the principal functions of the lawyer—counseling and litigating. A third is drafting legal instruments. A fourth, which is not strictly the practice of law, is negotiating the substance of agreements, as distinguished from giving legal expression to a consensus arrived at. The roles are combined in the American attorney, but in England divided between solicitor and barrister. The solicitor does not go to court; he drafts papers and gives his client legal advice, often mixed with business advice. The barrister's place is in court, although he may also give advice on what the outcome there is likely to be. This is not simply custom, but a matter of regulation. In the United States, on the other hand, admission to the bar is a license to perform all these functions. But it is a license not fully used. In fact, particularly among large law firms, there is a division that approximates the British system, and there is further specialization along other lines.

The practice of law in the United States, which is considered a single profession, is actually a great congeries of occupations, with only certain habits of thought in common, and sometimes less than that. The tax specialist, for example, is necessarily an unofficial accountant, and is kept so busy following the Internal Revenue Code and its interpretations that he has little time for other fields. Counsel to Wall Street houses will be quite at home among the regulations of the Securities and Exchange Commission and quite lost in the Copyright Office. Criminal cases, in the cities at least, are left pretty much to attorneys who do little else. A trial lawyer for an insurance company will be in court most days, in the library very seldom. He is concerned with establishing his client's view of the facts, the legal principles applicable to his cases being a monotonous few. He is usually more of an expert on, say, postconcussion syndromes than *inter vivos* trusts. (There are exceptions, of course—intellects capacious enough for both expertise and a good all-around knowledge of the law—but they are rare.)

There is specialization not only because the law itself has grown so large and complicated, but also because the client expects the lawyer to be familiar with the client's business. Lawyers for film companies know a great deal about producing a movie, and nothing about running a railroad; railroad lawyers *contra*. Real estate lawyers, besides being busy with deeds, leases, gores and easements, often act as negotiators for their clients, and sometimes are themselves the principals; they may be better able to judge the value of a building than the value of a motion for summary judgment. Sometimes a lawyer comes to know more about his client's business than the client does. Theatrical lawyers make so many decisions for producers that some of them eventually dispense with the client, adding the entrepreneurial function may not seem much of an additional burden, and the financial rewards are greater. The phenomenon of the attorney-turned-corporate-executive is a common one. A lawyer, for example, not a pilot, is the head of Trans World Airlines. (They had a pilot, Howard Hughes, and got rid of him, despite the fact that he owned eighty percent of the company.)

The degree of specialization varies, of course, and two of the variables are the size of the city and the size of the law firm. But the body of the law is at least ten times as great now as it was fifty years ago, and only specialization can make one an authority. The cost is a circumscription of view: the complete lawyer needs peripheral vision.

Too much time spent in court prevents the trial lawyer from learning the substance of the law, while an office lawyer, who rarely has to persuade a judge that the opinion he gave his client is correct, runs the risk of losing touch with legal reality; he may become either too confident or too timid about what can be done in court. The lawyer who does a number of different things will have less detailed knowledge of specific subjects, but he will tend to have a better-conditioned judgment, a more enjoyable practice, and a lower income tax to pay.

FANNY HILL *IN SCOLLAY SQUARE*

United States v. *Married Love* is at 48 F. 2d 821. The Macaulay quotation is from Vol. III of his *Critical and Historical Essays*.

FANNY HILL *IN HACKENSACK*

After the Supreme Court's decision, we thought that the Bergen County prosecutor might consent to a reversal, but he did not, arguing that the decision amounted to no more than a ruling that the Massachusetts court had committed legal error, which, he contended, Judge Pashman had avoided. In the fall of 1966 the New

Jersey Supreme Court reversed Judge Pashman on the basis of the tests stated in *Memoirs* v. *Massachusetts*—the same tests I had urged upon Pashman (before *Memoirs* v. *Massachusetts*) and he had said he accepted.

THE MAJORITY BELOW

A distinguished appellate lawyer, Frederick Bernays Wiener, says ". . . there exists and flourishes—let us be realistic—a judges' union. Let the higher judges reverse, correct and admonish the lower judges. Counsel should not even try. . . ." ("On the Improvement of Oral Argument," *New York State Bar Journal*, June 1967, p. 189.)

I disagree. Obviously, counsel can not "reverse" and will not, sensibly, "admonish," but Mr. Wiener's implication is that counsel should not assail the lower-court opinion, no matter how courteously, for fear of union solidarity, and on this I must depart from my respected brother.

"The best of us suffer lapses"—some examples closer to home:

In 1917, a Supreme Court majority managed to render a decision unsound, unjust, and unbecoming. Holmes and Brandeis were two-fifths of the majority.

The decision was on the Mann Act, passed to provide a federal deterrent to prostitution. The defendant took a trip from Sacramento to Reno with a woman to whom he was not married, "for the purpose of debauchery" said the indictment, "and for an immoral purpose, to wit, that the aforesaid woman should be and become his mistress and concubine." The Court affirmed a verdict of guilty.

The Act made it unlawful to transport a woman across state lines "to become a prostitute and to give herself up to debauchery or to engage in any other immoral practice." Everything after the word "prostitute" is shotgun legislative language, and quite plainly cannot be given a literal reading. Suppose the defendant had taken along his friend (who insisted on separate bedrooms) in order to assist him in a crooked game of poker, or to participate in drunken revels. Surely the one involves an "immoral practice"; the other involves "debauchery." Since the language was at best ambiguous, other evidence of legislative intent was relevant. The other evidence violently contradicted the majority's view of the statute. The report of the congressional committee handling the bill shows it was only organized prostitution that Congress meant to deal with. Moreover, the statute itself proclaims that it is to be known as the "White-Slave Traffic Act."

The usually realistic Holmes was also the writer of a 1922 opinion, for a unanimous Supreme Court, holding that the corporations which operate professional baseball teams are not engaged in interstate commerce, and hence may conduct their monopoly without regard to federal law. A suit brought against them under the antitrust act was dismissed. Some months later, at the same term of court, Holmes again spoke for a unanimous bench in another antitrust suit. This time the alleged monopoly was in vaudeville rather than in baseball, and this time the Court ruled that the suit should not be dismissed. In the baseball case, justifying the conclusion that interstate commerce was not involved, Holmes had said:

> The transport [in interstate commerce] is a mere incident, not the essential thing. That to which it is incident, the exhibition, although made for money, would not be called trade or commerce in the commonly accepted use of those words. As it is put by the defendant, personal effort, not related to production, is not a subject of commerce.

In the vaudeville case, called upon to distinguish the baseball case, Holmes said:

> in the transportation of vaudeville acts the apparatus is sometimes more important than the performers. . . .

Holmes' distinction is not only insulting to the performers (vaudeville may have died of hurt feelings); it assigns a peculiarly diminished role to the apparatus of baseball. The two decisions make sense together only on the assumption that the traveling baseball team must leave its equipment home. This envisages games in which the visitors play without bats or gloves, the catcher without his mask or chest protector. Perhaps this explained to Holmes why more often than not the home team wins.

These opinions, and the concurring votes of Holmes and Brandeis in the Mann Act case, do not alter the fact that Holmes and Brandeis were great men. The law is a difficult discipline; there are severe demands on the time of judges and lawyers, and even great men make mistakes.

The Mann Act case is *Caminetti* v. *United States,* 242 U.S. 470. The others are *Federal Baseball Club* v. *National League,* 259 U.S. 200 and *Hart* v. *Keith Exchange,* 262 U.S. 271.

THE BRIEF FOR THE SUPREME COURT

The quoted final paragraphs of the brief involve, though they make no attempt to spell out, the concepts of privacy and public decency. They are concepts that may have a positive importance in future obscenity cases (as distinguished from their negative importance—my argument that they are not relevant to books—in the *Fanny Hill* case).

When we think of privacy as a legal concept we usually think of the need to keep things to ourselves. The need is expressed in the contemporary alarm about electronic spying and recording. On this aspect of privacy, there are explicit constitutional safeguards. The Fourth and Fifth Amendments put a screen between the citizen and his government; the Fourth prohibits unreasonable searches and seizures, and the Fifth prohibits forced disclosure. These provisions, properly interpreted, can protect us; the technology is new, but government's propensity to pry is old, and the eighteenth-century language is broad enough to cover what is going on now. The protection cannot be absolute; a nation needs some information about the individuals who inhabit it, and the government of a complicated modern society needs more than would have sufficed when the nation was smaller and its economy simpler.

Technological eavesdropping by those outside the government is perhaps an even graver problem, but there is no question about the legal means to deal with it: we can pass whatever laws we wish (within the limits of due process) to forbid and punish snooping.

Another kind of privacy has been in the news lately—the option to keep one's name and history out of public sight. This is not a constitutional right; it was created in this century, by statute, and to some extent by the common law process. It owes its origin to an 1890 law review article by Samuel Warren, a celebrated teacher of law, and Louis Brandeis, the future Justice—or at least it entered the law sooner than it would have if they had not had their ideas and argued them so well. Lately, as I have said, the right has been severely limited by the Supreme Court because it impinges upon free speech. It is usually invoked not by those who wish to remain anonymous, but by those who wish to be paid for the exploitation of their celebrity. It is more a right of publicity than a right of privacy. Perhaps the wryest assertion of privacy under these statutes was made in the case of a fresh-faced Hollywood starlet who sued when a photograph of her (in clothes) was used in an advertisement without her consent. The court agreed that she could call on the law to shelter her privacy, and awarded a judgment for damages. Some time afterward she appeared, thoroughly public, in a *Playboy* photographic essay, typically exploratory (by arrangement, one assumes, since no legal action followed).

But there is another, a third kind of privacy, that concerns us here—one that gets less attention, and is less important than the first one mentioned, yet important enough to engage the law's attention. It is the right to be free from intrusion itself, even when the intrusion does not have the aim of extracting information. There is a need to remain at peace; we must not be too often forced to respond to unpleasant stimuli. The common law recognizes the need in its doctrine of nuisance; certain activities that are loud or smelly or unsightly will be enjoined.

The Fourth Amendment to some extent deals with this, but it is primarily an amendment designed to limit investigation. Just one part of the Constitution deals solely with what I am now speaking of, and it is the least known section in the Bill of Rights, the Third Amendment:

> No soldier shall in time of peace be quartered in any house, without the consent of the owner, nor in time of war but in a manner to be prescribed by law.

This is resistance to an unwanted presence, not merely resistance to disclosure. The archaic sound only serves to demonstrate that threats to liberty come from different sources in different ages.

The need cannot be completely satisfied, for here again the First Amendment is confronted. If speech is free, we are bound to hear some things we do not like. But we should not be too tightly bound. We ought not to be defenseless against every impact.

Privacy may be invaded by the speaker as well as by the listener, and while we are abroad as well as at home. It is not only a man's home that is his castle; it is also his nervous system. We want more than a curtain against the eavesdropper; we also want some defenses against the man with a sales pitch. Go away, don't bother me, get your finger off my chest.

It is not remarkable that the authors of the Bill paid little attention to this aspect of privacy. In the sparsely settled colonies, where communication was so difficult, loneliness was more a problem than intrusion. Even when they thought of the more populous nation to come, they could hardly have imagined the devices of assault that our technology would bring—public-address systems, neon signs, sky-writing, letters addressed to Occupant.

It is not unreasonable to allow people the choice of not listening when the message is being delivered in a form they feel is obnoxious, and anti-obscenity legislation may serve a valid purpose where the audience is captive. Even if the kind of privacy I speak of has no independent status in the Constitution, it ought to be taken into account when we are considering the scope of the enumerated guaranties. The right to express oneself freely (explicit in the Constitution) may collide with other rights, among them (probably implicit in the Constitution) a general right to be let alone.

Here the concept of privacy and the concept of public decency mix. Words on a billboard are not the same as words in a book. Speaking on radio is not the same as speaking on the telephone. Hanging a painting or photograph in a store window is not the same as hanging it in a gallery.

Public decency is a shifting, unstable concept, distorted and abused by those who would have it serve a thoroughgoing censorship. Nevertheless, that public things should be decent is not, intrinsically, a bad idea. Perhaps the orthodox libertarian will find the idea more acceptable if it is put in terms of aesthetics. Consider it a form of zoning. The ugly destruction of open space may be regulated by law, and the fact that some individual rights are trampled on—the freedom to build freshly minted slums in this instance—does not bother us. Nor should it bother us that the law may regulate displays on theater marquees. The interference with the free interchange of ideas is minimal.

When we go out into the common places, the places that are there to be used by all of us, we have a right to enjoy them. There are certain things, many people feel, that ought not to assail their senses, or their sensibilities. Their pleasure is spoiled by them. Their pleasure is worth preserving.

This is not confined to what is commonly thought to be obscene; what I say applies as well to any expression whose manner or method, as distinguished from its content, is odious: a public-address system too loud, for example, a hand on one's lapel. Where we deal with speech that is disapproved for substantive reasons—disapproved because of the essential ideas that are being transmitted—then public decency is not, cannot be, a consideration.

Privacy is an element in the concept of public decency. There is nothing of paradox in this. When a public display offends, the right to be let alone is breached. Both concepts may be described in terms of the captive audience, but the two are not congruent. An offensive letter sent to an unwilling recipient is not a public expression; neither is the obscene telephone call (party lines having disappeared). Only privacy is involved. On the other hand, though privacy is breached by an obtrusive public display, the very fact that it is public makes a difference. Things trivial in an exchange between individuals become more objectionable in crowds; the jostling of social molecules raises temperatures. Moreover, the general public includes children as well as adults, and persons of widely varying sensitivities. A degree of pleasantness, order, sanitation—call it what you like—may be demanded for public places, over and above the preservation of private tranquillity.

Elements of hypocrisy invade the concept of public decency. No wonder, considering its traditional sponsors. It suffers from the implication that we make a public show of disapproving what we secretly approve. But there is no inconsistency, and no hypocrisy, in the proposition that certain things which freely occur in private should not occur in public. In public, a variety of rights run their course, and the traffic must be regulated. Along with the right of privacy, there can be said to exist a duty of privacy.

Table of Judges

ROTH

For the Statute	Against the Statute
Warren	Black
Frankfurter	Douglas
Burton	Harlan
Clark	
Brennan	
Whittaker	

ALBERTS

For the Statute	Against the Statute
Warren	Black
Frankfurter	Douglas
Burton	
Clark	
Harlan	
Brennan	
Whittaker	

LADY CHATTERLEY

For the Book	Against the Book
Clark	Summerfield
Waterman	
Moore	
Bryan	

TROPIC MASSACHUSETTS

For the Book	Against the Book
Spalding	Wilkins
Whittemore	Williams
Cutter	Kirk
Spiegel	

TROPIC NEW YORK

For the Book	Against the Book
Dye	Desmond
Fuld	Burke
Van Voorhis	Foster
	Scileppi

FANNY HILL MASSACHUSETTS

For the Book	Against the Book
Whittemore	Wilkins
Cutter	Spalding
Spiegel	Kirk
	Reardon

FANNY HILL NEW YORK

For the Book	Against the Book
Dye	Desmond
Fuld	Burke
Van Voohris	Scileppi
Bergan	

GINZBURG SUPREME COURT

For Conviction	Against Conviction
Warren	Black
Clark	Douglas
Brennan	Harlan
White	Stewart
Fortas	

MISHKIN SUPREME COURT

For Conviction	Against Conviction
Warren	Black
Clark	Douglas
Harlan	Stewart
Brennan	
White	
Fortas	

FANNY HILL SUPREME COURT

For the Book	Against the Book
Warren	Clark
Black	Harlan
Douglas	White
Brennan	
Stewart	
Fortas	

Index

About the Author

CHARLES REMBAR *was born in New Jersey,
educated at Harvard College and Columbia Law School
and has practiced law in Washington, D.C.,
and New York, where he now lives
with his wife and two sons.*